LET SOMETHING GOOD BE SAID

Let Something Good Be Said

Speeches and Writings of Frances E. Willard

Edited by

CAROLYN DE SWARTE GIFFORD

AND AMY R. SLAGELL

UNIVERSITY OF ILLINOIS PRESS

URBANA AND CHICAGO

∞ This book is printed on acid-free paper.

Library of Congress Cataloging-in-Publication Data

Willard, Frances Elizabeth, 1839–1898.
Let something good be said : speeches and writings of Frances E.
Willard / edited by Carolyn DeSwarte Gifford and Amy R. Slagell.
p.   cm.
Includes bibliographical references and index.
ISBN-13 978-0-252-03207-3 (cloth : alk. paper)
ISBN-10 0-252-03207-1 (cloth : alk. paper)
1. Temperance—United States—History—19th century.
2. Alcoholism—United States. 3. Woman's Temperance Crusade,
1873–1874.
I. Gifford, Carolyn De Swarte. II. Slagell, Amy R., 1962– III. Title.
HV5232.W6A5   2007
322.4'4092—dc22   2007005142

To Mark, Carter, Kenny, and Bill, with gratitude for their support

CONTENTS

Frances Willard's office, which she called "the den," is a focal point of the museum tour of Rest Cottage, Willard's longtime home in Evanston, Illinois. From this room she conducted her presidency of the Woman's Christian Temperance Union (WCTU) for many years, writing letters, speaking into a Dictaphone, crafting speeches, giving interviews, and planning meetings. Here Willard sat among bookcases full to overflowing, surrounded by stacks of newspapers and journals piled on her desk; papers spilling out of her battered briefcase, which stood open on the floor; and photographs of the famous and not-so-famous pinned on screens and fastened to the walls. Willard's office was an important center of activity where she kept in touch with WCTU white ribboners[1] all over the world. When she was not on the road speaking and organizing, she was in her office reading, writing, discussing, and dictating.

Near her desk is a modest fireplace with an inscription painted across its brick face: "Let Something Good Be Said." Several stories have surfaced over the years about how that particular saying came to be on the fireplace, though none of them can be verified. We do know that the source of the inscription is the title of a poem by popular Hoosier poet James Whitcomb Riley.[2] Willard chose it as her motto for 1888, writing in *The Union Signal*, the WCTU's weekly newspaper, "I had resolved to have this motto, before dismissing any person's case or character, 'Let something good be said,' always something good."[3]

This phrase epitomizes Willard's way of participating in public life. It was the way she built relationships with those around her, a strategy that enabled her to facilitate the growth of the WCTU as it became the largest organization of women in the world during the closing decades of the nineteenth century. The principle of saying "something good" infused her written and spoken word, encouraging her listeners and readers and setting a high moral tone for WCTU members and others who joined her in reform activities. In the estimation of a large segment of American society during the late nineteenth century, Frances Willard exhibited integrity, good will, optimism, and concern for others; for them, she was the embodiment of "character."

As a young woman, Willard purposefully set out to develop a good character. She felt strongly that one of the bases of good character was geniality, a word that has gone out of fashion in the twenty-first century, but, in Willard's era, indicated a virtue that was much admired in both men and women.[4] A genial person was one filled with a welcoming kindness and sympathy toward others, a tendency to downplay disagreement and hostility, a willingness to seek the good in all people, and a desire to encourage that good nature to manifest itself in good actions.

One of Willard's first published works, an inspirational biography about the life and death of her younger sister Mary, closed with a moving deathbed scene. Just before she dies, Mary begs her family to "tell everyone to be good!"[5] Her beloved sister's dying request made a lasting impression on Willard, deepening her developing sense of purpose. Three years earlier she had confided to her journal, "There are many that shall yet thank God that I was created—I feel sure of this! There are words of love & comfort for me to speak—faint hearts for me to encourage."[6] Twenty-five years later in *How to Win,* Willard aimed to spread this ambition to do good to a new generation of young women. She called them to follow her example, to see themselves as active agents of reform, to "be not simply good, be good for something."[7]

Through her work as an organizer, visionary, speaker, and writer, Frances Willard became a powerful inspiration for her followers. As one of the nineteenth century's most dynamic and influential public figures, she helped shape American opinion on a number of political, economic, and social issues of great concern in the last quarter of the century. One way to understand Willard's success at mobilizing thousands of women and men for reform work is to explore a broad sample of her discourse. This volume brings together twenty-two examples of her speeches and writings, spanning the period from the beginning of her association with the Woman's Christian Temperance Union in 1874 to her final presidential address to the WCTU in 1897. The speeches and writings included in this collection capture particular moments in Willard's effort "to *be* and to *do good.*"[8]

This is the first time that such an extensive sample of Willard's thought has been readily available. Previously, someone curious about her words and thoughts could find only brief examples in rhetoric texts or women's history anthologies. These examples, excerpts of a speech or a few paragraphs of a book or article she wrote, though useful for acquainting readers with Willard, cannot convey the depth of her intellect, the eloquence of her oratory, or the intense reasoned passion of her argument. This text offers readers the opportunity to delve more deeply into Willard's thought. It presents a number of Willard's speeches delivered in a variety of settings: presidential addresses given at national WCTU conventions and meetings of other women's organizations; talks to church groups and temperance gatherings; and orations delivered to political conventions, state legislatures, and at Fourth of July celebrations. It also reproduces several examples of Willard's writing: articles she wrote for the WCTU's weekly newspaper, one that she published in a reform journal, excerpts from an advice book for girls, sections from handbooks she produced for her organization; and chapters from a popular book she wrote about learning to ride a bicycle.

Each of these texts is preceded by a headnote that explains the context of the discourse and guides the reader to its key ideas. These headnotes are intended to assist readers in tracing the development of Willard's thought over the quarter century of her public life. Through Willard's own words, readers can see the broadening and radicalization of her reform goals over time. In addition to these headnotes, the following detailed timeline of Willard's life and the introduction to this text provide an overview of the major themes and goals that emerged in the course of her work on the public stage as well as the biographical forces that shaped her as a reformer.

As editors of this collection of speeches and writings, we hope that readers gain a better understanding of this brave woman who we have come to admire for her lifelong work to make the world a better, more just place, especially for women and children. During the years in which we prepared the manuscript, often meeting together within a mile of Rest Cottage—Willard's home from 1866 until her death in 1898—we had moments of disagreement, but also a lot of laughter as we struggled through the voluminous papers of this prolific speaker and writer. We aimed to select texts that would illustrate the variety of issues, forms, and strategies Willard employed and to introduce and annotate those texts with enough detail to support twenty-first-century readers as they make sense of the nineteenth-century ideas, people, and events alluded to in the texts. Through it all we have remained fast friends and great fans of Willard. We think she would be pleased to know that across the decades women leaders have continued to rise and speak up for social justice, "letting something good be said."

Notes

1. WCTU members wore a small white ribbon, shaped in a bow and pinned on the front of a dress or shirtwaist blouse, to signify their allegiance to the organization and its tenets.

2. The full text of the poem (written in 1880) can be found in Edmund Henry Eitel, ed., *The Complete Works of James Whitcomb Riley* (Indianapolis, Ind.: Bobbs-Merrill, 1913), 2:209.

3. *The Union Signal,* January 19, 1888, quoted in Lori Osborne, "Notes from the Research Files" in *F[rances] W[illard] H[istorical] A[ssociation] Newsletter,* July 2000.

4. Many entries in Willard's journal from 1859 through the 1860s contain passages relating to Willard's shaping of her character and the importance of geniality to good character. See, for example, Carolyn DeSwarte Gifford, ed., *"Writing Out My Heart": Selections from the Journal of Frances E. Willard, 1855–96* (Urbana and Chicago: University of Illinois, 1995), 9–14, 41, 56, 83.

5. Willard, *Nineteen Beautiful Years* (New York: Harper, 1864; rpt. Chicago: Woman's Temperance Publishing Association, 1885), 172.

6. Willard, Journal, September 11, 1861, in Gifford, ed., *Writing Out My Heart,* 139.

7. Willard, *How to Win: A Book for Girls* (New York: Funk & Wagnalls, 1886), 125.

8. Willard, Journal, January 12, 1866, in Gifford, ed., *Writing Out My Heart,* 222.

ACKNOWLEDGMENTS

The editors have received a good deal of help and encouragement from many colleagues and friends as we compiled this collection. Both Carolyn and Amy would like to thank Virginia Beatty, archivist and librarian at the Frances E. Willard Memorial Library, for her enthusiasm for our project and her ability to track down elusive dates and obscure references. Her knowledge of the library and its collections is prodigious, and we have benefited from it. Before his death, Virginia's husband Bill Beatty, colibrarian and archivist at the Willard Library, also participated willingly in the hunt for information we needed for the volume. His gentle wit and his talent for recalling just where to locate the exact answers to our many questions was much appreciated. We will miss him.

We are also indebted to Lori Osborne, past president of the Frances Willard Historical Association, for putting us on the trail of the book's cover illustration. She remembered having seen what may possibly be the only extant photograph of Willard speaking. We'd also like to express our gratitude to members of the Social Gospel Lunch Group in Evanston, Illinois, who read and commented on several texts and introductions.

Carolyn wishes to thank the Evangelical Scholars Program of the Pew Charitable Trusts for naming her a research fellow for 1997–98. During that year she developed her understanding of Willard as an early leader in the social gospel movement. She also thanks the Department of Gender Studies, Northwestern University, for appointing her a research associate in 1996 and renewing the appointment yearly.

Amy extends her appreciation to Stephen E. Lucas, who directed her dissertation on Willard at the University of Wisconsin; his guidance then and continued support over the years have been more significant than he knows. Colleague and friend, Susan Zaeske offered sound advice and encouragement and even sponsored writing retreats, without which the project might never have been completed. Iowa State University's program for humanities research provided a summer salary grant to support this work. Many colleagues at Iowa State, Susan Yager, Maggie LaWare, Michael Mendelson, Donna Niday, as well as members of the English 611 graduate seminar on women's oratory, listened patiently and expanded her thinking about Willard's complexities. And to her parents, Norman and Rose Hibinger, she adds her thanks for their faith and love.

No book reaches its readers without the support of many hands and minds.

Debra Lynn-Neppl, with her knowledge of Microsoft Word, played a key role in preparing the manuscript. Joan Catapano, associate director and editor-in-chief and our editor at the University of Illinois Press, has been supportive throughout the publication process. Her colleagues, Rebecca Crist, managing editor, and Dawn McIlvain, copy editor, have made the process smooth and pleasant. We would like to thank the two anonymous readers for the University of Illinois Press who pointed out some very important changes that needed to be made in the manuscript. Thanks also to our indexer Carol Roberts for her contribution to the volume. We are grateful to our friend and colleague Rachel Bohlmann for her timely and incisive critique of the first draft of the introduction to the text.

Finally, we would like to thank Bill Gifford, and Mark, Carter, and Kenny Slagell for their patience and their good-natured willingness to put up with our endless conversations about Frances Willard.

TIMELINE OF FRANCES WILLARD'S LIFE

1839
- Born on September 28 in Churchville, New York.

1841
- Moved with her family to Oberlin, Ohio, where her parents attended Oberlin College.

1846
- Moved with her family to a farm outside of Janesville, Wisconsin, for her father's health.

1856
- Attended a one-room public school near the Willard farm, beginning in January.

1857
- Attended Milwaukee Female College, a preparatory school, as a boarder, for one term, from April to July.

1858
- Attended North Western Female College, a Methodist secondary school in Evanston, Illinois, beginning in March; later in 1858 the entire family moved to Evanston.

1859
- Graduated from North Western Female College in June.

1860
- Joined the Evanston Methodist Episcopal Church in January as a probationary member.
- Taught in a one-room public school in Harlem, Illinois, for one term, from June to September.
- Taught from October to December at a Methodist-sponsored academy in Kankakee, Illinois.

1861
- Baptized in May, becoming a full member of the Methodist Episcopal Church.
- Taught again in Harlem, June to August.
- Engaged in September to Charles Fowler, a young Methodist minister and recent graduate of Garrett Biblical Institute.

1862

- Ended her engagement to Charles Fowler in February and remained single throughout her life.
- Taught spring term at the newly opened Evanston public school.
- Younger sister Mary died in June of typhoid fever.
- Taught at North Western Female College, September to December.

1863–64

- Taught at the Pittsburgh [Pennsylvania] Female College, a Methodist secondary school, for several terms, from January through July, 1863, and again in late fall 1863 through midsummer 1864.
- Traveled through the eastern United States from October to December, visiting New York City, Philadelphia, and New England. While in New York, negotiated with Harper Brothers to publish *Nineteen Beautiful Years,* a memoir of her sister.

1864–66

- Taught at Grove School, Evanston, Illinois, a private elementary school, from fall 1864 through June 1866.
- Moved in 1966 with her family to the newly built Rest Cottage, her home for the rest of her life.
- Began to establish connections among Methodists around the nation as corresponding secretary of the American Methodist Ladies Centenary Association, a group organized to raise money for a dormitory for the Garrett Biblical Institute.

1866–68

- Held position of preceptress (principal) of Genesee Wesleyan Seminary, Lima, New York, from September 1866 to July 1867.
- Helped care for her father Josiah Willard at his family home in Churchville, New York, from November 1867 until his death from tuberculosis in January 1868.

1868–70

- Traveled and studied in Europe and the Middle East with her friend Kate Jackson from June 1868 until September 1870.

1871

- Became the president of the newly established Evanston College for Ladies in February; began fund-raising for a college building, hiring teachers, and planning the curriculum.
- Awarded an honorary master's degree from Syracuse University in June.

1873

- Named dean of women and professor of rhetoric and aesthetics when the Evanston College for Ladies formally merged with Northwestern University in June.

- Participated in the National Woman's Congress in New York City in October.

1874

- Resigned from her positions at Northwestern in June after a disagreement with the administration and faculty over the governance of women students.
- Became president of the Chicago, Illinois, woman's temperance organization in September, formed in the wake of the Woman's Crusade, a protest campaign against liquor dealers, which began in Ohio in December 1873, then spread through the Midwest, the Northeast, and the far western United States by spring 1874.
- Attended the organizing convention of the Woman's Christian Temperance Union (WCTU) held in Cleveland in November; elected as the organization's corresponding secretary.

1875

- Traveled throughout the year in the Midwest and the East, delivering speeches and organizing local unions, setting a pattern for the rest of her reform career.
- Published *Hints and Helps in Our Temperance Work*.

1876

- Spoke publicly for the first time on "Women's Duty to Vote," at Old Orchard Beach, Maine, at an August temperance camp meeting.
- Gave a speech on "Home Protection" to the Fourth Women's Congress in Philadelphia in October; spoke again on the topic at the October National WCTU convention; WCTU president Annie Wittenmeyer disavowed the organization's support for women's suffrage.

1877

- Stepped down from the presidency of the Chicago WCTU in February.
- Joined Dwight L. Moody's evangelistic campaign in Boston in February and stayed with the campaign until September. During the campaign, met Anna Gordon, who became her personal secretary, serving in that capacity until Willard died.
- Resigned as corresponding secretary of the National WCTU in October 1877.

1878

- Spoke before the U.S. House of Representatives Judiciary Committee in February and presented petitions calling for men's votes and women's signatures on whether to legalize the sale of alcohol in U.S. territories and the District of Columbia.
- Briefly coedited the *Post*, a Chicago newspaper, with her sister-in-law after her brother Oliver's death in March.
- Elected president of the Illinois WCTU in October; orchestrated an

unsuccessful but highly publicized campaign for the home protection ballot that continued through the spring of 1879.

1879

- Elected president of the National WCTU in October at its sixth annual convention in Indianapolis.

1880

- Presented her WCTU credentials to the General Conference of the Methodist Episcopal Church in May and was rebuffed. After a debate, the body voted in favor of allowing her to speak, but she declined.
- Presided for the first time over the seventh annual National WCTU convention held in Boston, in October. The home protection ballot was endorsed, and work among foreign women and African American women began.

1881

- Spoke before U.S. President James Garfield in March at the unveiling of a portrait of former First Lady Lucy Webb Hayes, commissioned by the WCTU for her support of temperance.
- Made a three-month tour of the South during the spring, from the Carolinas to Texas, speaking and organizing local WCTUs.
- Participated in the National Temperance Society meeting at Saratoga, New York, in the summer; attended temperance convocation at Lake Bluff, Illinois, meeting there with Prohibition Party leaders.
- Presided over the eighth annual National WCTU convention in Washington, D.C., in October, at which she launched the "Do Everything" policy and established both the Franchise (women's suffrage) and the Health and Heredity Departments.

1882

- Attended the Prohibition Party meeting in Chicago, where she persuaded party leadership to change the party's name to the Prohibition Home Protection Party; was chosen member of the party's central committee, serving until 1891.
- Presided over the ninth annual National WCTU convention in Louisville, Kentucky, in October.

1883

- Went on an organizing trip to the far western parts of the United States during the spring and summer, extending that tour to every state in a "Crusade roundup," celebrating the tenth anniversary of the Women's Crusade.
- Led the tenth annual National WCTU convention in Detroit from the end of October through early November where the WCTU adopted an equal suffrage resolution; formed a committee to resurrect the World's WCTU.
- Published the first edition of _Woman and Temperance_.

1884

- Visited the four major political party conventions during the summer; addressed the Committee on Resolutions of the Republican national convention in June.
- Gave a seconding speech for the nomination of John St. John, the Prohibition Party presidential candidate at the party's national convention in July.
- Persuaded WCTU officers to endorse Prohibition Party presidential candidate St. John, at the eleventh annual National WCTU convention in St. Louis in October, provoking a reaction from nonpartisan WCTU leaders.

1885

- Began to speak out on social purity issues at the twelfth annual National WCTU convention in Philadelphia, held from late October to early November; called for reinvigoration of the social purity department (begun in 1875). Presented Polyglot Petition, written by her in 1884, to the National WCTU for the first time.
- The World's WCTU formally re-established after remaining dormant since its establishment in 1876.

1886

- The National WCTU sent a delegation to the national convention of Knights of Labor in May, at her urging, indicating her public support for labor issues.
- WCTU national headquarters officially moved in July from New York City to downtown Chicago.
- Presided over the thirteenth National WCTU convention in Minneapolis in October.
- Published *How to Win*.

1887

- Joined the Knights of Labor.
- Presided over the fourteenth annual National WCTU convention in Nashville in November.

1888

- Acted as delegate to the International Council of Women called by the National Woman Suffrage Association and held in late March and early April; chosen president of the National Council of Women, which was founded then.
- Addressed the U.S. Senate Committee on Women's Suffrage in April.
- The Methodist Episcopal Church General Conference in May refused to seat her and four other women elected lay delegates from Annual Conferences.
- In the summer, chosen president of the Chicago Women's League, the first local group of the National Council of Women.

- Read Bellamy's *Looking Backward* and embraced Nationalism, a form of evolutionary socialism described in the book.
- Presided over the fifteenth annual National WCTU convention in New York City in October, at which the Department of Peace and International Arbitration was created.
- Published *Woman in the Pulpit.*

1889

- Became an associate editor of *The Dawn,* a journal of Christian socialism, in July.
- Presided over the sixteenth annual National WCTU convention in Chicago in November
- Published *Glimpses of Fifty Years: The Autobiography of an American Woman.*

1890

- Spoke in November at the laying of the cornerstone of the Woman's Temple Building, future headquarters of the National WCTU in downtown Chicago.
- Presided over the seventeenth annual National WCTU convention in Atlanta, Georgia, in November.

1891

- Presided over the triennial meeting of the National Council of Women in February.
- Met Isabel (Lady Henry) Somerset, British women's temperance leader, at the eighteenth annual National WCTU convention in Boston in November; the World's WCTU also met then, and elected Willard its president.
- Published *Evanston: A Classic Town.*

1892

- Attended the Industrial Conference in St. Louis in February, called by reformers seeking to create a third party challenge; unsuccessfully attempted to place support for women's suffrage and temperance on the platform of the proposed new party.
- Her mother Mary Hill Willard died in early August. Traveled with Anna Gordon to England later that month at the invitation of Isabel Somerset, president of the British Women's Temperance Association (BWTA). Attended meetings of the BWTA, encouraging the organization to broaden its reform perspective and adopt some of the WCTU methods.
- Returned to the United States with Isabel Somerset and Anna Gordon for the nineteenth annual National WCTU convention in Denver in late October and early November.
- Traveled back to England in November to work with Isabel Somerset and with the World's WCTU.

1893

- Spoke to a huge crowd at Exeter Hall, London, in January, at the start of a month-long speaking tour of the British Isles.
- Showed early signs of pernicious anemia, which continued through summer and fall.
- Joined the Fabian Society, a British socialist group, in August.
- Became too ill to travel back to the United States for the twentieth annual National WCTU convention and the second World's WCTU convention in Chicago at the Columbian Exposition in October; Isabel Somerset delivered Willard's speeches for her.
- Edited, with Mary A. Livermore, *A Woman of the Century: Fourteen Hundred-Seventy Biographical Sketches, Accompanied by Portraits of Leading American Women in All Walks of Life.*

1894

- Returned to the United States in June after one and a half years in England.
- Received an honorary Doctor of Laws degree from Ohio Wesleyan College in June.
- Presided over the twenty-first annual National WCTU convention in Cleveland in November.
- Published *A Great Mother,* written with her cousin Minerva Brace Norton.

1895

- Presented the Polyglot Petition, calling on world leaders to end the traffic in liquor and opium, to President Grover Cleveland in February. Isabel Somerset presented a copy of the petition to Queen Victoria.
- Traveled back to England in March.
- Presided over the third World's WCTU in London in June.
- Returned to the United States in September and presided over the twenty-second annual National WCTU convention in Baltimore in October.
- Published *Do Everything: A Handbook for the World's White Ribboners* and *A Wheel within a Wheel: How I Learned to Ride the Bicycle.*

1896

- Returned to England by May, suffering from recurrent illness.
- Traveled with Isabel Somerset to Marseilles, France, in September, as vice-president of the Armenian Relief Committee in America, to help resettle Armenian refugees fleeing Turkish persecution and seek support for Armenian relief from the United States.
- Returned to the United States for the twenty-third annual National WCTU convention in St. Louis in November.
- Edited, with Helen Winslow and Sallie White, *Occupations for Women.*

- Embarked in December on a journey to her ancestral homes in Vermont and New Hampshire.

1897

- Continued her journey, visiting her birthplace in western New York and seeing old friends in the Northeast and Midwest.
- Presided over the fourth World's WCTU convention in Toronto, Canada, and the twenty-fourth annual National WCTU convention in Buffalo, New York, from late October to early November.

1898

- Traveled to Janesville, Wisconsin, in January, the town where she had spent much of her childhood and adolescence, and gave her last speech there.
- Prepared to sail for England in New York City from mid-January on; became too ill to travel.
- Died February 17 at the Empire Hotel, New York City, from pernicious anemia, complicated by influenza. Funeral service held February 20 in New York City's Broadway Tabernacle. Special funeral train carried her casket to Chicago with a stop in Churchville, New York, her birthplace. At stops along the train's route, members of local WCTUs gathered to bid their leader farewell.
- Lay in state in Willard Hall, the Woman's Temple, Chicago, on February 23. Final funeral service the following day at the Methodist Episcopal Church, Evanston, Illinois. Cremated and interred in Rose Hill Cemetery, Chicago.

1905

- State of Illinois placed her statue in Statuary Hall of the United States Capitol Building, Washington, D.C, in February.

At the close of the nineteenth century, Frances E. Willard was recognized as the most famous woman in America. In 1905, seven years after her death, Willard's statue was placed in Statuary Hall in the U.S. Capitol Rotunda by the state of Illinois. At the ceremony marking this event, she was hailed as "the uncrowned queen of purity and temperance" and lauded as one "whose name is familiar wherever the English language is spoken."[1] As president of the National Woman's Christian Temperance Union (WCTU) from 1879 to 1898, she led the largest women's organization of her time, inspiring its members with her vision of a new ideal womanhood—self-reliant, independent, and dedicated to equality with men. A reformer of international renown and influence, she ably and passionately championed many of the most significant reforms of her day, advocating a broad agenda for social change that would bring about a better, more just society. Willard's speaking ability was legendary; her power to shape public opinion undisputed. One prominent minister declared that Willard's "annual messages to her constituents are better worth reading than the messages of the president of the United States for the same time."[2] Her books, articles, and pamphlets were avidly read and discussed. She was a towering figure, respected, listened to, and loved by countless thousands of followers throughout the world.

Preparing for a Life of Reform[3]

Many aspects of Willard's early years prepared her for a life devoted to reform. Her family, community, and church instilled in her a belief in civic responsibility and taught her that to be a good Christian one must be a good citizen. For the antebellum world of evangelical Protestantism in which the Willard family was immersed, strengthening the American experiment in democracy was understood to be a religious duty as well as a political goal. The volumes of Willard's journal written when she was a young girl reveal a staunch patriotism and loyalty to her country's highest political ideals. Yet her devotion to American democracy did not preclude strong criticism when she felt that the nation had fallen short of its democratic promise, a practice she continued into adulthood.[4]

When Willard was still a small child, her family moved from western New York to Oberlin, Ohio, so her father could prepare for the ministry at Oberlin

College. There, in a climate of abolitionist agitation, her parents' conviction that slavery was sinful and a stain on the young American nation's reputation was confirmed and strengthened. They brought those sentiments with them to the southern Wisconsin frontier, settling in a farming community of transplanted easterners who shared their view of slavery's ills. In her autobiography, Willard recalled that *The Slave's Friend,* an abolitionist tract for children, was her earliest reading, which "stamped upon me the purpose to help humanity, the sense of brotherhood, of all nations as really one, and of God as the equal father of all races."[5] These ideas implanted in childhood remained with Willard throughout her life, guiding her reform thought and action.

Like many of the New Englanders who moved to Wisconsin, the Willard family espoused firm temperance convictions. Temperance reform, which began in earnest during the early nineteenth century, was a response to excessive drinking among Americans.[6] First championed mainly by members of Protestant congregations concerned about the prolific use of alcohol among all classes, both sexes, and both adults and children, the reform soon included some Roman Catholics and many who claimed no religious affiliation. Early Temperance reformers were appalled by the scenes of public drunkenness that accompanied political, social, and even religious events and feared that alcoholism threatened to ruin the new nation, which depended on sober, clear-brained citizens. Fueled by emerging medical knowledge about the physical effects of alcohol as well as by increasing awareness of the toll of alcohol abuse on families and communities, the movement grew rapidly during the antebellum period. The Willards' belief in temperance was manifested by signing personal pledges to abstain from drinking and supporting temperance candidates in local elections.[7] When the Willard family moved to Evanston, Illinois, a new suburb of Chicago, in the late 1850s, its Methodist founders had already established a dry town; temperance reform was securely lodged in the hearts of Evanston's citizens and enshrined in the town's ordinances. As Willard put it: "Temperance was a matter of course in this 'Methodist heaven.'"[8]

The town was also a stronghold of the emerging Republican Party. Arriving in Evanston in 1858, the Willard family immediately entered a lively political atmosphere similar to the one they had left behind in Janesville, Wisconsin. Several prominent Evanstonians, neighbors and friends of the Willards, were leaders in the new party, and engaged in vigorous efforts to build a strong state and national political movement. As a young woman, Willard gained significant insight into how the American political process worked by observing the organization of grassroots support for the Republican Party.[9] These practical lessons in political organizing stayed with her as she instructed WCTU members in strategies designed to make an impact on the country's political system.

Willard found politics exciting and challenging but also a source of great dissatisfaction and grievance because of the limited role women could play in that crucial sector of American life. Many times during her reform career, Willard publicly recounted her bitter disappointment as a teenager, watching her father and brother set off for Janesville to vote in the 1856 presidential election and realizing that, as a woman, she might never be able to participate in that basic act of democracy.[10] In 1860 she transcribed into her journal large portions of an address by popular minister Henry Ward Beecher in which he supported women's suffrage. "I should not have copied all of this" she wrote, "save that it expresses so truthfully, & so much better than I could, my views on the subject of 'Women's Rights.'"[11] During her twenties, she continued to form strong opinions on the inequalities women experienced in American society, but she confined her critique to the relatively private medium of journal keeping.

Willard completed her formal education in 1859 and taught school for nearly a decade, first in newly established public schools and, for much of her teaching career, at Methodist-sponsored girls' preparatory schools in Illinois, Pennsylvania, and New York. She delighted in the slight degree of independence her small salaries gave her, but, at the same time, she began to realize just how difficult it was for women to support themselves without relying on their husbands or male relatives to provide essential economic backing. Work opportunities for women, especially middle-class women, were quite limited. In her public reform career, she would urge creating more employment possibilities as a crucial element in realizing the goal of women's economic independence.

As an educator, Willard took pleasure in helping educate a generation of young women, encouraging them to envision wider, less constricted roles than she believed her contemporaries had been given. She chose to teach rhetoric and composition to her students, seeing these courses as important tools for young women's self-expression. Living in a time when skilled orators and writers expressed America's dreams in stirring speeches and essays, Willard understood the power of the spoken and written word to shape opinion and belief.

It was, in fact, a speech delivered by Theodore Tilton in Evanston in March 1868 that was the catalyst for Willard's decision to become an active advocate for women's rights. After hearing Tilton's address "The American Woman," in which he argued vigorously for women's suffrage, Willard exclaimed in her journal: "I never heard anything better—or that so much inspired me. Theodore Tilton is the bright, fearless apostle of woman in the 19th century & doesn't utter a word to which my heart fails to respond." She wrote a few days later: "I believe in the *Woman Question* more & more. I'm going to give my little help to it in all possible ways. . . . Some how, since I heard Tilton lecture, my purpose is confirmed—my object in life clearer than ever before. What I can do in large & little ways by influence, by pen, by observation, for *woman,* in all Christian ways, that I will do. And may God help me."[12]

In this journal entry, Willard set forth both the foundation of her commitment to women's rights and the motivation from which that commitment sprang. It was her strong Christian faith that impelled her toward a life of active reform and gave her strength and determination to pursue such a life. Whereas several leading women's rights reformers, such as Elizabeth Cady Stanton and Matilda Joslyn Gage, denounced Christianity as an enslaving force, oppressing women and constricting their freedom, Frances Willard saw within Christianity, properly understood and interpreted, the possibility of women's emancipation, offering them the promise of a higher status than any other societal institution she knew.[13] Her experience within her Methodist community had been one of nurture and support; it gave her an education in liberal ethical values and ideals from both male and female mentors and teachers. In her future reform career, she would continue to count on men as well as women of good will to work for women's rights, realizing that male supporters were absolutely necessary to bring about the fundamental changes in public opinion and legislation that she sought.

Shortly after hearing Tilton speak, Willard prepared for an extended trip to Europe, fulfilling a dream she had long cherished. During her time abroad, she resolved to study the "Woman Question," investigating women's status in Europe and the Middle East. Upon her return to the United States, she would "study the same subject carefully in relation to my own land . . . *talk in public* of the matter, and cast myself with what weight or weakness I possess against the only foe of what I conceive to be the justice of the subject—unenlightened public opinion."[14] As she traveled, she pondered the development of a rhetorical strategy that would help her avoid facing what she described as the "grim visage of public prejudice."[15] She worried about the objections to women's public speaking that still existed among many Americans, even after a generation of antislavery and women's rights orators had paved the way for the women who came after those pioneers. "[M]ay I be brave enough," she hoped, "to speak in a womanly voice my honest word in behalf [of women's rights]."[16]

Discovering an appropriate "public voice" was of paramount concern to Willard. She did not intend to antagonize those in her audiences who were either unaccustomed to hearing women speak in public or who disapproved of the notion that women should be allowed to do so. Girls of her generation had grown up hearing and reading about "strong minded" women speakers,[17] who were criticized in disparaging tones and accused of stepping out of their proper sphere by acting like men on the platform. Their women's rights message was too often lost as audiences focused on their bold and "unwomanly" behavior.

Willard was determined that those to whom she spoke would pay primary attention to her ideas and not be distracted by what they perceived as an improper public persona. Perhaps her most significant contributions to the late nineteenth-century reform scene were her ability to convince mainstream Americans that the public sphere was an appropriate place for women's voices, and her success at enlisting thousands of women as reformers. To accomplish this she modeled what she and the reporters who covered her speeches called a "womanly" speaking style early in her reform career. Her delivery was acceptable, even admirable, to her listeners. On the platform she dressed conservatively in either black or brown dresses with high collars; only those sitting near the front took in the vivid blue eyes behind her pince-nez glasses. Slender and of medium height, Willard drew people toward her. Susan B. Anthony once called her "a bunch of magnetism . . . possessing that occult force which all leaders must have."[18] Yet her manner was that of the self-assured conversationalist rather than that of the self-aggrandizing orator. Sincerity combined with passion, warmth, and good humor were the hallmarks of her style. "As a speaker," noted one contemporary, "she is fervent, forcible, and withal most womanly."[19] The causes she championed in her speeches were unacceptable at first for many—probably a large majority—of her audiences. Yet, because of her engaging, conversational manner at the lectern and her ability to couch her reform goals in language that did not frighten or offend her hearers, she was able to persuade vast numbers of Americans to listen closely to what she had to say, consider it seriously, and work actively for the goals she advocated.

At first Willard believed that she was called to pursue her commitment to women's rights and equal opportunities within the milieu of women's higher education. In 1870 after she returned to Evanston from her European sojourn, she became president of the newly formed Evanston College for Ladies, a sister school of Northwestern University. With the institution's all-female board of trustees and its faculty comprised mostly of women, the college might have become a perfect place to develop an environment where young women could flourish within a space designed and nurtured by women, rather than a college planned and directed by men.[20] But this educational experiment was short-lived. Many of the college's donors lost their fortunes in the aftermath of the Great Chicago Fire of 1871 and could not honor their pledges to support the enterprise. To remain in existence in some form, the Ladies College merged with Northwestern in 1873; Willard was appointed professor of rhetoric and aesthetics and served as the university's first dean of women. One year later, after continued disagreements with Northwestern's administration over the governance of the university's women students, Willard reluctantly chose to resign her position.

Mobilizing the WCTU as a Vehicle for Reform

In summer 1874, Willard enthusiastically joined the women's temperance movement sweeping the country at that time. A surge of women's participation in temperance reform was sparked by the Women's Temperance Crusade, a series of spontaneous demonstrations against saloons and liquor dealers in winter and spring 1873–74. Though women had long been actively involved in temperance reform, these demonstrations marked the beginning of their leadership in the movement.[21] The Women's Crusade spread throughout the Midwest and the northern part of the United States, and leaders began to call for a convention to establish a permanent national organization of women temperance reformers. Willard attended the convention held in November 1874 and was elected corresponding secretary of the WCTU. The duties of her new position included traveling around the country, speaking about the WCTU and its goals, and forming local branches—all efforts to build a large grassroots reform movement with a religious base.

In 1879 she became the WCTU's national president, serving in this office until her death in 1898. Under her leadership, the WCTU grew from a few thousand members to two hundred thousand members by the 1890s, most—but not all—of whom were white, middle-class Protestants.[22] Willard's speaking, writing, and organizing skills were vitally important to the rapid growth of her organization nationally, as she worked to bring the WCTU from its eastern and midwestern base into the South and West during the 1880s. Traveling tirelessly throughout the United States, she appealed to the WCTU membership in language filled with the biblical references and evangelical phrases familiar to them from their upbringing in a religious milieu similar to her own. Often the meetings she conducted felt like church services, and her speeches resembled sermons. Like a powerful preacher, she inspired WCTU members with the certainty that theirs was a religious mission and that God called them to save their homes, families, and nation by creating a more just and equitable world. Willard's inspirational speeches evoked a strong response from audiences, who eagerly joined the WCTU to participate in its mission of reform. Once activated as reformers, many of these WCTU women took on a new sense of personal authority and power that revolutionized their identities. They came to perceive themselves as capable of self-definition and as agents of social change.

During her presidency, Willard led the WCTU to espouse a broad-based reform agenda, urging her constituency to support women's rights and the aims of the rising labor movement, as well as temperance goals, which remained the foundation of the WCTU's impetus toward reform. She envisioned the WCTU as a training place for women reformers, providing them with opportunities to acquire the self-confidence and skills needed to become activists. Well before women gained the vote, she and other WCTU leaders taught members to be strong and influential participants in the nation's political process at all levels. They became skilled lobbyists at the state and national level with a number of legislative accomplishments to their credit during the 1880s and 1890s.

Early successes came in the form of legislative mandates for public schools requiring scientific temperance instruction—education about the harmful effects of alcohol, narcotics, and stimulants. WCTU workers also participated in the passage of many local and state laws prohibiting or restricting the sale of liquor. Before long, some unions were pressing for physical education and sex education in the schools, for prison reforms including the hiring of police matrons to better protect women who were in police custody, and for equal enforcement of prostitution laws—so that the men who hired women for sex were held equally responsible before the law. In response to Willard's call for reform of existing rape legislation, the WCTU successfully lobbied to raise the age females could legally consent to sexual activity from ten years old to sixteen or older in nearly every state. In several communities, WCTU women established institutions such as free kindergartens, night schools for working women and men, Sunday schools, reading rooms, women's shelters, or homes for reformed prostitutes. At the same time, Willard and her organization continued to push for women's suffrage, championing women's limited suffrage on temperance and educational issues where that approach seemed most likely to succeed, but also taking a leading role in campaigns for full women's suffrage where that goal appeared to be within reach. By the late 1880s, Willard aimed to broaden the WCTU's political work on behalf of working-class women. She challenged WCTU members to support the Knights of Labor and the Farmers' Alliance in their struggle to improve the lives of working women through support of legislation such as the eight-hour day and factory safety rules that would improve working conditions.[23]

Willard's reputation as a powerful reformer reached its height in the United States in 1888 with her election as president of the National Council of Women, an umbrella group that brought together dozens of women's organizations sharing common concerns for human betterment. Her active leadership in the American reform community placed her within a network of influential male and female reformers. Her friends and colleagues included many of the most well-known reform figures of the era, from women's suffragists Susan B. Anthony and Mary Rice Livermore to Terence Powderly, Master Workman of the Knights of Labor; from utopian novelist and Nationalist Edward Bellamy to key figures within the Prohibition Party and senators such as Henry William Blair of New Hampshire, who supported the WCTU's efforts toward national prohibition.

In the mid-1880s, Willard called for the rejuvenation of the World's WCTU, first formed in the 1870s but dormant until a decade later. As president of both the National and World's WCTUs, she implemented a plan to send American WCTU missionaries on world tours, introducing the aims and goals of the organization to women in many different countries and establishing local World's WCTUs. This effort put members in the United States in touch with the concerns of women around the world, making "The Woman Question" truly global in scope.[24] WCTU missionaries from the United States worked with World's WCTU members on six continents on a number of issues including investigating the treatment of prostitutes in Indian brothels frequented by British troops; circulating the Polyglot Petition, which called on governments of the world to stop the international traffic in alcohol and opium; and collaborating with local World's WCTU members to institute scientific temperance instruction in schools. With the successful launch of the World's WCTU by the early 1890s, the organization was recognized as a significant partner in global reform and Willard's reputation as a leader had become a transnational one.

Beginning in 1892, Willard spent half of her time in England, working with the British Women's Temperance Association (BWTA) and its president Isabel (Lady Henry) Somerset. The two colleagues sought, with some success, to introduce American WCTU methods and goals, such as women's suffrage, to the more conservative British organization. While in England, Willard formed ties with a number of British reformers, including social purity leader Josephine Butler; women's suffragist Millicent Fawcett; Fabian Socialists Sidney and Beatrice Webb; and temperance leaders such as Canon Basil Orme Wilberforce, leader of the Church of England Temperance Society, Methodist minister Hugh Price Hughes, and Sir Wilfrid Lawson, Liberal M.P., who helped guide temperance legislation through Parliament. Willard thrived within this stimulating intellectual and activist climate, continually expanding her own ideas about reform. She studied the methods of municipal reform in British cities and the strategies of the British labor movement, and deepened her understanding of socialism as an alternative to the unrestrained capitalism she had come to deplore in her own country.

During the 1890s, the broad reform agenda Willard had developed over two decades came under criticism by vocal and influential temperance advocates on both sides of the Atlantic. Her critics insisted that hers was a scattershot approach to reform that dissipated the concentrated energy temperance advocates should direct toward achieving sobriety. They accused her of squandering the strength of her organization on activities and goals that were peripheral to the grand aim of prohibition. But these single-issue reformers did not comprehend the interconnected nature of Willard's notion of reform.

As president of the WCTU, Willard articulated a sweeping vision of reform, one that looked beyond the immediate goals of temperance and women's rights, toward the creation of a world where justice and equality prevailed. In her very first presidential address, she set forth her overarching goal for the organization she was to lead for the next two decades: "Our work," she announced, "is not along the woman question merely, but the deeper, higher, and far more sacred human question."[25] Far from a scattershot plan, Willard maintained that the true path toward reform required a two-pronged approach that would first overcome restrictions on women's self-development and exercise of power, and then unleash that formerly suppressed energy in lines of work that would transform human societies and establish a world founded on equality and justice.

"Translating Women from the Passive to the Active Voice"[26]

"The Woman's Christian Temperance Union is doing no work more important than that of reconstructing the ideal of womanhood," Willard announced in her 1887 presidential address.[27] To carry out the enormous tasks of broad-gauge reform, she insisted that WCTU women must leave behind restrictive notions of womanhood and woman's sphere dominant during much of the nineteenth century and embrace a new vision of woman and her possibilities. Willard realized that a new ideal of womanhood would require a corresponding new ideal of manhood as well as fundamental change in the nature of all relationships between the sexes.[28]

At the very beginning of her public speaking career, Willard tackled the issue of reconstructing gender relationships. In "The New Chivalry,"[29] delivered in 1871 to an audience interested in higher education for women, she confronted the popular middle-class notion of the nineteenth-century male as a chivalrous knight protecting the females under his care—his wife, daughters, and mother—from danger. For his protection, the traditional model held, they owed him deference and obedience. In this patriarchal world, powerful men defined women's roles and limits. Willard proposed a different ordering of gender relations. According to her, the "knight of the new chivalry" would be the man who championed equality for women and supported their struggle for independence, helping them gain the knowledge and power they must obtain to become full members of society. In her optimistic vision, such men would ultimately welcome women into an equal partnership with them in all areas of life.[30] By the mid-1870s she had begun to write about a "chivalry of justice" shown by men toward women and their aspirations.[31]

Although Willard began her reordering of gender relationships by focusing on the redefinition of manhood, she soon turned her attention and effort primarily toward redefining womanhood. When she joined other women temperance activists in 1874, the protection of women and children was one of their greatest concerns. In the wake of the Woman's Temperance Crusade, however, these women began to understand the extent of their lack of power in the public world of politics, business, and the law.[32] They were dismayed, and sometimes extremely angered, by their inability to enforce the regulatory measures against the sale and abuse of alcohol that had been put in place in response to several months of demonstrations by women in towns and villages across the Midwest and beyond. Once the excitement and good intentions generated by the Crusade died down, saloon keepers returned to their lucrative businesses, courts dismissed cases of drunkenness and abuse of wives and children, and political parties ignored women's calls for the election of temperance candidates. The role of protective chivalry women had come to expect from good men was disintegrating in the face of more powerful political and economic interests over which women had little control.[33]

Willard entered into this charged environment at the first convention of the WCTU in October 1874, as a young, enthusiastic recruit to what was characterized by more seasoned leaders as a war against male drunkenness. Since the male protectors, on whom women had relied, were not fulfilling their part of the gender bargain, women would have to become their sisters' protectors, guarding their safety and that of their children. When Willard enlisted in this war, she brought with her ideas she had already formed about women's right to both higher education and suffrage, along with less well thought-out notions about women's economic disabilities and their need to become economically independent. As corresponding secretary of the WCTU, she was assigned the tasks of developing the image and role of the WCTU reformer and building the organizational vehicle through which WCTU members could enlarge their public presence and power more effectively.

By the 1870s, Willard saw women's suffrage not simply as a right, but, crucially for women reformers, as one of the most indispensable weapons in their struggle to bring about change.[34] Women's "Home Protection" ballot, Willard insisted, would make them far more able to protect their sisters. With the vote, women could also help to save their country from the devastation wrought by alcohol. Voting would be the mark of women's responsible citizenship and their patriotic duty.

Although Willard placed great emphasis on the political image of "woman as voter" during the late 1870s, she also attempted to broaden that image by identifying the most fundamental characteristic necessary to the new womanhood she imagined. Drawing on her earlier career as a school teacher who had spent many years observing and mentoring girls and young women, she concluded that the power and ability of "self-definition" was the single most important quality to instill in women at this stage in the evolution of the ideal of womanhood. In a series of newspaper articles written in 1878,[35] she described the new woman as one who possessed the courage and will to define herself, refusing to accept being defined by societal expectations, whether those of her family, community, religious tradition, or government. She urged women time and again to move from "the passive to the active voice," taking charge of their own futures and breaking out of the constricting definitions of others.[36]

A crucial aspect of a woman's self-definition was her ability to determine her greatest talent and pursue it with the goal of earning her own living. Becoming economically independent would not only bolster a young woman's self-confidence and self-reliance, it would also mean that she could choose whom she would marry and not feel compelled to wed an undesirable man because of her need for economic support. Woman's new role as wage earner would necessitate a concurrent change in gender relationships within marriage. The traditional bond grounded in the inequality of power between husband and wife must be transformed to a new relationship built on equality. Such a marriage would move well beyond a nineteenth-century notion of chivalry—woman's protection in a basically unequal relationship—to a true partnership between husband and wife. It would mean the fundamental re-creation of the marriage relationship. The doctrine of spheres—the notion that men and women were created to play separate and predetermined roles in public and private life—would evolve into a new conception of shared responsibilities in all walks of life. This new partnership would be a model of equality and civic responsibility for the children raised by such a couple, thus instilling the ideal of egalitarian relationships in future generations.[37]

Willard predicted that women's power of self-definition and their economic independence would eventually lead to the reconstitution of all male–female relationships. However, as she had noted in "The New Chivalry," men would need to change as well as women. She continued to develop her ideal of the new manhood during the 1880s, always redefining it from the perspective of the woman who was struggling for self-definition. The ideal man would value women as independent beings with their own aspirations and goals and not as male possessions over whom he could assert his rights. He would think of women as comrades and companions in every area of life.[38]

For Willard, one of the most significant requirements for the realization of the new ideal of manhood was the elevation of men's sexual moral standards to the high level that the nineteenth-century male-dominated society had imposed on middle-class women. The belief that women were by nature more moral than men was widespread and resulted in the tacit acceptance of a sexual double standard due to the assumption that men could not control their sexual drives. Although Willard often seemed to embrace that essentialist position in her early reform career, by the mid-1880s she had begun to modify it, suggesting that women's higher standard of morality was the result of socialization into a moral role that was convenient for men. If women could be relied on to uphold a high standard of morality in regard to sexual behavior, then men could—and would—act as they pleased sexually.

This sexual system founded on a moral double standard fostered a class of women and girls dependent for their livelihood on catering to male sexual needs. Such women were usually scorned by both the men they served and "good women," those not forced by circumstance to support themselves and their children. Both types of women were, in different ways, victims of an unequal sexual system. Willard sought to attack the entrenched sexual double standard. She called on the upcoming generation of young women to insist on the same high level of morality from young men that young men had traditionally expected from the girls they hoped to marry. Only truly independent women, self-sufficient and self-confident, could challenge prevailing sexual standards and behaviors by demanding a higher level of morality from men.[39]

Women's individual self-definition and self-confidence were vitally important to Willard's understanding of a new womanhood. But for her, a further step was essential. Women must come together to create a force able to stand up to male domination. To build a strong women's movement, Willard urged the WCTU to unite with other rising middle-class women's groups and with working-class women to achieve mutually agreed upon aims. By the mid-1880s, many local and state WCTUs worked together with equal suffrage associations and benevolent groups, and the national organization made overtures toward women labor leaders.

In 1888, with her election as the first president of the National Council of Women, Willard held out great hopes that the council could serve as a "republic of women,"[40] an alternative body resembling the nation's (male) government in structure, but made up entirely of women and primarily focused on issues of paramount importance to themselves and their children. The National Council of Women, she believed, could become a united and powerful "voice" for women, one which would command the attention of male leaders and enter into dialogue with the "male voice" of Congress and other branches of government. Likewise, Willard hoped that the International Council of Women, also formed in 1888, could become a similar voice for women globally. From these two strong, united bases, women could assume their "true position as the equal partners of men in the great world and its work."[41] They would be ready to align themselves with those male reformers who exemplified the "chivalry of justice" toward women, the quality that she had first envisioned more than a decade earlier. Together they would form partnerships of equals, the logical outcome of a reconstructed ideal of womanhood, and its corollary, a new manhood. In her 1895 presidential address, she dubbed this partnership "The New Pair," who would bring about "the joint rule of a joint world by the joint forces of its mothers and its fathers."[42]

This joint rule was desirable not only as a matter of justice, but equally important for Willard, because women brought something unique to the partnership. A decade and a half earlier, in her first WCTU presidential address, Willard had chosen an ingenious image—"the stereoscopic view,"[43]—to illustrate why the ideas and concerns of both women and men must be brought to bear on all institutions of society. As a young teacher in the early 1860s, Willard had been fascinated by the stereoscope, then a relatively new invention, that gave depth of vision and added clarity to flat, two-dimensional scenes by merging into one the images on two pictures taken from slightly different angles.[44] In a similar manner, "the stereoscopic view" would bring women's and men's differing angles of vision together and focus them on an issue or problem, thus achieving a deeper and fuller, more complete perspective on the subject before them. Through her work over the years with women in all kinds of situations, Willard had seen that their traditional roles as mothers and heads of households, coupled with their experience of relative powerlessness outside their homes, gave them a very different perspective from men's on the role that basic institutions such as government should play in their lives. "To get a stereoscopic view in full-orbed perspective," she declared, "we must have the two angles of vision formed by the eyes of man and woman."[45] Women's perspective must be considered in the forming—and reforming—of societal institutions. Men's perspective alone was simply not adequate to envision the fundamental changes that must occur to bring about the true equality of women and men and the evolution of society.

Responding to "The Cry of the Human"[46]

During the first decade of her WCTU presidency, Willard directed most of her energy toward "the woman question." From time to time, however, she challenged women to confront the larger, more all-encompassing "human question."[47] She most often meant, by this phrase, the terrible conditions of poverty in which the struggle to survive took far too great a toll on both body and spirit. As a young woman traveling in Europe, Willard felt an overwhelming sorrow at discovering the great poverty that existed in the shadow of magnificent cathedrals and grand public buildings. The contrast between wealth and poverty was displayed most dramatically for her in Italy. She was moved to write in her journal: "I never dreamed, in those lethargic days at home, what a wide world it is, & how full of misery. Indeed it was Rome's office to teach me this. . . . Whoever can fail to feel the fires of a quenchless philanthropy kindling in his breast as he contemplates such scenes is either too frivolous for thought or too hardened for emotion. For myself, whatever I have not learned here, Rome has taught me an intense love & a tender pity for my race."[48] Filled with compassion for the suffering of the poor, she wrote just a few days later, "In the spirit of Charity may I go hence—in the spirit of gentlest, humblest, bravest labor for my race, in whatever sphere of life a wise and kindly Providence may open to my advancing steps."[49]

In the mid-1870s, Willard became more intimately acquainted with conditions of poverty when she worked for a brief time with the Chicago WCTU at its office in the city's downtown business district. There she counseled and prayed with men suffering from unemployment and homelessness as well as the ravages of alcoholism. She met their wives, who struggled to hold together families when there was no money for food or rent. Although at that point she and her coworkers tended to see temperance as the only remedy for the many ills the poor suffered, she came into direct contact with dire situations of need and became more aware of the extent of poverty within her own country.[50]

As she encountered firsthand the plight of the poor, her compassion for them grew. She began to understand the complicated nature of "the human question" and realized the enormous effort that would be required to solve the intractable problem of poverty. At this point, her position as WCTU corresponding secretary demanded that she put all of her energy into building the organization. "The woman question" became her most pressing cause, while the plight of the poor moved to the back of her mind for nearly a decade. However, she returned to the issue of poverty by the mid-1880s, at least partly impelled to face it once again by the work of local WCTUs, who had already begun to address the issue in their towns and cities. Willard learned from these efforts and proposed that the WCTU tackle the problem of poverty on a national scale. One of the ways she devised to do this was by enlarging the new ideal of womanhood still further.

To meet the challenging "human question," she envisioned an army of women imbued with the ideal of service to others, pursuing a "new and magnificent profession for women, now being brought to almost scientific accuracy and completeness: PHILANTHROPY."[51] What she had in mind was a redefinition of *philanthropy* that blended her idea of a new womanhood, the changing ideal of charity that was emerging in the second half of the nineteenth century, and the classic notion of Christian service. Willard had long understood service to others as a way of life to be pursued above all else. Belief in Christian service as a vocation began early in her life. Her journal reveals a young soul passionately struggling to find ways to serve others, "to *be* and to *do good*."[52] The ideal of woman as philanthropist that Willard developed in the 1880s was, to a great extent, the public articulation of the course she had determined for herself and had conscientiously tried to maintain and deepen.

She hoped that by encouraging a career in philanthropy she might inspire a generation of young WCTU women dedicated to "the human question." They would understand themselves as professionals in the sense that they would receive salaries sufficient to take care of their basic needs. But they would also be fulfilling a vocation of service to others, similar in intent to the growing numbers of young women who became home and foreign missionaries, deaconesses, and settlement workers during the last three decades of the nineteenth century. In Willard's 1891 presidential address, she mapped out the vast arena for such work, declaring that "women's mighty realm of philanthropy encroaches each day upon the empire of sin, disease and misery that has so long existed we thought it might endure forever. But there remains an immense territory to be possessed."[53]

The new philanthropists she envisioned would need to acquire a number of qualities and skills to fit them for their chosen profession. They must prepare themselves to be resourceful, flexible, creative, and courageous. They must master the tools of analysis being taught by sociologists and political economists seeking ways to grapple with the tenacious problem of poverty. Their Protestant faith should be marked by tolerance and inclusiveness, setting aside any narrow, sectarian prejudices in order to work together with people of different religious backgrounds as well as those who professed no religious belief. Though mostly white and middle class, they ought to be able to move beyond their own social, economic, and racial identities, reaching out to understand the situation of working-class women and men, including immigrants and people of color, joining with them in their struggle for a better life. Although their roots were in a particular geographic region, they would welcome opportunities to become acquainted with people from other areas, seeing them as part of a national and an even larger global community. Willard strove to model these qualities herself and to make the WCTU an organization in which women could acquire them.[54]

Her vision of woman as philanthropist was accompanied by an expanded understanding of the scope and aims of reform. During the 1880s and 1890s, Willard created a vocabulary of broad reform, producing a number of powerful slogans that appeared regularly in speeches, newspaper articles, and books. Mottoes such as "Do Everything"; "Everything is not in the temperance reform but the temperance reform should be in everything;" and "The white ribbon includes all reform; whatever touches humanity touches us"[55] announced the WCTU's commitment to broad-based reform and continually reminded members of it. Although each slogan had a specific meaning, the underlying message in them all was that the WCTU was not an organization devoted to a single issue—even one as fundamental to its history and mandate as temperance. "We are all by nature narrow," Willard warned. "We are inclined to take one item of the social program and work for it to the exclusion of others quite as important. It has been the curse of all reformers that they . . . held to their stereotyped, narrow gauged track."[56] Furthermore, she insisted, the single-issue strategy ignored the fact that situations in need of reform had multiple causes requiring that they be addressed in more than one way.

Even as Willard was extending the scope of the WCTU's reform efforts in the 1880s, she was becoming dissatisfied with the very notion of reform, as applied to American economic, political, and social systems. Amelioration and alleviation were the standard goals of reform; they would bring sorely needed improvements while basic structures would remain the same. But by the late 1880s, she began to insist on the radicalization of reform to result in transformation. Willard saw that massive change involving complete restructuring, particularly of the nation's economic system, was imperative to correct the injustice and suffering inflicted on large numbers of people through the greed, corruption, and indifference to poverty that characterized Gilded Age capitalism. She was also appalled at the apparent unwillingness of most Protestants to act in any way other than a grudging charity to address these deep-seated problems. Joining her efforts with social gospel preachers, ethicists, labor leaders, and civic reformers, she sought a lasting solution to "the human question" that had nagged her conscience for so long.

Embracing the Promise of Christian Socialism

By the end of the 1880s, Willard believed she had found a powerful transformative vehicle in Christian socialism, a movement that called for replacing unrestrained capitalism with a gradualist, nonviolent form of socialism.[57] Combining economic theory, political insight, moral and religious fervor, and expressing itself in the familiar language of the Old Testament prophets and the commandments of Jesus, Christian socialism promised to inaugurate an age of "Golden Rule justice," universal brotherhood and sisterhood, and the replacement of competition with cooperation.[58] Willard became an eloquent champion of this radical expression of reform during the last decade of her life. In the face of established Protestantism's reluctance to espouse radical reform, she exhorted the women of the WCTU to espouse the tenets of radical Christian socialism and persevere in broad reform efforts, no matter how difficult and dangerous they might be or how unpopular with the majority. For her, a life dedicated to such reform was the life that the Christian faith called forth; those pursuing that life would be sustained by the Spirit of God.

By the mid-1890s, Christian socialism claimed Willard's whole allegiance. It was, for her, *the* grand reform, encompassing and transcending all the many others she had championed in her years as WCTU president. In 1897, shortly after delivering her eighteenth, and final, presidential address to the WCTU, she confided to a friend, "I believe in the things that Christian Socialism stands for and, were I not 'tee-totally' occupied, would go into the movement heart and soul, as, indeed, I have done in public utterances for many years. Oh, that I were young again, and it should have my life! It is God's way out of the wilderness and into the Promised Land. It is the very marrow and fatness of Christ's Gospel. It is Christianity applied."[59] For Willard, the aims of Christian socialism, with their transformative possibilities, offered the best response to "the human question" of poverty. Under its banner, reformers could confidently go forward toward the future age of Golden Rule justice in which poverty and inequity would be vanquished.

During the 1890s, while Willard continued to call for broader and more radical reform, many other leaders, particularly in temperance groups and women's suffrage organizations, stepped up their demands for a single-issue focus. Willard persisted in efforts to convince her organization of the interconnection between the host of reforms she supported during her WCTU presidency. Temperance, women's suffrage, the eight-hour work day, the expansion of women's access to financial independence through education and free choice of occupation (including ordained ministry), health education in the schools, physical fitness, reform of the political system to root out corrupt machine politics, dress reform, peace and international arbitration, social purity and reform of the double standard, vegetarianism, and even animal rights—none of these was sufficient, by itself, to bring into reality the vision of social justice that Willard proclaimed. But if WCTU members continued to work for all of them, their struggle for thoroughgoing reform would help to usher in the just and egalitarian future for which Willard and many other late nineteenth-century reformers yearned.

In February 1892, pursuing her belief in broad-based reform, Willard participated in the St. Louis Industrial Conference, a gathering that included delegates from labor unions, Farmers' Alliance members, economic reformers, and temperance leaders. Their aim was to create a strong reform coalition, a People's party capable of competing with the existing political parties. Willard failed in her effort to include both national prohibition and women's suffrage in the new party's platform. Disappointed at this outcome and saddened by the death of her mother that summer, she left the United States for the first of four recuperative trips to England. But by the spring of 1893, physically exhausted and suffering from anemia, she was ordered by her doctors in Great Britain to take a year off from the public platform. Though she continued to dictate letters and articles, and resumed giving speeches within a year, she severely curtailed her schedule and even took up bicycling to improve her health.

This respite restored some of her earlier energy, but it was clear to those close to her that her years of constant work and travel had taken a toll. Nevertheless, by the mid-1890s Willard returned to a busy travel schedule. In February 1895 she presented the WCTU's Polyglot Petition to President Cleveland; then in June she sailed to England to prepare for and preside over the World's WCTU convention in London. Back in the United States in October, she addressed the National Purity Congress in New York and then chaired the National WCTU Convention in Baltimore, Maryland. In November of 1895 she launched a four-month tour of the southern United States, speaking and organizing in twelve states. During this final major speaking tour, Willard made particular efforts to persuade southern WCTU members to continue talking to men about women's need for and right to the ballot. She celebrated the fact that "in three states of the Republic women are full fledged citizens today. In one they have municipal [suffrage]; in twenty-five they have the educational ballot."[60]

In the summer of 1896 Willard took part in a major international effort to respond to the crisis precipitated by the genocidal policy of Turkish Sultan Abdulhamid II toward Armenian Christians. In addition to writing and speaking about the plight of the Armenian refugees to gain the attention of the Western world, Willard persuaded some local WCTUs to sponsor Armenian families wishing to immigrate to the United States. She and Isabel Somerset also traveled to the port of Marseilles, France, to help direct relief efforts among the Armenian refugees seeking asylum in Europe. Willard's work during the Armenian crisis, as well as her concern for Russian peasants injured and trampled to death during the coronation ceremonies of Czar Nicholas II in late May of 1896, reveal her deep conviction that the WCTU must respond to human suffering worldwide.[61]

During the last years of her life, Willard took an increasingly radical stance on economic and political reforms. Arguing for the absolute interconnectedness of all members of society, she asked for a commitment to social justice so deep "that there could be no rest while any lacked food, clothing or shelter, or while any were so shackled by the grim circumstances of life that they were unable to develop the best that was in them both in body and mind."[62] By the early 1890s she was also arguing for corporate ownership of the nation's major industries.[63] These positions, as well as her emerging view that alcohol abuse was as much as a consequence as a cause of poverty and related social ills, stretched the limits of her persuasive powers within the National WCTU. Though the size of the WCTU still provided her with a base of power within the reform community, by 1893 her sway over the organization had weakened, and her ability to mobilize its members to tackle the complex political and economic ills she identified was limited. As biographer Ruth Bordin makes clear, it was not only Willard's ideological overreach that led to a weakening of her leadership within the WCTU. Her repeated absences from the United States; various financial crises facing the organization, in particular those related to the Woman's Temple Project; and serious personal conflicts between several members of the organization's executive committee all contributed to her inability to sustain the organization's enthusiasm for her broadening vision of reform.[64]

Though Willard's persistent call for the increasingly radical reforms of Christian socialism did not shape the agenda of the National WCTU for the twentieth century, she continued to wield considerable influence as an internationally acclaimed reform leader and thinker even outside that organization. The program for peace and social and economic justice articulated by Christian socialists was not fully realized in Willard's day, nor has it been today; however, many of their ideas were adopted by the Progressive movement of the late nineteenth and early twentieth centuries. The settlement movement, municipal and election reforms, industrial safety and health regulations, workman's compensation, public lands, tax reform, as well as prohibition and women's suffrage are some of the early twentieth-century social movements and legislative accomplishments that grew out of the constellation of ideas for which Willard and many of her fellow reformers agitated throughout the 1890s. Their work built the ideological foundations and nurtured the idealism of the next generation of both female and male reformers. This fact was not lost on Reverend J. W. Bashford, the president of Ohio Wesleyan University. Shortly after Willard's death he declared that though her "title to heavenly fame is the fact that she left the world better than she found it," her push for farsighted and fundamental reforms in economic and political structures meant that she "belonged to the twentieth century rather than to the nineteenth."[65]

Women's suffrage and prohibition were the two particular reform victories of the early twentieth century with which Frances Willard is most readily identified. Though she would have viewed the passage of either of these reforms as cause for celebration (she always commemorated each positive step on the long road to reform), she would not have been surprised by the failure of each to bring about the total transformation of society that she envisioned. Her speeches and writings are infused with optimism, but Willard was not naïve about the complexities of social transformation. She saw suffrage as a necessary step, but never believed it was sufficient to establish women's equality. For her, such a goal would be accomplished only through decades of persistent work aimed at overcoming many additional obstacles, including the sexual double standard, the assumption that women's differences from men were evidence of women's physical and mental incompetence, and the habit of treating the ambitions of girls and boys quite differently. Even more important, she believed, would be the revolution of men's and women's roles within the home. Equal responsibility in caring for family and home, resolving the inconsistency she saw between the widespread attention to demands for the eight-hour work day for men and the absence of concern for "the sixteen hour day of the wife," would be necessary before women's equality could be approached.[66] In this sense, Willard's analysis of women's rights, though seen through her white, middle-class lens, prefigured second-wave feminism.

Neither did Willard believe that the adoption of a national prohibition amendment was a complete answer to the problems linked to alcohol and drug use. Twentieth-century movements such as Alcoholics Anonymous, the War on Drugs, and even Mothers Against Drunk Driving attest to the intractable nature of these problems. Nor did Willard insist that ridding the nation of alcoholism would be sufficient to alleviate poverty. Understanding that "Poverty causes intemperance and intemperance causes poverty and that is the whole of it," Willard did not view prohibition as a panacea that would solve the problems of poverty and protect the nation's citizens.[67] Rather, persistent attention to the integrated set of economic and social issues addressed by Christian Socialists was necessary to transform society. Prohibition was only one piece of a complex puzzle that reformers around the world were solving by taking one step at a time toward the advancement of humanity.

Willard never stopped urging WCTU members to push for those specific reforms as well as to participate in the everyday work of philanthropy. Yet in the last years of her life, she also hoped to convince them, as well as reform-minded men and women outside the WCTU, that the dramatic transformation Christian socialism promised to bring was the best possibility for fulfilling the dream of a truly just society. When she died of influenza, complicated by chronic anemia, on February 17, 1898, she was only fifty-nine years old. Willard knew that the struggle for social justice would go on, even as she hoped that she might be called on to wage "battles for God upon some other star."[68] In her works as well as her words, today's social activist can find inspiration and strategies for creating change. "I wonder why we don't set at work and abolish poverty in this great generous land within the next half century?" she asked in her final presidential address before the National WCTU.[69] It is a question that still haunts us today. We witness hunger in the midst of plenty and see the widening gap between the wealthy and the poor. We know that poverty, far from being a sign of the moral failure of the impoverished, is rather an indictment of our dominant culture's neglect and its perpetuation of nineteenth-century economic and power structures. Within this context Willard's voice and vision continues to speak and to spur broad-minded and compassionate activism.

Notes

1. The first quotation is from a tribute by Illinois Senator Shelby M. Cullom, and the second is from a prayer by Rev. Henry N. Couden, chaplain of the House of Representatives, published in *Statue of Miss Frances E. Willard, Erected in Statuary Hall of the Capitol Building at Washington: Proceedings in the Senate and the House of Representatives on the Occasion of the Acceptance of the Statue from the State of Illinois* (Washington: Government Printing Office, 1905), 43, 11.

2. Rev. Edward Everett Hale, Unitarian minister and longtime Chaplain of the Senate,

in a tribute to Willard included in Anna A. Gordon, *The Beautiful Life of Frances E. Willard: A Memorial Volume* (Chicago: Woman's Temperance Publishing Association, 1898), 381, and quoted by Illinois Representative George E. Foss at the ceremony of reception of Willard's statue in Statuary Hall, *Statue of Miss Frances E. Willard*, 51.

3. Several book-length biographies of Frances E. Willard have been published, including Ruth Bordin, *Frances Willard: A Biography* (Chapel Hill and London: University of North Carolina, 1986); Mary Earhart (Dillon), *Frances Willard: From Prayers to Politics* (Chicago: University of Chicago, 1944); Ray Strachey, *Frances Willard: Her Life and Work* (Fleming H. Revell, 1913); and Anna A. Gordon, *The Beautiful Life of Frances E. Willard* (Chicago: Woman's Temperance Publishing, 1898). Readers may also refer to the detailed "Timeline of Frances Willard's Life" in this present text.

4. For an early expression of Willard's patriotism, see her journal entry for July 4, 1855. For an example of her criticism of the country with regard to slavery, see her entry for December 2, 1859, the day of abolitionist John Brown's execution, in Gifford, *"Writing Out My Heart"*, 511–53. Historian Richard J. Carwardine masterfully depicts the religious/political environment the Willards and their midwestern communities inhabited in *Evangelicals and Politics in Antebellum America* (New Haven and London: Yale University, 1993).

5. Frances E. Willard, *Glimpses of Fifty Years: The Autobiography of an American Woman* (Boston: Geo. M. Smith, 1889), 7–8.

6. See William Rorabaugh, *The Alcoholic Republic: An American Tradition* (New York: Oxford University, 1979), for a thorough description of excessive drinking during the first half of the nineteenth century and the rise of the temperance movement during that time period.

7. Willard, *Glimpses of Fifty Years*, 351.

8. Willard, *Glimpses of Fifty Years*, 332.

9. See Willard's journal entry for May 19, 1860, describing her father's and brother's attendance the previous day at the Republican national convention when Abraham Lincoln was chosen as the party's presidential nominee. A complete transcription of the fifty volumes of Willard's journal, transcribed by Carolyn DeSwarte Gifford, is deposited at the Frances E. Willard Memorial Library, National WCTU headquarters, Evanston, Illinois, along with the original journal volumes. Quotations from the transcription will hereafter be cited as Willard's Journal.

10. See "Home Protection [I]," document 3 in the present volume, and "Exeter Hall Speech," document 18. The story appeared in several other speeches and articles from the 1870s through the 1890s.

11. Journal entry for February 21, 1860, in Gifford, ed., *"Writing Out My Heart"*, 60. Willard had read the text of Beecher's address "Woman's Influence in Politics" that appeared in the *Independent,* a popular religious newspaper, on February 16, 1860. Henry Ward Beecher (1813–87), famous Congregationalist preacher and author, was an influential spokesman for American middle-class Protestants during the height of his popularity in the 1860s.

12. Willard, journal entries for March 10, 20, and 21, in Gifford, *"Writing Out My Heart"*, 265–66 (emphases in original). Theodore Tilton (1835–1907), the editor-in-chief of the *Independent,* was on a speaking tour as a representative of the American Equal Rights Association, formed in 1866 to secure equal rights, especially suffrage, for all citizens regardless of race, color, or sex.

13. See Willard's journal entry for March 13, 1869 in Gifford, *Writing Out My Heart,* 298,

for a brief but illuminating statement on the freedom that Christianity, in both its theology and its practice, could offer women. See also Carolyn DeSwarte Gifford, "American Women and the Bible: The Nature of Woman as a Hermeneutical Issue" in Adela Yarbro Collins, ed., *Feminist Perspectives on Biblical Scholarship* (Chico, Calif.: Scholars Press, 1985), 25–30, for a comparison of Stanton's and Willard's understanding of Christianity's definition of womanhood and women's status.

14. Willard, journal entry for February 6, 1869, in Gifford, *"Writing Out My Heart"*, 292 (emphasis in original).

15. Willard, *Glimpses of Fifty Years*, 196.

16. Willard, journal entry for March 13, 1869, in Gifford, *"Writing Out My Heart"*, 298.

17. In Willard's story about watching her father and brother set out to vote in 1856, her sister cautions Willard not to voice her belief that women should also be able to vote. "If she did," her sister warned, the girls would be "called strong-minded." "Home Protection I," document 3 in this present text.

18. Quoted in R. F. Dibble, *Strenuous Americans* (New York: Boni and Liveright, 1923), 183.

19. *Life*, February 18, 1893, in Woman's Christian Temperance Union National Headquarters Historical Files (joint Ohio Historical Society and Michigan Historical Collections), *Temperance and Prohibition Papers*, microfilm edition, reel 40, frame 161. Hereafter, references to this microfilm series will be cited as WCTU series, followed by the appropriate reel number and frame number. For further discussion of Willard's womanly style see Amy Rose Slagell, "A Good Woman Speaking Well: The Oratory of Frances E. Willard" (PhD dissertation, University of Wisconsin-Madison, 1992), 20–86.

20. For Willard's vision of higher education for women, see her speech delivered on October 17, 1873, at the founding meeting of the Association for the Advancement of Women in Willard, "A New Departure in Woman's Higher Education," in Amy Rose Slagell, "A Good Woman Speaking Well," 147–59.

21. See Jack S. Blocker, *American Temperance Movements: Cycles of Reform* (Boston: Twayne Publishers, 1989), especially chapter 3, "Women Take the Lead," which ably presents the history of the WCTU in the context of the American temperance movement.

22. The WCTU claimed 150,000 dues-paying members in 1892. The combined membership of the WCTU and its children's and young women's auxiliaries was 200,000. Figures cited by Ruth Bordin in *Woman and Temperance: The Quest for Power and Liberty, 1873–1900* (Philadelphia: Temple University, 1981), 3.

23. See Ruth Bordin, *Woman and Temperance,* chapters 6 and 7 on the WCTU's legislative tactics and accomplishments.

24. For an excellent study of the World's WCTU within the context of the expansion of American and European ambitions toward empire around the world, see Ian Tyrell, *Woman's World, Woman's Empire: The Woman's Christian Temperance Union in International Perspective, 1880–1930* (Chapel Hill and London: University of North Carolina, 1991).

25. Willard, "First Presidential Address—1880," document 6 in this present text. Willard often repeated her insistence that "the human question" should be WCTU members' ultimate reform goal, for example in "The Dawn of Woman's Day," document 14 in this present text.

26. Willard, "Talks to Girls—No. III," from the *Chicago Post*, Scrapbook 6, 30, Frances E. Willard Memorial Library. Willard repeated this phrase in several key speeches and writings, including "Home Protection [II], document 5 in this present text.

27. Willard, "President's Annual Address" in *Minutes of the National Woman's Christian Temperance Union* (Chicago: Woman's Temperance Publication Association, 1888), 90.

28. For a different interpretation of Willard's concept of "womanhood," see Bonnie J. Dow, "The 'Womanhood' Rationale in the Woman Suffrage Rhetoric of Frances Willard" in *Southern Communication Journal* 56 (Summer 1991), 298–307. Also see Karlyn Kohrs Campbell's "Social Feminism: Frances Willard, 'Feminine Feminist'" in *Man Cannot Speak for Her: A Critical Study of Early Feminist Rhetoric* I (New York: Praeger, 1989), 121–32.

29. Willard, "The New Chivalry" can be found in Amy Rose Slagell, "A Good Woman Speaking Well," 124–41.

30. See Carolyn DeSwarte Gifford, "'The Woman's Cause Is Man's'? Frances Willard and the Social Gospel" in Wendy Deichmann Edwards and C. Gifford, eds., *Gender and the Social Gospel* (Urbana and Chicago: University of Illinois, 2003), 23–25, for an analysis of this speech.

31. Willard, in a letter written December 18, 1877, to the editor of the *Boston Daily Advertiser,* found in Willard, *Glimpses,* 550. Over the course of her WCTU presidency, she dubbed several male reformers "knights of the new chivalry," for example, Henry B. Blackwell, husband of women's rights and antislavery reformer Lucy Stone, and a famous reformer in his own right (inscription by Willard on the back of a photo of Blackwell, dated 1887, in the photograph collection, Willard Memorial Library).

32. See Jack S. Blocker, Jr., *"Give to the Winds Thy Fears": The Women's Temperance Crusade, 1873–1874* (Westport, C.T. and London: Greenwood, 1985) and Susan Dye Lee, "Evangelical Domesticity: The Origins of the WCTU under Frances Willard," (PhD dissertation, Northwestern University, 1980), for interpretations of the Woman's Temperance Crusade.

33. See Suzanne M. Marilley, *Woman Suffrage and the Origins of Liberal Feminism in the United States, 1820–1920* (Cambridge, Mass.: Harvard University, 1996), chapter 4, "The Feminism of Fear."

34. See "Home Protection II," document 5 in this present text, and Amy R. Slagell, "The Rhetorical Structure of Frances E. Willard's Campaign for Woman Suffrage, 1876–1896," *Rhetoric and Public Affairs 4* (Spring 2001), 1–23.

35. Willard, "Talks to Girls," an eight-part series in the *Chicago Post,* Spring 1878, in Scrapbook 6, 29–35, Willard Memorial Library. These articles form the basis of Willard's book *How to Win: A Book for Girls* (See document 12 in this present text.)

36. Willard, "Talks to Girls—No. III," from the *Chicago* Post, Scrapbook 6, 30.

37. See Amy R. Slagell, "Making the World More Homelike: The Reform Rhetoric of Frances E. Willard," in Martha Solomon and Thomas Burkholder, eds., *A Rhetorical History of the United States, Volume 5* (Lansing: Michigan State University Press, forthcoming).

38. Willard, "The New Ideal of Manhood," in *How to Win,* document 12 in this present text.

39. Willard, "The New Ideal of Womanhood" and "The New Ideal of Manhood," in *How to Win,* document 12 in this present text and "Social Purity," document 11 in this text.

40. Willard, "Woman and Organization," 1891, document 16 in this present text.

41. Willard, "The Dawn of Woman's Day," in *Our Day,* 2 (November 1888), document 14 in this present text.

42. Willard, Presidential Address (Chicago: Woman's Temperance Publishing Association, 1895), 60, 59.

43. Willard, Presidential Address, 1880, in *The Minutes of the Woman's National Christian Temperance Union* (New York: The National Temperance Society and Publication House, 1880), document 6 in this present text.

44. See Gifford, *Writing Out My Heart,* entry for March 21, 1863 (210–11), in which she described her delight at viewing scenes of Europe and the Middle East through a stereoscope at the home of a Pittsburgh art collector.

45. Willard, "1891 Presidential Address," (Chicago: Woman's Temperance Publishing Association, 1891), 133. Willard used the image often in speeches and writings, expanding its scope and implications for the meaning of the partnership of women and men. Reference to "the stereoscopic view" occurs, for example, in "Personal Liberty," document 8 in this present text, where she argued for the necessity of prohibition and in *Woman in the Pulpit* (Chicago: Woman's Temperance Publishing Association, 1889), 21, where she insisted on training women scholars to interpret scriptures previously given a patriarchal interpretation by men.

46. As a young woman, Willard recorded in her journal her love for Elizabeth Barrett Browning's poem, "The Cry of the Human" (entry for March 28, 1861, in Gifford, *Writing Out My Heart,* 109). She often quoted the poem's title in her own speeches and writings, using it as a phrase indicating a plea to feel compassion for the entire human race.

47. Willard, "Home Protection—II" *The Independent,* July 10, 1879, 13 (see document 5 in this present text).

48. Willard Journal, January 6, 1870. A slightly different version of this quote occurs in Willard, *Glimpses of Fifty Years,* 274.

49. Willard Journal 34, January 10, 1870, Willard Memorial Library.

50. Willard, journal entries for early 1875 in *Glimpses,* 342–47.

51. Willard, *How to Win,* 42, (below). See also Willard, "Woman and Philanthropy (1887)" in Amy Rose Slagell, "A Good Woman Speaking Well," 395–406.

52. See Preface, note 8.

53. Willard, "1891 Presidential Address," *Minutes of the National Woman's Christian Temperance Union* (Chicago: Woman's Temperance Publishing Association, 1891), 93.

54. See Willard, "The Dawn of Woman's Day," document 14 in this present test, especially section titled "Some of the Reflex Results."

55. For examples of Willard's use of these slogans, see *Do Everything: A Handbook for the World's White Ribboners* (Chicago: Woman's Temperance Publishing Association, 1895); Willard, "The Do Everything Policy," in Willard, 1893 Presidential Address, document 19 in this present text; and Willard, 1891 Presidential Address, 88.

56. Willard, "1893 Presidential Address," document 19 in this present text.

57. See Richard W. Leeman, *"Do Everything" Reform: The Oratory of Frances E. Willard* (New York and Westport, C.T.: Greenwood Press, 1992), especially chapter 4, "Christian Socialism."

58. Willard, 1897 Presidential Address, "President's Annual Address," document 22 in this present text. See also Willard, "The Coming Brotherhood," document 17, and Willard, 1889 Presidential Address, document 15.

59. Letter quoted in George T. B. Davis, "The Greatest Woman. Miss Frances E. Willard's Last Autobiographical Interview" in *Our Day* (March 1898, v. 18, 107–16) on http://prohibition.history.ohio-state.edu/Willard/Willard_last_interview.htm.

60. Willard, "Address at the Nashville Tabernacle," December 15, 1895, in Amy Rose Slagell, "A Good Woman Speaking Well," 641.

61. Willard, "1896 Presidential Address" in Amy Rose Slagell, "Good Woman Speaking Well," 664.

62. Willard, "Thirteenth Presidential Address," October 16, 1893, document 19 in this present text.

63. See Willard, "Eighteenth Presidential Address," October 29, 1897, document 22 in this present test.

64. See, Bordin, *Frances Willard,* chapter 12, and Bordin, *Woman and Temperance,* chapter 8. As Bordin suggests, the narrowing of the reform interests of the National WCTU in the years following Willard's death indicate that by the end of her career, her leadership of that organization had come to be grounded more in the admiration its members had for her than in their assent to her sweeping reform agenda.

65. Quoted in Anna A. Gordon, *The Beautiful Life of Frances E. Willard,* 398.

66. Willard, "Women and Organization" February 23, 1891, document 16 in this present text.

67. Willard, "Thirteenth Presidential Address," October 16, 1893, document 19 in this present text.

68. These are the closing words from Willard's 1897 Presidential Address, document 22 in this present text.

69. See document 22 in this present text.

Our goals in producing this collection are, first, to represent the wide range of Frances E. Willard's ideas and strategies as well as the varied audiences to whom she spoke and wrote during her reform career; and second, to present texts that are accurate and readable for a twenty-first-century audience. Our commitment to demonstrating a spectrum of Willard's works made it impossible to include full versions of several of her more lengthy texts, especially her published presidential addresses. It became necessary to excerpt these texts, using ellipses to indicate each time original text was edited for brevity. Throughout the process we aimed to preserve Willard's voice and to respect her considerable skill as a writer. At the end of the head note for each document is a full citation of the source for the text, allowing readers to refer to the original document if they wish.

We have added occasional bracketed comments or footnotes when needed for clarity. Our concern was to provide the kind of information necessary to understanding the gist of Willard's ideas in the passage and to facilitate understanding of the significant nineteenth-century figures who influenced Willard's thought and helped carry on the work of the reforms she championed. To avoid overwhelming readers with such explanations, we adopted several guidelines.

1. Insert brackets to explain or translate occasional obscure or uncommon foreign language terms.
2. Insert brackets to indicate the source of biblical quotations and paraphrases of them.
3. Insert footnotes to briefly explain references to historical events or figures necessary to understanding Willard's point in the passage.
4. Insert footnotes to identify the first mention of the significant individuals Willard names in her speeches and writings.
5. Insert brackets to indicate the full name of individuals mentioned in the texts whose historical impact or influence on Willard were not especially significant.

We have applied these guidelines to the best of our ability. In some cases we have been unable to confirm birth or death dates for our identifications or to uncover a first name for a temperance organizer in the western states. The decision to refrain from adding citations for each poem, hymn, or other literature quoted or alluded to in the texts was made both because such citations are not necessary to understand the meaning of the passages and also to limit interruptions for the reader. Biblical references are included because they infuse Willard's discourse, say much about her worldview, and are an important marker of the cultural meanings she shared with her audience. Among academics today it is easy to misread the language of nineteenth-century liberal evangelical Protestantism and to associate it with the contemporary discourse of the religious right. But like the discourse of many civil rights leaders and liberation theologians, Willard's use of biblical language may remind readers that liberal religion and biblical ideas have often laid the foundation for powerful liberal and progressive reforms.

The documents in this collection have been printed as they appeared in the original sources with the following silent changes:

1. Obvious printing errors have been corrected.
2. Nineteenth-century punctuation, spelling, and capitalization have been modernized when deemed necessary to avoid confusion or misreading. The spelling of British terms has been changed to those of American English (except for Document 18, which is a text given in England). Terms such as *woman's* (as in Woman's Christian Temperance Union) or *women's* (as in "women's suffrage) have been made consistent.
3. Paragraphing and punctuation have been added as needed to aid clarity.
4. Titles, usually descriptive, have been given to speeches in cases where no title was indicated in the text or in newspaper reports.
5. Brackets in printed documents have been converted to parentheses.
6. Obvious titles of books and newspapers have been italicized when they were not italicized in the original.
7. Section headings in texts that were found in newspaper reports have been removed. Section headings Willard used when publishing her presidential addresses have been retained.

Speeches and Writings

ONE

"Everybody's War," Fall 1874

Frances Willard's earliest temperance speeches, represented below in "Everybody's War," were linked to the widespread surge of protest against alcohol by middle-class women in the winter of 1873–74. In what came to be known as the Woman's Temperance Crusade, thousands of women in dozens of midwestern towns and cities took to the streets to protest the negative impact of alcohol use and the liquor industry on homes and their communities. From its beginnings in Hillsboro, Ohio, Crusade participants marched, sang, and prayed their way into the hearts of both those who drank and those who sold them liquor, imploring them to reform. By early spring of 1874 the spark of the Crusade had reached Chicago, where local church women asked Willard to lend her skills to the movement. On March 30, 1874, while still dean of women at Northwestern University, Willard gave what she considered her first temperance speech. She delivered it at Chicago's Clark Street Methodist Church. "What I said I do not know," she recalled years later in her autobiography, "except that I was with the women heart, hand and soul, in this wonderful new "'Everybody's War.'"[1]

This speech marked the beginning of Willard's move from the field of education to reform. During the spring of 1874 she made a handful of temperance speeches and resigned her position at Northwestern. That summer she set off for the East Coast, where she conversed with leaders of the movement, attended several temperance camp meetings, and participated in the tail end of the Crusade in Pittsburgh, visiting a saloon with a band of protesting women. By September, Willard had returned home as the president of the Chicago Woman's Temperance Union. Soon she became secretary of the Illinois Woman's Christian Temperance Union (WCTU) and in November was sent as a delegate to the first national meeting of women temperance leaders, in Cleveland, Ohio. There she was elected corresponding secretary of the newly formed National WCTU.

Willard's sense of urgency concerning the movement against the saloon was reflected in her discourse during this period. She called liquor selling a "crime," a combination of "theft, arson, murder, and treason," which had to be "warred upon."[2] At this time Willard's war work combined the direct action outreach programs housed in downtown Chicago's Farwell Hall with the organizational work of mustering more women and resources. No record has been found of the Gospel Temperance talks she gave at the weekly meetings downtown, but the following text is an excellent example of her early temperance rhetoric aimed to recruit workers and funds. Most likely given in October 1874, the speech, titled "Everybody's War," aimed to awaken her audience, largely women and children, to the harms of alcohol use in America and motivate them to play an active role on the temperance battlefield.

This address shows the range of Willard's arguments, from the theoretical to the imminently practical. She argued, for example, that the temperance fight was linked to patriotism. The very nature of American democracy made demands on citizens quite different from those made in a hereditary monarchy. The safety of the republic required that ballots be cast by clear-thinking citizens rather than by those who "stagger up to the polls." At the same time, however, she encouraged listeners to show their support for temperance in very practical ways, such as eschewing alcoholic celebrations of New Year's Day or contributing money to the cause. Even in this early temperance speech Willard asserted her faith that the ballot was a source of vital power and its appropriate use was inextricably linked to the success of the temperance cause.

"Everybody's War" stands as an example of Willard's earliest contributions to the movement. Though less sophisticated than her later discourse, it introduces some of the themes and devices on which she would rely throughout her career. The war metaphor developed here must have had considerable resonance to a generation that lived through the Civil War. Willard's war cry made it clear that though the saloon visits of the Woman's Temperance Crusade had passed, women had been awakened to the effects of alcohol on their lives, on their communities, and on the destiny of the nation. As "daughters of America" they would continue to find ways to ameliorate these harms.

The transcript from which this text is derived was found in a speech file at the Frances Willard Memorial Library in WCTU headquarters in Evanston, Illinois. It is not in Willard's hand and its conversational quality suggests that it is a stenographer's recording.

* * *

At one of the meetings of the Woman's Temperance Union there was a poor fellow present, written all over from head to foot with evidences of a dissolute life. He came to the altar after the meeting and said to [the speaker] "I want you to remain a few moments when the rest are gone for I have something I propose to show you."

Now boys and girls I want you to listen—what do you suppose it was? He took out of his pocket an old soiled package—he took off a paper and inside of that was another, a little cleaner—he took that off and inside was *another* and inside of that was a tissue paper, nice and white, and inside of all this there was a photograph. The [speaker] looked at the photograph—it represented a young man about eighteen years old, a pleasant nice looking, young fellow. She looked at this man who was standing there before her so distressed an object in every way and she said curiously, "this photograph represents a friend of yours perhaps." And what do you suppose he answered her? "Well lady I ain't showed myself much of a friend to him, that photograph is me, before I took to drinking whiskey and I thought I ought to show it to you for my mother's sake." She looked at the frank open face of the photograph and at the blurred sad wrinkled face of the man, at the nice white collar and nice tie in the photograph, then at the thin collarless shirt of the man. She thought of the time when this man, standing before her now so weary and troubled—once, lay in his happy boyhood days sleeping upon his mother's breast. She thought of the time when first his footsteps wandered beyond the shelter of the quiet happy home towards the sinful resorts that we legalize on either side along our street. Then she turned to the man and photograph and turned her eyes to heaven with that old cry, "How long, Oh God how long" [Isaiah 7:11].

This sort of thing might do for others—for other lands, but it will not do for the land of the star-spangled banner. It may have done for other times but it will not do for the nineteenth century. It might do for other people but it will not do for the descendants of the Pilgrim Fathers and William Penn.[3] I say there is a war about it in America—a war about that sort of thing which changes men so that their mothers after a few years would not know them, for though all mothers may not have their hearts broken—may have no sons—no boys who carried on to destruction, yet our Christian republic may not legalize the deadly traffic in that which they know by observation is likely in all cases to lead to that precise result.

Ladies of the north side I am sad but frank to say it, there has not been so much interest shown in this quarter of the city as in others in the temperance movement by the women. I want to ask you now if you have not joined before in this work, hadn't you better in the name of these boys and girls sitting here, hadn't you better? I came here today through blocks and blocks of saloons and almost under the very shadow of great grinding distilleries. There are no insurance policies upon your homes, the rum shops have the free run of the whole place—the home of the American Eagle.

Remember it is simply a matter of fact that from the rum shops every year in America sixty thousand of our citizens reel out into eternity and taste a drunkard's death. There are half a million steady drinkers, behind this a million moderate drinkers, behind *them* two millions occasional drinkers, behind them all little boys go tramp, tramp, tramp to a drunkard's tomb; And remember these unfurling ranks, for they are always full you know, must be recruited from somebody's cradle, from somebody's fireside, perhaps your own, no matter how stately or proud that home may be. Some ladies say to me with all sobriety . . . "I wish the best in the world for your grand cause—I hope it will succeed but then I have no boys." Perhaps you have daughters—if you have not somebody has and somebody has boys. If you have daughters and not sons try to fathom the unfathomable lessons of these words "*A drunkard's wife.*"

There is a war about this in America, a war of mothers and daughters, sisters and wives. There is another sort of war and I want to have the boys and girls follow me as I talk to them and I think I can make you understand me. There is a war between the rum shops and religion. They stand over against each other, unsurmountable and unalterable foes. You know the late pen of Seward wrote of our late war as an irrepressible conflict.[4] We have an irrepressible conflict, a war to the knife and the knife to the hilt. Only one can win, the question is which one is it going to be? Now think about it. In this war with them, I take it, we Christians of the church, we [don't] outnumber them.

Did you ever think of it little people? There are in this city for instance a certain number of churches and for every church there are from twenty-five to thirty whiskey shops. There are for every minister twenty-five or thirty barkeepers and while the churches only meet and open their blessed doors once or twice or at most four or five times a week, the whiskey shops grind on their mill of destruction all the days of every week, all the weeks of every month and all the months of every year.

We are outnumbered, are we not? We are outgeneraled by the people who keep the rum shops—we who keep the Sunday school and the church. They have a series of lessons, international if you please, with which ours of the Sunday school does not compare at all. They have their music of which I would not speak, their literature free by license, of which I would not think. One of our reformed men was talking with me one day of a friend of his who had signed the pledge and broken it; he was discouraged; he had taken a binding pledge and broken it again and again. This is what the reformed man said to me: "I said you don't understand the business, that is all. You are new in the business. You must not get discouraged; don't you give Tim up or anything of the sort. You remember he is a graduate in a seven-years course in a saloon. It took him seven years to learn all that education in the saloon, now give him a year or two to unlearn it—the education of the saloon."

Then the man went on to say "do you know that in the saloon conscience is considered a fraud and a jest. Do you know that in the saloon the religion of Christ is counted just simply an old wife's fable, that Christ is an exploded myth, the Christ of whom you women like to talk about is only the fevered fancy of woman's dream?" I tell you my eyes have been opened with wonder to see things I didn't use to see at all. I saw dear friends going up and down our streets. I saw things I liked to see. I saw pleasant homes on every side of the way. I saw churches which are suggestive of immortal hope. I saw bookstores at once honey hives of thought.

Do you know that, until the Woman's Crusade came sweeping up over our prairies, I never cared? I never saw a saloon. It was a question with which I had nothing to do. It was nothing to me. I hoped [the Crusade] would succeed, but I did not see it the same as I do today. Let me tell you young people the way I seem to see it now—you just reflect—I go up and down the streets here in Chicago. I go up and down the streets of other town[s] and cities throughout the west on the errand I believe God sent me to go upon. If I did not believe it I would not go. I see on one corner church spires, tall and stately pointing heavenward. I see over on another corner of the same street a schoolhouse with doors opening wide, and little boys and girls, youths and maidens drinking at the pure fountain of knowledge. And between these two are institutions called saloons, equally guaranteed by our laws, equally fostered by our nation and more than equally patronized by our people. There is no boy or girl so high that they don't know what I mean. It has a sanded floor, its curtains halfway down. It has a screen across the front so you can't see what is going on inside. It has fumes and odors coming out of its doors that make you wish you had passed on the other side. You know I mean the rum shop.

Let us go in with this man who was taught in our Sunday schools. When he was the least bit of a boy he sat in his father's pew Sunday after Sunday, with an honorable and useful life stretching before him, [as] the minister spoke of life, duty and destiny and another life coming on afterwards. Let us go in here with this boy who later was taught in our public schools until he knew something of [the world?].

But he got in the way of going in here. He did not go at first because he wanted to but because someone asked him to. He did only as other young men did, and he thought it the proper thing to do, to be social. As the habit grew upon him, he failed in business, his friends deserted him; he lost those who were dearer to him than life. Then he did not care.

Let us go in with some friend and see this transaction. Behind the counter stands avarice, before the counter appetite, and between the two a transaction that puts a few dimes into the till of the proprietor and drives voluntary insanity into the brain of the patron. The man goes out, he goes to the primary meeting and election, he loiters away his time, he fritters away his earnings. He goes to the house where he is best beloved, to the best friends he has in the world, where they love *him* better then they do anybody else. Yet upon that wife that loves him so well and little children clinging about his neck, he inflicts atrocities which imagination cannot picture and no tongue dare describe. Now I am not telling you anything that does not happen in Chicago a hundred times a day. If it had happened away up among the Eskimo, if it had happened down among the South Sea Islanders or on the prairies where the wild Indians live, we would say it is just what we should expect of such people. But these rum shops do exist and this rum traffic is going on by permission and apathy of well-born, well-bred and well-taught Americans. These rum shops exist in the shape of Juggernaut's old car.[5] They stand in the shadow of the sacred wide arms of the Cross of Christ, the Jesus Christ our Lord. That is why there is a war about it in America.

I shall not dwell long on that, but pass on to the taxpayers revolt. We people don't see the effect of all this. You know we used to say we must have this money to help pay the taxes, this liquor tax of seventy millions a year but we have found out that the liquor traffic makes a cat's-paw of the taxpayers to rake in the hot chestnuts of ninety millions a year for extra paraphernalia. I want the boys particularly to remember this—that more than all the revenue derived from the whiskey shops must go to build prisons, must go [to] the hospital, the home for the friendless, police justices and police officers to take care of these people who go crazy on purpose and to pay all that, so that it costs us yearly the difference between seventy and ninety millions of dollars. We have lost yearly on that old financial basis twenty millions a year—twenty millions lost. I want you to think about that—that is the very thing we do.

Another thing—I don't suppose everybody who is listening to me knows what all these drinks are made out of—out of the nice clean grain that grows out of the ground, wheat, rye, barley, corn. We use in America forty millions of bushels of nice clean grain [that] is turned over into alcoholic drinks every year. Now a good man has found out by mathematical calculation that we drink enough to pay for paving a good wide street long enough to reach all the way from Chicago to New York. Our yearly drink bill in Illinois is forty-two millions of dollars and in the country six hundred millions. There is no use in stopping to dwell longer upon these statistics. These are facts and figures which we cannot deny. We have to take this money out of our pockets and pay it to the very last cent. This we find out from Secretary [of the U.S. Treasury, Benjamin H.] Bristow in his last report, so it is plain enough.

There is another kind of war; it is the patriot's war. I do not believe there is one boy or girl here tonight that he or she does not revere the old flag, the red white and blue. I remember when I was a little girl, away up in Wisconsin, the 4th of July, I remember, when we had our little procession and flags made from a pillow case with red calico stripes sewed on and gold stars pinned on the corner. I was going to talk about the harm the liquor traffic does to the country and the flag we love so well, for I tell you I always loved the flag. Yes it is a patriot's war because in our country we get up public opinion—everybody thinks one man's vote is as good as another even though he staggers up to the polls and drops in the ballot on election day. Our people are made to think you cannot change the habits and drinking customs they had over across the sea where one man is not as good as another on election day—where they have such a different government altogether. We should, I think, remember what difference there is between them and us. We are taught to pray: "Thy Kingdom come, Thy will be done." Where? "On earth." [Matthew 6:10]. We sing the sacred hymn: "bring forth the Royal diadem and crown Him Lord of all." We as a people believe what this good book says when it plainly again and again declares that Christ is again going to rule on earth. How is he going to rule until we get all the rum shops out of the way?

Now let us take the contrast—there is Germany. Let us take that. Germany is a country governed by a hereditary monarch. They know who is to be the next king; this king he rules until he is relieved by death. Then his son rules and so on with the never-ending formula. They never ask who is going to be the next President; they know who is to be the next king. In America every man is King—King over whom? King over his own self. In Germany they are nudged on by two million bayonets. In America ballots are bayonets. Every drunkard, every rum seller holds that in his hand which may shake the very President in his chair. In America there are one million drunkards and rum sellers who stagger up to the polls and exercise that sacred right. They are in every ward, in every precinct, and every election district. They stagger up to the polls and drop in their bleared ballots. What fruits can we expect but salary grabbers, [corner?] rings, whiskey rings, post tradership rings, and every sort of ring except the ring of the true metal? Going on at this rate no one needs to be a prophet to see what this thing will lead to.

It is a patriot's war indeed; it is everybody's war great and small, from the least to the greatest, and what a war it is. We must guard [against] it as we would a foreign foe. I like the idea of marching along with men and women who have their eyes open. I like to go along keeping time to the same music ever singing that good old song: "I'm glad I'm in this army, I will battle for the cause." You think maybe the Crusade is dead and its banner trailing in the dust, I tell you no—the women who marched with the crusade, don't you believe they are somewhere? The children of these men and women are being sworn at the home altars against this traffic as Hannibal was sworn against Rome.[6] The method is changed but the movement is just the same. [Even] if the world was asleep, you young people would understand that, but the world is awake, its heart is sad, its lips are apart and its eyelids wide.

I am here tonight dear friends, an American woman forever grateful to the land that has been so good to me and whose path in life has been turned out of the expected channel by the crusade, I am here to ask you just this simple question: Is all this anything at all to you? How is your stand affected by it? How are you toward the temperance reform? How are you in the sentiments you cherish in your hearts? That is it. You know what Mrs. Stowe[7] said about it—if you can't say anything about it, you can feel right. How are you in the sentiments you express? How are you on election day when Aldermen are to be elected? How are you when a notice comes for a primary? How do you stand upon the question on New Year's Day? How do you stand in the social sanctity? Let me tell you it makes all the difference in the world how you *stand* though you never say one word or give one dollar toward our cause—if you only just care.

There is a noble fellow on the board of trade in this city who said to me the other day, "I can't do much for the cause; I read about it and think about it, but it has just come into my head what I could do. I often am asked when closing a bargain to go out and take a glass of beer or even something stronger. I always used to and used to say to them 'I don't care,' and thought it was the proper thing to do. I just stopped short off—I will not do it. When men ask me I will say I have joined the temperance ranks. I believe as the women do." That man is a regular temperance lecturer—for he *acts*. I think we are all sympathetic on this subject. I don't believe there is any difference between us in the contest. We are moving on the enemy's track. I think if I were to ask any little boy or girl here the reason why these people carry on this business, the answer would be because there is money in it. That goes straight to the mark; that answer is just exactly right. There is this about it, there [are] large sums of money invested in this traffic. Ours is no light reform. There [are] seven hundred millions invested in this rum traffic this very day and you know the way to get at these men is to touch their pocket books. Every man who is informed by our efforts makes that much less revenue for them. This seven hundred millions ought to be taken out of this rum traffic and be invested in other branches of trade which would go toward making up our national life and prosperity.

I want to say a few words more before I close; I want to say just this one thing more on this subject. In a few days from now you will be called upon to go to the polls inasmuch as there are to be thirty-six or thirty-eight aldermen to be elected in the city of Chicago. It is a vital question to us what sort of men they are. Although the women cannot go to the polls to vote, let me urge upon them to send their sons and their husbands there. Will you remember good sirs that when you go to the election you represent more than you did once; you represent more thoughts, more work, more prayer; remember whom you want and whom you will have. Let us work and pray for the good time coming when this city shall be redeemed. Although we are not voters, we are daughters of America, as much as you are sons and patriots. We need money to carry on this war—we cannot like King Midas turn everything into gold. I know that times are hard. You have your office rents to pay and all your other expenses, but we need money to buy temperance literature and different things we have to have to carry on the war; and when you can give a dollar, remember, you cannot give it to a more worthy cause than ours. Then I want the boys to remember that men are only boys grown tall. We count on you to help our cause. We should have the aid of the young men in the strength and vigor of their youth, in the glory of their manhood, and I want the young ladies to support them in their work. You who are sheltered at home must remember that they are tempted and tried. I want you to remember that your words and acts in the social circle have everything to do with the way in which young men stand affected by this temperance question.

And often to me nowadays comes the thought of something in my life very dear and distant—something which I do not hesitate to speak to you about. I want to speak to you about my sister loved and lost.[8] Many years ago away up in Wisconsin, where we spent our girlhood days, that little girl was my only playmate. And there upon a fallen tree trunk, little Lizzie she would stand and make a temperance speech to me, little thing, and I in turn would make one to her just for play. And now I think as I go about in this new and strange work that she knows about it and cares about it—that I am not alone. I am reminded of the sad sweet message she left when she went away from us. . . . [S]he laid her dying head upon the pillow and looked at me with that strange look in her eyes, which were growing dim; she uttered these last words, "Sister I want you to tell everybody to be good." Then she turned her face away and when I saw it next, it had upon it that smile of God's eternal peace.

I say tonight I want to leave in your hearts these burning words. I do not think I shall ever forget her sweet dying message. I wish it might be remembered as she so gently expressed it, "be good." Be good and help everybody to be good who needs help. God grant that each of us this night may have a clear formula of life, which should be nothing more nor less than to be *good*.

Notes

1. Willard, *Glimpses of Fifty Years: The Autobiography of an American Woman* (Chicago: Woman's Temperance Publishing Association, 1889), 336.

2. *Chicago Tribune*, April 6, 1874.

3. Penn (1644–1718) was a prominent English Quaker and founder of the American colony of Pennsylvania.

4. William Henry Seward (1801–72), U.S. Senator and antislavery politician, delivered his famous speech on the Civil War, "The Irrepressible Conflict," on October 25, 1858, in Rochester, New York.

5. *Juggernaut* refers to an image of the Hindu god Krishna in Orissa, India, which was loaded onto a cart during an annual festival and drawn through the streets where some devotees reportedly threw themselves under the wheels to be crushed.

6. Hannibal Barca (247–183 BCE) was the General of Carthage during the Second Punic War; at the age of nine he was said to have sworn before an altar to oppose Rome.

7. Harriet Beecher Stowe (1811–96), an American author of moral fiction, is best known for her novel *Uncle Tom's Cabin* (1852), which brought many people to support the anti-slavery movement.

8. Willard's sister, Mary Eliza Willard, referred to as "Lizzie" here, though Willard usually called her Mary, died in June 1862 of typhoid at the age of nineteen. In her first book, *Nineteen Beautiful Years* (New York: Harper and Bros., 1864), Willard tells the story of Mary's life and death including the injunction from this speech that Willard should tell everyone to "be good."

TWO

Hints and Helps in Our Temperance Work, 1875

Willard composed her how-to manual *Hints and Helps in Our Temperance Work* to provide detailed "information for everybody who wants to know how to go to work." As corresponding secretary for the National WCTU, Willard's most formidable task was organizing local WCTUs throughout the country, recruiting the women's "temperance army" that would fight in the reform she had earlier dubbed "Everybody's War." As she began traveling to cities and towns in the Midwest, speaking to church groups and parlor meetings, and corresponding with those who wished to enlist in the reform effort, Willard discovered that many women had almost no idea of how to build and run an organization or even how to chair a meeting. With a sense of great urgency, she wrote her colleague Annie Wittenmyer, the newly elected president of the National WCTU: "Letters from all parts of the country reveal the utmost interest and ignorance combined. The women are eager for the fray but untaught as to the tactics."[1] To meet this pressing need for training, Willard quickly put together her handbook *Hints and Helps in Our Temperance Work.*

The manual contained every bit of information that Willard could think of at that point that might be helpful for women forming local unions. The bulk of the document (omitted here) consisted of sample temperance pledges; constitutions for local, district, and state groups; instructions for founding and maintaining local unions; and "The Plan of Work" authorized by the National WCTU. It even included an exhaustive list of temperance publications, complete with publishers' addresses so WCTU women could immediately send away for tracts and pamphlets for distribution to new members and others interested in learning about the reform.

The section called "General Hints" (included here) was packed with suggestions that reflected both sweeping aims and specific targets. No aspect of organizing was too small to merit her attention, as evidenced, for example, by her warning to prayer meeting leaders to choose a place that is "*centrally located* and *not* up several flights of stairs*." With humor and dedication, Willard did her best to prepare WCTU women for their task. Armed with her manual, women could go forth with confidence to do battle against their formidable foe: the liquor industry.

The methods and strategies Willard proposed in *Hints and Helps* showed that WCTU leaders understood from the organization's beginning stages that the "peaceful war" against alcohol would be waged in several ways and on several fronts. Recruits would be drawn mainly and most easily (but not exclusively) from Protestant churches, traditionally the strongest supporters of the temperance movement. The organization would have a deeply religious tone and spirit; prayer would always remain its basis of strength. Its members, however, would move beyond home and church to act in the political realm as a legitimate expression of their responsible Christian citizenship. WCTU women would seek to influence the moral climate in the business world as well, believing that this sphere required women's presence and interest as much as the political sphere. They would also work to build the next generation of temperance reformers by founding groups for children and young women and men.

In order to accomplish all this, Willard knew very well that most WCTU women needed to be convinced of their ability to do what their organization asked of them. They must receive large doses of encouragement and support in their efforts. The underlying message in her manual was that she and the rest of the WCTU leadership were available to women new to the work, open to their questions and suggestions, and willing to help them as they began "the long campaign" for a sober America.

The following excerpts are from Frances E. Willard, *Hints and Helps in Our Temperance Work* (New York: National Temperance Society and Publication House, 1875), 7–8, 59–70.

* * *

To the Women of America

The world's "Banner Nation" and our mother-land has ten times as many liquor-saloons as it has churches and school-houses. These cost us, annually, fifteen and one-half times as much as our schools of all grades, and more money than we have used in carrying on Christ's church since the landing of the Pilgrims. Fifty per cent of the insanity in America comes of strong drink. Seventy-five per cent of all the murders grow out of drunken brawls. Eighty-six percent of all our criminals became such while crazed by alcohol. Ninety-five per cent of our vicious youth emerge from the homes of those who drink. Each year, one hundred thousand of our citizens reel out into eternity through the awful doorway of a drunkard's death.

Beloved sisters, as you read these facts, will you, each, ask this question earnestly, thoughtfully, of God for you will meet it at the last:

"Is all this anything to me?"

If it is not, just put my little book aside—give it to "somebody who cares." But if it is, read on; and may your zeal be kindled and your hands strengthened for the blessed service in Christ Jesus.

Such "Hints and Helps" as follow are the fruit of personal experience, of conversations, letters from ladies and gentlemen prominent in the temperance work, and of a careful examination of documents and current temperance literature. The providential uprising of women known as "The Crusade" has been as providentially succeeded by the "sober, second thought" of organization. An attempt has here been made to anticipate questions that arise in the minds of Christian women who are willing to labor in the temperance cause, but not informed concerning plans of organization or methods of work. . . .

General Hints

Occasional *days of fasting and prayer* are a great help. Select a subject and appoint a leader for each hour in the day. Let the place of your prayer-meetings (daily or otherwise) be *centrally located* and *not* up several flights of stairs. In some towns a room at the rail-road depot has been used as the rendezvous of the Woman's Temperance Union, and also as a public reading-room. Call out home talent as much as possible in mass-meetings.

Write to your state secretary for a list of the best speakers available to you. Observe the 23rd of December, the anniversary of the crusade, by special exercises, in which men, women, and children all participate.

Get correct statistics of intemperance in *your own town,* and have them kept before the people. These will tell more than imported figures. Interest the press in your work. Give your editors facts. Wherever practicable, edit a column in the local newspaper in the interest of the reform, and strive, by all honorable means, to enlist the press as our most powerful ally.

Offer prizes, so far as practicable, in Sabbath-schools, secular schools, and seminaries,[2] for essays on different aspects of the temperance question, and offer prizes of temperance stories to the child bringing the largest number of new members into Juvenile Unions.

Organize *Temperance Glee Clubs* of young people, also Social Clubs and Young Ladies' Unions, where the exercises and influences shall all strengthen *the total abstinence sentiment.* Get music of Mr. Stearns,[3] 58 Reade Street, New York, and of music publishers in your town.

Have a "Pulpit and Press Secretary" to attend to special notices, and select that rare treasure—*somebody who will actually do the work assigned her.* Get the Address and Plan of Work of the Woman's National Union published in just as many papers as possible.

Whatever you neglect, *keep up your prayer-meeting,* and so far as possible get men and women in the bondage of strong drink to come there and sign the pledge and seek "the Lord behind the pledge." *But* while you are thus caring for the sick and wounded, do not forget that, after all, your most effective work is *drilling the juvenile troops,* and carrying your peaceful war right into the ranks of the men who vote, and the men who sell intoxicating liquor.

Much has been said about our negligence in rendering our homes attractive and our *cuisine* appetizing; and not always without reason. We therefore recommend that in our unions essays on the science and art of making home outwardly wholesome and attractive be read, books on that subject circulated, and all possible effort made to secure a more scientific attention to the products of the kitchen, and a higher aesthetic standard for the parlor.

Remember that your Union is no more nor less than a *Home Missionary Society.* Remember that to *help evangelize the masses,* from the children up, is one of the chief features of your work, and that piety, persuasion, and prayer are the weapons with which God has furnished you for this sacred warfare. So far as possible, enlist *the pastors and the churches.* Seek to influence each church to become practically a *Temperance Society.* A *Young* Ladies' Temperance Union—a sort of social club, with music, reading, kindly faces, and the pledge-book—would do much to influence young men right, and would greatly aid your work.

Write in a blank-book this agreement:

We, the undersigned, believing it to be for the greatest numbers' greatest good, agree to pay our employees on Monday (or the first of the week) instead of on Saturday night, from this time henceforth.

Get all the business men to sign it, at the same time offering the pledge to them and to their men.

Our Unions should visit landlords and get them to agree not to rent buildings for any use involving the sale of intoxicating drinks.

Have plenty of signs out to show where your headquarters are and how kindly you will welcome any who will come.

Get out and circulate a neat "business card," with the name of your Union, location of headquarters, announcements of meetings and *"Everybody Welcome!"*

Organize, just the same, even if you are so fortunate as to live where some men are not allowed to make other men drunk. Get everybody pledged; get the young folks started right; elevate public sentiment; and keep clandestine liquor-dens out of your town.

Seek to multiply places and sources of rational recreation for the young. If possible, induce each church in the town to fit up one of its apartments as a reading-room and place for social gatherings. Let it not be said by young men away from home, and shut up in uncongenial boarding places, that the church takes no cognizance of their youthful love of company and of variety, but that the saloon and billiard-hall alone do this.

Let not any woman whose heart is in the work imagine she cannot "talk temperance" to public audiences. The truth is that the nimble tongue so long employed in utterances less noble has a power not easily excelled, when the high themes of human destiny engage it; and this the world is just beginning to find out.

Homes for Inebriates—both men and women—should be established in our cities, and the Women's Unions can do much to aid in this enterprise, by soliciting aid from the state and municipal governments and from the public generally. They can also greatly help those who enter these homes, by their sympathy, Christian counsel, and prayers.

The Temperance Reform Clubs recently projected in New England, will be powerful auxiliaries in our work, and we urge the Women's Unions to help establish them in every community. Temperance Reform Clubs are doing a great work, both East and West. Fifty have been organized in Illinois within five months, and have a membership of thousands. For information, write (with postage stamp) to J. K. Osgood,[4] Gardiner, Maine, who organized the first club about two years ago.

Drinking fountains for "man and beast" ought to be erected by our Unions in every city, town, and village. They can be cheaply made, and should have appropriate inscriptions. Send for information as to style, cost, etc. This is good summer work.

In cities, the ladies have found 4 o'clock P.M. on Sunday (just after Sabbath-school) a good time for a religious temperance meeting, with prayers, experience of newly-converted men, and appeals to Christian women. In cities, especial effort should be made to have *at least one lady* to represent *each church.*

During the session of the legislature the Woman's State Union should plan for a convention or a series of mass-meetings at the capital. While we must labor earnestly to reclaim the drunkard, we must not neglect to make the influence of our organization felt at the sources of power, the centers of influence, where opinion crystallizes into law.

Do not let us imagine that women can do this work without the aid of men. Let us be of a teachable spirit and tolerant of those opinions which differ from our own, while we still strive to show the reasonableness of ours.

Let each one work in the direction for which she seems best fitted, and to which her sympathies incline her, at the same time encouraging those who feel called upon to take up another method or department of the same work.

Do not concentrate all efforts upon cities and towns. Go out and hold meetings in school-houses, and endeavor to arouse the country people to the necessity for action. The moral sense and virtue of the rural population are of vital importance to our cause, as an offset to the aggregated vice of cities.

While this is a religious work, do not refuse the help and sympathy of those who are not Christians in name, although, so far as this work is concerned, they act like Christians.

Select persons for any responsible position in our Unions with reference to their fitness for that particular place, rather than on account of their social position.

Go to the saloon-keeper and the liquor-dealer in a spirit of courtesy and kindness. He is not so very much more to be blamed than the thoughtless or selfish but respectable voters who have legalized the traffic in which he is engaged. Meet him on the high plane of human kindness and of your common need of a Redeemer from sin and a regenerated heart. Talk less to him of what he does than of what he is, and proclaim to him the good news of Jesus, Savior of men.

Do not let us expect every one to think well of our work at once, but let us go on patiently until the results attained shall disarm prejudice and demonstrate the righteousness of our cause. And let us strive to win others to cooperation rather than estrange them by criticisms and complainings.

In one of the daily Gospel Temperance meetings in Chicago, a young man who was trying to reform asked permission to write "another pledge" besides that of total abstinence. He prepared and signed the following, and though we do not urge, we offer it when we deem it judicious to do so:

> Believing that the use of tobacco (smoking and chewing) acts as a feeder, and is likely eventually to lead to the use of intoxicating drinks, I solemnly promise, by the help of God, to quit the practice.

The general spirit of our organization is shown in the following resolution, adopted at the Woman's National Christian Temperance Union, at its first meeting, in Cleveland, November, 1874:

> Resolved, That recognizing the fact that our Cause is, and will be, combated by mighty, determined, and relentless forces, we will, trusting in Him who is the Prince of Peace, meet argument with argument, misjudgment with patience, denunciation with kindness, and all our difficulties and dangers with prayer.

Use your influence to make the location and surroundings of the ballot-box respectable, and then spare no pains to urge upon voters who have a conscience *the duty of going to the polls and voting for the best men.* But, before this, bring all the influence of your Union to bear to get good men to attend the primaries, or caucuses, where more mischief is done by demagogues and their tools than you can undo in a lifetime.

It is sometimes best, in a state, after the preliminary convention which results in organization has been held, to call a *Mass Convention* to represent the churches, Sabbath-schools, and all temperance organizations.

If thought best, the fifty cents membership-fee may be raised by taking a "mite collection" at weekly, monthly, or public meetings.

Amusement must be largely combined with instruction in the Juvenile Unions, and the teaching will consist mostly of general exercises, questions. etc., from the "Temperance Text-Book" and Catechisms.

Let the Juvenile Union give entertainments with admission fees, and use the proceeds to start a *Temperance Library.*

Please send suggestions that will help on our work—results of experience, or "bright ideas" that come to you. Write freely, *whenever you have anything to suggest or to ask,* and all letters will be promptly answered, if addressed to the Corresponding Secretary of the [National] W.C.T.U., 148 Madison Street, Chicago, Illinois.

"Finally,

Let us be strong in the Lord and in the power of his might" [Ephesians 6:10]. Be this our motto: "*I pledge myself* to the temperance cause, to work for it with brain, and heart, and hand, and money (if I have it), until we win the day or I am 'mustered out.'"

Dear sisters, we have laid before you the plan of the long campaign. Will you work with us? We wage our peaceful war in loving expectation of the day "when all men's weal shall be each man's care," when "nothing shall hurt or destroy in all my holy mountain, as saith the Lord," [Isaiah 11:9] and we may live to see America, beloved mother of thrice grateful daughters, set at liberty full and complete from foamy king Gambrinus[5] and fiery old King Alcohol.

Notes

1. Willard to Annie T. Wittenmyer, December 11 and December 1, 1874, Correspondence file/1874, Frances E. Willard Memorial Library, National WCTU.

2. Seminaries were private elementary and secondary schools established by Protestant denominations.

3. John Newton Stearns (1829–95), prominent temperance reformer, was the publishing agent and editor for the National Temperance Society and Publishing House from 1865 until his death in 1895.

4. Joshua Knox Osgood (1816–85) began organizing clubs for reformed drinkers in Maine in 1872 and later served as president of the State Reform Club Association.

5. Gambrinus was a legendary king and the patron saint and guardian of beer and brewers.

THREE

"Home Protection [I]," October 5, 1876

Frances Willard called for women's suffrage in an address entitled "Home Protection" given in Philadelphia, Pennsylvania, at a meeting of the Association for the Advancement of Women. Although her personal commitment to women's voting rights was long-standing, she first publicly supported the women's ballot in August 1876, in Maine at the Old Orchard Beach camp meeting. While at that camp meeting she heard a speech by Letitia Youmans[1] of Canada, who had adapted the phrase "home protection" from tariff debates going on in her country. In this slogan Willard found further inspiration for her argument for a women's temperance ballot, a line of reasoning she believed would be persuasive even to conservatives among reform-minded women. During the next two months she reworked the prosuffrage speech she had introduced at Old Orchard Beach and unveiled this new version in Philadelphia.

The "Home Protection" speech set forth the case for what was known as a temperance ballot, arguing that the votes or signatures of women should be required in a community before licenses for the sale of alcohol could be granted. The rum power was growing, Willard warned, and a new source of virtuous power was needed to offset it; women's suffrage, in this argument, was primarily a vehicle to defeat the evils of alcohol. In addition to setting forth this rationale for putting the ballot in the hands of women, Willard considered objections to a women's temperance ballot and refuted them. The conclusion of the speech—beginning with "it is women who have given the costliest hostages to fortune"—became one of the most famous passages in Willard's repertoire. In 1878 she delivered a version of her "Home Protection" address before the U.S. House Judiciary Committee. The conclusion of that speech echoed the words from her 1876 address and excerpts from it are inscribed at the base of the Willard statue that stands in Statuary Hall at the United States Capitol.

Some leaders in the suffrage movement enthusiastically embraced their new comrade. Susan B. Anthony wrote to Willard, "I wish I could see you and make you feel my gladness, not only for your sake, personally, but for the *cause's sake*—

for Temperance and Virtue's sake—for Woman's sake."[2] Anthony's joy was not surprising; in the early 1870s, the women's suffrage movement was still an unpopular reform in the minds of many Americans. Its leaders and their actions were often characterized as extreme, and the movement was making little headway. Disagreements among leaders over goals and strategies led to a split into two factions, and the movement faced several serious setbacks, including Anthony's guilty verdict at her trial for voting in New York (1872) and the Supreme Court decision in *Minor v. Happersett* (1874) declaring that the right to vote was not an inherent part of citizenship.

In July of 1876 Anthony interrupted a mass meeting at the nation's centennial celebration in Philadelphia to present copies of the "Declaration of the Rights of Woman." This bold assertion of women's equality further risked alienating mainstream America from the suffrage cause. Willard's more circuitous suffrage argument, focusing primarily on home protection and the benefits of suffrage for the nation, appealed to the wide range of women who perceived a grave threat to themselves and their children, their homes and communities from male drunkenness. As she presented it, the ballot was no radical demand; rather, it was a powerful means to counter this threat. Arguing from the grounds of women's need for the ballot and working to rehabilitate the image of the ballot, Willard was able to appeal to conservative and reform-minded audiences whose interest in the ballot lay more in their determination to make the world a better place than in the exercise of their natural rights.

Willard delivered "Home Protection" addresses throughout the rest of her public career, but as early as 1879 her arguments and reasoning aimed at full suffrage rather than simply the temperance ballot. By the 1890s Willard included strong arguments grounded in women's right to the ballot alongside her claims about women's need for suffrage. As the WCTU broadened its goals beyond temperance, the woman's ballot became a crucial weapon in enacting its reform agenda.

The text of "Home Protection I" is taken from the proceedings of the *Association for the Advancement of Women: Papers Read at the Fourth Congress of Women in Philadelphia* (Washington, D.C.: Todd Brothers, 1877), 81–87.

* * *

The rum power looms like a Chimborazo[3] among the mountains of difficulty over which our native land must climb, to reach the future of our dreams. The problem of the rum power's overthrow may well engage our thoughts as women and as patriots. Tonight I ask you to consider it in the light of a truth which Frederick Douglass[4] has embodied in these words: "We can, in the long run, trust all the knowledge in the community to take care of all the ignorance of the community, and all of its virtue, to take care of all its vice." The difficulty in the application of this principle lies in the fact that vice is always in the active, virtue often in the passive. Vice is aggressive. It deals swift sure blows, delights in keen-edged weapons and prefers a hand to hand conflict; while virtue instinctively fights its unsavory antagonist at arm's length—its great guns are unwieldy and slow to swing into range. Vice is the tiger with keen eyes, alert ears and cat-like tread, while virtue is the slow paced, complacent, easy going elephant whose greatest danger lies in its ponderous weight and consciousness of power.

So the great question narrows down to one of methods. It is not, when we look carefully into the conditions of the problem: How shall we develop more virtue in the community to offset the tropical growth of vice by which we find ourselves environed? but rather how the tremendous force we have may best be brought to bear; how we may unlimber the huge cannon now pointing into vacancy, and direct their full charge at short range, upon our nimble, wily, vigilant foe?

As bearing upon a consideration of that question, I lay down this proposition: All pure and Christian sentiment concerning any line of conduct which vitally affects humanity, will, sooner or later, crystallize into law. But the keystone of law can only be firm and secure when it is held in place by the arch of that keystone, which is public sentiment.

I make another statement, not so often reiterated, but just as true, viz: The more thoroughly you can enlist in favor of your law the natural instincts of those who have the power to make that law, and so select the officers who shall enforce it, the more securely stands the law. And still another: First, among the powerful and controlling instincts in our nature stands that of self preservation, and next after this (if indeed, it does not claim superior rank,) comes that of a mother's love. You can count upon that every time—it is sure and resistless as the tides of the sea, for it is founded in the changeless nature given to her from God.

Now the stronghold of the rum power lies in the fact that it has upon its side two deeply-rooted appetites; namely, in the dealer, the appetite for gain; and in the drinker, the appetite for stimulants. We have dolorously said, in times gone by, that, on the human plane, we have nothing adequate to match against this frightful pair. But let us think more carefully, and we shall find that, as in nature, God has given us an antidote to every poison and in grace a compensation for every loss; so in human society, He has prepared, against alcohol, that worst foe of the social state, an enemy under whose weapons it is to bite the dust.

Think of it! There is a class in every one of our communities—in many of them far the most numerous class—which, (I speak not vauntingly, I but name it as a fact,) has not, in all the centuries of wine, beer and brandy drinking, developed, as a class, an appetite for alcohol, but whose instincts, on the contrary, set so strongly against intoxicants, that if the liquor traffic were dependent on their patronage alone, it would collapse this night as though all the nitro-glycerine of Hell Gate reef had exploded under it.[5] There is a class whose instinct of self-preservation must forever be opposed to a stimulant which nerves, with dangerous strength, arms already so much stronger than their own, and so maddens the brain God meant to guide those arms, that they strike down the wives men love and the little children for whom, when sober, they would die. The wife, largely dependent for the support of herself and little ones upon the brain which strong drink paralyzes, the arm it masters and the skill it renders futile, will, in the nature of the case, prove herself unfriendly to the actual or potential source of so much misery. But, besides this primal instinct of self-preservation we have, in the same class of which I speak, another far more high and sacred—I mean the instinct of a mother's love, a wife's devotion, a sister's faithfulness, a daughter's loyalty. And now I ask you to consider earnestly the fact that none of these blessed rays of light and power from woman's heart, are as yet brought to bear upon the rum-shop at the focus of power. They are, I know, the sweet and pleasant sunshine of our homes; they are the beams which light the larger home of social life and send their gentle radiance out even into the great and busy world. But I know, and as the knowledge has grown clearer, my heart has thrilled with gratitude and hope too deep for words, that in a Republic, all these now divergent beams of light can, through that magic lens, that powerful sun-glass which we name the ballot, be made to converge upon the rum-shop in a blaze of light which shall reveal its full abominations, and a white flame of heat which, like a pitiless moxa,[6] shall burn this cancerous excrescence from America's fair form. Yes, for there is nothing in the universe so sure, so strong, as love, and love shall do all this—the love of maid for sweetheart, wife for husband, of a sister for her brother, of a mother for her son. And I call upon you who are here today, good men and brave—you who have welcomed us to other fields in the great fight of the angel against the dragon in society—I call upon you thus to match force with force, to set over against the liquor-dealer's avarice our instinct of self-preservation; and to match the drinker's love of liquor with our love of him! When you can center all this power in that small bit of white paper which falls

> As silently as snowflakes fall upon the sod,
> But executes the freeman's will as lightnings
> do the will of God,

the rum power will be as much doomed as was the slave power when you gave the ballot to the slaves.

In our argument it has been claimed that by the changeless instincts of her nature and through the most sacred relationships of which that nature has been rendered capable, God has indicated Woman, who is the born conservator of home, to be the Nemesis of Home's arch enemy, King Alcohol. And further, that in a Republic, this power of hers may be most effectively exercised, by giving her a voice in the decision by which the rum-shop door shall be opened or closed beside her home.

This position is strongly supported by evidence. About the year 1850, petitions were extensively circulated in Cincinnati (later the fiercest battle ground of the Woman's Crusade) asking that the liquor traffic be put under the ban of law. Bishop Simpson,[7] one of the noblest and most discerning minds of his century, was deeply interested in this movement. It was decided to ask for the names of women as well as those of men, and it was found that the former signed the petition more readily and in much larger numbers than the latter. Another fact was ascertained which rebuts the hackneyed assertion that women of the lower class will not be on the temperance side in this great war. For it was found—as might, indeed, have been most reasonably predicted—that the ignorant, the poor, (many of them wives, mothers, and daughters of intemperate men) were among the most eager to sign the petition. Many a hand was taken from the washtub to hold the pencil and affix the signature of women of this class, and many another, which could only make the sign of the cross, did that with tears and a hearty "God bless you." "That was a wonderful lesson to me," said the good Bishop, and he has always believed since then that God will give our enemy into our hands by giving to us an ally still more powerful—Woman with the ballot against rum-shops in our land. It has been said so often that the very frequency of reiteration has in some minds induced belief, that women of the better class will never consent to declare themselves at the polls. But, tens of thousands from the most tenderly sheltered homes have gone, day after day to the saloons, and have spent hour after hour upon their sanded floors, and in their reeking air—places in which not the worst politician would dare to locate the ballot box of freemen—though they but stay a moment at the window, slip in their votes and go their way.

Nothing worse can ever happen to women at the polls than has been endured by the hour on the part of the conservative women of the churches, in this land, as they, in scores of towns, have pled with rough half-drunken men to vote the temperance tickets they have handed them and which, with vastly more of propriety and fitness, they might have dropped into the box themselves. They could have done this in a moment and returned to their homes, instead of spending the whole day in the often futile endeavor to beg from men like these, the votes which should preserve their homes from the whiskey serpent's breath for one uncertain year. I spent last May in Ohio, traveling constantly, and seeking on every side to learn the views of the noble women of the Crusade; they put their opinions in words like these: "We believe God led us into this work by way of the saloons; he will lead us out by way of the ballot. We have never prayed more earnestly over the one than we will over the other. One was the Wilderness, the other is the Promised Land."

A Presbyterian lady, rigidly conservative, said: "For my part, I never wanted to vote until our gentlemen passed a prohibition ordinance so as to get us to stop visiting saloons, and a month later repealed it and chose a saloon keeper for mayor."

Said a great grand-daughter of Jonathan Edwards,[8] a woman with no toleration toward the Suffrage Movement, a woman crowned with the glory of grey hairs—a central figure in her native town—and as she spoke, the courage and faith of the Puritans thrilled in her voice: "If with the ballot in our hands, we can, as I firmly believe, put down this awful traffic, I am ready to lead the women of my town to the polls as I have often led them to the rum-shops."

We must not forget that for every woman who joins the Temperance Unions now springing up all through the land, there are, at least, a score who sympathize with us but do not join. Home influence and cares prevent them, ignorance of our aims and methods, lack of consecration to Christian work—a thousand reasons, sufficient in their estimation though not in ours, hold them away from us. And yet they have this Temperance cause warmly at heart; the logic of events has shown them that there is but one side on which a woman may safely stand in this great battle, and on that side they would indubitably range themselves in the quick, decisive battle of election day; nor would they give their voice a second time in favor of the man who had once betrayed his pledge to enforce the most stringent law for the protection of their homes. There are many noble women too, who, though they do not think as do the Temperance Unions about the deep things of religion, and are not as yet decided in their total abstinence sentiments nor ready for the blessed work of prayer, are nevertheless decided in their views of Woman Suffrage, and ready to vote a Temperance ticket side by side with us. And there are the drunkard's wife and daughters who from very shame will not come with us or who dare not—yet who could freely vote with us upon this question; for the folded ballot tells no tales.

Among other cumulative proofs in this argument from experience, let us consider briefly, the attitude of the Catholic Church toward the Temperance Reform. It is friendly at least. Father Matthew's spirit lives today in many a faithful parish priest.[9] In our procession on the Centennial Fourth of July, the banners of Catholic Total Abstinence Societies were often the only reminders that the Republic has any temperance people within its borders, as they were the only offset to brewers' wagons and distillers' casks, while among the monuments of our cause by which this memorable year is signalized, their fountain in Fairmont Park [Philadelphia]—standing in the midst of eighty drinking places licensed by our Government—is chief. Catholic women would vote with Protestant women upon this issue for the protection of their homes.

Again, among the sixty thousand churches of America, with their eight million members, two thirds are women. Thus, only one third of this trustworthy and thoughtful class, has any voice in the laws by which, between the church and the public school, the rum-shop nestles, in this Christian land. Surely all this must change before the "Government shall be upon His shoulders" [Isaiah 9:6] who shall one day reign King of Nations as he now reigns King of Saints.

Furthermore, four fifths of the teachers in this land are women, whose thoughtful judgment expressed with the authority of which I speak would greatly help forward the victory of our cause. And finally by those who fear the effect of the foreign element in our country let it be remembered that we have six native for every one woman who is foreign born, for it is men who emigrate in largest number to our shores.

When all these facts (and many more that might be added) are marshaled into line, how illogical it seems for good men to harangue us as they do about our "duty to educate public sentiment to the level of better law," and their exhortations to American mothers to "train their sons to vote aright." As said Mrs. Governor Wallace, of Indiana,[10] until the Crusade an opponent of the franchise, "What a bitter sarcasm you utter, gentlemen, to us who have the public sentiment of which you speak, all burning in our hearts, and yet are not permitted to turn it to account."

Let us then, each one of us, offer our earnest prayer to God and speak our honest word to man in favor of this added weapon in Woman's hands, remembering that every petition in the ear of God and every utterance in the ears of men, swells the dimensions of that resistless tide of influence which shall yet float within our reach all that we ask or need. Dear Christian women who have crusaded in the rum-shops, I urge that you begin crusading in halls of legislation, in primary meetings and the offices of excise commissioners. Roll in your petitions, burnish your arguments, multiply your prayers, go to the voters in your town—procure the official list and see them one by one—and get them pledged to a local ordinance requiring the votes of men and women before a license can be issued to open rum-shop doors beside your homes; go to the Legislature with the same; remember this may be just as really Christian work as praying in saloons was in those other glorious days. Let us not limit God, whose modes of operation are so infinitely varied in nature and in grace. I believe in the correlation of spiritual forces and that the heat which melted hearts to tenderness in the Crusade is soon to be the light which shall reveal our opportunity and duty as the Republic's daughters.

Longer ago than I shall tell, my father returned, one night, to the far-off Wisconsin home where I was reared; and sitting by my mother's chair, with a child's attentive ear, I listened to their words. He told us of the news that day had brought about Neal Dow,[11] and the great fight for Prohibition down in Maine, and then he said: "I wonder if poor, rum-cursed Wisconsin will ever get a law like that?" And Mother rocked a while in silence, in the dear old chair I love, and then she gently said: "Yes, Josiah, there'll be such a law all over the land some day, when women vote." My father had never heard her say as much before. He was a great conservative; so he looked tremendously astonished, and replied, in his keen, sarcastic voice: "And pray how will you arrange it so that women shall vote?" Mother's chair went to and fro a little faster for a minute, and then, looking not into his face, but into the flickering flames of the grate, she slowly answered: "Well, I say to you as the apostle Paul said to his jailor: 'You have put us into prison, we being Romans, and you must come and take us out'" [Acts 16:37].

That was a seed-thought in a girl's brain and heart. Years passed on, in which nothing more was said upon this dangerous theme. My brother grew to manhood, and soon after he was twenty-one years old, he went with father to vote. Standing by the window, a girl of sixteen years, a girl of simple, homely fancies, not at all strong-minded, and altogether ignorant of the world, I looked out as they drove away, my father and brother, and as I looked I felt a strange ache in my heart, and tears sprang to my eyes. Turning to my sister Mary, who stood beside me, I saw that the dear little innocent seemed wonderfully sober, too. I said, "Don't you wish that we could go with them when we are old enough? Don't we love our country just as well as they do?" and her little frightened voice piped out: "Yes, of course we ought. Don't I know that; but you mustn't tell a soul—not mother, even; we should be called strong-minded."

In all the years since then, I have kept those things, and many others like them, and pondered them in my heart [Luke 2:19]; but two years of struggle in this temperance reform have shown me, as they have ten thousand other women, so clearly and so impressively, my duty, that I have passed the Rubicon[12] of Silence and am ready for any battle that shall be involved in this honest declaration of the faith that is within me. "Fight behind masked batteries a little longer," whisper good friends and true. So I have been fighting hitherto; but it is a style of warfare altogether foreign to my temperament and mode of life. Reared on the prairies, I seemed predetermined to join the cavalry force in this great spiritual war, and I must tilt a free lance henceforth on the splendid battlefield of this reform; where the earth shall soon be shaken by the onset of contending hosts, where legions of valiant soldiers are deploying; where to the grand encounter marches today a great army gentle of mien and mild of utterance, but with hearts for any fate; where there are trumpets and bugles calling strong souls onward to a victory which Heaven might envy, and

> "Where behind the dim unknown
> Standeth God, within the shadow,
> Keeping watch above His own."

I thought that women ought to have the ballot as I paid the hard-earned taxes upon my mother's cottage home—but I never said as much—somehow the motive did not command my heart. For my own sake, I had not courage, but I have for thy sake, dear native land, for thy necessity is as much greater than mine as thy transcendent hope is greater than the personal interest of thy humble child. For love of you, heartbroken wives, whose tremulous lips have blessed me; for love of you, sweet mothers, who in the cradle's shadow kneel this night, beside your infant sons, and you, sorrowful little children, who listen at this hour, with faces strangely old, for him whose footsteps frighten you; for love of you, have I thus spoken.

Ah, it is women who have given the costliest hostages to fortune! Out into the battle of life they have sent their best beloved, with fearful odds against them, with snares that men have legalized and set for them on every hand. Beyond the arms that had held them long, their boys have gone forever. Oh! by the danger they have dared; by the hours of patient watching over beds where helpless children lay; by the incense of ten thousand prayers wafted from their gentle lips to Heaven, I charge you to give them power to protect, along life's treacherous highway, those whom they have so loved. Let it no longer be that they must sit back among the shadows, hopelessly mourning over their strong staff broken, and their beautiful rod [Jeremiah 48:17]; but when the sons they love shall go forth to life's battle, still let their mothers walk beside them, sweet and serious, and clad in the garments of power!

Notes

1. Letitia Creighton Youmans [also spelled Yeomans] (1827–96) was a Canadian temperance leader, president of the Ontario Woman's Christian Temperance Union for a number of years until she became president of the Dominion WCTU in 1883.

2. Susan B. Anthony to Willard, September 18, 1876, WCTU series, reel 11, frame 543.

3. The highest point in Ecuador, Mount Chimborazo was once thought to be the highest in the world.

4. Frederick Douglass (1818–95) was the most prominent African American antislavery reformer of the nineteenth century; he also endorsed women's suffrage.

5. Nitroglycerin was detonated on September 24, 1876, in order to clear the passage through Hell Gate reef in New York City's East River.

6. The moxa is a stick or cone of the mugwart root that is set on fire and then placed on the body as a "cure" for various ailments.

7. Matthew Simpson (1811–84), a longtime friend and mentor of Willard's, was named a Methodist bishop in 1852. Like many Methodists, he was a strong supporter of temperance and also of wider leadership roles for Methodist women.

8. Jonathan Edwards (1703–58) was one of the most prominent Calvinist preachers and thinkers in eighteenth-century America.

9. Irish priest, Father Theobald Matthew (1790–1861), led a total abstinence crusade in the United States in 1849.

10. Zerelda Sanders Wallace (1817–1901), one of the founders of the Indianapolis Equal Suffrage Society in 1878, served as president of the Indiana WCTU in the early 1880s and later headed the Department of the Franchise for the National WCTU.

11. Neal Dow (1804–97), renowned nineteenth-century temperance reformer, was known as the "Father of the Maine Law," prohibitory legislation passed by the Maine legislature in 1851, which became a model and impetus for further prohibition efforts at the state level.

12. This phrase invokes the notion of an irreversible decision. In 49 B.C.E. Julius Caesar decided to cross the river Rubicon with his army, a move that triggered a civil war in Rome.

FOUR

Address before the Illinois Senate, April 10, 1879

Two and half years after her first public call for a women's temperance ballot, Willard stood before the Illinois State Senate arguing for passage of the Hinds bill—named for Illinois House Representative Andrew Hinds, a strong supporter of the bill. The proposal would require that both men and women have a voice in the decision to offer liquor licenses to dealers in their communities. This moment was the culmination of more than two years of agitation on the issue throughout the state. By the late 1870s the Illinois WCTU had come to be strong supporters of women's suffrage on the temperance question; in fact, many Illinois WCTU members had already moved beyond the idea of a limited vote for women to support full suffrage, a view Willard herself held but mostly chose not to voice at that time.

Having delivered her home protection speech at the state WCTU convention in October 1876, Willard called on Illinois WCTU members to conduct a statewide campaign for a home protection ballot. Mass meetings were held in all nineteen Illinois congressional districts to launch a petition drive asking that women have an equal say with men in whether liquor dealers were permitted licenses in their communities. The petition, with more than seven thousand signatures, was presented to the state legislature in March 1877 but was virtually ignored by legislators. Undeterred by this apparent failure, the Illinois WCTU stepped up the campaign, sending lecturers throughout the state to speak on home protection and build public sentiment for the cause.

In the fall of 1877 Willard resigned her office with the National WCTU largely due to conflicts with the more conservative leaders over the appropriateness of her support for women's ballots. Elected president of the more progressive Illinois WCTU in October 1878, she immediately began to rally her troops for a massive petitioning effort, focused on the spring 1879 legislative session. In January and February WCTU workers went door to door throughout the state collecting signatures on the home protection petition. Meanwhile, Willard moved to Springfield, the state capital, to be at the center of campaign activity. In the weeks before the opening of the legislative session, she and other WCTU leaders held mass meetings and lobbied individual legislators to gain their support. When the Illinois house of representatives convened in early March, WCTU women draped the entire house chamber with a giant petition featuring 110,000 signatures—the largest ever presented in the legislature up to that time. Willard was quick to point out that nearly half of the signers were voters (that is, men) who had the power to determine the political fate of legislators, even though women who signed did not.

A month later, the petition, with 70,000 additional signatures, was presented in the senate. Willard and other WCTU representatives had spoken on behalf of the Hinds bill in a regular house session, but after a lengthy and bitter debate in the senate over whether it was appropriate for a woman to address that body, Willard was refused permission to speak during the session. In a compromise measure, she was allowed to address senators during a half-hour recess. As she rose to speak, three senators walked out of the hall in protest. Several others turned their backs on her and busied themselves reading throughout her speech. Strengthened by hundreds of supporters observing from the balcony and by her faith that she spoke for thousands of Illinois women, Willard was undaunted by these gestures of disapproval. She proceeded to deliver a strong speech tailored to the specific concerns of male politicians.

Willard laid out several arguments that answered the kinds of objections to the home protection ballot she had heard from individual legislators before the session began. Countering concerns about potential loss of revenue, objections from their German immigrant constituencies, and legislators' beliefs that local option laws didn't really work, she urged lawmakers to see the bill as good public policy. Willard also warned legislators that if they did not pass the home protection bill, the WCTU would bypass them and go directly to counties and municipalities whose officials had the power to hold a referendum on licensing questions. By summer 1879 the house had narrowly voted down the Hinds bill, and the senate version had died in committee. WCTU workers immediately began to push for local referendums; according to the WCTU, 645 Illinois communities did vote against licensing liquor dealers in the following year. At the same time, the WCTU began to campaign for an amendment to the state constitution that would allow women to vote on temperance questions.

The text of "Address before the Illinois Senate" is from a clipping from the *Citizen's League,* June 14, 1879, in Scrapbook 32, WCTU Papers.

* * *

The last words of the great statesman De Tocqueville to our Charles Sumner,[1] when the latter left the shores of France, were these: "Life is neither a pleasure nor a pain. It is a serious business, to be entered on with courage and in a spirit of self sacrifice." If I did not believe these words expressive of the true philosophy of life, be assured, gentlemen, that in the face of the desire of many, which they have so plainly expressed, not to hear my voice within these walls, it would not here be raised. After all, this is to you an hour of not so very much great significance. You have in courtesy adjourned, and given thirty minutes to the temperance women of Illinois. To us this hour is fraught with pathos which no words of mine may measure, and with a hope which reaches high as that of a saint and deep as a drunkard's despair. I want to remember that though I stand here solitary, I am not alone. There are hundreds of thousands of the good and brave and gentle whose prayers are with me, who have genuine womanly sympathy, and I do not feel other than buoyed up and helped along as I shall try to speak on their behalf. And it is not to me a little thing that here beside me is the president of the Senate [Lieutenant Governor Andrew Shuman], a friend for many years, whose only child and daughter was my well beloved pupil; a gentleman who knows that I have never *sought* the opportunity to speak on any question or in any presence.

We have come before you with a petition numbering over 175,000 names; 75,000 to 80,000 voters of Illinois have said to us women, "We believe that good will come out of your movement and we will stand by you," just as you honorable gentlemen who granted us this "hearing" have stood by us this morning. I wish to speak of some of the reasons why we believe that our movement will not prove futile. I had thought that I would like, if we might so long trespass upon the valuable time of senators, to speak concerning prohibition or "local option," which is the phase of prohibition we have adopted in our work—not saying "You shall, whether you will or not," to a locality, but saying "you may, if you will, have the saloon as one of the institutions of your town, or you may not." That is what we would like to have become the law of this our land, and we would like all who are to be affected in their homes and in their happiness and in their personal prosperity by these saloons, to have a voice in saying whether they shall be among the institutions of the town in which they live. We have believed that if this could be achieved, it would have the effect to banish saloons from our fair state. Not in a year, gentlemen.

In some of your localities you have had license for a year, and no license for another, and license for a third, and the swing of the pendulum to and fro has not given a fair demonstration as to what local option might do for your communities. In Maine, when they first secured their law they found there were 520 open bars in as many hundred hotels. They said, "What can we do about it?" But they went right straight on along that line, and in a few years the growth of sentiment and the continual and more rigid enforcement of the law wiped out these bars, and today there is not a hotel bar in Maine from Kittery to Calais, and not even a newspaper correspondent who is inimical to the temperance cause will say that he has found one. It takes years to demonstrate whether a local option law is a success or a failure, and we beg time in which our demonstration may be wrought out. We claim we are not trying to make men "total abstainers by law," as the phrase is in many of our journals. Suppose they say you are trying to make men and women love one another by law because we have capital punishment for men and women who hate one another enough to take one another's lives? We have a law against one person poisoning another. That is not trying to make people friends by law. Any person may poison himself. Suppose we have a law that during an epidemic cabbages cannot be exposed in the market. That is not saying that any man shall not buy cabbages and make himself sick by using them, when the conditions are such as to render it dangerous, but it is saying that a traffic in that which produces such results cannot go on safely, and that the voters and law makers will not give such a traffic, under such conditions, the sanction of a vote for which they are responsible before the bar of the people, no less than before the bar of God.

The question is brought forward that the revenue will be greatly interfered with if our measures should succeed. Is that worth any consideration when you remember that 80 percent of the crimes which it costs us so much to punish were caused by alcohol, and that the criminals back of these crimes have to be taken care of by the state? Ninety percent of all the prisoners in the Joliet penitentiary have their names on this petition. We know that eighty percent of them committed their crimes under the influence of liquor, or else they were brought to it through the machinations that took place in the saloons and in the company of those who make the saloons their headquarters. Chicago, you say, gets great revenue from the liquor traffic. What about the $670,000 Chicago spends annually for its police force? It is an added expense, that comes in on that line vastly more than offsetting the revenue we get by the other.

Gentlemen, it is said that there are many of you who are in your hearts favorable to the movement which we have introduced, but that you have no belief it would succeed. May I mention the state of Mississippi, which certainly is not very far advanced in temperance sentiment? It has had a law like this. I will mention to you some of the points, showing that that law is not a failure. A gentleman who deals in beer and ice, and who is not friendly to the temperance movement, but who, when I was entertained in the same family where he lives, talked kindly to me about these things, (suspending hostilities for an hour) enlightened me considerably upon the subject of woman's influence. When I asked him about his trade in Mississippi, and how it was interfered with,—the effect of this law allowing women the right of signature,—he said, "Well, since you ask I will have to acknowledge to you that our drummers and our men who are out through the state of Mississippi getting orders for our ice and beer and such products as those"—and he is a wholesale dealer—"they say that this law most unmercifully interferes with them, especially through the country districts, not much as yet in the large cities." It seems to me this is a good temperance argument in favor of such a law.

There is another question that has been often brought forward in the days I have spent at the capital. Gentlemen who are very friendly to the efforts we are making, say, "We believe in your Home Protection measure, and we wish there were not saloons. We know they ought not to be. Some day they will not be, but women are so given up to any one subject they fix their gaze upon that, and they forget how varied are the subjects that we must discuss, how manifold the interests entrusted to our hands. They forget that there is no party which wishes to give its alliance to this new subject of the woman's temperance ballot, and thus to enlist against itself the strength of that vote and constituency which always votes solid, the strength of those who, whether we are vigilant or not, are always on hand, and will make themselves felt in political caucuses, and in all branches of political manipulation." In reply to that objection may I say briefly this: Has anybody called the campaign which placed this petition around these walls a political campaign? Is any party in Illinois responsible for this attempt? Do you call it a democratic measure? Do you call it a republican measure? Is it the nationalists who have stood at the front and have worked out this result which has cost so much time and labor? Is it the socialists? What party is it that is responsible for the 175,000 names gathered up in the last few weeks in Illinois? Let me then say to you brothers, that if this has not been a political campaign neither will any further effort of ours be political.

A prominent member of one of the houses of the legislature said to me, "If you women—if you only could—I don't see how you can—if you only could lift up this subject out of the rut of party politics, if you only could enlist the men of all parties so it would in no way be a party issue, your success is assured; until that is done it will never be assured." Gentlemen, suppose you place this question so sad, so complicated—this question which has been an elephant in the hands of the parties always—place it at last in the hands of those who, while they have most at stake in its decision, yet belong to no party—then do you not lift it out of this "rut" of which this party leader spoke? Is it not right that we should have placed in our hands by you a constitutional amendment? Will you not say, "It is fair, it is just, it is equitable; many of us are judges of the law, many of us are lawyers, and we feel it is not right utterly to ignore in the halls of legislation such a petition as this. We will transfer the burden to the shoulders of the people. We will allow them to say what they will do."

Suppose you should do that. Then may I frankly sketch for you what I believe our action would be. We have in Illinois today 200 women's temperance societies. We are organizing others constantly. If you gave us the long arm of the lever in that fashion we would organize them faster than ever. In each locality where the Woman's Temperance Union had headquarters we would open books of record. We would ask our brothers frankly, straightforwardly, just as we have done here—and the most of them have frankly and straightforwardly replied—"Are you for an amendment that will let us women have a voice in determining the legal status of the saloon, or are you against it? Will you let us put your name down in our book?"

That is what we should do in every town, in every hamlet, in every village, in every city. We should know no democrat, no republican. We should only know humanity striving by every means to lift itself up to the level of a better life. Some of you say, "Oh well! They would promise you one way and go and vote another." Would they, then? We don't believe it. There was a Judas among the twelve, but there were eleven who stood firm and true, and I believe we should find more than that proportion. You may say it is a woman's ignorant faith. It is my honest faith, founded on evidence as all true faith must be, that we should find the same men standing by us who put their names on the petition, who two days ago by tens of thousands voted "no license" in scores of towns in Illinois.

My brothers, considering this, considering that in the house, where we have been specially working for the last few days we have had the strong support of both democrats and republicans; considering we did not ourselves know, except as we found out through one and another who came to tell us, which belonged to one party and which to another, will you not adjust this question by putting it before the people and giving us a chance to try to lift that which after all is more a social than a political question, up into the more vital air of an individuality which knows no politics, no party, no creed; which knows nothing but the best interests of the tempted and the tried, and those who suffer and can make no sign?

May I just tell you what we are going to do, whether or not you grant us our request? We have found out something that we didn't know before, for we were very ignorant of the laws. We have found out that county supervisors could, if they chose, declare that they would give no licenses except the majority of the adult population of the county desired it, women as well as men. We intend to go to them and take to them our petitions, urging them to make this declaration. We have found out that a corporation can say, if it chooses, by special ordinance, in many of the localities, "We will not license the saloons unless the majority of the adult population come to us by petition." We intend to work that up. We know we can in towns and villages, and after a while it will spread wider and work out more broadly, and so you see we have transferred our prayer, because in five years' honest work we found where the sources of the fountain of power were. At first we didn't know—we just went to the saloons because the saloons had cost us so much misery. We went straight there with our prayer and our pleading and petition, but we traced slowly back to its source this awful flood, and we found the fountain from which came the power to make the saloon something against which we in vain labor and struggle, was located on a high hill which has the capitol on top of it! For you stand upon a vantage ground my brothers. This capitol is on the highest point in Illinois. If only here we can persuade them to let us have some voice in this matter, then with the weapons of faith and work, of persuasion and home teaching which we have always had, we believe that your hearts and our hearts shall be made glad by a new and better future for the state of Illinois.

May I say a word about the Germans? Don't let me trespass on the time allotted to me. I am so interested I may forget its expiration. I will take it as a kindness if some gentleman will rise and remind me if I should exceed the limit.

I have lived in Berlin, Dresden and Leipzig. I have enjoyed many a beer garden. I have sat whole evenings with kindly friends, with their glasses of beer in those beer gardens, and listened to the beautiful music, and thought it was all right. It never crossed my mind that I was doing anything out of the way. I had just as kind a heart toward humanity then as I have now. I had just as great an interest in Illinois then as I have now, but certain arguments have come before me since then; certain sympathies have pleaded with me; certain voices that I have heard in prayer have argued with me. I have noticed what the beer act was of which the Duke of Wellington said it was a greater victory when he got it through Parliament than his battle of Waterloo. I have noticed what wretchedness it brought to England as attested by hundreds of intelligent and disinterested witnesses; I have carefully studied the official report of the Convocation of Canterbury, and I would that every gentleman here had done the same;[2] also [read] the scientific argument and heard the experience of an army of reformed men and practical temperance workers. I, for one, have been persuaded. I know there are no more instructed and truer heads on human shoulders than the heads of the honest-hearted Germans of Illinois. I know the German women are kindly and the race pre-eminent in love of home. I used to know a good deal about the German language. I mean to brush that up. I mean to go before them and talk to them about the good sense of our cause. I mean to ask them if they won't give over the idea that we are fanatics, and let us reason about it, as the Scripture has it, and see if there are not reasons why I have changed my mind, which may perhaps prevail to make them change their minds, and with patience and earnestness and with the reasoning faculty as developed as it is in our time. I believe we shall have the Germans coming to our side. Did you hear what Miss Kimball[3] said? She told us of the German whom she met on the streets of Chicago and whom she asked: "Are you for our petition?" and he said, "I can't give up my beer, but I want to help the ladies." We shall enlist that chivalric German spirit on our side. It is going to be, just as sure as you live. It is going to be a conquest of reason and gentleness, and this is going to be a popular movement in Illinois.

Now one last word. I take it from a German's lips. He is a member of this Legislature. I would it might be remembered that when the voice you have listened to so kindly shall be heard no more within the walls of the Capitol. This is the noble utterance I would leave with you. He said: "I am here to represent the voters who sent me to the House. I am here to represent also a constituency larger than the voters. I am here to represent the women and the children. They have a right to be represented by me, and they shall not be forgotten when I vote on the Hinds bill and the constitutional amendment."

O, may that voice and that argument be written on your memory, and may you who sit here in this spacious hall beneath the dome of the Capitol, with its waving flag of the red, white and blue, remember that though other measures are local, this is general; though other measures are temporary in their value, this is lasting and universal, and may you act as patriots accountable to your brothers and sisters, and, as human souls, accountable to God.

I thank you for your courtesy. I represent the women. I have spoken for them only. I thank you not on my behalf alone, but on behalf of the temperance women of Illinois.

Notes

1. Alexis de Tocqueville (1805–59), prominent French statesman and author of *Democracy in America* (1835, 1840) met Charles Sumner (1811–74), a young Massachusetts lawyer, in France in the late 1830s. Sumner, an antislavery advocate, became a U.S. senator in 1852 and served until his death.

2. In 1830 Arthur Wellesley, Duke of Wellington (1769–1852), led the fight for the Beer Act, which attempted to reduce hard liquor consumption by removing all taxes on beer and allowing inexpensive licenses to sell beer. By 1869 the Convocation of Canterbury published a report detailing the harms resulting from the sharp increase in drinking establishments in working-class communities.

3. Lucia E. F. Kimball was the chair of the WCTU's National Sunday School Committee during the late 1870s. She became the Superintendent of the National Sunday School Department in 1880.

FIVE

"Home Protection [II]," July 4, 1879

Frances Willard's frequent speaking engagements and well-publicized work on the petition drive in Illinois established her as a national temperance leader. On July 4 she spoke at the Independence Day celebration in Woodstock, Connecticut, sponsored by *The Independent*, one of the most widely read reform newspapers. On the platform with her were several prominent men, among them the governor of Connecticut, four U.S. congressmen, a Methodist bishop, and a professor from the Chicago Theological Seminary.

Willard used this national platform to refine and extend her arguments for the home protection ballot, calling on New England women to take the lead both in using educational and temperance ballots where they were available and in working for universal women's suffrage. Only with full suffrage could women gain support for their cause from politicians and ensure the enforcement of prohibitory legislation once it was passed. Her argument once again was based on establishing women's need for the ballot. Yet Willard's appeal was not simply on behalf of a wife's or daughter's need to protect her loved ones, but also to protect her nation from harm. Willard grasped this Fourth of July opportunity to emphasize women's patriotic duty to participate in the civic realm.

Most of the address was devoted to setting forth the rationale for the women's temperance ballot, defending the claim that women would vote for prohibition, and refuting the arguments of those opposed to the women's ballot. In this speech Willard asserted her belief in woman's natural right to the ballot; equally clear was her belief that what people needed to be persuaded about was not that women had the right, but that the world would be a better place if women exercised that right.

Willard also devoted a major portion of the address to sharing the story of the political consciousness raising experienced by some conservative women during their work for the home protection ballot in Illinois. Their awakening was prompted by the realization that elected representatives were at the mercy of those who had the power to vote in elections. Temperance legislation, the women discovered, must be supported by constituents with ballots; women had very little chance of persuading legislators to act on their behalf if they were unable to demonstrate that such action secured, rather than threatened, the representatives' re-election.

In addition to the extended argument for the women's ballot, the speech also contains a strong case for the efficacy of prohibition legislation. Unlike the philosophical case Willard would make in favor of prohibition in her address "Personal Liberty" three years later (document 8 in present text), in this speech she maintained a practical focus celebrating the success of prohibition in Maine. Prior to the passage of Maine's prohibition amendment the state had hundreds of bars and saloons, but thirty years after prohibition was put in place the sources of liquor had dried up in all but a few hidden dives in the cities.

The text of Willard's address circulated nationally in the pages of *The Independent.* It was also republished as part of *The Home Protection Manual,* a detailed guide modeled on the Illinois campaign, for those WCTU workers embarking on similar campaigns in their states. Perhaps the most important measure of the success of Willard's case for the home protection ballot came later that fall at the WCTU national convention in Indianapolis when the liberal faction of the organization, the one led by Willard and championing women's suffrage, came up against the conservative wing, led by current president Annie Wittenmyer, in a battle for the presidency. As it turned out, Willard easily won the election. Though four years passed before the National WCTU officially endorsed full suffrage for women, this later version of the home protection argument made clear Willard's case that the evolution from the temperance ballot to complete enfranchisement of women was inevitable.

The following excerpt from "Home Protection [II]," is from the report published in *The Independent,* July 10, 1879, 11–13.

* * *

Once more will the time-honored declaration be made today, by a thousand Fourth of July orators, that "the Americans are a free people." But I insist that we are governed by the most powerful king whose iron rule ever determined the policy, molded the institutions, or controlled the destinies of a great nation.

So pervasive is his influence that it penetrates to the most obscure and distant hamlet with the same readiness, and there wields the same potency as in his empire's capital; nay (with reverence be it said), he is like Deity in that his actual presence is coextensive with his vast domain. Our legislatures are his playthings, our congressmen his puppets, and our honored President the latest child of his adoption. We do not often call him by his name, this potentate of million hands and myriad voices; but to my thinking, nothing is today so vital to America as that we become better acquainted with our ruler. Let me then present to your thought his Majestic Highness King Majority, Sovereign Ruler of these United States.

Permit me now to introduce a different character who comes to the court of King Majority as chief ambassador from the empire of Satanic Majesty. Behold! I show you the skeleton at our patriotic banquet. It has a skull with straightened forehead and sickening smile; but bedecked with wreaths of vine, clusters of grape, and heads of golden grain—King Alcohol, present at court in radiant disguise. With a foaming beer mug at his lips, he drinks the health of King Majority; and, placing at his feet a chest of gold labeled "Internal Revenue," he desireth conditions of peace.[1]

Behold in these two figures the bewildering danger and the ineffable hope of the Republic! How can we rouse the stolid giant, King Majority? How light in those sleepy eyes the fires of a holy and relentless purpose? How nerve once more, with the resistless force that smote African slavery to death, the mighty sinews of the Republic's sleeping king?

How? Only by "sweet reasonableness"; only by ceaseless persuasion; only by noble examples; only by honest hard work based upon fervent and effectual prayer.

Human heads and hearts are much alike. I remember that the great Temperance Crusade of 1874 found me with a beer keg in my cellar, a fatal haziness in my opinions, and a blighting indifference to the temperance reform upon my will. But how did its intense pathos melt my heart; how did its mighty logic tune the lax cords of opinion to concert pitch; how did its miracle of prayer bring thousands to their knees, crying: "Lord, what wouldst thou have me to do?" [Acts 9:6]. For myself, I could never be the same after that. As a woman, a patriot, a Christian, my heart is fixed in deathless enmity to all that can intoxicate. The same influences which so transformed one brain and heart are steadily at work today in a thousand quiet ways.

The sober second thought of the Woman's Temperance Crusade was organization. The voice of God called to them from the lips of his prophet: "Make a chain, for the land is full of bloody crimes and the city is full of violence" [Ezekiel 7:23]. And so in every town and village we are forming these chains of light and of loving helpfulness, which we call "Woman's Christian Temperance Unions." We have already twenty-three states organized, with thousands of local auxiliaries. Every day brings fresh accessions of women, translated out of the passive and into the active voice on this great question of the protection of their homes. Of the fifty-four thousand papers published in this country eight thousand have temperance facts and figures regularly provided by members of our societies. Temperance literature is being circulated; *Our Union,* the official organ of the [WCTU], has a large subscription list; Sabbath schools are adopting our plans of temperance instruction; and hundreds of juvenile societies are inscribing on their banners: "Tremble, King Alcohol! We shall grow up." Friendly inns and temperance reading rooms are multiplying; Gospel meetings conducted by women are reaching the drinking class in hundreds of communities; the Red and Blue Ribbon Movements have attained magnificent proportions; and all this many-sided work is fast concentrating its influence to place the ballot in the hand of woman, and thus capture for the greatest of reforms old King Majority. Magnificent is the spectacle of these new forces now rallying to the fray. Side by side with the 500,000 men whose united energies are expended in making and selling strong drink, we are working day by day. While they brew beer we are brewing public sentiment; while they distill whiskey we are distilling facts; while they rectify brandy we are rectifying political constituencies; and ere long their fuming tide of intoxicating liquor shall be met and driven back by the overwhelming flood of enlightened sentiment and divinely aroused energy.

"To be sure, King Majority gave prohibition to Maine; but prohibition doesn't prohibit," interrupts Sir Sapient, whose remark furnishes a striking illustration of the power of the human mind to resist knowledge. Just take the spyglass of observation, and behold from Kittery to Calais the gleaming refutation of your error.

Less than thirty years ago they had four hundred open hotel bars and ten miles of saloons. Today Dr. Hamlin, of Constantinople,[2] tells us that, coming home, after forty years' absence, he finds his native state thoroughly renovated from the liquor traffic. General Neal Dow testifies that the law has absolutely driven the sale of strong drink out of all rural districts; and in the larger towns, instead of the free, open sale of former years, it is crowded into secret places, kept by the lowest class of foreigners. Ex-Governors Dingley and Perham and Senator Blaine and Representative Frye declare that it is as well enforced as the law against stealing; and even sensational journalists have not told us that thieves flourish in the Pine Tree State.[3] Mr. [Henry] Reuter, of Boston, president of the National Brewers' Convention, held in St. Louis four weeks ago, says: "Formerly Maine produced nearly ten thousand barrels of beer annually; but this has fallen to *seven barrels,* in consequence of the local enforcement of prohibitory law." Surely, this gentleman should be considered as good authority on this subject as a convict is of the strength of his prison bars!

But you say "Maine is different from any other state." Why so? Are not its citizens of like passions with other men? Turn your glass upon a panorama of Maine as it was in former days. See yonder stalwart workers in the harvest-field paying vigorous addresses to the little brown jug; observe its ubiquitous presence at the logging bee, the "raising," the wedding, and the funeral; see it pass from lip to lip around the fireside circle; observe the Gospel minister refreshing himself from the demijohn of his parishioner and host; and be assured that within the memory of men now living these were everyday events. I have this testimony from the most honored residents of Maine, whose recitals involved the words "all of which I saw and part of which I was." But, as gallant Neal Dow hath it, "Maine was sown knee-deep with temperance literature before we reaped the harvest of prohibition." Let us note the evolution of this seed-planting. Landowners found that two-thirds of their taxes resulted from the liquor traffic (largely in cost of prosecuting criminals and taking care of lunatics and paupers); so they concluded that legalizing saloons for the sake of the revenue was penny wisdom and pound foolishness. Businessmen discovered that the liquor traffic is a pirate on the high seas of trade, that the more the grog-shop is patronized the fewer customers there are for flour and fuel, boots, shoes, and clothes; and so, in self-defense, they declared for prohibition. Church people found that fifteen times as much money went to the dramshop as to the church, and that the teaching of the one more than offset those of the other with the young men of the state; so they perceived they could not conscientiously ally themselves with the liquor traffic by their votes. Those interested in education learned that enough money was swallowed in drinks that deteriorate the brain, to furnish a schoolhouse for every fifty boys and girls, and to set over them teachers of the highest culture; and they saw it was unreasonable to defend the liquor traffic. In short, the majority came to believe that between the upper and nether millstones of starving out saloons, on the one hand, and voting them out, on the other, they could be pounded to death; and they have so pounded them. The question of selling as a beverage the drinks which we know by centuries of demonstration will so craze men that they will commit every crime and show the subtlest cruelty to those they love the best, is not today in Maine an open question with either party, any more than trial by jury or imprisonment for theft. True, the people had a thirty years' war before the declaration of this blessed peace; but what are thirty years when crowned at last by the surrender of King Alcohol to King Majority?

"Ah! but," pursues our doubting friend, "Maine is a peculiar state, in this: it has few foreigners, with their traditions of whiskey and beer."

I grant you, there we are at disadvantage. But go with me to the Cunard wharves of Boston and to Castle Garden of New York, and as the long procession of emigrants steps across the gangway, you will find *three times as many men as women.* How can we offset their vote for free liquor, on Sundays and all days? Surely, the answer to this question is not far to seek. Strengthen the sinews of old King Majority, by counting in the home vote to offset that of Hamburg and of Cork and let American customs survive by utilizing (at the point where by the correlation of governmental forces "opinion" passes into "law") the opinion of those gentle "natives" who are the necessary and tender guardians of the home, of tempted manhood and untaught little children.

Hands which have just put aside the beer mug, the decanter, and the greasy pack of cards are casting ballots which undermine our Sabbaths, license social crimes that shall be nameless, and open 250,000 dramshops in the shadow of the church and public school. I solemnly call upon my countrymen to release those other hands, familiar with the pages of the Book of God, busied with sacred duties of the home and gracious deeds of charity, that they may drop in those whiter ballots, which, as God lives, alone can save the state!

Kind friends, I am not theorizing. I speak that I do know and testify what I have seen [John 3:11]. Out on the Illinois prairies we have resolved to expend on voters the work at first bestowed upon saloon-keepers. We have transferred the scene of our Crusade from the dramshop to the council room of the municipal authorities, whence the dramshop derives its guarantees and safeguards. Nay, more. The bitter argument of defeat led us to trace the tawny, seething, foaming tide of beer and whiskey to its source; and there we found it surging forth from the stately capitol of Illinois, with its proud dome and flag of stripes and stars. So we have made that capitol the center of our operations; and last winter, as one among our many branches of work, we gathered up 175,000 names of Illinois's best men and women (80,000 being the names of voters), who asked the legislature for a law giving women the ballot on the temperance question. In prosecuting our canvass for these names, we sent copies of our "Home Protection Petition" to every minister, editor, and postmaster in the state; also to all leading temperance men and women, and to every society and corporation from which we had anything to hope.

In this way our great state was permeated, and in most of its towns the petition was brought before the people. The religious press was a unit in our favor. The reform clubs of the state, with ribbons blue and red, helped us with their usual heartiness and efficiency. And what shall be thought of the advance in public sentiment, when (as was often done) all the churches join on Sabbath night in a "Union Home Protection Meeting," and ministers of all denominations (Presbyterians included) conduct the opening exercises, after which a woman presents the religious duty of women to seek and men to supply the temperance ballot; and, to crown all, conservative young ladies go up and down the aisles earnestly asking for signatures, and the audience unite in singing

> "Stand up, stand up for Jesus,
>   Ye soldiers of the Cross;
> Lift high His royal banner,
>   It must not suffer loss."

Friends, it means something for women of the churches to take this radical position. America has developed no movement more significant for good since the first dawning of the day we celebrate.

The state of Indiana stands with us; only there the temperance women have worked out the problem of deliverance further than we, and asked the ballot on all questions whatsoever. They do the same in Minnesota and in Iowa; while at the East the WCTU of grand old Maine endorses the temperance vote, and Rhode Island sends to Illinois resolutions of approval, while Massachusetts, under Mary A. Livermore,[4] has declared for Home Protection and is preparing for the fall campaign; and within a few days Ohio, the Crusade State, which is the mother of us all, has fallen into line. The most conservative states are Connecticut, New Jersey, Pennsylvania, and New York; but in each of these there are many brave women, who but bide their time for this same declaration, and the whole twenty-three states already joined in the National Woman's Christian Temperance Union will ere long clasp hands in the only work which can ever fulfill the glorious prophecy of the Crusade. History tells us that on the morning of December 23rd, 1873, when in Hillsboro', Ohio, the pentecostal power fell on the "praying band" which first went forth, the leading men of that rum-cursed town went out from the church where their wives and mothers had assembled, saying: "We can only leave this business with the women and the Lord." History has repeated itself this winter in our Illinois crusade. Men have placed money in our hands to carry on the Home Protection work, saying: "The women of America must solve this problem. Our business relations, our financial interests, our political affiliations and ambitions have tied our hands; but we will set yours free, that you may rid us of this awful curse."

Yet a few men and women, densely ignorant about this movement, have been heard to say: "Who knows that women would vote right?" I confess that nothing has more deeply grieved me than this question from the lips of Christian people. Have distillers, brewers, and saloon-keepers, then, more confidence in woman's sense and goodness than she has herself? They have a very practical method of exhibiting their faith. They declare war to the knife and the knife to the hilt against the Home Protection Movement. By secret circulars, by lobbyists and attorneys, by the ridicule of their newspaper organs, and threats of personal violence to such women of their families as sign of our petition, they display their confidence in womankind.

The only town in Illinois which sent up a delegation of citizens openly to oppose our petition was Belleville, with its heavy liquor interest and ten thousand German to three thousand American inhabitants; and among our 204 legislators there were no other dozen men whose annoyance of the Home Protection Committee was so persistent and so petty as that of the senator who openly declared he was there to defend the vested interests of his Peoria constituents, who in 1878 produced eight million dollars' worth of ardent spirits. Nay, verily, woman's vote is the way out of our misery and shame, "our enemies themselves being judges" [Deuteronomy 37:31]; and none see this so clearly as the liquor dealers, whose alligator eye is their pocketbook, and the politicians, whose Achilles heel is their ambition. The women of the Crusade must come once more to judgment—not, as aforetime, with trembling lip and tearful eye; but reaching devout hands to grasp the weapon of power and crying with reverent voice: "*The sword of the Lord and of Gideon!*" [Judges 7:20].

But, after all, "seeing" is a large part of "believing" with this square-headed Yankee nation; so let us seek the testimony of experience.

In Kansas the law provides that the signatures of women shall be requisite to a petition asking for a dramshop before that boon shall be conferred upon any given community. This arrangement wrought such mischief with the liquor dealers that they secured an amendment exempting large towns from such bondage. But in small towns and villages it has greatly interfered with the traffic and has so educated public sentiment that prohibition can—with impunity!—form the theme of a governor's inaugural, and Kansas is on the warpath for a law hardly less stringent than that of Maine.

In Des Moines, Iowa, a few weeks since, as a test of popular opinion, the women voted on the license question; twelve declaring in favor of saloons and eight hundred against them. In Newton, Iowa, at an election ordered by the council, 172 men voted for license to 319 against—not two to one against it; while the women's vote stood one in favor to 394 against licensing saloons. In Kirkville, Missouri, ten women favored the liquor traffic, twenty declined to declare themselves, and five hundred wanted "no license." In our Illinois campaign, which resulted in 95,000 names of women who expressed their wish to vote against saloons, not one woman in ten declined to affix her name to our petition.

The attitude of the Catholic Church was friendly to our petition, many priests urging their people to sign. Irish women, as a rule, gave us their names, and saloon-keepers' wives often secretly did so. Scandinavians were generally enthusiastic for the petition. Germans opposed us; but the reply of one of them indicates the chivalric nature which will come to our aid when our invincible argument against beer shall be brought in contact with German brain and German conscience. He said: "If it is not the pledge, I will sign it. I cannot give up my beer; *but I want to help the ladies.*" To be sure, German saloon-keepers were universally and bitterly antagonistic, and had much to say about "women keeping inside their proper sphere." . . .

"But women should content themselves with educating public sentiment," says one. Nay, we can shorten the process; for we have the sentiment all educated and stored away, ready for use in brain and heart. Only give us the opportunity to turn it to account where in the least time it can achieve the most! Let the great guns of influence, now pointing into vacancy, be swung to the level of benignant use and pointed on election day straight into the faces of the foe! "No; but she should train her son to vote aright," suggests another. But if she could go along with him, and thus make one vote two, should we then have a superfluous majority in a struggle intense as this one is to be? And then how unequal is her combat for the right to train her boy! Enter yonder saloon. See them gathered around their fiery or their foamy cups, according to the predominance in their veins of Celtic or of Teuton blood. What are they talking of, those sovereign citizens? The times have changed. It is no longer tariff or no tariff, resumption of specie payments, or even the behavior of our southern brethren that occupies their thought. No. Home questions have come elbowing their way to the front. The child in the midst is also in the marketplace, and they are bidding for him there, the politicians of the saloon. So skillfully will they make out the slate, so vigorously turn the crank of the machine, that, in spite of the churches and temperance societies combined, the measures dear to them will triumph and measures dear to the fond mother heart will fail. Give her, at least, a fair chance to offset by her ballot the machinations which imperil her son.

"But women cannot fight," you say, "and for every ballot cast we must tally with a bayonet." Pray tell us when the law was promulgated that we must analyze the vote at an election, and throw out the ballots of all men aged and decrepit, halt and blind? . . . I venture the prediction that this Republic will prove herself the greatest fighter of the nineteenth and twentieth centuries; but her bullets will be molded into printers' type, her Gatling guns will be the pulpit and the platform, her war will be a war of words, and underneath the white storm of men's and women's ballots her enemies—state rights, the saloon, and the commune—shall find their only shroud.

Of the right of woman to the ballot I shall say nothing. All persons of intelligence, whose prejudices have not become indurated beyond the power of logic's sledge-hammer to break them, have been convinced already. For the rest there is no cure save one—the death cure—which comes soon or late and will open more eyes than it closes. Of the Republic's right to woman's ballot I might say much. Well did two leaders of public thought set forth that right when Joseph Cook[5] declared that "woman's vote would be to the vices in our great cities what the lightning is to the oak"; and when Richard S. Storrs[6] said: "If women want the suffrage they will be sure to have it, and I don't know but when it comes it will turn out to be the precious amethyst that drives drunkenness out of politics"?

"But women do not care to vote." This is the "last ditch" of the conservatives. The evolution of temperance sentiment among women hitherto conservative refutes this argument; yet I confess there are many who do not yet perceive their duty. But Jack's beanstalk furnishes only a tame illustration of the growth of women in this direction in the years since the Crusade. Of this swift growth I have already given abundant proof. It is, in my judgment, the most solid basis of gratitude on this national anniversary.

During past years the brave women who pioneered the equal suffrage movement, and whose perceptions of justice were keen as a Damascus blade, took for their rallying cry: "Taxation without representation is tyranny." But the average woman, who has nothing to be taxed, declines to go forth to battle on that issue. Since the Crusade, plain, practical temperance people have begun appealing to this same average woman, saying, "With your vote we can close the saloons that tempt your boys to ruin"; and behold! they have transfixed with the arrow of conviction that mother's heart, and she is ready for the fray. Not rights, but duties; not her need alone, but that of her children and her country; not the "woman," but the "human" question is stirring women's hearts and breaking down their prejudice today. For they begin to perceive the divine fact that civilization, in proportion as it becomes Christianized, will make increasing demands upon creation's gentler half; that the Ten Commandments and the Sermon on the Mount are voted up or voted down upon election day; and that a military exigency requires the army of the Prince of Peace to call out its reserves.

The experience which opened the eyes of one cultured conservative in Illinois is here in point.

Mrs. Pellucid was my companion at the Capitol, where, with other ladies, we spent several weeks in the endeavor to secure legislative support for our Home Protection measures. One of the members, when earnestly appealed to, replied, with a rueful grimace: "Ladies, when I tell you the leading towns in the district I represent, you will see that I cannot do as you wish," and he rattled off such names as "Frankfort, Hamburg, and Bremen," wished us "the success that our earnestness merited," and bowed himself out.

"Why—what—does—he—mean?" inquired my lovely Conservative, in astonishment.

A committee clerk stood by, who answered, briskly: "Why, ladies, Mr. Teutonius represents a district in which German voters are in the majority; therefore, he cannot support your bill."

"Why, I thought a lawmaker was to represent his own judgment and conscience," murmured the sweet-voiced lady.

"His judgment, yes; for that tells him on which side the majority of votes in his district is located. His conscience, no; for that would often cost him his chances for a political future," answers the well-instructed youth.

"O-o-oh!" softly ejaculated Mrs. Pellucid, in the key of E flat, minor scale.

By this time Mr. Politicus entered; in response to our invitation, of course—he never would have come on his own motion. After a brief conversation, he pledged himself to vote for our bill and to make a speech in our favor. Nevertheless, if you should glance over the list we are carefully preserving and industriously circulating in Illinois, of men who voted against us, you would find his name. But he is an honest fellow in his way, and we owe it to a motion made by him that women were, for the first time in history, allowed to speak before the legislature of Illinois. He explained his desertion of the temperance cause on this wise: "I tell you, ladies, I've got to go back on you. I'm leader of my party in the House, and they've cracked the party whip mighty lively around my ears. The long and short of it is, I've got to represent the men that voted me in."

Poor Mrs. Pellucid! How appealing was her voice, as she replied: "But I am sure your better nature tells you to represent us." Mr. Politicus brought his great fist down on the table with a stalwart thump, and said: "Course it does, Madam; but, Lord bless you women, you can't stand by a fellow that stands by you, for *you hain't got any votes.*" Just here a young lady of the group piped up: "Oh! but we would persuade our friends to vote for you." "Beg pardon, Miss; but you couldn't do nothin' of the kind," said he. "Don't you s'pose I know the lay o' the land in my deestrict?" The young lady now grasped the other horn of the dilemma, saying, desperately: "But we will get the temperance men in your district to vote against you if you desert us in this manner." His rejoinder was a deplorable revelation to our simple-minded company: "Never a bit on't, Miss. The temperance men are an easy-going lot, and will vote the party ticket anyhow. Old dog Tray's ever faithful! We've ignored them for years; but they come up smilin' and vote the Republican ticket all the same. You'll see!" "But won't you stand by us for God and home and native land!" pleaded Mrs. Pellucid, with a sweetness that would have captured any man not already caught in the snares of a gainsaying constituency. The worthy politician thumped the table again, and closed the interview by saying: "You women are altogether too good to live in this world. If you could only vote, you'd have this legislature solid. But, since you can't, I'm bound to stand by such a conscience as I've got, and it tells me to stick to the fellows that voted me in. Good morning!" And he got speedily out of the range of those clear, sad eyes. Mr. Readyright (an ex-senator) came in. With all the vehemence of his Irish nature he anathematized the "weak-kneed temperance men." "Sure as you're living, Politicus told you the truth," said he. "The temperance men are the football of parties. There's none so poor to do 'em reverence. Where are the plucky young fellows that were here when we gave Illinois her present local option law?" (By the way, that law bears the name of this valiant senator, who is, by the same token a Democrat.) "Where are they? Out in the cold, to be sure. Did the temperance folks remember their services and send 'em back? Not a bit of it. But the whiskey men didn't forget the grudge they owed 'em, and they're on the shelf today—every last man of 'em." "I tell you," and the wise old gentleman gesticulated wildly in his wrath, "until you women have the power to say who shall make the laws and who enforce 'em, and to reward by re-election them that are faithful to your cause and punish by defeat them that go back upon it, you may hang your bonnets on a very high nail, for you'll not need 'em to attend the funeral of the liquor traffic!" "Why," exclaimed one of the ladies, confusedly, "you don't mean to say that the temperance ballot is not enough, and that we must follow in the footsteps of Susan B. ——?" The sturdy old gentleman walked to the door, and fired this Parthian arrow back at us: "Susan could teach any one of ye your a-b-cs. This winter's defeat'll be a paying investment to ye all, if ye learn that a politician is now and ever will be the drawn image, pocket edition, safety-valve, and speakin'-trumpet of *the folks that voted him in.*"

The ladies drew a long breath. "I begin to see men as trees walking," [Mark 8:24] slowly murmured sweet Sister Pellucid.

"But we must bide the Lord's time," warningly uttered an old lady, who had just arrived. To her the brisk committee clerk ventured this answer: "But Senator Readyright says you'll find the Lord's time will come just about twenty-four hours after the women get their eyes open!"

A temperance member of the House is the last caller whom I will report. He spake in this wise: "Ladies, I pretend to no superior saintship. I am like other men, only I come from a district that would behead me if I did not stand by you. I have a pocket full of letters, received today from party leaders at home, assuring me I run no risk." At the close of three weeks of such a school as this, one of our radicals asked Mrs. Pellucid, chief of conservatives, this pointed question: "Are you still for the Home Protection vote alone, or for the ballot on all questions?" She replied, in thrilling tones and most explicit words: "Any woman who could have shared our bitter experience here without desiring to vote on every officer, from constable to President, would be either a knave or a fool."

This lady reasoned that, since we are solemnly bound to be wise as serpents [Matthew 10:16], we must harness self-interest to our on-moving chariot. The great majority of men who are in office desire to be re-elected. By fair means, if they can; but to be re-elected anyhow. Only in one way can they bring this to pass, by securing on their side old King Majority. If we furnish them with a constituency committed to the proposition "The saloon must go," then go it will, and on the double quick. Let the city council know that women have the ballot, and will not vote for them if they license saloons, and they will soon come out for prohibition. Let the sheriff, marshal, and constable know that their tenure of office depends on their success in executing the law thus secured, and their faithfulness will leave nothing to be desired. Let the shuffling justice and the truckling judge know that a severe interpretation of the law will brighten their chances of promotion, and you will behold rigors of penalty which Neal Dow himself would wince to see.

There is also great force in the consideration that, if women, *not themselves eligible to office,* had the power to elect or to defeat *men* (who will alone be eligible for a long while yet), the precise check might by this arrangement be supplied which would keep politics from forming with the worst elements of society that unholy alliance which is today the grief of Christians and the despair of patriots. Belonging to no party ourselves, we might be able to lift the Sabbath, the temperance movement, and kindred moral questions out of the mire of merely partisan politics into which they have fallen. It is, at least, worth trying. Into the seething caldron, where the witch's broth is bubbling, let us cast this one ingredient more. In speaking thus I am aware that I transcend the present purpose of my constituency, and represent myself rather than "the folks that voted me in!"

Our temperance women in the West are learning that, while the primary meetings are the most easily influenced, they are the most influential political bodies in America. Ere long the WCTUs will attend these, beginning in the smaller and more reputable communities. We are confident that nothing would be so effective in securing the attendance of the respectable voter as the presence at the primaries of "his sisters and his cousins and his aunts." To be "in at the birth" of measures vital to the well-being of society seems to us, in the light of last winter's experience, a more useful investment of our influence than to be "in at the death." At

Springfield we found the enemy entrenched, while in the primaries his soldiers are not yet even recruited. We intend also to open in each locality books of record; and, by thorough canvass, to secure an informal registration of all men and women—the former as to how they will and the latter as to how they would (mournful potential mood!) vote on the question of permitting saloons. Every such effort helps to obliterate party lines; or, more correctly, to mass the moral elements by which alone society coheres, against the disintegrating forces, which of themselves would drive us into chaos and old night.

New England must lead. Let not the West outstrip you in this glorious race. I appeal to the women of the East. Already New Hampshire and Massachusetts have placed in your hands the educational vote, which has a direct bearing on the temperance question, since by its use the mothers of this land can place on the school committees those who will make the scientific reasons for total abstinence a regular study of the children. I beg you, by its use, to testify your fitness and desire for the more powerful weapon it foretells. It comes to you as the gift of a few earnest, persistent women, who steadily asked your legislators to bestow it, even as they will the larger gift, if you as diligently seek it. Your undertaking will not be so gigantic as ours in Illinois, for with us 34 in the senate and 102 in the house must first agree to a constitutional amendment, and then the concurrence of two-thirds of our voters must be secured. Another contrast further illustrates the favorable conditions here. Negro suffrage at the South was forced upon wide areas occupied by a voting population bitterly hostile to the innovation. Here woman's vote must first be granted by free consent of a majority of the representatives chosen directly by those who are already citizens; and by operating over the small area of a single state at a time it would arouse no violent upheaval of the opposition. Besides, the large excess of women here makes this the fitting battleground of a foregone victory.

Women of New England! among all the divisions of our great White Ribbon Army you occupy the strategic position. Truly, your valiant daughter, Illinois, earlier flung down the gauge of the new battle; but your blood is in our veins, your courage nerves our hearts, your practical foresight determines our methods of work. I come from the prairies, where we are marshaling forces for a fresh attack, and solemnly adjure you to lead us in this fight for God and home and native land. Still let dear old New England take her natural place in the forefront of the battle; and from an enemy more hateful than King George let the descendants of our foremothers deliver Concord and Lexington, and wield once more in Boston, with its eight miles of grog-shops, the sword of Bunker Hill! To chronicle the deeds by which your devotion shall add fresh luster to names renowned and hallowed, the Muse of History prepares her tablet and poises her impartial pen.

Friends, there is always a way out for humanity. Evermore in earth's affairs God works by means. Today he hurls back upon us our complaining cry: "How long? O Lord! How long? [Isaiah 7:11]. Even as he answered fainthearted Israel, so he replies to us: *What can I do for this people that I have not done? "Speak unto the children of Israel that they go forward"* [Exodus 14:15]. . . .

Notes

1. With the repeal of the income tax law in 1872, the federal government returned to funding itself largely through liquor taxes which gave it a vested interest in the continuance of the liquor industry.

2. Cyrus Hamlin (1811–1900) was a well-known missionary to Turkey who was founder and president of Robert College in Constantinople.

3. Willard was establishing the success of prohibition by citing Maine's most prominent politicians. Nelson Dingley (1832–99) was governor of Maine from 1874–76; he followed Sidney Perham (1819–1907), who was governor from 1871–74. James Gillespie Blaine (1830–93) also known as the "Plumed Knight," was a politician from Maine who served in both houses of the U.S. Congress during the years from 1863–81 and was the Republican nominee for the presidency in 1884. William Pierce Frye (1830–1911) was another national politician from Maine; he served in the House of Representatives from 1871–81 and in the Senate from 1881–1911.

4. Massachusetts WCTU president Mary Rice Livermore (1820–1905) was a strong supporter of women's suffrage. Before moving to Massachusetts in 1870 she helped found the Illinois Equal Suffrage Association (1869).

5. Reverend Joseph Cook (1838–1901) was a nationally prominent advocate of temperance and other reforms best known for his popular Boston Monday lecture series.

6. Reverend Richard Storrs (1819–1900) was an eloquent speaker and author, and was also an editor of *The Independent*.

SIX

First Presidential Address, October 27, 1880

The WCTU convention held in Boston in October 1880 provided Willard with a national platform from which to present her vision for the organization to the membership and the wider public. She outlined the direction the WCTU should take, the goals it should pursue, and the way to realize them. This was Willard's first opportunity as the WCTU's top leader to determine its future and she took full advantage of it, presenting a blueprint for the work of the WCTU that would engage its members for the next decade and beyond.

Willard began the address by reviewing advances in temperance reform not only nationally, but also internationally during 1880, thus illustrating the breadth of her understanding of the movement in its global context. The opening section ended with a stirring new metaphor: "the greatest lawsuit of the century . . . the women of the nation versus the liquor traffic." This image complemented her earlier powerful description of the struggle as a war, a martial metaphor that she continued to employ in this speech as well as those given later. It also signaled an important change in the organization's battle strategy that could already be seen in the activities of local and state temperance unions. The battlefield had now moved from the streets where the Crusade was fought to the legislatures and courts—especially the "court of public opinion"—where the WCTU's efforts would be focused for the coming decades. The tendency toward using political and legal means in addition to moral suasion had been growing among reformers for several decades, and Willard clearly embraced this trend in her championship of the home protection ballot.

As Willard expanded on the WCTU Plan of Work for the coming years, she urged her constituency to enlarge their vision of reform beyond merely temperance, calling on them to direct their efforts toward the challenge of creating a better environment for those living in the nation's rapidly expanding cities. Pointing to WCTU innovations such as hiring police matrons and petitioning legislatures to fund reform schools for girls, Willard endorsed various programs that anticipated by nearly a decade the work of settlement houses and civic betterment organizations, thus placing the WCTU in the vanguard of the Progressive movement.

The address also illustrates Willard's strong organizational skills as she articulated her ideas for restructuring the composition of WCTU committees and increasing the organization's financial base. She also proposed altering its system for choosing delegates and creating a cadre of paid WCTU field workers who could devote their full energy and time to reform, complementing the efforts of the majority of members whose domestic commitments made full-time reform work difficult. By the mid-1880s, all three of these organizational reforms were in place, helping to make possible the tremendous growth and effectiveness of the WCTU during the 1880s.

The most important moment in Willard's address came at its conclusion, in the portion she called "Reflex Influence of This Work Upon the Workers." It marked her first effort as WCTU president to engage her organization in a thoroughgoing critique of traditional gender relations, as she began to conceive an alternative, more egalitarian mode of male–female relationships. Temperance reform could offer women a way out—one that had God's sanction—from their enslavement within a narrow and confining domestic existence. Armed with the virtues of morality and caregiving that they had honed over centuries, WCTU women would move into the world under the banner of "Home Protection" using their gifts in whatever sphere of action they chose "for purposes of wider blessing to humanity." Employing a provocative image—"the stereoscopic view"—to suggest the added scope and depth of vision that women would bring to bear on the nation's public institutions, Willard built her case for women to become active in the world beyond the home. For the duration of her long presidency, temperance and "the cause of woman," would remain inextricably linked.

These excerpts from Willard's first presidential address are from *The Minutes of the Woman's National Christian Temperance Union* (New York: The National Temperance Society and Publication House, 1880), 9–10, 18–25.

* * *

Progress

Beloved Sisters and Co-workers: This has been the most encouraging year the world has ever seen in the history of temperance reform. Even in Germany it was proposed at the last session of the Reichstag to tax the beer-trade because of its harmful effects on the health and morals of the people. In England, Gladstone's Ministry secured the malt-tax and the House of Commons passed Sir Wilfrid Lawson's Local Option Resolution.[1] The Scott Act of Canada[2]—which has no peer among prohibitory laws in its machinery for enforcement—triumphantly sustained the ordeal of an appeal to the Supreme Court to test its constitutionality, and has been adopted by the Province of Prince Edward Island with the favorable results which, among a people educated in temperance sentiment, have always followed such enactments. In Maine the law was greatly strengthened in its penalties by the last Legislature, and a thorough temperance man is elected governor. The Legislature of Iowa has placed a prohibitory constitutional amendment before the people, and Kansas will vote on the 2nd of November, on a similar provision, which will undoubtedly prevail; while, despite the utmost efforts of the rum-Democrats and beer-Republicans, Governor St. John of Kansas,[3] that stalwart defender of the faith, was overwhelmingly successful in securing a renomination.

In this year, too, the Crusade state of Ohio sent the largest petition its annals show, asking the ballot for women on all temperance questions; while, under a local ordinance prepared by a leading lawyer and circulated by the Woman's Christian Temperance Union of Illinois, women have actually voted in five municipalities on the question of license; and all of them—the high and low, illiterate and educated, Catholic and Protestant—voted "to close the dram-shop door over against their homes."

But let us thank God most of all that in the supreme court of public opinion the greatest lawsuit of the century is set for trial. Long quibbled over and frequently postponed, it has at last come squarely to the front; it heads the docket, and the clear-cut issue is stated in these words: *The Women of the Nation* versus *The Liquor-Traffic.* . . .

Work which We May Inaugurate and Inspire

While as temperance women we keep to our own work, there are many other philanthropic efforts which, in various localities, have been projected by our societies. In Dover, N.H., an evening school for employees, originating in the Union, was taken up by the proprietor of a large manufactory, who assumed all the expenses. In Rochester, N.Y., the Young Woman's Temperance Union gives temperance lessons to the public-school children on Friday after hours, awaiting the time when the proper authorities shall incorporate the work into the system of public education. In Portland, Maine, the employment of a member of our Union to attend the police-court and look after the interests of arrested women resulted in the appointment of a woman policeman (pardon the philanthropic paradox) by the municipal authorities in a distant city, who were moved thereto by their knowledge of the Portland experiment. In Michigan, the State Woman's Christian Temperance Union last year induced the Legislature to appropriate thirty thousand dollars for a Girl's Reform School.

It has long seemed to me that our Unions, by their unsectarian character and representative aims, were fitted incidentally to furnish the incitement to noble enterprises closely related to our work, in which women who will not as yet, engage in our direct temperance endeavor would gladly employ their steadily-arousing energies. In large cities we might call a meeting and do the preliminary work which would result in organizing the associated charities so beneficently operative in Philadelphia and in Boston, or the founding of an Industrial and Temporary Home like that of which the pastor of this church [A. J. Gordon, Clarendon Street Baptist Church, Boston] is the chief presiding officer; or the inauguration of a Citizens' League in the interests of the Sabbath and the protection of children from the liquor-traffic, an enterprise which has had notable success in Chicago. We might go even beyond all this and petition municipal authorities to establish public fountains, free bathing-houses and gymnasiums, all of which, conducing directly to improved sanitary habits in the public, would accomplish much toward diminishing the feverish and unnatural thirst for stimulants. Let us not insist that all shall work with us, but rather be sedulous in the endeavor so to increase the aggregate "enthusiasm of humanity," so as to glorify the sentiment of *other-hood* as opposed to the sense of *self-hood,* that all may find the secret of a happy life in working *somewhere.*

How Shall We Do All This?

But how shall all this work be carried on? More and more, as it develops, by increasing the number of paid laborers in the field. Every state and all the chief local Unions must have headquarters with paid secretaries. Consider the experience of the Young Men's Christian Association. Its local auxiliaries had a most uncertain tenure of life and its work grew slowly until it adopted this plan of commanding consecrated talent in the departments of organizing, writing, and speaking, and now what a vast and growing power it has become! Look over our state and local Unions to see where most has been accomplished, and you will invariably find that it is where this same plan was early adopted by our women. This is the age of experts and specialists. We must find out what each woman who makes this cause her life-work can do best, then set her at that and see that she is taken care of—a moderate but stipulated sum, being paid from our treasury, on which her collections in public meetings shall apply. Of this I may speak freely, never having received a penny's salary from the National Union, and being determined that I never will, just for the pleasure of tilting a free lance, as I am doing now.

By having more workers, both in state and nation, who devote themselves to special lines, we can dispense with many of our standing committees, but I suggest, that if a chairman has done well we observe in her case the rules of civil-service reform—which admit no change except "for cause." Especially should this be the case in view of the fact that under our present loose system of scattering members of committees through several states, and giving no opportunity for consultation at the National Meeting, the chairman who has saved any time from committee correspondence for real work must be a person of marvelous executive ability. In the accompanying schedule the committees are more compactly classified than heretofore, and your attention is asked to the suggested changes. Perhaps the national standing committees should consist of one person each, and be similarly duplicated in the different states, down to the local Unions. If this plan is not adopted, we must in all conventions appoint these committees early in the session, so that consultation may be had before they separate. Or, possibly, a still more effective plan is the one indicated in the schedule, by which our most important lines of work are entrusted to superintendents, national, state, and local. Much advantage will result from a more specific definition of the duties of our general officers, that upon each may be fixed the responsibility for her appropriate lines of work.

Where Shall We Find the Special Workers?

Not by levying a draft upon the home women, to the neglect of those duties which, if performed with reverence and intelligence, will help humanity as no other efforts can.

But while the beloved home-makers and home-keepers give us scraps and fragments of their time, finding in our Unions a nobler form of social interchange than in the ceremonious calls and visits of the olden time—those scraps and fragments can be braided together into coherent form by the steady fingers and deft skill of the once "anxious and aimless," but now cheery and efficient class which we name "*our Protestant nuns.*"

Thousands once called "spinsters" because society had found nothing for them to do but spin; thousands more whom death, or that death-in-life called dissipation has bereft of "their strong staff and beautiful rod" [Jeremiah 48:17]; and yet other thousands who, when their nest was left unto them desolate because the birds were fledged and flown, once sat with folded hands through life's long afternoon—are now finding a place where their activities exactly fit into the varied and musical machinery of our beautiful and blessed work. To empty-hearted young women in homes of luxury our Unions come with loving invitations; to the dormant talent in Christ's Church the call is: "Arise, ye who are at ease in Zion; hear my voice, ye careless daughters" [Isaiah 32:9] to the over-crowded ranks of teacherdom (and here I can speak out of long experience) the invitation is, come with us; we need each other. Hard as our work is, a teacher's occupation is harder still. Though I could point you to a score of women in our work who speak on an average of once a day all the year round, who organize, write and travel without respite, and nearly all of whom were healthier, and in better spirits than ever in their lives before. The breezy life, the tonic of change, the inspiration of variety have much to do with this. Moreover, if one is in earnest and has something to say, the average audience need have no terrors for a woman who can instruct and hold the interest of a high-school class. Indeed, the former requires more stress of nerve, for your class instinctively matches its united intellectual vigor against its teacher and is full of questionings; while an audience is in receptive rather than combative mood, and is also to the last degree good-natured and cannot answer back! Let the voice of invitation go forth, then, to the teachers and the young women in our colleges, certifying to them that in delightful service for Christ a new vocation is open to the persuaders of the race. Nor do I hesitate to predict the day as not far distant when we shall have scores of educated women, where we now have one, engaged in the sure and steady occupation of educating and refining public sentiment, with voice and pen, against the use of poisonous beverages. Fields are waiting for them in half a dozen states today, as I know by urgent applications from leading officers. They will be welcome and beloved, the sisters of all homes, societies, and people, for their work's sake. Custom's pinched lips have ceased to mutter their tyrannical "Thus far, no farther," which in less Christian centuries checked the buoyant steps of woman, and God's loving "Thus far, no farther," written in our nature, asserts its kindly sway.

Finances—Basis of Representation

What is the essential prerequisite to these enlarged plans for our work? I do not hesitate to answer that it is the silver and gold which belongs to God, but has not yet found its way into the temperance treasury. The ring of the consecrated dollar is as genuine a sign of consecrated character as this world can show, and a basis of representation which requires the payment of a moderate membership fee, say a penny a week, from each woman who unites with us, will gird our feeble treasury with the sinews of war. At first many of us did not perceive this need, and, though a membership fee was usually incorporated into our constitutions, it was practically a dead letter. But among the best lessons of our experience has been that which leads us to desire the enforcement of this rule, not only in the basis of national, but of state and local representation. Surely a penny per week from each member is a little thing to ask from those whose hearts God has touched with the spirit of temperance work, but that amount *paid in* would enable us to reverse the magic of classic story, which says the touch of King Midas turned everything into gold, for our Christian alchemy would transmute gold into everything—into the temperance reading-room, the literature, the organizer's clear brain, the speaker's voice, the writer's pen.

Let us not be so illogical as to imagine an antagonism where none exists—by which we set *paying* and *praying,* always in God's economy two parts of one tremendous whole, over against each other. What would the church be if we did not both pray *and* pay? What would the Missionary Society accomplish without its well-lined treasury? And what can this home missionary work of temperance hope to achieve, if we call that unclean which God hath cleansed [Acts 10:15]? This fallacy is akin to that which objects to paying salaries or accepting money for any kind of temperance work. It seems to creep in at the beginning of every form of Christian enterprise, the ministers of new sects being usually unsalaried, but is always detected in the clearer light of experience.

We do the public a positive harm when we deprive them of the pleasure of giving their substance to those philanthropic workers who, though necessarily dismissing the expectation of material wealth, nevertheless perform such labors as are worthy not only the priceless hire of souls and of public good will, but of a comfortable maintenance as well. "He that provideth not for his own household is worse than an infidel" [1 Timothy 5:8], and there is hardly a worker in our ranks who would not speedily perceive the bottom of the coal-bin and the flour-barrel were those for whom she labors unmindful of her needs.

These things being true, let us look the financial question squarely in the face, and I suggest that to the membership fees be added, in all local Unions, the system of monthly subscriptions by card, the circulation of individual subscription-books by leading members, and the effort to secure the Thanksgiving Day collection for the home work. The little "red books" sent out from our National Headquarters this year have materially added to our resources, and I am confident that, if you decide to put a Financial Agent in the field, next year will witness a surprising augmentation of our income.

But the basis of representation by which each delegate represents a fixed number of paying members is not only financially helpful, it is *just,* since by means of it each delegate represents a *certain number of temperance women,* rather than (as heretofore) a certain area of population, large numbers of whom sell, drink, and vote for the sale of intoxicating liquors. Still farther, the new basis gives the additional influence which is their due to localities where the largest numbers have been enlisted, and thus becomes an honorable incentive to energetic efforts in the work of organization. . . .

Reflex Influence of This Work upon the Workers

Having surveyed the field to learn what women are doing for the temperance cause, let us, in conclusion, gratefully consider what the temperance cause is doing for women. It is leading us outside the hedges of a narrow sectarianism. Going into the streets to pray meant going beyond denominational walls, and clasping hands with all who love our Lord Jesus Christ in such sincerity as leads them to "rescue the perishing." This temperance work is also revealing to us the absurdity of always standing below the cataract to grasp, often vainly, for those who have made the fearful plunge, instead of stationing guards above it to keep the ignorant and unwary from falling in. It has taught us also that, as God has given us eyes which can look up and around but not within ourselves, the most healthful Christian life is one that gazes lovingly into the face of Christ and helpfully around upon humanity, instead of tiring itself out with morbid introspection. Slowly we are discovering with happiness that mocketh speech, that this fight against home's bitterest enemy is God's highway of the exodus for half the race. Wonderful indeed are the orderings of Heaven by which today in thousands of communities our Unions are the nucleus of such study as women of the church and home have never before given to the structure of the human body and God's Health Decalogue written therein. Think what it means for her who is priestess of the cradle to follow lines of work and study which keep steadily before her thought the fact that the body is sacred and that the rules of its well-being are religious, inasmuch as they are the ritual of the temple of the Holy Ghost written in natural law.

The medieval monastery taught men to despise the body; the modern home will teach them to reverence and ennoble it by sedulously cultivated habits of pure living. Steadily cherishing this thought, our temperance women will go beyond the study of the pitiful effects of the alcohol and nicotine habits upon their sons, to the closely related topics of diet, dress, cleanliness, ventilation, and exercise, as helps or hindrances not to their sons only but to the best development of themselves. Indeed, I have heard more than one of them say already that she never drank a cup of water, partook of food, or provided for the ventilation of her sleeping room as a *religious* act until this temperance work had wrought into her thinking and her conscience this reverent appreciation of God's revelation written in our members. Dressmakers and shoe merchants are receiving instructions for more generous measurements and sizes than formerly from temperance women, and a simpler style of diet and adorning is among the reflex influences upon the home, for which we thank God and take courage. As the work goes on, and our study of these solemn and beautiful truths of God grows deeper, the dense ignorance and heart-breaking indifference of both men and women to the laws that govern that incomparable sacrament, the genesis of an immortal spirit, will be slowly overcome.

Our Dr. Richardson[4] whose "Temperance Text-Book" we are studying, says this whole subject of inherited tendencies waits and will go on waiting till women take it up. But they will do so as one reflex of our work: and when its sacred laws are understood, taught, and obeyed, we shall see the banished pair returning to Eden early lost, and our sorrowful race, so long defiled, shall come back to its Father and its God. Oh! If those close-clasped hands had never parted company our poor old world had been a happier place today. It is not good for man to be alone [Genesis 2:18]. In college, camp, and court his deterioration is the patent obstacle against which even our Christian civilization contends in vain. Until we get the stereoscopic view from the different angles of vision which man's eye and woman's furnish, Government will remain the Chinese picture that it is, without the vividness and perspective of truth. We are learning that our work is not along the line of the woman question merely, but the deeper, higher, and far more sacred *human question.* The laws of heredity and six thousand years of education have developed in woman the instinct of speech and the faculty of government. She has always been chief legislator in the little principality of home, and no queen ever had subjects more loving or more loyal. The scientific method and the teachings of the Gospel (invariably harmonious when both are reverently studied) have always favored the exercise of these two predominant gifts of what will always be "the gentler sex." Literature was the first field opened to us, then coeducation, then occupation, then—in the widest sense—philanthropy. Prejudice predicted failure in each, but was mistaken. Conservatism prophesied the loss of womanly character and deportment as the too costly price of preferment in all, but its fears have not been realized.

Ere long the Christian womanhood of our country will come to Church and state asking that, for the highest good of each, woman's full power of speech and legislation shall be exercised in both. I make this prophecy not as *your* representative, but as my own. The masses who drink and sell intoxicants are not reached by the usual means of grace; but two-thirds of Christ's church are women, whose persuasive voices will be a reinforcement quite indispensable to the evangelizing agencies of the more hopeful future. A horde of ignorant voters committed to the rum power, fastens the dram shop like a leech on our communities; but let the Republic take notice that our Unions are training an army to offset this horde, one which will be the only army of voters specifically educated to their duty which has ever yet come up to the help of the Lord against the mighty. For slowly but surely the reflex influence is educating women to the level of two most solemn and ominous ideas: 1st. *That they ought to vote.* 2d. *That they ought to vote against grog-shops.* The present generation will not pass away until in many of the states this shall all be fulfilled, and then, America, beloved Mother of thrice grateful daughters, thou shalt find rallying to thy defense and routing the grimy host that reel about thee now, an army of voters which absenteeism will not decimate and money cannot buy. Under the influence of our societies may be tried the great experiment that agitates the age, and which upon the world's arena most of us have feared.

When we desire this "home protection" weapon American manhood will place it in our hands. Though we have not taken sides as yet in politics, we cannot be insensible to the consideration shown us in the platform of the Prohibition party—a prophecy of that chivalry of justice which shall yet afford us a still wider recognition. These benign changes will not come suddenly, but as the result of a profound change in the convictions of the thoughtful and conscientious, followed by such a remolding of public sentiment as this class always brings about when once aroused. First of all the best and truest men must be convinced that *womanliness* can never be legislated out of being, but that, as it has survived the days when women wove and spun, picked their own geese and did their own dyeing; as it has borne bravely up amid the crash of old theories concerning how much a woman might know and how little she might do, womanliness is likely to prove the grandest recorded instance of survival of the fittest based on natural law.

Beloved friends, among the reflex influences by which this temperance work has broadened my own outlook and enriched my hopes, may I speak of the sweet and tender lesson of your homes to me? I have learned how such solemn vicissitudes as come into the lives of women only, help to confirm your faith in the world invisible. The breath of eternity falls on your foreheads like baptismal dew in those hours of unutterable pain and danger when a little child is born into your home. Your steps lie along the borderland of this closely-curtained world,

> "And palpitates the veil between
> With breathings almost heard."

Into your eyes fall the first mystic glances of innocent and trusting souls. Tender little hands folded in prayer and winsome voices saying

> "Gentle Jesus, meek and mild,
> Look upon a little child,"

have done more than all traditional restraints to keep your hearts loving and unworldly. Always this will be so; always from manhood's more exterior view of life's significance you are separated by the deepest and most sacred experiences which human hearts may know. That anchor holds. But God has given the mother-heart for purposes of wider blessing to humanity than it has dreamed as yet. Let us go gently forward until that loving, faithful heart shall be enthroned in the places of power; until the queens of home are queens indeed.

And, best of all, the hand of Him whose Gospel has lifted us up into these heavenly places in Jesus Christ; of Him who was a brother to the Marys, and who, in His hour of mortal agony, did not forget His mother—that pierced hand points the way.

Notes

1. William Ewart Gladstone (1809–98), an English legislator and reformer, served four times as prime minister of Great Britain, including a term running from 1880 to 1885. British Parliament member Lawson (1829–1906) was also the president of the British temperance organization, the United Kingdom Alliance, from 1879 until his death.

2. Passed in 1878, the Canada Temperance Act, named for Secretary of State Richard William Scott, was a local option bill.

3. Prominent politician and temperance leader, John Pierce St. John (1833–1916), was governor of Kansas from 1879 to 1883 and was the Prohibition Party's presidential candidate in 1884.

4. Benjamin Ward Richardson (1828–96), British physician and one of the earliest doctors to work in the field of public health, was known for his research on alcohol. His *Temperance Lesson Book,* a series of short lessons on alcohol and its effects on the body, was widely used in public schools in Britain and the United States.

SEVEN

Three Articles from the WCTU Newspaper, 1881–83

Throughout the early years of Willard's WCTU presidency, the *Union Signal,* the official newspaper of the national organization, served as one of her most powerful communication tools. The paper, like the organization, evolved over time. The WCTU first launched a monthly paper in 1875 and was soon publishing a weekly called *Our Union.* By 1883 that paper had merged with the newspaper of the Illinois WCTU, the *Signal,* as well as several other papers, to become the nationally circulated paper, *The Union Signal.* Through its pages Willard communicated the WCTU's mission to her constituents and beyond. In the late 1870s, the newspaper had a circulation of only a few thousand, but by 1891 the number of subscribers had grown to 85,000, making it one of the most widely distributed organizational newspapers of the time.

The following three excerpts from the WCTU newspaper indicate two of the types of writing Willard did for the WCTU in its pages. The first, "The Dragon's Council Hall: A Temperance Allegory," which appeared in *Our Union* in January 1881, is a satire describing the range of ways the liquor industry worked against both temperance and women's role in the reform by co-opting religion to subvert the WCTU's efforts. In it, Willard depicted a top-level meeting called by Satan so his lieutenants could report on the advance of his sinful Kingdom. The satire forcefully, yet quite humorously, presented the kind of very real opposition WCTU women met from pastors and church members they might have expected to be their allies in the fight for sobriety. This short piece served to heighten women's awareness of their opponents' machinations, strengthening them in their struggle against formidable enemies.

The second and third excerpts illustrate Willard's practice of reporting to her readers during her extensive travels as a temperance lecturer and organizer for the WCTU. The letters are typical of the public correspondence she produced for the newspaper throughout the 1880s and 1890s, which kept the membership in touch with her thoughts and activities as she built the WCTU into a truly national organization. The letters also served to introduce her readers to new leaders in the organization and new regions enlisted in the reforms she championed. "A Rapid Transit Letter," which appeared in *Our Union* in April 1881, was one of a series of reports from Willard on her first southern tour. Over a period of three months she visited "nearly one hundred towns and cities," speaking about the goals of the WCTU, forming local unions, and recruiting members.[1] Her public letter noted some of the challenges she faced as a northern woman speaking in public, but made clear that she was enthusiastically received. Her hopes that the WCTU could play a leading role in the post–Civil War reconciliation of North and South, seemed to be substantiated during this early southern tour.

In "Across the Continent—VI," from the *Union Signal*, August 16, 1883, Willard wrote a lively account of the special difficulties of organizing during her "Western Round Up." During this 105–day tour of six western states, Willard and her personal secretary Anna Gordon held 116 meetings.[2] In her public letters during the tour, Willard vividly described the many hardships they endured as they traveled through the northwestern states by train, river steamer, stage coach, and buckboard. Difficult as it was for visitors like Willard and Gordon, middle-class women settlers who moved to the far northwest faced natural and social conditions that continually tested their strength and determination. Even by the 1880s, western towns and cities were rough, lawless places where alcohol, gambling, and prostitution were rampant. The WCTU, with its message of home protection and prohibition carried by Willard and other organizers, supported the reform work undertaken by church women, ministers, and civic leaders in the region.

Willard's reports from both her 1881 southern visit and her 1883 western trip give detailed illustrations of her methods of organizing. This reporting served a dual purpose: to keep in touch with her constituency and to offer a model for WCTU organizers throughout the country. The letters reveal that Willard was adept at making contacts with the Protestant establishment in the towns she visited, meeting with "leading citizens," and building a network of supporters wherever she traveled. These extended tours also linked women in all parts of the nation with a strong sisterhood that shared their beliefs and goals. Willard's insistence on keeping in touch with her constituency proved to be a crucial strategy in building a committed and effective membership.

"The Dragon's Council Hall: A Temperance Allegory" is from *Our Union*, January 27, 1881, 3. This article is reprinted in Frances E. Willard, *Woman and Temperance* (Chicago: Woman's Temperance Publishing Association, 1883), 389–92. The excerpts from "A Rapid Transit Letter" are from *Our Union*, April 14, 1881, 2. The excerpts from "Across the Continent—No. VI" are from *The Union Signal*, August 16, 1883, 5.

* * *

"The Dragon's Council Hall: A Temperance Allegory," 1881

Behold His Satanic Majesty in Cabinet Council assembled with his minions and his emissaries, newly returned from this sin-stricken earth. Each brings the latest news concerning the endless conflict between darkness and light; ignorance and wisdom; sin and righteousness. Each gives the most carefully considered suggestions for the building up of Satan's kingdom—for the multiplication of murders, robberies, outrages and conflagrations. "Permit the suggestion, Your Majesty," says one brimstone-colored satellite, "that you will build a new distillery at Spiritsville, for at that point the church people are growing rapidly in power."

"Not at all," tartly replies he of the horns and hoofs, "well you know better than to be always showing your hand in that fashion! Do this instead: Put it in the heart of John Barleycorn, proprietor of the distillery I have already there, to subscribe ten thousand dollars toward finishing that church."

The order was entered in lurid letters on the books. No. 2 proceeded to report.

"In Temperanceville they have so few saloons that the young men are rapidly getting out from under the sway, and I humbly suggest the imperative necessity of a special order, on the Stygian Manufactory for six well instructed and experienced imps, who shall put it into the heads of six men now engaged in other business, to open these saloons as business is so lively at Cincinnati and Peoria, that we can spare none of our already enlisted forces."

"Tut, tut!" roared the devil, "I can beat that device, with only half trying. Send a beer-drinking pastor to Temperanceville and let him preach in favor of the Business Men's Moderation Society and show up the idiot theories of those stiff-necked teetotallers."

No. 3 now ventured to suggest that in Tippleton, the women had opened a Sunday afternoon meeting and had given out that they should offer a free lunch at the polls on the approaching election day. He therefore asked for a detailed escort of fiends who should be commanded to set fire to the Temperance Reading Rooms and drive the President of the W.C.T.U. raving distracted.

"You are a callow young limb of perdition to go so clumsily about your business," roared the devil; "I won't send a special squad, for they are all employed in the saloons working up the voting-lists against the next election, in the interests of the whisky governor, but do you go and put it into the head of Deacon Setbones to prove to the W.C.T.U. President that the Scriptures do plainly teach that it's a sin and a shame for a woman to speak in any public place, and that the whole spirit of Christianity is set against the insane notion of a woman's undertaking to preside at an electioneering lunch down at the polls."

And now came the last, and most lugubrious-looking messenger, with this doleful story to relate:

"I ask that pestilence and famine be let loose, for I am terribly alarmed for the stability of the Kingdom in the Province, of which Chicago (otherwise Beeropolis) is the chief city; for be it known unto your Majesty, there is a serious revolt among those whom thou hast kept in strict subordination, lo, these centuries! For *the women* are rousing themselves to the cry of 'Home Protection!'; studying into the structure of the government; tracing back to their source the temptations that have so admirably succeeded in capturing boys and men for thy great armies. These frightful women, neglecting their proper sphere and the submission so long their convenient characteristic, have actually dared to publish figures showing that the majority of voters are on thy side, and that thus thou dost hold thyself in power by keeping thine ambassador King Alcohol, entrenched among the people."

Here the fiendish messenger turned a sickly yellow, and gasped with rage, as he concluded his awful revelation in these words, "They even ask—and many ministers, church editors, and other strong allies of Him whom thou didst tempt and crucify are asking for them—the power to vote upon all questions relating to the sale of alcoholic drinks."

O, what a scene was that! The devil quaked in every limb; his sharp knees smote together and a howl of hellish hate and rage rang through the sulphurous air of the dark Council Chamber, "Away with you, fools that you are! Talk of letting loose famine and pestilence! If things have reached this pass—if the women have discovered that *the side always wins which has the most votes*—let me make haste, I'll send no stupid, clumsy-footed subaltern, in an emergency like this! I'll steal in among those timid and silly rebels who have always hated me and sought the triumph of Him who wore the thorn-crown, and from a thousand pulpits I'll declare that woman leaves her home on this vile errand at the peril of society;—that you can not carry temperance, much less the Gospel, into politics, and that on the day when woman votes, the Home will fall into everlasting ruin and woman turn herself into a Jezebel! *Exeunt omnes* [exit all].

"A Rapid Transit Letter"

On the cars en route for Savannah, Apr. 1, 1881.

After three weeks of Southern experience I am glad and grateful to send you word it is the most rewarding work of my whole life. Not financially of course, for we charge nothing, take no collections, and the subject of money is not to be "once named among ye" [Ephesians 5:3]. But the hospitality is boundless. Invitations to breakfast, dinner, and tea; calls, carriage rides, flowers, dainty dishes, and kind words by the dictionary-full.

When we get to the railroad station some gentleman insists on buying our tickets and then suddenly disappears, after placing them in the hands of our *major-domo,* Mrs. McLeod.[3] Nay more, by the efforts of Mrs. Doctor Thomas and Mr. E. S. Young, assistant general passenger agent of Baltimore and Potomac, and of Mr.

John B. Peck, of Atlanta, whose wife is earnest in our work, we have secured some passes and several reduced rates, so that expenses have been very much diminished. It is a new experience to go "Scot free" in a strange land. We are spending a good deal in literature for which the demand is strong, and by this means shall be able to spread the knowledge of our work and methods, far and wide. Three weeks of blessed work for the homes and loved ones of a most genial, intelligent and heartily responsive people, have made me quite in love with the South. To think they should have received me as a sister beloved, yet with full knowledge that I was that novel and unpalatable combination (as a Richmond gentleman said) "A *woman;* a *Northern* woman; a Northern *temperance* woman!" I had been told that to speak in public in the South was "not to be thought of"—that "all would be lost" if I attempted anything beyond "parlor meetings." But, instead of this, their liberality of sentiment has been abundantly equal to the "strain"; their largest churches fill with the best, the most influential and thoughtful people; their ministers more united and earnest in the temperance cause than ours at the North; their editors, without the slightest "subsidizing," as kind and helpful as my own brother could have been. Nay, the only grief I have is to be spoken of so much better in every way than my own consciousness bears me witness that I merit.

Let me give you an idea of our *modus operandi.* Dear Mrs. McLeod, a "Southron of the Southrons," sends letters to leading ladies and pastors, secures their interest, goes on before and speaks, perhaps in some church prayer meeting, giving accounts of our work, arranging for afternoon meetings of ladies and evening engagements in some church. Arriving, a committee is at the depot, and from that hour everything is done to express the welcome of generous and honest hearts. In the evening after an address, often with all the leading pastors of the city present, papers are circulated through the audience asking ladies to put down their names for membership in the W.C.T.U. The Huguenot pastor of Charleston, Rev. Dr. [Charles Stewart] Vedder, says that means "*We come to unite,*" and "*We come to upset.*"

The conditions of membership are signing the total abstinence pledge and agreeing to pay a penny a week into the treasury. Gentlemen become honorary members on the same terms. I have seldom or never had responses so hearty at the North as we find here. Next day we hold a ladies' meeting, the pastors assisting, and elect officers, agree upon practical methods of work, as: organizing temperance cadets with the military drill; circulating temperance literature by means of tin boxes put up in markets, depots, shops, etc.; securing a "Loan Library," to be placed in the hands of those we wish to influence; getting a temperance column in the local papers; holding union prayer and gospel meetings in the churches; giving temperance lessons regularly in the Sabbath school; recruiting for members in all the churches, etc., etc. The Southern ladies take up these quiet, systematic lines of work with an intelligence and zeal which I have never seen exceeded and seldom equaled. Would that instead of two we had two hundred of our workers actively engaged in the fourteen southern states. That would be a "peace policy" worthwhile to plan and execute. Politicians would be unable to keep "the two sections" from being one after a few years of such fraternization. There is an "our folks" air in audiences, cars, and on the streets here, that is quite refreshing. The colored population are of such home-like nature, and the foreign element so insignificant in influence and numbers, that temperance has an immense advantage in the South. Beer has no such grip on the habits or the politics of the people as at the North. Almost without exception the gulf and seabound states have taken advance ground here this winter. The time is ripe: "the sound in the mulberry trees" [2 Samuel 5:24] is plainly audible; total abstinence and a prohibition ballot commend themselves to a people proud of their chivalry, when presented as a plea from women's point of view.

The colored population is very readily influenced to make common cause with the whites for the defense of their homes, and the foregleams of the "era of good feeling" between the two classes are the dawning light of the temperance awakening. God speed the day! We have already eight new unions at Richmond, Va; Wilmington, N.C.; Aiken, S.C., (which Anna and Bessie Gordon[4] are helping to build up); Columbia, Spartanburg, Greenville—three in the last named, one white, one of young ladies in the Baptist college, and one of colored people.

Mrs. John Crenshaw of Richmond; Rev. Dr. Yates of N.C.; Mrs. Leonard Chapin,[5] President of our work in South Carolina; Bishops Wightman and Stevens; Dr. Vedder, Rev. Coke Smith and Rev. Mr. Chrietzburg, of Charleston; Rev. Dr. Wells and Stokes of Columbia; Hon. Wm. Blake and Rev. Dr. Wightman of Spartanburg, S.C.; Gen. Ellison Capers and Rev. J.O. Willson, of Greenville, S.C., have been our chief coadjutors thus far. Mrs. McLeod says that in these three weeks I have spoken twenty-six times, which, with correspondence, travel and constant social visits, is quite a "portion," but my health is excellent. We are now *en route* to Savannah, Ga., thence Jacksonville, Fla., Atlanta, Augusta, Macon, &c., Ga., possibly Mobile and New Orleans, afterward Raleigh, N.C., where we have been warmly invited to the State Convention Apr. 27. A prohibition petition two hundred thousand strong was presented there to the last legislature, which submitted the question to the people, and they vote upon it August 1st. The time is thus propitious for the introduction of our organization.

How goes dear old Illinois? Have heard nothing for weeks. Please ask God's blessing on our Southern work.

"Across the Continent—No. VI"

En route, Idaho to Oregon, 1883

Dear *Union Signal:*

Two days ago, after our night of unexampled misery in a hotel room without a window and the thermometer almost beyond the nineties, we made our contemplated *detour* into Idaho. Leaving the railroad at Texas Ferry, we took the pleasant steamer John Gates for an eighty miles trip up the Snake River to Lewiston, the oldest town in Idaho. . . . So far as I can learn, no organized temperance work has ever been attempted for this most inaccessible of territories. Even we who "stay not for break and stop not for stone," have felt constrained to relinquish the hope of penetrating to its capital: Boise City, or "Boissie," as the people here have endearingly nick-named it. But we have been receiving the kindest invitations from Mrs. Norman Buck, our National vice president, since we reached California, and we determined to call for a convention and to plan the outline map of a territorial W.C.T.U.

Mrs. Buck's position gave her special facilities for working up such a meeting, as her husband is United States Judge, appointed by President Hayes and well liked by the people. Besides, she is a woman of antecedents, gifts and experience. . . . [She told me:] "I graduated at the university in Appleton [Wisconsin, Lawrence University], lived in Winona, Minnesota, nineteen years and was county president of the W.C.T.U., came here a year ago with six children, staging it five days and four nights across the hills. Found myself appointed as representative of the W.C.T.U. in this part of the moral vineyard, and felt I must do 'what I could.'" Mrs. Buck is the sister of Professor Julius H. Kellogg, of the Northwestern University at Evanston [Illinois], and was at the Lake Bluff convocation last summer. So we are fortunate in having as our Idaho president a woman so thoroughly of us and so recently with us.

Well, this dear, bright little woman had set to work, first of all, to form a W.C.T.U. in her own town of Lewiston. It was accomplished on this wise and I do not give the links in the chain of circumstances without a purpose. Joining the church of her choice (Methodist) she proposed a ladies society which should meet four times per month—the first time for prayer that they might themselves be better Christians, the second for the church and to do "Church Aid Society" work, the third for the temperance cause *in Lewiston,* and the fourth for foreign missions. A few months later, the Presbyterian pastor, Rev. Mr. Boyd, preached a temperance sermon and urged the good people to enter upon some form of organized effort. Whereupon Mrs. Buck who chanced to be present, told of the little prayer meetings, and stated her earnest hope that it should be expanded into an unsectarian society of the very name and nature of the W.C.T.U. This met with a hearty response and steps were at once taken to carry out the plan. Mrs. S. A. McAlister, wife of the Universalist minister, was chosen president and has filled the position with marked ability, until now, when her family is removing to Eugene City, Oregon—here she has "taken a letter" to the flourishing W.C.T.U. of that go ahead University town. (By the way, this is a seed thought. Why should we not always give a letter in due official form to our women when they migrate thus? Perhaps for the sake of "belonging" they would even start a Union if they found none in their new homes.) Lewiston has been a very godless town, at first a mining camp—and later on, almost a prey to saloons and their nameless twin abominations. Its latest phase has afforded more hopeful symptoms, but temperance sentiment is at a low ebb. How to get at the great out-doorsy people

> "The tired Humanity that beats
> Its life along the stony streets,"

that was the question.

"We prayed that question through," said Mrs. Buck, and proceeded to tell me of a pleasant place with grass and shade, right in the heart of the town, which she coveted (with righteous coveting) for an outdoor gospel meeting. She found this place belonged to a Catholic lady, and after much prayer for strength, she went to her, although quite a stranger, proffered her novel request and was so kindly received that, as she said, "ever since we've had those shady grounds to preach and pray." Governor [William] Newell of Washington, Rev. Dr. Lindley, Pastor of the Presbyterian Church in Portland, and chief authority on Alaska, have both spoken for the ladies, as has Rev. Mr. McAlister, husband of the president, and a noble hearted, earnest temperance man—a son of the Pine Tree state [Maine], across whose lips not a drop of alcoholic stimulants has ever passed.

And so the local W.C.T.U. was started, the call for a mass convention issued, the programme determined, four addresses of welcome arranged for, we took the cars and came on our winding way from Walla Walla. When lo! At Texas Ferry we were met by this telegram: "The authorities forbid Convention. We accept as gracefully as possible. Mrs. Norman Buck." We had five minutes in which to decide, I ejaculated two expressions of opinion thus: "The saloon interest is back of this pronunciamento" and "I shall go right on and outline a W.C.T.U. for Idaho all the same." And so we started for a long, hot, monotonous day and night upon the Snake River itself, eleven hundred miles in length, rising near Salt Lake and emptying into the Columbia after the most unaccountable meanderings. Strange basaltic formations hedge in our sight on either hand, indolent undulations of sky line, cliffs, promontories, valleys, all of a pale green now, but like green velvet, we are told, earlier in the season. Without bird or herd or flock in sight save at long intervals a strip of farm hugging the narrow "Car" between the hills and river, this winding landscape best answers the description of a place the Hardshell Baptist asked the Lord to bless: "Where the eye of God has never seen and the foot of man has never trod." Yet, it has a certain fascination for restless voyagers like us, its imperturbable calm, its high, sweet, wholesome silences and all over the quiet sky and later on a crescent moon like a gold shield. Our steamer tied up for the night, and we went to sleep in peace with stateroom doors partially open on account of the great heat and the slow lapping river lulling us to sleep.

Next day we reached Lewiston, named for the celebrated explorer [Meriwether Lewis] who came with [William] Clark in 1804. We beheld a long, rambling town, of about fifteen hundred inhabitants, its great age—twenty years; shadowed forth by its tall gleaming lines of Lombardy poplars. . . . A Jehu [coach driver] from the hotel, with a spirited span of white horses, conveyed me to Mr. Buck's house, where the first thing we saw—except her two little sons, her "boy telegraph" for the W.C.T.U., as she facetiously called them—was a writing table with *The Union Signal,* reports of superintendents, Mrs. Barnes'[6] new leaflet, catalogues of temperance publication houses, and J. Ellen's[7] and my own [writings]. . . .

Pretty soon in came Mrs. Buck, who had missed us at the wharf, whither she went in dutiful mood, although she had evidently supposed that telegram would put a quietus upon us. Then the mystery we explored of the exploded convention. Diphtheria had been in Lewiston on and off for some weeks. Perhaps a dozen children had had it, of whom five had died. It was not getting worse, but rather better, and yet, two days before our advent the Board of Health had forbidden all public meetings.

The temperance ladies declined to attribute this to the liquor ring, but leading citizens declared it had no other animus. However, not to rouse antagonism, it was resolved to heed the admonition, but in the parlors of Mrs. Billings, a noble-hearted Presbyterian lady, we assembled the leading women of the city, and after earnest waiting upon God, we proceeded to organize the convention, adopt the constitution, select the officers and launch our W.C.T.U. life boat as if there were no Board of Health nor other impediment in our way.

Miss Kate Thatcher, a native of Idaho, an accomplished musician and as clear-headed a young woman as I have anywhere seen, was made corresponding secretary. Miss Rena Poe, another dear, bright girl, was recording secretary. Mrs. Conley, the generous Catholic lady was present. The pastors' wives stood firm for "going right on with business" and became vice presidents and superintendents, and we divided the territory, separated as it is by the Blue Mountains from Southern Idaho, arranging to place the four northern counties, Nes Perces, Idaho, Sho-shones, Kooteni, under Mrs. Buck's care as president of Northern Idaho. I shall look after the Southern part by correspondence, but we can do very little there at present, as it is largely a mining country. Mrs. Buck will send you a full list of officers, etc. Mrs. E. W. Thatcher is agent for our own paper, and is a woman who cannot fail in any undertaking that commands her heart. You would know this by [a] look into her face. Mrs. Vining had us stop at her door in our packed coach and taste her nice ice cream. The whole convention went with us to the boat, and with waving of handkerchiefs we steamed down the river and left the faithful W.C.T.U. women of Idaho upon its distant shores. All blessings be upon their loyal hearts!

Notes

1. Willard, *Glimpses,* 372.
2. Bordin, *Frances Willard,* 115.
3. Georgia Hulse McLeod of Baltimore was the president of the Maryland WCTU in

the late 1870s. She accompanied Willard on much of her 1881 tour through the southern states.

4. Anna Adams Gordon (1853–1931) began working with Willard in 1877 during the Moody Revivals in Boston. Gordon soon became indispensable as Willard's personal secretary until Willard's death in 1898. Especially active in temperance work among children, she became the fourth president of the WCTU. Her sister, Bessie Gordon, was also active with the WCTU, serving as corresponding secretary for the Massachusetts WCTU. She was the author of *Women Torch-bearers: The Story of the Woman Christian Temperance Union*, published for the organization's fiftieth anniversary in 1924.

5. Sallie Flournoy Moore Chapin (1830?–96), author and temperance lecturer, was the president of the South Carolina WCTU and a member of the executive committee of the Prohibition Home Protection Party in 1882. She was one of Willard's major southern connections throughout her life.

6. Frances (Fan) J. Barnes (1846–1922) was the national superintendent of Young Women's Unions.

7. Judith Ellen Foster (1840–1910), a lawyer from Iowa, was the WCTU's national superintendent of legislation and a great ally of Willard's at this time.

EIGHT

"Personal Liberty," June 11, 1882

In the late spring of 1882, Willard joined temperance and prohibition workers from all over the nation as they converged on the state of Iowa to assist local prohibitionists in their effort to pass a state prohibitory constitutional amendment. "Personal Liberty," the address she repeated in twenty Iowa communities, was her particular contribution to the work of the so-called Army of the Amendment. Reading "No person shall manufacture for sale, or sell, or keep for sale as a beverage any intoxicating liquor whatever, including ale, wine and beer," the proposed amendment had already passed each part of the legislature and would be submitted to a vote of the people of Iowa on June 27, 1882. One of the largest audiences Willard faced was in Des Moines on June 11, 1882. The local newspaper report described the crowd at the Lewis Opera House, noting: "every inch of sitting and standing room . . . was filled at a very early hour, as were all the halls leading to the audience room, and thousands who came to attend the meeting were unable to gain admittance." "It was a noble audience that listened to the speaker," the report continued, "and it had a noble orator in Miss Willard."[1]

"Personal Liberty" contains Willard's most developed theoretical statement of the political philosophy that justified prohibitory legislation. Offering a counterpoint to theories of individualism, Willard sets forth in clear accessible language how the nature of an individual's sense of selfhood was immediately constrained once he or she became a member of a community. The foundations of community lie not in an individual's rights, but rather in an individual's responsibilities. Successful democracy, she insisted, was grounded in a consensus that each member should act not simply out of self-interest, but also out of a consciousness of the needs and interests of others in the community.

From this foundational principle, Willard raised both moral and practical arguments to demonstrate the immorality of the liquor industry's claim that their "personal liberty" was constrained by prohibitory legislation. By asserting an analogy between the arguments of the saloon keepers and those of slave owners during the late eighteenth and early nineteenth centuries, Willard invoked public memory of the personal liberty debates of that era. The personal liberty laws of many northern states aimed to curtail abuses of fugitive slave laws by guaranteeing the presumption that an African American living in the state was free and requiring evidence presented to a court to support any claim to the contrary. These policies overturned the presumption existing in the slaveholding states that African Americans were presumed to be slaves unless they had papers to establish that they were not. On a practical level Willard spelled out the harms of the liquor industry that justified the public's right to prohibit the business. The question, she asserted, was one of public safety.

The "Army of the Amendment" was successful in its campaign to bring out the temperance vote in support of the constitutional amendment. The amendment passed with a margin of nearly 30,000 votes. One Iowan thought Willard the most effective speaker in the campaign: "I am not in favor of women speakers generally, and on temperance they are usually especially bad; but this is an exception, and I venture Miss Willard's address would make more votes for temperance than any man's speech during the campaign."[2] The celebration, however, was short-lived. By January 1883 the amendment had been overturned by the state supreme court on a technicality concerning the wording of the amendment in the public record of the debate in the legislature and the wording on the ballot. Although temperance sentiment was strong throughout the state, there was little heart to begin again the five-year-long process of a state constitutional amendment fight. Such disappointments at the state level encouraged national temperance leaders to consider seeking a national prohibition amendment.

The text presented here is from a printed flyer of the Des Moines address in Willard's papers in the Frances E. Willard Memorial Library, at WCTU headquarters, Evanston, Illinois. A revised version of "Personal Liberty" is included in Willard's *Woman and Temperance*, 486–503.

* * *

Kind Friends: The stereoscopic view is more complete than any other because it presents the same object under two angles of vision. By plain analogy, Prohibition like all other moral issues gains in clearness and perspective when we bring to bear upon it the united vision of manhood and womanhood. Fitting is it that Governor [John] St. John's lecture should be followed by one from Judith Ellen Foster and other representatives of the Temperance Alliance [and] by those of the WCTU. There is moreover, historic and poetic as well as scientific justice in a woman's plea for prohibition. Sitting beside Neal Dow in his Portland home, he told me that thirty years ago, into that very room came a broken-hearted wife beseeching him to bring her drunken husband home to her from a saloon, the name of which she gave. General Dow went at once to the proprietor—stated the case—made a plea on behalf of the sorrowful wife, and was ordered out of the saloon, the keeper saying "There's my license on the wall, this man is one of my best customers—I'll not offend him." General Dow left the saloon with these words: "The people of the state of Maine will have something to say about how long you'll go on selling!" For then and there was born in his soul the purpose of a deadly contest with the liquor traffic through the ballot and the law. Remember then dear friends, that I am speaking in behalf of homes no less bereft and women no less desolate than those which touched the compassionate heart and moved the mighty will of him whose name stands peerless upon history's page, as the Father of the prohibitory law.

As the "Cunarder" is the evolution of Robert Fulton's North River steamboat, so is your amendment the bright consummate blossom of Maine's statutory law. What to put in, as well as what to omit, you have learned from the hard-earned experience of other states. The difference between the man who built his house upon the sand, and him who built upon a rock [Matthew 7: 24, 26], is illustrated by the difference between prohibition built upon statutory, and on constitutional law. The first shifts with the changeful character of legislatures, the last based on the people's will, is a foundation that standeth sure. We do not regulate the man that buys—his instinct of self-preservation ought to be law enough, and will be by the growth of scientific intelligence under the tutelage of law.

There are several hair-splitting questions to which the opposition has been reduced, and which are being most ably set at rest by your own clear-headed workers. That they should be asked at all illustrates the lamentable weakness of a cause that will be "lost" on the 27th of June.

But in general terms the question now before the People's Jury in the state of Iowa is this: Ought a civilized nation to legalize and derive revenue from the sale of alcoholic compounds to be used as a beverage when it has been proved by centuries of awful demonstration that such use results in untold misery and sin? Ought an intelligent nation to protect a traffic which sets two schools of ignorance and vice over against each school house in the land? Ought a home loving nation to tolerate an institution which is the arch foe of woman's peace and childhood's purity? Ought a Christian nation to foster the saloon system which empties churches, scoffs at the law of Christ, and can succeed only in proportion as His gospel fails?

Twenty years hence it will seem as unaccountable that on this subject there should be a difference of opinion among good men as it does now that men just as good took texts out of the New Testament from which to prove African slavery divine.

But at the present stage of public enlightenment it will be urged, not among the ignorant alone, but also as the honest opinion of intelligent and estimable men, that a law prohibiting the liquor traffic is an infringement of "personal liberty." Let us seek the meaning of this current phrase.

The poet [William] Cowper represents Robinson Crusoe in these familiar lines:

> I am monarch of all I survey.
> My right there is none to dispute,
> From the center all round to the sea.
> I am the lord of the fowl and the brute.

But when Crusoe saw upon the shore of his desolate island a footprint not his own, that very moment he was no longer monarch and no longer lord. From that time his personal liberty was divided by two, selfhood—that pitiful pivot on which so many human windmills turn—had to take cognizance of otherhood. Always after "I"—that tall telegraph pole of a pronoun—had to take note of y-o-u, with its pathetic echo, "I owe you!" Or, to put the matter somewhat differently: out on his Island Robinson could reach forth his nimble fingers and gather whatever seemed to him good for food—and there was none to interfere. But, suppose him transferred to this Iowa city, and practicing the same light-fingered method in your grocery store, good citizens, or at your pantry shelf, dear lady. What a catastrophe would then occur? Out on his island he could appropriate whatever was adapted to his use as clothing—let him try the same method in your tailoring establishment, my friend, and his personal liberty will be at once upset by interference of the figure in blue coat and brass buttons—the policeman, that guardian of the liberties of all. Behind the star on the policeman's breast gleams the star of Empire—nay, I speak it reverently—the star of Bethlehem. For it has taken centuries of Christian teaching to make us willing thus to relinquish much that is dear to hearts untutored, for the greatest numbers, greatest good.

Out on his island Crusoe had the freedom of the place, and might shout and halloo at the top of his voice; but just let him attempt to try it in this audience. Why, I have scores of brothers present, not known to me by name, who would take the intruder by the collar and march him down the aisle upon a double quick. Indeed, this audience itself, by its kindly attention, is a splendid object lesson to illustrate my point that a citizen's liberty is relative, not absolute. I am confident you will accept the definition I would now offer, viz: that all law, from the days of Justinian's code, to your own Iowa Amendment that is to be, is but the drawing of the circle of a person's liberty, just so large around, and far across, as is consistent with the number of circles to be drawn within a given space. Take this pleasant audience again, it is an illustration perfectly in point. Within these four walls the circle must be small, for there is only so much space, and there are so many circles to be drawn. Think of it! You have all resigned the abstract right of unrestricted locomotion and vocal utterance. Why? Because it is a law of assemblies—*pro bono publico* [for the public good].

But it is Nature's benignant law that by the relinquishment of some part of a savage personal liberty, you gain a freedom vastly broader, higher and more fruitful. For society abounds in proofs that the human being who most unconsciously obeys most laws, is really most free. The man in this audience who has so conformed his life to the laws of good society that he obeys them without thought, is the most perfect gentleman. The printer who makes his hand the bond-slave of the types, gains in due time complete control of them. We stoop to conquer. Three classes are outside the calculation we have made—the idiot, the savage and the child. As for the first, he has no brain to build upon, and we consign him to an asylum, where he is well cared for. The savage has the freedom of all out doors, and yet, unless he is the very last of the Mohegans, he observes certain unwritten laws of brotherhood.

"Baby is King," has passed into a proverb; he pulls your hair or doubles up his little fist, and thrusts the same into your eye. But let anybody else try it, and how soon you will develop that unconscious theory of a restricted personal liberty on the basis of which you live, and move, and have your being [Acts 17:28]. Behold with what resistless energy the enginery of civilization takes that child in hand to teach it what are the dimensions of the home circle of personal liberty. Before he can speak he has learned to share his toys and dainties, to keep the peace; to fold his little hands while papa asks the blessing. The little angular fragment of human character, under the attrition of home life grows smooth and symmetrical, as the pebbles on the shore of my own Lake Michigan are rounded and polished by the untiring waves. Then after a while the mother hands her child over to the school. Having taught two thousand pupils, I know how our work supplements that of the home. "You must not be tardy, little man," the teacher says. "Why?" "Because the rest of us can't wait for you." And so on with respect to silence, order and good lessons. Then comes the church to teach the reasonableness of all these inroads upon liberty; that they are based upon the golden rule, and that what is "good for the hive is good for the bee." Now, if these three agencies have done their work well, a man's personal liberty never will be, consciously to him, restricted by law. I am happy to address an audience, the greater part of whose members doubtless have relinquished the crude notion of personal liberty so dear to savage men, and have been content to accept civil liberty instead. I mean the liberty of civilized men, and I mean by that, brotherly men. Most of us have been so well trained in home and school, and church, that we were never yet wounded by contact with the clear-cut circle of law, because that circle is so far outside our own voluntary and habitual concessions to the public weal. For my own part, and I say it with profound gratitude, I was so fortunate in my inheritance from an upright ancestry, as well as in my mother, teachers, and church training, that I have never fallen into the clutches of the law, and never shall. Instead of being a terror, it is to me a friend. It is the law that gives my mother the title-deed to her quiet home. It is the law that surrounds her steps and mine with guarantees and safeguards. It is the law that I often bless as I ride, an average of three hours a day, on railway trains, for its protecting presence is everywhere, and can check up even the snorting steam horse, saying to him: "Thus far, and no farther." But no man feels the halter draw with good opinion of the law. So is it with the man who sells intoxicating liquors as a drink. Not one of them has had and heeded the teaching of home, and schools and church. Not one of them has so put away childish things as to hold himself in the circle of a liberty which will not harmfully intrude upon the interest of other men.

In whose personal liberty is the saloonkeeper most interested? Is he not like the slaveholder of other days, who meant by that expression, his own liberty to enslave another class? And does not the saloonkeeper practically seek the liberty to enslave the drinker? He knows that is the tendency with all his patrons, and the actual condition of many. But this very fact binds them more closely to him—their liberty diminishing as his own is increased. We do well to look carefully at this phrase—perchance it may be found to prove too much.

I do not wish to speak harsh words of them. They are "in their conditions," as a kind old lady said, who had learned what we reformers are apt to forget, that "vinegar never catches flies." If the liquor dealers of this country would give up their harmful trade and become "the butchers, the bakers, the candle-stick makers," the members of our WCTU would go a long distance out of their way to give them patronage. We do not look upon them as alone responsible for the evil against which we strive. In the assessment of responsibility we are willing to take our share for the indifference and inactivity of earlier years; we think the government greatly to blame; also the heedless voter, who throws his influence in favor of saloons rather than home protection. But when all is said, we can but speak harsh words about the business of a man who settles down on a community like a leech to get his support from the sale of intoxicating liquors as a drink giving no equivalent for value received, and ignoring the foundation principle *pro bono publico*. A business from which comes 60 percent of the insanity in America; 75 percent of our criminals become such when crazed by alcohol; 80 percent of our worthless youth are schooled in dram shops; 90 percent of our paupers emerge from drunkards' homes, and yet you wish to make your living out of strong drink? Don't ask us to deal leniently with the business.

Society invites the solitary to sit down at the sunny fireside of the human family. It says to Robinson Crusoe, "Come in with us and we will do you good." "All that art yields and nature can decree" shall be poured out like a libation at your feet. "The long result of time" shall be your heritage. For you our poets shall sing, our artists paint, our musicians evoke the harmonies of orchestra and organ. For you our inventors shall keep their magic brains at work, our scientists seek out the mysteries of nature, our artisans bestow their manly toil. For you the railroad shall climb the mountaintop and spin along the valley, and the telegraph murmur under the seas. The white pinions of the press shall speed their tireless flight for you to gather up the thought, the sympathy, the purpose of a world and lay them daily at your feet. The very viands on your table, the very clothes you wear, gathered from every clime, shall be the products of the prowess, industry, the skill of a thousand men who spend their lives for you, where commerce stretches forth her myriad hands. We will thus consider you, *but you must in your turn consider us.* What will you yield, and what will you bring? Society coheres by mutual and myriad concessions. Will you make them?

Edmund Burke[3] says that man emerging from the solitary, and entering upon the civil state, does by the very act renounce the first of personal rights, that of self-defense. He may not avenge himself nor plead his own cause, but must hand both over to the laws, the witnesses, the courts. Having conceded this much to enter our charmed circle at all, you should surely be prepared to yield many minor points. For instance: You cannot say what you please (though the "personal liberty" advocates declare you do). Words, indecent or profane, you may not utter with impunity. We hope you do not wish to, but we have legal safeguards if you do. Neither may you wear what suits you. The prescribed garb involves at least two imperious requisitions, failing to meet which, you will be marched off to the calaboose [jail]. You may not build the kind of house you please within our fire limits. Call yours a "castle" never so sacred in fancy, but you will find in fact, that we will rattle it down about your ears if not of our prescribed material *pro bono publico.* You may not open a shop for the sale of impure books or pictures—we will confiscate them. You may not open a tannery, glue factory, slaughter house, gun-powder mill, alongside our homes. Neither may you fit up an opium shop in our midst, to tempt the innocent and unwary, nor to attract the base. For do you not perceive that we have pooled our individual rights of self-protection and handed them over to the state, through those sworn to represent us, as the capital stock on which her laws are based? Hence her first principle must be the aggregate protection of the weak against the strong. Whatever clouds the clear brain or gives tremors to the steady hand, involves grave danger to society. Opium does. Taken in small amounts it may be used with impunity at first, but its law is the law of habit—the tendency of yesterday becomes the bondage of tomorrow. We cannot permit its sale, because the only force it introduces into our social compact is a deteriorating, a disintegrating force. Precisely for the same reason we cannot permit you to trade in, to manufacture, or to sell intoxicating liquors as a drink. Your circle of personal liberty in such a case, trenches too much upon that other's well-being, and on the government in which, as Gladstone says, "It must be made as easy as possible for everybody to do right."

Remember, we say nothing about men's drinking habits. We urge them, in our gospel meetings to enact a prohibitory law for one, in the legislature of their own intellect to declare it constitutional in the Supreme Court of their own judgment, and to vigorously enforce it by the executive of their own will. That is the basis of the total abstinence movement. But the public trade in strong drinks we believe should be outlawed, and not protected by the government. We believe the drinking men themselves are largely on our side in this. This saloon system is well known by them to be evil, only evil, and evil continually, and we confidently count upon their co-operation, even though they may oppose our total abstinence views. It is men who get gain by the manufacture and sale who are interested to urge the specious plea which I have this evening attempted to combat. Sadly are we reminded by their conclusions of the cry of the devoted and patriotic Madame Roland on the scaffold, to which the frightful fanaticism of the French revolution had condemned so many of earth's purest and best: "Oh, Liberty, what crimes have been committed in thy name!"

Notes

1. *Iowa State Register,* June 13, 1882.
2. *Evanston Index,* July 1, 1882, clipping in WCTU series, reel 30, frame 434.
3. Edmund Burke (1729–97) was a British statesman and political theorist during the last third of the eighteenth century.

NINE

Woman and Temperance, 1883

Frances Willard had spent nearly a decade as a WCTU organizer when she produced *Woman and Temperance: or, the Work and Workers of the Woman's Christian Temperance Union.* By then she had become a seasoned campaigner, having traveled thousands of miles giving hundreds of speeches and founding several thousand local unions throughout the country. Although her first brief manual *Hints and Helps in Our Temperance Work* (1875) served for a number of years as a useful guide for women who wanted to begin work in their own communities, *Woman and Temperance,* at over 600 pages, provided a better, more complete resource than Willard's earlier booklet. The organization now had an impressive ten-year history of activism, causing longtime temperance leader John Gough to declare that the WCTU was "doing more for the temperance cause today than all others combined."[1]

Willard gave her version of that history in *Woman and Temperance* so that local organizers would be able, in turn, to recount it for prospective members, letting them know that they would be allying themselves with a powerful force for reform. For Willard and many other nineteenth-century readers, history came alive through biography, the stories of heroes and heroines of important events and eras. Biographical sketches of fifty WCTU leaders—Woman's Crusaders, state presidents, and superintendents of national departments—make up nearly forty percent of the volume. These leaders modeled dedication, innovation, and daring in their efforts, all qualities which Willard hoped new members would emulate.

Women needed instruction as well as inspiration, however, to become knowledgeable and committed reformers. *Woman and Temperance* presented both, with a lively and sometimes humorous style that would engage readers as they learned. During the many years she was on the road founding WCTUs, Willard had learned a great deal about what to do and, perhaps more important, what *not to do* in the process of establishing enduring local and state unions. "How ought a Local WCTU to conduct a Public Meeting?" (below) demonstrates how Willard laid out in detail the kind of advanced planning and publicity necessary to attract good sized audiences, leaving nothing to chance—or mischance. She also included steps to be followed that would insure an interesting, spirited meeting, resulting in listeners eager to commit themselves to the goals and activities of the WCTU. The practical suggestions for meetings were complemented by specific advice for women speakers new to the public platform. Societal prejudice against women speaking in public was still strong in the last quarter of the nineteenth century, especially in some quarters where the WCTU hoped to gain a hearing, such as conservative church groups and the southern United States. In this work Willard presented a unique rhetorical theory and strategy suited to women orators, one that would enable them to speak with the kind of confidence and self-possession that she had developed during her teaching and reform career.

Woman and Temperance was reprinted many times, and the section in chapter 36 titled "How to Conduct a Public Meeting" was reprinted as a pamphlet and widely distributed. In 1893 Willard wrote a third manual, *Do Everything: A Handbook for the World's White Ribboners,* intended for World's WCTU organizers, which featured an updated version of "How to Organize a WCTU." The aphorism she chose to place on the title page of *Do Everything* explains her motive for producing the multitude of instructional materials she churned out for her organization: "The joy of life is doing good according to a plan." Certainly Willard provided her WCTU sisters with a plan, one that would enable them to become vital and effective participants in public life.

Excerpts are from Willard, *Woman and Temperance: Or, the Work and Workers of the Woman's Christian Temperance Union* (Hartford, Connecticut: Park, 1883), 618–29, 636–38.

* * *

How to Organize a W.C.T.U.

How ought a Local W.C.T.U. to conduct a Public Meeting?

I. THE PRELIMINARIES.   These are of two kinds: First, Notices to the public. Second, Opening exercises.

Your notices should be printed in all the local papers at least one week beforehand, and sent to each pulpit on the Sabbath previous. The following form is recommended:

To the ladies of _____:
    The National W.C.T.U. has nearly fifty auxiliaries, and is the largest and most influential society ever composed and conducted exclusively by women. It has nearly ten thousand local auxiliaries and thousands of juvenile organizations. It is a lineal descendant of the great temperance Crusade of 1873–4, and is a union

of women from all denominations, for the purpose of educating the young, forming a better public sentiment, reforming the drinking classes, transforming by the power of Divine grace those who are enslaved by alcohol, and removing the dram-shop from our streets by law.

Mrs. _____ of _____, duly authorized by _____ W.C.T.U. to undertake this work, will speak in _____ on _____ at _____ o'clock on the history, aims, and methods of this society. All ladies are earnestly requested to attend. The presence of all pastors is respectfully invited.

On the same slip put the following:

Attention Boys and Girls!
You have a friend who would like very much to meet and talk with you at _____ on _____ at _____ o'clock. She will show you some interesting experiments, blackboard exercises and charts. Please come, and we will try to organize a Band of Hope. Yours for clear heads and true hearts. Mrs. _____

This should be sent to Sunday-schools and public schools as well as to pulpit and press. It is a false—let us rather say an ignorant—indelicacy which hesitates to give full information through all legitimate channels, of the time, place, and object of any attempt to build up Christ's kingdom by benefiting the race for which he died. But our workers have gone hundreds of miles to form a local union only to find a single stray line in the corner of one newspaper as the only notice given, or a brief mention at a rainy Sunday morning service their only herald. Not thus does the enemy permit his opportunities to go by default.

Second, the opening exercises. Let these be informal but full of earnestness. Many a time I have seen the devotional spirit frozen out by the mechanical air of the leader, added to the slow process of hunting up and distributing hymn books, waiting for the organ key to be sent for; persuading some reluctant musician to come forward, and so on to the doleful climax of failure. Suppose you just omit all that—come forward at once with some pleasant allusion to a familiar hymn "as one of the special favorites of our work," strike up yourself, or have someone ready to do so without loss of time. As to Scriptural selections, I could spend a whole day exhibiting the choice cabinet of jewels in delightful variety and marvelous adaptation to our needs, which the past years of study have disclosed. As I listen to our women, East and West, in local meetings and conventions, I am impressed by none of their beautiful gifts so much as that they are indeed workmen who need not be ashamed, rightly dividing the Word of God [2 Timothy 2:15]. From Mrs. [Abby Clement] Leavitt of Cincinnati, with her "Saloon Keeper's Psalm (the tenth), to Mrs. [Clara H. Sully] Carhart of Iowa, reading Miriam's Song at the jubilee in June; whether it be Sanballat, Gideon's Band, Deborah and Barak, Queen Esther, Joel (second chapter) or the Prodigal Son and Good Samaritan, our workers have proved themselves mighty in the Scriptures ever since those wondrous school days when they learned to read their Bibles in the grog-shops of the land. Their "Crusade Psalm" (the 146th) is unrivaled for expository use. It is capable of being wrought into a delightful evening's "Bible Reading," but this must be greatly abridged in your opening exercises. Suppose you study its ten verses for the purpose of finding our bugle call, our key word, exhortation, basis, complete plan of work, prophecy, and philosophy, and song of jubilee—for all of these and vastly more are there!

If the pastor is present ask him to offer prayer.

II. THE ORGANIZATION.   And now, with preliminaries arranged, the spirit of praise and prayer evoked, a secretary *pro tem* appointed to keep the important record of "first things," and a group of women gathered around you in home or church parlor, what are you to say and do that they shall love our cause and work with us?

First, don't take too much for granted. Don't think because these are women of general intelligence and Christian experience they are also clear in their respective minds as to the history, mystery, and methods of the W.C.T.U. On that subject you had better take it for granted they are outside barbarians. At least I was of this description when the Crusade of 1874 struck the classic suburb of Evanston. Fancy the ignorance of one who had never, that she knew of, seen a saloon and yet had lived for nearly twenty years within a few miles of Chicago. Imagine the illiteracy that had never once laid eyes upon a temperance paper nor heard the name of J[ohn] N[ewton] Stearns. Conceive of the crudity that let me in my sober senses to make a bee line to Boston, that I might learn of Dr. Dio Lewis[2] the whole duty of a W.C.T.U. woman, and for the same reason to Portland that I might sit at the feet of Neal Dow.

But all this is hardly more absurd than the revelation of failure (after I thought myself a veteran in our ranks) made to me most unwittingly by a dear old lady down in Delaware, who, after I had talked an hour by the clock on the "Aims and Methods of the W.C.T.U." said in a droll soliloquy, as she scrawled her name upon my membership card: "I'm sure I don't know what she wants us to do, but I reckon it's a good deal in temperance work as it is in goin' to prayer meetin' of a dark night—I can't see but a step at a time, but when I've taken one step, why I'm there and the lantern's there too, and we just go along to the next. So if the Lord has got temperance work for me to do he'll give me light to do it by." Learn then, dear temperance workers, that in this day of specialists you are safe in assuming that your group of good women have minds as vacant as a thimble, and about as much expanded on the scope and working and laws of the W.C.T.U. Their interest is general, not specific; they have come on purpose to find out what it is your business (not theirs) to know. Therefore take nothing for granted save that each of them is fitted out with brain and heart and conscience on which you are to act by knowledge, sympathy, conviction.

Second, don't assume the role of Sir Oracle. Teach without seeming to do so. Carefully skip around all such "hard words" as "take notice," "I call to your attention," "Do you understand?" and on no account conclude a sentence with that irritating grammatical nondescript "See?" Put yourself in the attitude of a learner along with the rest. Thus your style will be suggestive and winsome rather than authoritative and disagreeable. I shall never forget Bishop Warren's[3] opening words to a room full of young people in a southern school. He stood before them with a face wise, kindly, and benignant, and gently called them "Fellow students."

Third, don't despise the day of small things. You have no reason to be discouraged because your audience is small. I have organized seventy women into a weak society and seven into a strong one. Well do I recall a winter afternoon in 1870, when, complying with an invitation previously given by my first Bible class teacher (of auld lang syne) Mrs. Governor [Helen Judson] Beveridge, as we call her now, half a score women of Evanston went to a missionary meeting in that lady's parlor. Its object was to organize a Woman's Foreign Missionary Society, and though I had traveled in several Oriental countries, and as a tourist seen something of evangelistic work there, I found myself rudimentary in knowledge beside one who had made the subject a specialty and brought Mrs. Willing's[4] thoroughness of grasp to the theme of woman's martyrology in lands unsunned by Christ. Less than a dozen names were that day enrolled to form our local auxiliary. A dozen years have passed, and through the influence—direct and indirect—of this society, nearly forty young people have gone out from Evanston to the foreign field, to say nothing of thousands of dollars gathered and dispensed through its treasury.

Fourth, don't fail thoroughly to premeditate your "impromptus." The Holy Spirit seems better pleased to inspire the process of reflection and composition than to atone for what Miss Ophelia called "shiftlessness," by an eleventh hour inspiration. We want no scattering fire in our public utterances, but the most sober second thought of your brightest and most studious hours. As a general outline speech I would offer the following:

1. Very brief allusion to the origin and progress of temperance movements, with earnest acknowledgment of what has been done by the Church, the Washingtonian movement, Good Templars, Catholic Total Abstinence Society, etc.
2. Brief and pictorial (not abstract) account of the Woman's Crusade.
3. Organization as its sequel—Origin of the National W.C.T.U. at Chautauqua in 1874.
4. Growth of the Society in the United States, in Canada, England, and elsewhere, evolution of its work, number and variety of its departments; notwithstanding this general uniformity, the National like a photograph of imperial size; the state a cabinet, the local a *carte de visite* [calling card].
5. Why we have superintendents instead of committees, viz.: to insure individual responsibility. Illustrate by blackboard with our departments written out.

6. Reasons why women should join us. I have often given these in anecdotal form, telling just what women, old and young, grave and gay, have said to me about the convictions resulting from their own observation and experience which had led them into temperance work.
7. Appeal for considerations embodied in our motto 1. For God; 2. For home; 3. For native land.
   This address, mixed with the Word of God, and prayer, both in its preparation and recital, should be followed by a humble petition for His blessing.

Fifth, don't fail to suit the action to the word. Ask for a motion to organize, stating it in due form and requesting any lady who has the matter at heart to make it. Get a second to the motion and make a few incidental remarks about the importance of that etiquette of assemblies which we call parliamentary usage. Recommend them to buy *Roberts' Rules of Order,* and learn a little of it at each meeting.

When it comes to a vote after the parliamentary interval for remarks, mention that you are tired of your own voice and anxious to hear theirs, adding in your clearest tones, "All in favor of that motion will please to say aye," and let your final word be in the most decided sense a rising circumflex. You will be surprised to see the readiness with which you can thus call out the voices of the timid, partly out of good nature and partly because their musical perceptions lead them to put a climax to your incomplete inflection by their own. Do not go through the dumb show of "the lifted hand," nor the imbecility of "manifest it by the usual sign" (when there are several signs), but call out that most inspiring response, the human voice divine. Remember too, that thus you educate women out of the silence which has stifled their beautiful gifts so long.

Next follows the form of constitution for local auxiliaries, which should be gone over rapidly, reading only the important points, and remarking that this is the form usually adopted and subject to revision at their regular meetings. (Mrs.[Caroline Brown] Buell, our National Corresponding Secretary, at 161 La Salle Street, Chicago, furnishes the best.) After a *viva voce* [voice] vote on this, read with emphasis our pledge. It includes total abstinence from wine, beer, and cider as a beverage. Explain about the annual membership fee; exhibit *The Union Signal,* stating price, and send out ladies previously appointed to solicit memberships and subscribers.

This moment is the crucial test. To it everything has pointed—failing to secure its objects you will fail indeed. But just at this point we are too often unpardonably heedless. What would be said of the angler whose awkwardness at the critical moment should frighten away the fish he was about to impale? Or the farmer who should forget his scythe when going to the hay-field? But how often have we seen such a stale, flat, and unprofitable half hour succeed the aforementioned address, that it seemed as though a premium was put upon a general stampede of the auditors. "Has any one a pencil to take names?" is a question equally pregnant and imbecile, while vandal hands have made a raid upon stray hymn-books and their fly-leaves have been ruthlessly confiscated to take the place of the enrolling tablets, conspicuous by their absence. The best way is for the leader of the meeting to keep up a running fire of pleasant explanation or of reply to questions invited by her from the pews. Among the questions which her clear-cut preliminary statements should anticipate are: "Must we pay the membership fee when we give our names?" (No, not unless it is convenient.) "Can young ladies join?" (Most gladly.) "Does this mean all kinds of cider?" (It does.) "Then I cannot join." Well, you can at least attend the regular meetings of the union to follow this, in which the cider leaflets will be discussed, and becoming a sustaining, if not a regular member (only the latter are eligible to vote). It should be explicitly stated that by our new basis of organization, adopted at Washington, we are entitled in the National Convention (beside our state officers) to one delegate for each 500 paying members, and as we desire a large representation, we are anxious to enroll the names of all women who are sufficiently intelligent and devoted friends of temperance to take the pledge and pay the fee, even though they are unable to do any work or to meet with us regularly. The use to be made of the fee should be distinctly stated. The amount differs in the various states. Explain the division of the fee, representing that one of its parts is to be used in the local work, the other going to the state treasury to extend the organization, save that ten cents must be taken out and sent to the National W.C.T.U. to carry on its work. Bring forward *The Union Signal* and solicit subscribers to the national organ. Refer to the Woman's Temperance Publication Association, 161 La Salle St., Chicago, with its great supply of Timely Talks, Leaflets, Readings for Local Unions, Temperance Manuals for the training of the children, and other helps for carrying on the work of the forty National W.C.T.U. departments, besides *The Union Signal, The Young Crusader* for the Children, the *Oak and Ivy Leaf* for the Y.W.C.T. Unions, and *Der Deutsch-Amerikaner,* the German paper. Urge the motto upon the new recruits: "First, *Consecration;* then *Information.*"

Distribute the Annual Leaflet of the National W.C.T.U., which conveys all needed intelligence as to who and where are our General Offices, superintendents of departments, presidents and corresponding secretaries of states, and a general outlook over the whole field. This leaflet forms an invaluable manual for reference for all our workers.

If there is a piece of fine music prepared, or if you have an interesting speaker present besides yourself, it will be well to mention that attraction as a counter-inducement to those inclined to go.

But all these exercises, from your first bow to your closing *Benedicite,* must be marked *staccato,* and must be made brief and crisp, or your group of guests (for such, do not forget, they are), will file out and hie itself away. The change from one exercise to another, if effected with sufficient ingenuity to avoid jumbling, will help to hold your audience, but most will depend upon your compliance with the suggestion.

Sixth, Don't fail to keep your wit, wisdom, and patience well to the front. Somebody will come to you then and there with *sotto voce* [whispered] gossip, with legends and histories of societies previously organized and now fossiliferous, or the prayer-meeting killer of the neighborhood will stray in and begin his sanguinary work upon your feeble bantling [infant] of a society; or Miss Contretemps, of the contrary part, will state her objections to the pledge, or Madame Pharisee feel called upon to explain that she never was cursed with this demon in her own home and therefore can not, etc., etc., drowsily oblivious of the statement you—should—have made, that ninety per cent of our members share the exemption which she, with small good taste, parades. Now is the time to prove what manner of spirit you are of. Does your courage rise with danger? Are you fertile in resource? You are being tested now as they test steam engine boilers. The force is applied—the tension noted—and the strong, well wrought metal holds its own, but the thin, flaw-eaten, gives way in its weakest part. Are you master of the situation? "He that ruleth his spirit is better than he who taketh a city" [Proverbs 16:32]. Now is your chance for *mastery*. Many of these annoyances may be prevented by circulating the question papers before the meeting opens and asking that any query, comment, or criticism be written and placed in the question-box, to be circulated before the meeting is closed. This gathering up of questions, as well as the circulation of the various documents I have mentioned, should be attended to by the Secretary *pro tem* [temporary]—to be appointed at the opening of the meeting.

Seventh, Don't be precipitate in choice of standard bearers. In this choice will be involved the success or failure of your entire movement. You are trying to launch a life-boat, but if the captain be near-sighted and the mate a blunderer, your craft will swamp before it gets beyond the breakers. The worst of it is that you are at the mercy of the raw hands who must select these officers from their own newly-enlisted crew. In this choice, the element of deliberation is important, for while you will often be urged to select the officers then and there, "for fear we cannot get the women together again," my experience is that in the long run we get better results by a careful canvass of the pros and cons. Too often when we try to finish up the business of electing at the first meeting, we discover, later on, that the finish was an extinguisher. From a recent confidential letter I make this extract: "A W.C.T.U. was recently organized in our village and there isn't a quarrel in the neighborhood that was not represented on our board of officers."

As you will naturally conclude, I do not expect the liquor traffic in that locality need stand in special fear of said society. This was away down east, but a remark made to me on the frontier has in it equal food for reflection. It was from a new worker, and was so simply said, and with so much of large-eyed wonder "for the cause," that if not so tragic I would have deemed it vastly comical: "Why, do you know, that until our new President was elected I did not know that anybody could be an officer at all and yet be such a poor one!"

Alas for the application of this utterance, which all of us have seen! Now, while we cannot hope to avoid these calamities in the present partially developed condition of woman's work; while it is doubtless true that girls now acquiring the systematic training of our public schools and colleges will make more efficient officers of our future work, it is nevertheless possible for us to secure, in a majority of instances, excellent services from the good women of the present. But here, as always, the preliminary part of the recipe is: "First catch your hare," and I am confident a choice specimen will be caught by appointing (by previous consultation) such a committee on nomination as will represent the different churches and social circles, and adjourning to a day not distant when said committee shall report. It should also include, among its duties, the preparation of a plan of work for the society, and the organizer should furnish it with a model from our state or national minutes, with a leaflet of the national containing our list of superintendents of departments. In appointing the list of Vice-Presidents, insist on one from each denomination, including Catholics, Jews, etc., and appoint one "at large" to represent the great and kindly outside fraternity which has this cause at heart. Insist on a Superintendent of Temperance Literature, who shall also be Librarian of your Loan Library and agent for the W.T.P.A. Make these Superintendents members of your Executive Committee—which should meet weekly, while the W.C.T. U. meets monthly and has a religious, literary, and business programme. Fix the quorum of both meetings at five—so that the exceeding deference which causes our good women to lose so much time rather than "act without the prescribed number," may not endanger their results of work. Wear the white ribbon yourself, and urge all to do the same. Close your meeting by singing "Blest be the Tie that Binds."

I have suggested that you follow this meeting at once by another for the children. This is of paramount importance for its own sake; and also to conciliate public sentiment and give your new society that *sine qua non* [indispensable condition] of its existence, to say nothing of its success—something to do. . . . .

"But, After All, What Can I Do?"

Many a Christian woman, earnest and true, will lay down the book I have written on purpose for her with this question in her heart. May I suggest some of the answers which have come to my own mind, first reminding my readers that they need not neglect home's sacred ministries for any other? Take the time, rather, that has been given to things that were unnecessary, to superfluous sewing, calling, visiting, reading, resting, reverie, and this alone for this "Home Missionary Work."

1. Dear sister in Christ Jesus, you can kneel before God and ask him to show you what he would have you to do. You can also ask his daily blessing on the field, and on the workers there.

2. You can begin in your own home in the lullaby song, the twilight story, the family pledge, with "line upon line and precept upon precept" [Isaiah 28:10], to train your sons and daughters to be total abstainers.

3. You can prepare the way for consistent precepts by a perfect example, abstaining scrupulously yourself, not only from ever partaking of or offering the beverage, but the *medicinal* use and *culinary* use of intoxicating drinks; and you can study to prepare food that shall be so wholesome that it will not "lie like lead" upon the stomach, which often craves a drink to "wash down" an ill-cooked meal.

4. You can study to make your own home so attractive, by reason of its cleanliness, its simple yet attractive adornings, its books, music, and games, and, above all, by its sweet, Christian atmosphere, that its attractions for your sons will not be outmatched by those of the saloon.

5. You can organize your Sunday-school class into a temperance society, getting each member to sign the pledge, and by prayer and personal influence securing the conversion of each; for, after all, as a reformed man said, with shaking voice and tearful eyes, "If I'm to stand ladies, it's got to be the Lord behind the pledge!"

6. You can personally pray for and appeal to any intemperate man of your own acquaintance; visit the homes of inebriates to lend them "the helping hand," if needed, to pray with and for them, and to use your influence for their restoration to manhood.

7. You can go to the prison in your vicinity, visit the inmates, talk with them of Christ, pray with them, leave little books and papers full of blessed lessons, and get them to sign the pledge.

8. You can circulate our temperance literature. A dollar bill will secure a good many papers, tracts, and little books for children.

9. You can go quietly, with the loving spirit of Christ in your heart, and gentle words on your lips, to the home of the saloon-keeper, and talk with his wife and family, and put some temperance publications in their hands.

10. You can, with one or two lady friends, go to any saloons in your neighborhood, and talk and pray with its keeper, and those who frequent its bar, taking your pledge-book and seeking signatures.

11. But you can never do these things at all, in any effective and true sense, until your own heart is full of Christ's love and consecrated fully to his service, and unless your practical good Samaritan help goes hand in hand with your prayer and faith. But *per contra* [by contrast], if you begin this day simply and honestly to do any of these things, or any other true and womanly thing in this cause which you own heart suggests, how you will "grow in grace!" [2 Peter 3:18] How your own deepest nature will be lighted up by God's own smile! How sweetly you will learn what Christ can become to the soul that goes gently and lovingly upon his errands!

Dear Christian sister who reads these lines, you are one of the "living epistles" [2 Corinthians 3:3] by which this critical age is deciding how it will answer the question, "What think ye of Christ?" [Matthew 22:42]. You are a leaf out of the world's Bible. It "wants facts." In God's name give it the shining fact of your loving, helpful life "hid with Christ in God" [Colossians 3:3].

Notes

1. Willard, in her preface to *Woman and Temperance*, 6. John B. Gough (1817–86) was a recovering alcoholic who became one of the most popular Temperance speakers of the nineteenth century.

2. Diocletian Lewis (1823–86) was a physician, educator, and temperance advocate. His temperance lecture in December 1873 in Hillsboro, Ohio, sparked the Woman's Crusade.

3. Rev. Henry White Warren (1831–1912) became a bishop in the Methodist Episcopal Church in 1880. Besides a keen interest in Methodist overseas missions, Warren was an enthusiastic supporter of Methodist educational institutions for African Americans founded in the South during the post–Civil War era.

4. Jennie Fowler Willing (1834–1916), an English professor at Illinois Wesleyan College during the 1870s, was for many years the corresponding secretary of the northwestern branch of the Women's Foreign Missionary Society of the Methodist Episcopal Church. She also chaired the organizing convention of the WCTU in 1874, served as president of the Illinois WCTU during the mid-1870s, and continued her WCTU activities until the end of the century.

TEN

Address to the Committee on Resolutions of the Republican National Convention, June 4, 1884

By the summer of 1884 the prominence of the temperance reform and of Willard as a national leader was underscored by her appearance at four national political conventions. At the Republican convention in Chicago she was granted fifteen minutes to address the Committee on Resolutions on behalf of the WCTU memorial calling for a national prohibitory amendment that had been forwarded to the Greenback, Democratic, Republican, and Prohibition parties. As she made clear in her address, her father had been active in the party, and she acknowledged that the party had been in the forefront of many of the significant reforms of the past. But, on the question of prohibition, the Republican Party was mute. Though Willard claimed to speak as a representative of the "women's party," and argued that the political party that best responded "to this plea from the hearts of women," would gain the support of thousands of politically active women, the Committee on Resolutions took no action. Although she had a ticket to sit on the convention stage, she had no votes to offer the party and there was no endorsement of prohibition in the 1884 Republican Party platform.

Willard later reflected that her experience at the Republican convention marked a turning point in her politics. While she "had already acted with the Prohibition Party for a brief period," she wrote, she had not until this time "given up the hope that the Republican Party might so retrieve itself that we could stand together for God and Home and Native Land."[1] After the 1884 convention, she decided to give her all to the Prohibition Party and to abandon the Republicans because she felt they had abandoned her and her cause.

A few weeks later Willard traveled to Pittsburgh for the Prohibition convention to present the WCTU memorial. She was welcomed enthusiastically, and the convention endorsed the memorial and women's suffrage. Willard was more than simply a major player within the party. She was seen by some as the "center of the present movement." A local reporter had overheard a conversation in which some delegates declared, "We should nominate her for President if it weren't for the kick that Nye and some of the other chaps are making against woman suffrage."[2] Though no presidential nomination was forthcoming, Willard did deliver the nominating speech for John St. John, the Kansas governor, who was one of the Prohibition Party's most successful presidential candidates.

Willard's rejection at the Republican convention and personal triumph at the Prohibition convention fueled her push to campaign for St. John and to use the WCTU's resources, such as the *Union Signal* to further that effort. To Willard and many others, this implied political endorsement meant that the WCTU had "crossed the Rubicon";[3] it was now a power to be reckoned with in national politics. The Prohibition Party, which had garnered just over ten thousand votes in the presidential election of 1880, polled nearly 150,000 in 1884. In the key state of New York, Prohibitionists drew enough votes away from the Republican candidate in November to ensure the election of Democrat Grover Cleveland. As a result, prohibition gained credibility as a serious political issue; however, Willard and the WCTU were vilified by many Republicans for their role in the party's defeat.

The text of Willard's speech to the Committee on Resolutions is from Willard, *Glimpses,* 392–94.

* * *

Gentlemen: The temperance women of America have never before asked for one moment of your time. Thousands of them have worked and prayed for your success in the heroic days gone by, but up to this hour they have laid no tax on the attention of the people's representatives in presidential convention assembled. Though the position is a new one, I cannot count myself other than at home in your presence, gentlemen, as you represent that great party, which, on the prairies of Wisconsin, my honored father helped to build, and whose early motto roused my girlish enthusiasm, "Free soil, free speech, free labor, and free men."[4] But I rejoice today in the sisterhood of the women's party—the Woman's Christian Temperance Union—where I may march side by side with that brilliant southern leader, Mrs. Sallie F. Chapin, of South Carolina, who, in our new antislavery war, the fight for a free brain, is my beloved coadjutor.

I am here in no individual character, but as the delegated representative of the Woman's Christian [Temperance] Union of forty-eight states and territories, including the District of Columbia, to present to you the memorial of the American home against the American saloon. You will notice that we make no note of foreign drinking customs, but speak and work directly against an institution which derives its authority directly from our own government. Our society is the lineal descendant of that whirlwind of the Lord known as the "Woman's Temperance Crusade," of 1874; and stands not only for total abstinence and prohibition, but for no sectarianism in religion, no sectionalism in politics, no sex in citizenship. We recognize state rights as to the adoption of these principles, but move forward in one grand and solid phalanx—a society as well known in Florida as it is in Oregon, by the results of the last ten years' work; a society that has an open hand for the Catholic and Protestant, for the foreign as well as the native born.

We know that in America the great clanging mill of government, kept in motion at enormous cost, turns out just one product, and that is protection for life and limb and property. But it seems to us women that the citadel of purity, the palladium of liberty, the home, our brothers have forgotten adequately to protect. Therefore, I am here today to speak on behalf of millions of women, good and true, but grieved and sorrowful, to ask that the guarantees and safeguards of law shall be stripped from the saloons of my country; that their tarnished gold shall no more pollute our treasury, and that the land we love may at once and forever go out of partnership with the liquor traffic.

Gentlemen, some political party will respond to this plea from the hearts of women asking for protection from a stimulant which nerves with dangerous strength the manly arm that God meant to be woman's shelter and protection, so that man's cruelty becomes the greatest toward those he loves the best. Some party will declare that when our best beloved go forth into life's battle they shall not have to take chances so unequal in the fight for a clear brain, nor run the gauntlet of saloons legalized and set along our streets. Some party will take to heart this object-lesson of the "Nation's Annual Drink Bill," shown in the chart I have had placed before your eyes today, with its nine hundred millions for intoxicating liquors, to five millions for the spread of Christ's gospel. The Greenback convention has already received with favor this memorial. Senator [William G.] Donnan, our gallant Iowa champion, has secured its reading in your own great convention and its reference to your committee. Tomorrow you will act upon it. On July 8 it will be presented to the Democratic convention in this city, and on July 23 to that of the Prohibition Home Protection Party in Pittsburgh, Pennsylvania.

A great chief of your party who was with us as the hero of your last convention, said that not in the turmoil of politics, but at the sacred fireside hearth, does God prepare the verdict of a great, free people. Let me say, gentlemen, that the party which declares for national prohibition in 1884 will be the one for which the temperance women of this land will pray and work, circulate literature, convene assemblies, and do all in our power to secure its success. Nor is the influence of these women to be forgotten or lightly esteemed as the past has sufficiently proved.

While I have tried to speak, my spirit has been sustained and soothed by the presence of that devoted army whom I am here to represent. As womanly, as considerate, as gentle as the women of the Woman's Christian Temperance Union, from Alabama to Wyoming, would wish me to be in this presence, I have tried to be—that I might justly represent them—good-natured as sunshine, steadfast as gravitation, persistent as a Christian's faith. I have no harsh word to speak of any.

The liquor traffic is the awful heritage of a less wise, less kind, and less enlightened past. For its existence in this gentler age we are all more or less responsible.

Let us combine to put it away, "with malice toward none, with charity for all."[5] Daughters of heroes and sisters of patriots are those for whose dear sake I have dared to speak today. De Tocqueville said: "Life is neither a pleasure nor a pain; it is a serious business, to be entered on with courage, and in a spirit of self-sac- rifice." Gentlemen, in that spirit I have tried to speak—not because I wished to be heard, but to represent, as best I could, the homes of America in their sacred warfare against the American saloon. May God lead and guide us all into lives and deeds of tenderest charity and divinest toil for the sorrowful and weak.

Some of us have sung the Miriam song[6] of this great party in other days, and whether we shall, erelong, chant its requiem depends upon whether or not the party shall be as true to living issues of the present as it was true to living issues in the past. For

> New occasions teach new duties,
>   Time makes ancient good uncouth;
> They must upward still and onward,
>   Who would keep abreast of truth.

We ask you to declare in favor of submitting to the people a national consti- tutional amendment for the prohibition of the liquor traffic.

Gentlemen, on behalf of the National Woman's Christian Temperance Union, I thank you for this courteous hearing.

Notes

1. Willard, *Glimpses,* 395.

2. Undated clipping from the *Pittsburgh Dispatch,* WCTU series, reel 34, frame 283. The reference here is likely to Frank Mellen Nye (1852–1935), who was a state legislator in Wisconsin in 1884 and 1885.

3. Willard, *Glimpses,* 409.

4. Slogan from the 1856 presidential campaign of Republican candidate John C. Fre- mont.

5. This quote is the closing line from the "Second Inaugural Address" of the first Re- publican president, Abraham Lincoln.

6. The "Miriam song" is a song of victory. The reference here is to Exodus 15:20–21 where Miriam led Israelite women in a song of celebration for their release from Egypt and the defeat of the Egyptians who were pursuing them.

ELEVEN

"Social Purity: The Latest and Greatest Crusade," April 22, 1886

"Social Purity: The Latest and Greatest Crusade" was delivered before the Central WCTU of Chicago on April 22, 1886, and was the first of many addresses Willard devoted solely to this cause. As Willard admitted in her speech, neither she nor the WCTU had been in the forefront on the issue of social purity, which, since the antebellum period, had been addressed by various female moral reform societies. Within the WCTU, some members in states such as Iowa and Maine had been active for several years in work among prostitutes. However, British journalist William T. Stead's startling July 1885 exposé of the "white slave" trade in London made it clear to Willard that the WCTU faced a moral imperative to increase activism on this issue.[1]

Stead's tale of young girls sold, forced, or seduced into lives of prostitution also made clear the connection between alcohol use and the trade in women. His story revealed that the parents who sold their daughters to procurers for brothels were often alcoholics and that girls seduced or raped within the brothels were typically made drunk beforehand. In her presidential address at the 1885 WCTU convention, Willard castigated herself and other uninvolved parties saying, "it is a marvel not to be explained, that we go on the even tenor of our way, too delicate, too refined, too prudish to make any allusion to these awful facts, much less to take up arms against these awful crimes."[2] She closed the discussion of social purity in that address by asking for a volunteer to superintend this work for the WCTU. When no one came forward, she took the job herself.

This text is foremost a teaching address that served to introduce Willard's Chicago audience to the history of the social purity movement, its major figures, goals, and ideological grounding. She reviewed the contributions of leaders in the social purity movement such as Josephine Butler, who led the fight against the United Kingdom's Contagious Diseases Act, which as an effort to protect men's health, allowed police to arrest women suspected of being prostitutes and force them to undergo an exam for venereal disease and to confine them for treatment if they showed signs of the disease. As characterized by Willard, Butler and many other social purity advocates based their arguments not on a simplistic Puritan ideal of sexuality, but rather on the protofeminist argument that such laws were grounded in gender discrimination. Willard expressed outrage at the wrongs inflicted upon women under a system of "iniquitous legislation" apparently designed to protect only the interests of men. Her denunciation of the sexual double standard, her ability to connect the economic oppression of women to the trade in women, her call for women to legislate on their own behalf, and her demand for moral reform among men as well as sex education for women all evidence an astute analysis of the issues within their nineteenth-century context.

According to Willard, the goals of the social purity movement were, first, to assist rather than shun "fallen sisters" and, second, to discard the double standard that protected men from suffering consequences for their ill-use of women. Educational and economic independence for women would provide a key first step. Women who were not financially dependent on men for their livelihood would be able to leverage their power to keep men away from tobacco, alcohol, and promiscuous sex. In her 1886 presidential address Willard took her economic argument even further, demanding that society "put a money value upon a wife's industry in helping to build up and maintain a home" and so help to foster women's independence.[3] In addition, organizations promoting social purity pledges, such as the White Cross for young men and the White Shield for young women, would help the next generation change cultural expectations of male sexual behavior.

The following excerpts are from *Voice Extra*, June 1886, found in the WCTU series, reel 35, frames 161–66.

* * *

In the year 1869, while studying in Paris, I used often to see passing along the pleasant streets, great closed wagons, covered with black. Inquiring of my elegant landlady the explanation of these somber vehicles, she answered, sorrowfully, "It is the demimonde [prostitutes], who go to be examined." I then learned for the first time that in Paris fallen women have a legal "permit" to carry on what is a recognized business, but must remain secluded in their houses at certain hours, must avoid certain streets, and must go once a week, under escort of the police, to the dispensary for examination and certificate that they are exempt from contagious disease. Always, after that, those awful wagons seemed to me to form the most heartbreaking funeral procession that ever [a] Christian woman watched with aching heart and tear-dimmed eyes. If I were asked why there has come about such a revolution in public thought that I have gained the courage to speak of things once unlawful to be told, and you may listen without fear of criticism from any save the base, my answer [would] be:

"Because law makers tried to import the black wagon of Paris to England and America, and Anglo-Saxon women rose in rebellion."

Even a worm will turn at last, and when her degradation was thus deliberately planned and sanctioned by the state on the basis of securing to the stronger partner in a dual sin the same protection from nature's penalty which society had granted him so long, and of heaping upon the weaker partner in that sin all the disgrace and shame, then womanhood's loyalty to woman was aroused, it overcame the silence and reserve of centuries, and Christendom rings with her protest today.

Thus do the powers of darkness outwit themselves, and evils evermore tend to their own cure. It is now solemnly avowed by thousands of the best and most capable women who speak the English tongue, not only that the contagious-diseases acts shall never be tolerated upon a single inch of British or American soil, but that houses of ill fame shall be not only prohibited but banished altogether. The system of license must not come. The "let alone" policy must go. The prohibitory method must be achieved.

"And He gave some prophets and some apostles and some teachers and some evangelists" [Ephesians 4:11]. This is the order in each new evolution of that gospel which would bring about equality between Jew and Greek, bond and free, male and female, in Christ Jesus [Galatians 3:28]. To see the prophet of this new civilization we must go to the beautiful old cathedral town of Winchester, England, and find a Christian mother with husband and sons about her. She lost her only daughter long ago, and with the chrism of this great sorrow on her heart, dedicates her rare gifts of faith and works of pen and voice to the lost daughters of mothers still more sadly stricken and bereft. History will record that Mrs. Josephine Butler,[4] wife of Canon Butler, of Winchester Cathedral, was the earliest public champion of the cause of social purity. For well-nigh twenty years this noble woman has battled against the odious contagious-diseases acts in England and on the Continent, and lives to see them rendered inoperative during six years past, and to witness an almost unanimous vote in the House of Commons for their repeal within the past few weeks....

The "Teacher" in this movement is Miss Ellice Hopkins,[5] whom we hope to welcome within a twelvemonth to the United States.... The preventive aspect of this work has been developed by Miss Hopkins as by no one else. She is the founder of the White Cross Army for young men, under the patronage of the Bishop of Durham, which in three years has extended over Great Britain, and now bids fair to take firm root in America, where it was introduced about one year ago by the Reverend Dr. B[enjamin] F[ranklin] DeCosta, of New York, rector of the Church of St. John the Evangelist. Miss Hopkins has prepared its literature and formulated its obligations, which are as follows:

1. To treat all women with respect, and endeavor to protect them from wrong and degradation.
2. To endeavor to put down all indecent language and coarse jests.
3. To maintain the law of purity as equally binding upon men and women.

4. To endeavor to spread these principles among my companions, and try to help my younger brothers.

5. To use all possible means to fulfill the command, "Keep thyself pure."

The principle on which this movement rests is that to be forewarned is the only way to be forearmed; that virtue based upon knowledge is safer than innocence based upon ignorance; and that the recital of the creative mysteries from a mother's lips imparts to the child's mind such a sense of their solemnity and sacredness as cannot be otherwise obtained. The girl and even more especially the boy who feels a confidential freedom in bringing to the home sanctuary the mysterious questions sure to be asked and answered somewhere will be likely to maintain purity of word and deed even amid youth's manifold temptations. Some author has beautifully said, "God could not be everywhere, so He made mothers." Happy the child whose mother has his entire confidence all his life long. I have been told by many a fortunate mother that her son indignantly repelled the degradation of the common schoolboy talk upon subjects he had learned to regard as sacred by reason of confidences exchanged between himself and her who bore him. Mothers' meetings for conference upon these themes are a part of our White Cross plan in the WCTU, and we have a list of topics that will be furnished on application at the *Union Signal* office, Chicago.

It is well for us to remember that the work of the two ladies I have named and the loyal followers whom such leadership could not fail to secure conducted directly to the mighty consequences involved in the *Pall Mall Gazette* disclosures. Through their efforts the criminal reform bill has been introduced into the House of Commons. Its principal provision was one which raised the "age of consent" (i.e., the age at which a girl could deliberately agree to her own ruin) from ten to sixteen years. By British law a little girl who was not old enough to make a legal sale of her own doll was declared sufficiently wise to protect her own honor. Also by British law it had been held that no child's testimony could be put in evidence unless the little creature was able to explain "the nature of an oath." By this ingenious but most iniquitous legislation the ravisher usually got off scot-free; for if the child was ten or more she was held to be old enough to consent, in which case her assailant went unpunished, and if less than ten she could seldom explain the nature of an oath, hence could not bear witness against him. Thus considerately have men from time immemorial legislated for woman. Their laws have shown the mercy that a wolf shows to a lamb. Similar laws are on the statute books of the United States. In the very particulars where women most needed protection they have been least protected.

How much longer must we wait before women will begin to beg the privilege of doing a little legislation on their own account? or at least having a voice in choosing the men who shall represent their interests and protect by law the physically weaker sex? This improved bill, which raised the age of consent to sixteen years (it should be eighteen, for sixteen is a most irresponsible age) [and] made a little girl's testimony valid as to who had injured her, was lying becalmed, and had been for years when Mrs. Butler and Miss Hopkins prevailed upon Mr. William T. Stead to be its champion. His brave record as a journalist had long been known to them, and his paper was one of leading influence. To my thought he is the apostle of this movement. Before taking up the bill he wished to learn for himself the correctness of some frightful statements made by its friends, and soon found that the half had not been told. So terrible were his disclosures and such dismay did they scatter among the libertines of high as well as low life that through their influence he was arrested and upon a legal technicality thrown into jail. But meanwhile Lord Shaftesbury,[6] England's foremost philanthropist, stood by him, the last public speech of that illustrious nobleman being in defense of Mr. Stead; the Parliamentary commission, with the Archbishop of Canterbury[7] at its head, appointed to test the truth of the disclosures, declared them substantially correct, and the criminal reform bill, its sails filled with the new tempest of the people's wrath, raised by intelligent opinion and aroused conviction, swiftly made the safe harbor of a well-nigh unanimous adoption.

I feel bound to utter and reiterate these facts out of my deep thankfulness to Mr. Stead, because men of the world have been industrious in their attempt to blacken the name of one to whom women owe a debt of eternal gratitude. His revelations have not only given to England such legislation for the protection of woman's honor as a year ago was deemed hopeless, but have hung out danger signals for every home, and rendered every little girl more safe. Publicity was precisely what was needed. A conspiracy of silence is almost always a conspiracy of sin. Whether conducted by boys in the pantry or by men in society, it is pretty sure to be at the expense of something precious to home-keepers. The hush-a-by policy has had ample time in which to disport its virtues, and it has miserably failed. Bad men would have good women think that a gulf like that which separated Lazarus from Dives [Luke 16:19–31] must separate them from women no worse than the very men who inculcate this shameful heresy. Bad men would have us believe that to be virtuous we must be ignorant, and that the least contact with such women as they hold themselves free to consort with would be to us a profanation.

No wonder that a subtle Frenchman said, in a view of the long subjugation of the gentler sex: "The virtue of women is the wittiest invention of men." Its earliest purpose was doubtless rooted in that passion for power, which has been the most enduring attribute of the physically strong. Having dominated a tribe during his lifetime, the chieftain wished a son to inherit his prowess and the prerogatives he could no longer grasp. But in order to satisfy the chieftain's sense of ownership and gain the tribe's submission, this son must be undoubtedly his own. Hence, to assure this fact, the most cruel expedients were resorted to. It is believed that we have here the origin of the cruel practice of binding up the feet of Chinese women of the higher class, so that they should be of necessity shut up in the house of their master. The faces of Mohammedan women were veiled, and they were hidden away in harems guarded by eunuchs, and a hundred other devices were invented too revolting for an occasion like the present; but we have here the origin of fashions and customs regnant today, for the examples of "chiefs," whether in a savage tribe or so-called civilized nation, are universally contagious, and by their tenacity of life illustrate the survival of the most unfit.

Even in our own day, Russian peasants, returning from wars in which the outrages inflicted by them upon women have been limited by their opportunity alone, will cut the tongues from their own wives or beat them to death, if in the husband's absence they have proved untrue.

Little does the fine lady on the avenue suspect that the smile with which she receives some dissolute young man who comes to spend the evening with her daughter is but the shading off of that same enforced subserviency which makes a Cossack's wife kneel to be whipped by a husband far more guilty than herself.

Little does the simpering belle who talks lightly of her future husband as one who has "sown a good many wild oats" reflect that she is unspeakably degraded by an admission which allies her to the women of the cruel past. Nothing will ever open the eyes of women to their duty of tender helpfulness toward their fallen sisters and the correlate duty of social ostracism toward their fallen brothers except to study this whole subject in the light of history and to adopt Christ's teachings, "Neither do I condemn thee; go and sin no more; let him who is without sin among you cast the first stone" [John 8:11, 7]. On these two hang all the law and the prophets [Matthew 22:40] in the dispensation of social purity.

The great naturalist, Darwin,[8] says that in no race except the human is the male ever unkind to the female. Guided by nature's instinct, even the tiger and the wolf are considerate toward their weaker mates, and never use their superior force to intrude upon or in any wise harm them. Nor is this done, in the whole realm of nature, save where animals have been trained by man to some faint imitation of their own inconsiderateness and cruelty.

It will be perceived that whoever touches this question of the origin of the social evil has come near finding the "origin of evil" itself. That the world's equilibrium is lost we all concede. That it shall be restored when woman takes her rightful place, and not till then, intelligent students of science, history, and the New Testament believe. On a low plane, and for sordid ends, primeval and medieval man wrought out, by fiercest cruelty, virtue as the only tolerated estate of one half the human race. On a high plane, and for the noblest purpose, Christianity, working through modern women, shall yet make virtue the only tolerated estate of the whole human race. For whatever standard women steadfastly insist upon, with power to enforce that insistence, men will attain. In practical life this greatest of reforms will work itself out on this wise: Whenever the young women of this nation or any other, able to earn their own living, ready for an independent life, yet sweetly drawn by the eloquent persuasions of their hearts to the old and sacred pathways of love, marriage, and home—whenever they can say to the young men: "You must choose between tobacco and me," "You must choose between strong drink and me," "You must choose between an immoral life and me," then, and not till then, these sensual indulgences will be relinquished by young men; then, and not till then, the cause of social purity shall grandly triumph.

Whenever it has dropped like leaven into the lump of human sin and sorrow, Christianity, like nature, has prescribed one code of morals to the male and female of the race. That code exists today wherever the teachings of Christ are made the law of daily life. When I said to women in France and Italy that I was confident a large majority of the men in my own social circle were as chaste as women, the statement was invariably received with shouts of laughter, and some such pitying comments as "L'Americaine has spent her life with books, 'tis evident; she does not know the world." But what I then believed I believe now. The manhood of America is the noblest and most masterful on earth, because it has most mastery of itself. Nor is there any explanation of this fact so adequate as that our everyday religion has so developed women and refined men that men think of us with respect and reverence; see us from many angles of vision; realize our power on the industrial plane; recognize the possibility of intellectual comradeship with us; count on our help in all religious and philanthropic movements, and, a little beyond the swinging door of the twentieth century, will seat us beside themselves upon the throne of Government. Then shall be enacted such a code of laws for the protection of woman's honor as the world has never seen or dreamed of, for it shall protect man's honor, too! For the first time in history he shall be held to equal penalties with woman, and his superior physical strength shall be counted at its just value as presumptive evidence against him in all cases of indecorous or cruel treatment toward the weak. Then shall woman, with all the avenues of development for brain and hand wide open to her, and women in the court and on the jury to defend her interests, begin to know her own value, and find her inclination and temptations to a debasing life reduced to zero.

A physician, who was also a phrenologist, told me that self-esteem seemed wanting in the craniums of women who had fallen, and it is so with those who consent to live with drunken husbands. Financial reasons are the chief consideration in the latter case, as I know from long and painful observation. This great uplift of the working classes has in it blessed hopes for women, and hence for social purity. Whatever takes the yoke from off the laboring man helps to a truer individuality the woman by his side.

But the outworking of this mightiest of reforms, which, in the last analysis, we have perceived to be part and parcel of the great temperance movement, is no more in the interest of woman than of man. For "they rise or fall together, dwarfed or Godlike, bond or free." No true reformer among women has harsh and bitter thoughts of men. Their inheritance from the dark ages, unsunned by Christ or science, the blessed revelators, is their misfortune rather than their fault, as ours is also. But, working side by side, be it theirs and ours to restore to this pitiful world the Eden it has lost. I am not here to speak alone about the "Woman Question;" that is but half my theme; it is rather the higher, broader, and more sacred "Human Question" that should enlist the interest and work of all true hearts.

While the electric forces of modern—which, to me, means Christian—civilization are all harnessed to the snow-white car of social purity, and will do more to speed it forward than any specific effort can, we, as white ribbon women, are bound to do our part in the great society that has grown out of that whirlwind of the law called "The Temperance Crusade." Organized in ten thousand towns and cities, with state and territorial auxiliaries embracing the entire republic, and now stretching out in the World's WCTU to every corner of the globe, we are, in the providence of God, the strongest single power yet raised up among women to do battle for this sacred cause. I believe we are called to become not its prophets, teachers, or apostles so much as its evangelists.

In the great departments of heredity and hygiene, of scientific instruction in the public schools relative to the laws of health (already introduced by statute into nearly a score of commonwealths), in the evangelistic work and young women's societies, in the equal franchise and literature departments, we can strike blows that will be mighty for the pulling down of this central citadel of iniquity, the degradation of women. Indeed, our thirty-nine departments all converge like the fingers of a hand upon this curse of curses, and will do more in the next twenty years to crush it than we dreamed of who did not clearly see, at first, their bearing on a cause even greater than the cause of temperance. . . .

The final question, here and evermore, must be the same: *Is all this anything to me?* I am told on good authority that Chicago has today no less than thirty thousand prostituted women. Have they any reason to think that we are grieved for their sake; that we desire to do them good; nay, that we are determined to help them if they will but accept our offers of sympathy and aid? What have we done, each one of us, for the amelioration of their hideous estate? Breathing the same air, walking the same streets, reading the same newspapers, we have no more knowledge of each other than if the thirty thousand fallen women lived upon the planet Venus. In saying this I would by no means ignore the exceptional Christian workers and institutions here and there, but I mean the great mass of us who have not specifically taken up this branch of philanthropic endeavor. We are professed followers of Him who, as He went about doing good, seemed, if possible, more compassionate toward the Magdalene and those like her than toward any other class of evil doers. And yet the fallen women of Chicago might justly rise up on the last day and accuse us of unfaithfulness, might justly say: "You belonged to the fortunate class, whose opulent and forceful lives were fed from a thousand springs of opportunity and blessing, but we were untrained, unwarned, uncared for. You were shielded in Christian homes, while we were motherless or unbefriended, and in our youth and inexperience exposed to manifold temptations. You had the discipline of education and the stimulus of intellectual development; we never knew the wholesome companionship of great thoughts and the self-control which only studious habits can impart. The love of Christ was a beacon of light to your lives, while we plodded on in shadowy paths of sin, and yet you never tried to match our weakness by your strength, our poverty by your riches, our ignorance by your knowledge, our sin by your saintship—you never tried at all." Dear sisters, who of us is willing to face such a record as that? Not one; and yet it is our own today. But, thank God, the account is not yet closed; the blessed opportunity is ours; the smallest effort made by a fervent heart will not be lost. Let us go home with the question reverberating through the halls of conscience, Lord, what wouldst thou have me to do?

Notes

1. William Thomas Stead (1849–1912), was an investigative reporter and editor first of *The Northern Echo* and later of the London daily, the *Pall Mall Gazette*. His exposé, "Maiden Tribute of Modern Babylon: The Report of Our Secret Commission" was published as a serial July 6, 7, 8 and 10, 1885, in the *Pall Mall Gazette*. The text is available online at: www.attackingthedevil.co.uk/pmg/tribute/. Later references to Stead are from this text.

2. Willard, 1885 Annual Presidential Address, *Minutes of the National Woman's Christian Temperance Union* (Brooklyn, New York: Martin and Niper, 1885), 74.

3. Willard, Annual Address before the National WCTU in *Minutes of the National Woman's Christian Temperance Union*. (Chicago: Woman's Temperance Publishing Association, 1886), 78.

4. Butler (1828–1906) was the foremost leader of the British social purity movement. She worked with the World's WCTU during the early 1890s, becoming the superintendent of its Social Purity Department. She was the major British figure in the fight against the contagious diseases act of 1864. This act aimed to protect the health of men by allowing the arrest and forced physical examination and treatment of any woman accused of being a prostitute. The act was repealed in 1886.

5. Jane Ellice Hopkins (1836–1904) was, with Josephine Butler, at the head of the social purity movement in Great Britain.

6. Anthony Ashley Cooper, Seventh Earl of Shaftesbury (1801–85), known as "The Working Man's Friend," was a British politician and activist who supported several key reform acts benefiting workers and child laborers.

7. Edward White Benson (1829–96) served as the archbishop from 1883 to 1896.

8. British naturalist Charles Darwin (1809–82) is best known for introducing the theory of natural selection in his 1859 book, *The Origin of the Species*. His extended discussion of male–female sex differences is in his 1871 book, *The Descent of Man*.

TWELVE

How to Win: A Book for Girls, 1886

In *How to Win: A Book for Girls* Willard spelled out the nature and implications of the new definition of womanhood she had been rethinking since her teen years. She had ventured a tentative attempt at redefinition in her 1871 speech "The New Chivalry" and in the early 1870s, as President of the Evanston College for Ladies, she gave several addresses along similar lines as she traveled to raise funds and generate public support for women's higher education. In 1878 during her brief tenure as editor of the *Chicago Post,* she wrote a series titled, "Talks for Girls" and published them in the pages of the newspaper. These early speeches and writings laid the groundwork for the more fully developed argument in the 125 pages of *How to Win.* Willard chose to address girls and young women because she saw them as the best hope for realizing the new ideal of womanhood she imagined. It was an audience dear to her from her teaching days. She often described herself as an "elder sister of girls," someone who had their best interests at heart. Her purpose in writing the book was to give her "younger sisters" the kind of advice that she and her generation had not received growing up in the 1850s and 1860s when expectations for their futures were far more limited.

The young women of the 1880s were likely to pay attention to what Willard had to tell them. By that time she was a nationally known reform leader much admired and beloved by thousands of American women. Furthermore, she had become something of a heroine and role model for the generation of college girls who joined newly organized sororities, campus Christian Endeavor societies, and the Young Woman's Christian Temperance Unions. It was to these bright young women that she chose to present in depth her notion of a reconstructed ideal of womanhood. *How to Win* was a guidebook for girls, aimed at empowering them to make their way successfully in the new climate of openness for women's larger ambitions that she sensed was on the horizon.

Willard wanted young women to be able to determine the course of their own lives rather than be confined by what were, in her estimation, outdated customs and traditions. She insisted that they become economically independent, so that they would not be victims of men's inability or unwillingness to provide financial support for them. Like other women's rights reformers, she had seen the bitter consequences of the failure of the prevailing middle-class ideal of marriage—the wife happily ensconced in her home with a reliable husband to protect and support her and their children. WCTU members knew well that the reality of some women's lives did not reflect the Victorian ideal of woman's domesticity. Whether the cause was the loss of husbands through death in the Civil War, the lack of marriageable men, or the collapse of families due to alcoholism, many women were struggling to support themselves and their children, with few ways of making a living. Such women faced a bleak future, which for a few meant turning to prostitution. For years, the WCTU and other benevolent and charitable organizations had been trying to aid such women through various rescue operations. Willard understood that the WCTU must now move beyond merely rescuing women to concentrate on developing a new generation of independent women that would no longer need to be rescued.

Distinguishing her volume from other advice books for girls, Willard maintained that realizing this new ideal of womanhood required a corresponding new ideal of manhood. The young men of the future must be willing to relinquish their dominant roles in male–female relationships and enter into a partnership of equals both within and outside of the home. They must also cease practicing a double standard of morality that allowed prostitution and other vices to flourish, and raise themselves to the moral level they required of the young women they desired to marry.

With characteristic optimism, she looked forward to a time not too far distant when women and men would become equal partners in reform. Together they would labor to "make the world homelike" through an intensified form of activism she termed "philanthropy," one that would bring the ethical attributes of a reformed ideal of marriage, home, and family life into all other institutions of society. Willard would elaborate further on the meaning of this slogan in subsequent speeches and writings. Its appearance in *How to Win* announced one direction Willard's thought and rhetoric would take in the 1890s, as she urged the WCTU to focus energy on the task of reconstructing the ideal of womanhood.

Excerpts are from Willard, *How to Win: A Book for Girls* (New York: Funk and Wagnalls, 1886), 11–15, 21–24, 27–32, 37–40, 42, 48–50, 63–64.

* * *

Why I Wrote of Winning

Long ago, and long ago it was, in the days when I used proudly to write "School Teacher" after my name, I bought a certain book for the express purpose of reading it to the girls I've left behind me. The book is one beloved by train boys, of which they and other venders have sold so many that the latest dodgers read, "Twentieth thousand now in press." It is sensible in matter, attractive in style, and goes by the enticing name of "Getting on in the World."[1] Naturally enough it was written in Chicago, and like most "Garden City" notions, is a success. But the trouble with this volume was that it didn't fill the bill. I wanted to read it to "my girls," to stir up their pure minds by way of remembrance that "life is real, life is earnest," and the rest of it. But as I scanned its bright and pleasant pages I found out—what do you think I found? Why, that with the light of a new dispensation blazing in upon him, and the soprano voices of several million "superfluous women" crying, "Have you no *work* for me to do? This honored author had written never a word about creation's gentler half! His book contained three hundred and sixty-five pages, but if you had read a page each day, all the year round, you wouldn't have found out at last that such a being as a woman was trying "to get on" in this or any other world. Not a bread-winning weapon had he put in the hand of the neediest among us, nor had he, even in a stray chapter, or "appendix," taken us off by ourselves and drawn us a diagram of our "sphere."

I was so pained by this that I wrote Professor Matthews (the gifted author, and my personal friend), asking him why he had thus counted out the women folks in his book upon success in life. I even ventured to hypothecate the reason, saying to him: "Dear Sir: I do not think you did this with malice aforethought or from lack of interest in our fate, but simply and only because, like so many of our excellent brethren, you 'done forgot all about us,' as *Topsy* would say." Whereupon came a prompt and gracious reply, with the frank admission: "You guessed aright; I simply forgot to speak of women."

Now, you perceive, it set me thinking—this obliquity of mental vision, which had led a writer so talented and wise to squint thus at the human race, seeing but half of it. I recalled the fact that, into most families, are born girls as well as boys; nay, that, as many an overburdened *paterfamilias* [father of the family] can testify, girls come not infrequently in largely superior, if not exclusive numbers. Having, also, at a remote period of my history, belonged to their helpless fraternity, I was haunted by the wish that I might write a sequel to the professor's excellent book, talking therein to girls and women about success in life. Perhaps my time has come—perhaps. I have now the largest audience that has yet consented to listen to my "views." Anyhow, I mean, in these offhand pages, to talk to girls of "How to Win" in something besides the sense treated of it in books of etiquette and fashion magazines, or systematically taught in dancing-schools.

And now, my dears, if you are patient and my small assistant keeps me in lead-pencils, I shall try to show that if every young woman held in her firm little hand her own best gift, duly cultivated and made effective, society would not explode, the moon would not be darkened, the sun would still shed light. As things are now, when I see an audience of young men, they remind me of a platoon of soldiers, marching with fixed bayonet to the capture of their destiny, while an assembly of young women, on the other hand, recalls a flock of lambs upon a pleasant hillside, that frisk about and nibble at the herbage and lie down in the sun. Above them soars the devouring eagle of their destiny, ready to pounce down upon them, while the meek little innocents turn their white faces skyward and mildly wonder "what that graceful creature is up yonder?" Girls remind me, too, of the reply given by a bright young friend of mine to the solemn exhortation that she should "make the most of life." "Humph! She exclaimed, with a rueful grimace, "I have no chance, for life is busy making the most of me!"

The trouble is, we women have all along been set down on the world's program for a part quite different than the one we really play upon its stage. For instance, the program reads: "Woman will take the part of Queen in the Drama of Society," but offtimes, before the curtain falls, the stage reveals her as a dressmaker, a school teacher—perchance that most abused of mortals—a reformer! The program reads: "This august actress will be escorted to the stage by Man, her loyal and devoted subject, to whom has been assigned the part of shielding her from the glare of the footlights, and shooting anybody in the audience who dares to hiss." But alas! offtimes the stage reveals her coming in alone, dragging her own sewing machine, while her humble and devoted subject, with tailors' goose [iron] in one hand and scissors in the other, indicates by energetic pantomime his fixed intention to drive her speedily behind the scenes. The program, my beloved innocents, attires you all in purple and fine linen and bids you fare sumptuously every day [Luke 16:19], but not infrequently the stage reveals you attired in calico gowns, and munching your hard-earned crackers and cheese. The world's theory furnishes every young lady that draws breath, with a lover loyal and true, but the world's practice shoots him on the battlefield, or stunts and poisons him with alcohol and nicotine, until he can only "rattle around" through life in the place God meant him to fill within home's sacred sanctuary. It is just this discrepancy that I complain of, and the generous age we live in is complaining of it with a thousand tongues, so that the logic of events that happen, rather than the logic of events that ought to happen, is impelling toward nobler fortunes that phenomenal creature whom a French author has called "the Poor Woman of the nineteenth century." . . .

"I am Little, But I am I.". . . .

In creating each of us with some peculiar talent, God has given us each "a call" to some peculiar work. Indeed, the time is almost here when the only call that will be recognized as valid, in any field, must involve in him who thinks he hears it both adaptation and success. Each one of us is a marvelous bundle of aptitudes and of capacities. But just as I prefer the active to the passive voice, I prefer to put the aptitudes first in my present inventory. Besides, the world has harangued us women on our capacities from the beginning, and it is really refreshing to take the dilemma of our destiny by the other horn, at last! Civilization (by which I mean Christianity's effect on the brains and hands of humanity) wonderfully develops and differentiates our powers. . . .

By some unaccountable perversion of good sense, the specialties of human beings who are women have been strangely circumscribed. But they were *there*, all the same, and now, under the genial sun of a more enlightened era, they are coming airily forth, like singing birds after a thunderstorm, and wonderfully do they help some of us to solve the toughest of all problems: "*What is life for?*"

Let us see. Lift the cover of your sewing basket: there are thimble, scissors, spools of thread, and all the neat outfit needful to a seamstress, but minus the needle they have no explanation and no efficiency. Unlock your writing desk: what are paper, ink, and sealing wax, without the pen? They are nothing but waste material and toys. So it is with you and me. We have no explanation that is adequate; we have no place in the work-box and portfolio of today; no place in the great humming hive of the land we live in, save as some predominating aptitude in each of us explains why we are here, and in what way we are to swell the inspiring song of voluntary toil and beneficent success. Suppose that here and now, you proceed to take an "inventory of stock," if you have not been thoughtful enough to do that already. Made up as you are, what is your *forte*, your "specialty," your "best hold," as the men phrase it? Be sure of one thing at the outset: The Great Artificer, in putting together your individual nature, did not forget this crowning gift, any more than He forgets to add its own peculiar fragrance to the arbutus [a ground cover plant], or its own song to the lark. It may not lie upon the surface, this choicest of your treasures; diamonds seldom do. Miners lift a great deal of mere dust before the sparkling jewel they are seeking gladdens the eye. Genius has been often and variously defined. I would call it *an intuition* of one's own best gift. . . .

As iron filings fall into line around a magnet, so make your opportunities cluster close about your magic gift. In a land so generous as ours, this can be done by every woman who reads these lines. A sharpened perception of their own possibilities is far more needed by "our girls" than better means for education. But how was it in the past? If there is one reflection which, for humanity's sake, grieves me as no other can, it is this thought of God's endowment bestowed upon each one of us, so that we might in some especial manner gladden and bless the world, by bestowing upon it our best; the thought of His patience all through the years, as He has gone on hewing out the myriad souls of a wayward race, that they might be lively stones in the temple of use and achievement, and side by side with this the thought of our individual blindness, our failures to discern the riches of brain, heart, and hand, with which we were endowed. But most of all, I think about the gentle women who have lived and died, and made no sign of their best gifts, but whose achievements of voice and pen, of philanthropy, might have blessed and soothed our race through these six thousand years. . . .

Aimless Reverie Versus a Resolute Aim—The New Profession

I am to give you reasons why you are to cultivate your specialty. And I claim, first, . . . that you should do this because you have a specialty to cultivate. . . . The second reason is, because you will then work more easily and naturally, with the least friction, with the greatest pleasure to yourself, and the most advantage to those around you. "Paddle your own canoe," but paddle it right out into the swift sure current of your strongest, noblest inclination. Thirdly, by this means you will get into your cranium, *in place of aimless reverie, a resolute aim.* This is where your brother has had his chief intellectual advantage over you. Quicker of wit than he, far less unwieldy in your mental processes, swifter in judgment, and every whit as accurate, you still have felt, when measuring intellectual swords with him, that yours was in your left hand, that his was in his right; and you have felt this chiefly, as I believe, because from the dawn of thought in his sturdy young brain, he has been taught that he must have a definite aim in life if he ever meant to swell the ranks of the somebodies upon this planet, while you have been just as sedulously taught that the handsome prince might whirl past your door "most any day," lift you to a seat beside him in his golden chariot, and carry you off to his castle in Spain.

And of course you dream about all this; why shouldn't you? Who wouldn't? But, my dear girls, dreaming is the poorest of all grindstones on which to sharpen one's wits. And to my thinking, the rust of woman's intellect, the canker of her heart, the "worm i' the bud" of her noblest possibilities has been this aimless reverie; this rambling of the thoughts; this vagueness, which when it is finished is vacuity. Let us turn our gaze inward, those of us who are not thoroughgoing workers with brain or hand. What do we find? A mild chaos; a glimmering nebula of fancies; an insipid brain-soup where a few lumps of thought swim in a watery grave of dreams, and, as nothing can come of nothing, what wonder if no brilliancy of achievement promises to flood our future with its light? Few women, growing up under the present order of things, can claim complete exemption from this grave intellectual infirmity.

Somehow one falls so readily into a sort of mental indolence; one's thoughts flow onward in a pleasant, gurgling stream, a sort of intellectual lullaby, coming no-whence, going no-whither. Only one thing can help you if you are in this extremity, and that is what your brothers have—the snag of a fixed purpose in this stream of thought. Around it will soon cluster the dormant ideas, hopes, and possibilities that have thus far floated at random. The first one in the idle stream of my life was the purpose, lodged there by my life's best friend, my mother, to have an education. Then, later on, Charlotte Brontë's "Shirley"[2] was a tremendous snag in the stream to me. Around that brave and steadfast character clustered a thousand new resolves. I was never quite so steeped in reveries again, though my temptations were unusual: my "Forest Home," by a Wisconsin river, offering few reminders to my girlish thought, of the wide, wide world and its sore need for workers. The next jog I got was from the intellectual attrition of a gifted and scholarly woman who asked me often to her home and sent me away laden with volumes of Wordsworth, Niebuhr, and the British essayists, not forgetting Carlyle and Emerson. Margaret Fuller Ossoli was another fixed point—shall I not rather say a fixed star?—in the sky of my thought, while Arnold of Rugby, to one who meant to make teaching a profession, was chief of all.[3] Well, is it possible that any word I have here written may set some of you thinking—that's it—*set* you a fixed purpose rather than a floating one—about a definite object in life toward which, henceforth, you may bend a steady, earnest gaze? I am not speaking of a thorough intellectual training only. It is to the life-work, which only a lifetime can fully compass, that I would direct your thoughts. Rather than that you should fail to have a fixed purpose concerning it, I would that your mental attitude might be like the one confided to me by a charming Philadelphia girl, whose letter of this morning has the following *naïve* statement:

"I feel such an aching in me to do or be something uncommon, and yet a kind of awful assurance that I never shall."

Nor do I here refer to that general knowledge of household arts which forms the sole acquirement inculcated in the regulation "Woman's Department" of the bygone-age newspaper, which in many localities remains in this, like the boulder of a past epoch.

It was once thought to be a high virtue for women, no matter how lofty in station or how ample of fortune, to do their own work with the needle. Homer represents Penelope spinning, surrounded by her maids, and the classic art abounds with illustrations of like character. But the virtues of one age often become the mistakes of the next. When loom, needle and broom were woman's only weapons, she did well to handle them deftly, no matter what her rank, for they were her bread-winning implements, and fortune has been proverbially fickle in all ages. But men, by their witty inventions, have perpetually encroached on "woman's sphere."

Eli Whitney, with his cotton gin, Elias Howe, with his sewing-machine, and a hundred other intricate-brained mechanics who have set steel fingers to do in an hour what women's fingers could not accomplish in a year; all these have combined to revolutionize the daily cares of the gentler sex. With former occupations gone, and the world's welcome ready when they succeed in special vocations new to them, it becomes not only the privilege but the sacred duty of every woman to cultivate and utilize her *highest* gift. There is no more practical form of philanthropy than this, for every one who makes a place for herself "higher up" leaves one lower down for some other woman who, but for the vacancy thus afforded her in the world's close-crowded ranks, might be tempted into paths of sin. There is an army of poor girls wholly dependent for a livelihood upon the doing of house-work. They have no other earthly resource between them and the poorhouse or haunt of infamy. There is another class to whom an honorable support can come only by sewing or millinery work. Whoever, then, fitting herself for some employment involving better pay and higher social recognition, graduates out of these lower grades and leaves them to those who cannot so advance, has helped the world along in a substantial way, because she has added to the sum of humanity's well-being. . . .

Let it not be concluded that I have meant to speak lightly of the intricate, skilled labor involved in making healthful and attractive that bright, consummate flower of a Christian civilization—the home. I have felt that this theme has been so often treated that it needed no amplification at my hands, but I will add that, having been entertained in scores of homes belonging to "exceptional women," "women with a career," etc., my testimony is that for wholesomeness, heartsomeness, and every quality that superadds home-making to housekeeping, I have never seen their superiors, and seldom, take them all in all, their peers. But as a rule, these women have earned the "wherewithal" to make a home, by the exercise of some good gift of brain or hand, and thus having been enabled to put a proxy in the kitchen, they direct, but do not attend personally to the minutiae of daily household cares.

Cultivate, then, your specialty, because the independence thus involved will lift you above the world's pity to the level of its respect, perchance its honor. . . .

In this century, when the wage of battle has cost our land an army of her sons, when widows mourn, and unwedded thousands are forced to meet the hard-faced world (from which rose-water theorists would shield them), America is coming to the rescue of her daughters! For the nearer perfect—that is, the more Christian—a civilization has become, the more carefully are the *exceptional* classes of society provided for. All our philanthropic institutions under state or private patronage illustrate this. In less enlightened days, your ideal woman composed the single, grand class for which public prejudice set itself to provide. She was to be the wife and mother, and she was carefully enshrined at home. But happily this is the world's way no longer. The exceptions are so many, made by war, by the thousand misunderstandings and cross-purposes of social intercourse, by the peculiar transition period in which we live, by the absurdly extravagant customs of our day, and the false notions of both men and women—that not to provide for those exceptions would be a monstrous meanness, if not a crime. And the provision made in this instance is the most rational—indeed, the only rational one which it is in the power of society or government to make for any save the utterly incapable—namely: *a fair chance for self-help.* Nor (to pursue the line of our argument still further) can we forget that skeleton hand which, in utter disregard for "the proprieties" in destiny's weird drama, thrusts itself so often into the charmed domestic circle, and snatches the beloved "provider" away forever, while it sets gaunt famine by the fireside in his stead. Furthermore, can we forget that, in ten thousand families, wives are this moment waiting in suspense and agony the return of wretched husbands to homes made hideous by the drunkard's sin—wives whose work of brain and hand alone keeps their children from want, now that their "strong staff is broken and their beautiful rod" [Jeremiah 48:17].

There are delicate white fingers turning the page on which I print these words that will never wear the marriage ring; there are slight forms bending over my friendly lines, which, not far down the years, will be clothed in widow's weeds. Alas, there are as surely others who, when they have been wooed and won, shall find that they are worse than widowed. And what of these three classes of women, sweet and helpless? Clearly to all of them I am declaring a true and blessed gospel, in this good news concerning honest independence and brave self-help! Clearly also, no one is wise enough to go through the assembly of my readers, and tell us who, in future years shall need a bread-winning weapon with which to defend herself and perchance also the helpless ones between whom and the world there may be no arm but hers. But it is a principle in public as well as private economy that *the wisest foresight provides for the remotest contingency,* and thus, in its full force, all that I have been saying applies to every woman who may read these thoughts on "How to Win." Suppose that many of you, dear girls, are destined to a downy nest, instead of a strong-winged flight—what then? Will the years spent in making the most of the best powers with which God has endowed you be worse employed than if you had given them to fashion and frivolity? These "*ad interim*" years which separate the graduate's diploma from the bride's marriage certificate, can they possibly be better invested than in the acquisition of some useful trade or dignified profession? And then aside from this, I would help the youngest of you to remember (even in the bewildered years of her second decade) what noble Margaret Fuller said: "No woman can give her hand with dignity, or her heart with loyalty, until she has learned *how to stand alone.*" It is not so much *what comes to you* as *what you come to,* that determines whether you are a winner in the great race of life. Never forget that the only indestructible material in destiny's fierce crucible is *character.* Say this, not to another—say it to yourself, utter it early, and repeat it often: "*Fail me not, thou.*"

Thus far I have been trying to impress upon you the reasons why you should cultivate individuality and independence in word and deed. I have claimed that each one of you has a "call" to some specific work, indicated by God's gifts to you of brain, or heart, or hand. But I would not have you only, or indeed chiefly, concerned with the evolution of your powers for your own sake. If you acquire, let it be that you may dispense; if you achieve, that others may sun themselves in the kind glow of your prosperity. The people who spend all their strength in absorbing are failures and parasites. It is alike the business of the sun and of the soul to radiate every particle of light that they contain. There is every reason to believe that this is precisely what they are for. And so, having made sure of your light, strength, and discipline, strike out from the warm and radiant center of a self-poised brain and heart, into the lives about you, and you will find that "What is good for the hive is also good for the bee." The luminous characters of history have done this, always. Losing their lives in those of other men, they have found themselves on the crest of the world's gratitude and fame. . . .

"Self-culture" is much in vogue nowadays, and has for its high priest some of the most incisive minds of this or any age. But self-culture stops in the middle of the sentence that I would fain help you to utter. It says: "Make the most of your power": it does not say "*for others' sake* as well as for your own." It claims that if we set the candle of our gifts upon the candlestick of modern society, its light will inevitably radiate according to its power of shining, and thus while brightening ourselves we shall have done our utmost toward lighting up the general gloom. But self-culture forgets that a candle is no type of you and me. We are human spirit-lamps, whose rays should be directed and intensified by the blow-pipe of unceasing purpose: for we are all so made that unless we *will* to light up other lives, we can never do so to the limit of our powers. Self-culture is never base; it is often noble, but it can never be the noblest aim of all. . . .

Just here let me add a personal appeal based on all that has preceded it, for the line of work that I deem most attractive and most urgently demanded by the exigencies of our time. It is that new and magnificent profession for women, now being brought to almost scientific accuracy and completeness—viz., PHI-LANTHROPY. . . .

The New Ideal of Womanhood

No doubt my readers have asked ere this the inevitable question: "Why does that seem natural and fitting for a young woman to do and to aspire to now which would have been no less improper than impossible a hundred years ago?" Sweet friends, it is because *the ideal of woman's place in the world is changing in the average mind.* For as the artist's ideal precedes his picture, so the ideal woman must be transformed before the actual one can be. In an age of brute force, the warrior galloping away to his adventures waving his mailed hand to the lady fair who was enclosed for safe keeping in a grim castle with moat and drawbridge. But today, when spirit force grows regnant, a woman can circumnavigate the globe alone, without danger of an uncivil word, much less of violence. We shall never span a wider chasm than this change implies. All our inventions have led up to it, and have in nothing else wrought out beneficence so great as they have accomplished here, purely by indirection. In brief, the barriers that have hedged women into one pathway and men into another, altogether different, are growing thin, as physical strength plays a less determining part in our life drama. All through the vegetable and animal kingdoms the fact of sex does not widely differentiate the broader fact of life, its environment and its pursuits. Hence, the immense separateness which sex is called in to explain when we reach the plane of humanity is to be accounted for largely on artificial grounds. In Eden it did not exist, nor in the original plan of creation, as stated in these just and fatherly words: "And God said, 'Let us make man in our own image, after our own likeness. Let them have dominion.' . . . So God created man in His own image, in the image of God created he him, male and female created he them, and God blessed them, and said unto them, 'replenish the earth and subdue it . . . and have dominion over every living thing'" [Genesis 1:26–28]. After the fall came the curse, which may have been no part of the original design, and from which the Gospel's triumph is releasing us, for there is "neither male nor female in Christ Jesus" [Galatians 3:28]. Who knows but that the origin of evil was contemporaneous with man's assertion of supremacy over one who was meant to be his equal comrade. If so, our Paradise regained will come only when the laureate's [Alfred Lord Tennyson] prophecy is realized:

> "Two heads in council, two beside the hearth,
> Two in the noisy business of the world,
> Two in the liberal offices of life;
> Two plummets dropped to sound the abyss of science
> And the secrets of mankind."

The times when a new ideal is molded, in church, state, or society, mark the epochs of history. Amid what throes did Europe pass from that of supreme authority in the Church to the incomparably higher one of supreme liberty in conscience; from the divine right of kings to the divine right of the people! But there was to come a wider evolution of the same ideal—namely, the co-equal power of the co-partners, man and woman, in working out the problem of human destiny. This newest and noblest of ideals marks the transition from physical force ruling to spiritual force recognized. The gradual adjustment of everyday occupation, custom and law, to this new ideal, marks ours as a transition period. Those who have the most enlargement of opportunity to hope for from the change, will, in the nature of the case, move on most rapidly into the new conditions, and this helps to explain, I think, why women seem to be climbing more rapidly than men, today, the heights of spiritual power, with souls more open to the "skyey" influences of the oncoming age.

More women study today than men; a greater proportion travel abroad for purposes of culture; a larger share are moral and religious. Half of the world's wisdom, more than half its purity, and nearly all its gentleness, are today to be set down on woman's credit side. Weighted with the alcohol and tobacco habits, Brother Jonathan will have to make better time than he is doing now, if he keeps step with sister Deborah across the threshold of the twentieth century. For the law of survival of the fittest will inevitably choose that member of the firm who is cleanliest, most wholesome, most accordant with God's laws of nature and of grace, to survive. To the blindness or fatuity which renders him oblivious to the fact that the coming woman is already well-nigh here, our current writer of the

W. D. Howells and Henry James school[4] owes the dreary monotony of his "society novel." Not more "conventional" was the style of art known as "Byzantine," which repeated with barren iteration its placid and colorless "type," than are the pages of this dreary pair, whose books put a period to the literary sentence of their age. The "American novel" will not be written until the American woman, a type now to be found in Michigan, Boston, Cornell, and other universities, shall have taken her place, twentieth-century product that she is, beside the best survivals of young men in similar institutions and wrought out the Home, the Church, the State that are to be. Measuring each other on all planes, these life partners will know each other's value, and no appeal to the divorce court will be made to relieve them, a few years after marriage, from an incompatibility that has ripened into open war. Happy homes will dot the country from shore to shore, in which both the man and the woman will do their best to lift the world toward God.

"Self-knowledge, self-reverence, and self-control: these three alone lead life to sovereign power," and these are fast becoming essential to any ideal of womanly character which the modern age will recognize as the product of its institutions. Of self-knowledge, these talks have said much. Self-reverence I would fain help you to develop in your character as a woman. If my dear mother did me one crowning kindness it was in making me believe that next to being an angel, the greatest bestowment of God is to make one a woman. With what contempt she referred to the old Jewish formula in which the less refined sex rolled out the words, "I thank Thee, O God, that Thou hast not made me a woman," and with what pathos she repeated the gentle prayer of the other, "I thank Thee, O God, that Thou hast made me as it pleased Thee," with the pithy comment, "What could have pleased Him better, I should like to know, than to make one so rare, so choice, so spiritual as woman is?" Perhaps some of you may have thought you wanted to be a boy, but I seriously doubt it. You may have wanted a boy's freedom, his independence, his healthful, unimpeding style of dress, but I do not believe any true girl could ever have been coaxed to be a boy. Reverence yourself, then if you would learn one of the first elements of "How to Win" in this great world race, with its "go-as-you-please" terms, but its relentless penalties for failure.

What will the new ideal of woman *not* be? Well, for example, she will never be written down in the hotel register by her husband after this fashion: "John Smith and Wife." He would as soon think of her writing "Mrs. John Smith and Husband." Why does it not occur to anyone to designate him thus? Simply because he is so much more than that. He is a leading force in the affairs of the Church; he helps decide who shall be pastor. (So will she.) He is, perhaps, the village physician, or merchant (so she will be, perhaps—indeed they are oftentimes in partnership, nowadays, and I have found their home a blessed one.) He is the village editor. (Very likely she will be associate.) He is a voter. (She will be, beyond a peradventure.) For the same reason you will never read of her marriage that "the minister pronounced them MAN and *wife*," for that functionary would have been just as likely to pronounce them "husband and woman," a form of expression into which the regulation reporter will be likely to fall one of these days, it being, really, not one whit more idiotic than the time-worn phrase, "man and wife." The ideal woman of the future will never be designated as "the *Widow* Jones," because she will be so much more than that—"a provider" for her children, "a power" in the Church, "a felt force" in the State. I think George Eliot is the first woman to attain the post-mortem honor of having her husband called "her widower," John W. Cross having been thus indicated in English papers of the period.[5] A turn about is fair play, and the phrase is really quite refreshing to one's sense of justice. The ideal woman will not write upon her visiting-card, nor insist on having her letters addressed, to Mrs. John Smith, or Mrs. General Smith, as the case may be, but if her maiden name were Jones, she will fling her banner to the breeze as "Mrs. Mary Jones-Smith," and will be sure to make it honorable. She will not be the lay figure made and provided to illustrate the fashions of Monsieur Worth and lesser lights of the same guild; but will insist that the goddess Hygeia is the only true modiste,[6] and will dutifully obey her orders. As the Louvre Gallery proves that when men were but the parasites of the court they, too, decked themselves with earrings, high heels, powdered hair and gaudy garments, so the distorted figures in the detestable fashion-plates of today are the irrefutable proofs of woman's fractional estate; but this will not be so tomorrow, when she finds her kingdom—which is her own true self. The ideal woman will cease to heed the cruel "Thus far and no farther," which has issued from the pinched lips of old Dame Custom, checking her ardent steps throughout all the ages past, and will be studious only to hear the kindly "Thus far and no farther" of God.

The ideal woman will play Beatrice to man's Dante in the Inferno of his passions. She will give him the clue out of materialism's Labyrinth. She will be civilization's Una, taming the Lion of disease and misery. The state shall no longer go limping on one foot through the years, but shall march off with steps firm and equipoised. The keen eye and deft hand of the housekeeper shall help to make its everyday walks wholesome; the skill in detail, trustworthiness in finance, motherliness in sympathy, so long extolled in private life, shall exalt public station. Indeed, if I were asked the mission of the ideal woman, I would reply: IT IS TO MAKE THE WHOLE WORLD HOMELIKE. Someone has said that "Temperament is the climate of the individual," but home is woman's climate, her vital breath, her native air. A true woman carries home with her everywhere. Its atmosphere surrounds her; its mirror is her face; its music attunes her gentle voice; its longitude may be reckoned from wherever you happen to find her. But "home's not merely four square walls."

Some people once thought it was, and they thought also, that you might as well throw down its Lares and Penates[7] as to carry away its weaving loom and spinning wheel. But it survived this spoliation; and when women ceased to pick their own geese and do their own dyeing, it still serenely smiled. The sewing machine took away much of its occupation; the French and Chinese laundries have intruded upon its domain; indeed the next generation will no doubt turn the cook stove out of doors, and the housekeeper, standing at the telephone, will order better cooked meals than almost anyone has nowadays, sent from scientific caterers by pneumatic tubes, and the debris thereof returned to a general cleaning-up establishment; while houses will be heated, as they are now lighted and supplied with water, from general reservoirs.

Women are fortunate in belonging to the less tainted half of the race. Dr. Benjamin Ward Richardson tells us that but for this conserving fact it would deteriorate to the point of failure. A bright old lady said, after viewing a brewery, distillery, and tobacco factory: "Ain't I thankful that the women folks hain't got all that stuff to chew and smoke and swallow down!" It behooves us to offset force of muscle by force of heart, that what our strong brothers have done to subdue the material world for us, who are not their equals in physical strength, may be offset by what we shall achieve for them in bringing in the reign of "Sweeter manners, purer laws." For the world is slowly making the immense discovery that not what woman *does* but what she *is*, makes home a possible creation. It is the Lord's ark, and does not need steadying; it will survive the wreck of systems and the crash of theories, for the home is but the efflorescence of woman's nature under the nurture of Christ's Gospel. She came into the college and hallowed it, into the business world and ennobled it. She will come into government and purify it, into politics and cleanse its Stygian pool[8], for woman will make homelike every place she enters, and she will enter every place on this round earth. Any custom, or traffic, or party on which a woman cannot look with favor is irrevocably doomed. Its welcome of her presence and her power is to be the final test of its fitness to survive. All gospel civilization is radiant with the demonstration of this truth: "It is not good for man to be alone" [Genesis 2:18]. The most vivid object lesson on history's page is the fact that his deterioration is in exact proportion to his isolation from the home of woman's pure companionship. To my own grateful thought, the most sacred significance of woman's philanthropic work today lies in the fact that she occupies the outer circle in this tremendous evolution of the Christian idea of home. Ours is a high and sacred calling. Out of pure hearts fervently, let us love God and humanity; so shall we be Christ's disciples, and so shall we safely follow on to know the work whereunto we have been called. "'Tis home where'er the heart is," and no true mother, sister, daughter, or wife can fail to go in spirit after her beloved and tempted ones, as their adventurous steps enter the labyrinth of the world's temptations. We cannot call them back. "All before them lies the way."

There is but one remedy: we must bring the home to them, for they will not return to it. Still must their mothers walk beside them, sweet and serious, and clad in the garments of power. The occupations, pleasures, and ambitions of men and women must not diverge so widely from each other. Potent beyond all other facts of everyday experience is the rapidly increasing similarity between the pursuits of these two fractions that make up the human integer. When brute force reigned, this *rapport* was at zero. "Impedimenta to the rear," was the command of Caesar and the rule of every warrior—women and children being the hindrances referred to. But today there is not a motto more popular than that of the inspired old German [Friedrich Froebel], "Come, let us live for our children"; and as for women, "the world is all before them where to choose."

No greater good can come to the manhood of the world than is prophesied in the increasing community of thought and works between it and the world's womanhood. The growing individuality, independence and prestige of the gentler sex steadily require from the stronger a higher standard of character and purer habits of life. This blessed consummation, so devoutly to be wished, is hastened, dear girlish hearts, by every prayer you offer, by every hymn you sing, by every loving errand of your willing feet and gentle hands. You are the true friends of tempted humanity, bewildered youth, and every little child. The steadfast faith and loyal, patient work you are to do, in the white fields of reform, will be the mightiest factor in woman's contribution to the solution of this Republic's greatest problem, and will have their final significance in the thought and purpose, not that the world shall come into the home, but that the home, embodied and impersonated in its womanhood, shall go forth into the world.

I have no fears for the women of America. They will never content themselves remaining stationary in methods or in policy, much less sound a retreat in their splendid warfare against the saloon in law and politics. The tides of the mother's heart do not change; we can count upon them always. The voice of Miriam still cheers the brave advance, and all along the line we hear the battle cry: "Speak unto the children of Israel, that they go forward" [Exodus 14:15].

The New Ideal of Manhood

Let us remember, then, that the Ideal of Womanhood, as it exists in the minds of the grandest-natured men, is changing rapidly. But as you study "How to Win," conforming your plan of life to the new ideal which you must see clearly "in your mind's eye, Horatio" before you can proceed to study, much less to win, a certain shy question is sure to haunt your brain. "Uttered or unexpressed," it will be there, and it will be this: "Elder sister, coming freshly from life's battlefield where banners wave and squadrons wheel, you tell us that the ideal of woman is gradually changing; but *how is it with the Ideal of Man?*" Ah, gentle hearts, you do well to ask that question; it is "part of the price": not to propound it, either in the silence of your own heart or the half-apologetic tone with which I grew familiar in my teaching days (when girlish confidences were reposed in me so often), would be confessing judgment as not downright womanly yourselves. Yes, the ideal of man is changing—as it must—to keep pace with its blessed correlate.

The ideal man is a "Brother of Girls," as the choice Arab proverb phrases it. He is chivalric, but the chivalry of justice outranks that of manner and romance upon his Bill of Rights. He never says, because he never thinks, "you are only a girl," for he has grown to be the antithesis of the Jew who thanked God who had not made him a woman, and honestly believes that she is "the crowning work of God." He values her esteem and love as the most priceless of all benedictions this side of heaven, and to make himself worthy of them he sedulously determines to be free from every habit which would be unworthy of or distasteful to her. He recognizes himself as her comrade, not her master, and rejoices in their joint-partnership in all this world affords. He asserts over her no rights whatever, but is a man so good and noble that his happiness is her law, even as hers is his delight. He would deem it beneath his dignity to lay commands upon his equal, and would be as much ashamed to hint at woman's subjection, as some crude, old time men and all barbarous nations are proud to assert it. Whatever property he may have or accumulate, he regards as one half hers, not of grace but of debt, and anticipates, by his own action, those laws which will erelong assert this equitable claim. He does not think that woman exists primarily for him or for the home, but as a daughter of God, whose duties are, first of all, to her own nature and to Him by whom that nature was endowed. Similarity, not differentiation, of surroundings and pursuits is what he seeks, perceiving this to be great nature's law in all the lower forms of mated life, and believing the departure from this rule in human history to have been a temporary concession to the age of brute force. He does not ask the narrow question, "Is she good enough for certain professions, avocations, and spheres?" but rather, "Are they good enough for her?" and this he leaves for her to settle, perceiving that "under grace" she may very properly inquire, "Who made thee a judge or a rewarder over me?" [Acts 7:27]. These are some of the traits of that great, high-souled, generous nature, that "Mother's boy" who is to be. Enough specimens have strayed into this century to show us his outline, and make us sure that "the coming man" is not far off. Womanhood, in the new age, shall rejoice in this companionship. . . .

I have long believed that when the question of a life-companionship shall be decided on its merits, pure and simple, and not complicated with the other questions, "Did she get a good home?" "Is he a good provider?" "Will she have plenty of money?"; then will come the first fair chance ever enjoyed by young manhood for the building up of genuine character and conduct. For it is an immense temptation to the "sowing of wild oats," when the average youth knows that the smiles he covets most will be his all the same, no matter whether he smokes, swears, drinks beer, and plays cards or not. The knowledge, on his part, that the girls in his village and "set" have no way out of dependence, reproach, and oddity, except to say "Yes" when he chooses to "propose": that they dare not frown on his lower mode of life; that the world is all before him where to *choose;* that not one girl in one hundred has been endowed with the talent and the pluck that make her independent of him and his ilk; all this gives him a sense of freedom to do wrong which, added to inherited appetite and outward temptation, is impelling the youth of our day to ruin with a force strong as gravitation, and relentless as fate. Then, the utterly false sense of his own value and importance which "Young America" acquires, from seeing the sweetest, truest, most attractive being on earth thus virtually subject to him, often develops a lordliness of manner which is too pitiful for words, in boys who, otherwise, would have been modest, sensible, and brotherly young fellows, such as we are, most of all, likely to find in co-education schools, where girls take their full share of the prizes, and many of them have in mind "a career." A thousand forces in law and gospel are today conspiring for the deliverance of our young men from the snares of their present artificial environment and estimate of their own value; but the elevation of their sisters to the plane of perfect financial independence, from which they can dictate the equitable terms, "You must be as pure and true as you require me to be, ere I give you my hand," is the brightest hope that gleams in the sky of modern civilization for our brothers; and the greater freedom of women to make of marriage an affair of the heart and not of the purse, is the supreme result of Christianity up to this hour.

Notes

1. By William Matthews, S.C. Griggs: Chicago, 1873.

2. *Shirley* (1849), by English novelist Charlotte Brontë, was a plea for more useful occupations for women. The novel's heroine was a woman with freedom and the power to act decisively in the world.

3. Willard's neighbor lent her a collection of William Wordsworth's poetry, a volume of correspondence of German historian Barthold Georg Niebuhr, a collection of essays by Thomas Carlyle and other British essayists, the essays of American Ralph Waldo Emerson, a memoir of American Transcendentalist Margaret Fuller Ossoli, and a popular biography of Thomas Arnold, headmaster of Rugby, a model English public school.

4. Novelists William Dean Howells (1837–1920) and Henry James (1843–1916) were pioneers of the realist school in American fiction. Willard found their portrayals of women characters too passive and dependent.

5. Willard referred to midnineteenth-century English novelist George Eliot (Mary Ann Evans, 1819–80), who married John Walter Cross (1840–1924) late in her life.

6. Charles Frederick Worth (1826–95) founded Maison Worth in both Paris and London and dictated elite women's fashions on both sides of the Atlantic in the late nineteenth century. Hygeia was the Greek goddess of health.

7. In Roman mythology Lares and Penates were groups of deities who protected the home and family, as well as the Roman state. Statues depicting these gods were worshipped at household shrines.

8. The term "Stygian pool" is a reference to the river Styx, the principal river of the underworld in Greek mythology, and indicates a dark, dismal, even hellish place.

THIRTEEN

"The Greatest Party," May 30, 1888

"The Greatest Party," was the address Willard delivered for the Decoration Day (now called Memorial Day) observance held in Indianapolis, Indiana, at the national convention of the Prohibition Party. During the mid-1880s both the WCTU and the Prohibition Party grew quickly in numbers and political influence and the connection between them strengthened. By the 1888 presidential campaign, the two organizations were nearing the height of their power and the Prohibition Party convention was a great celebration of that combined power. More than one thousand delegates gathered at the end of May—one hundred of them women. The convention attracted several thousand more supporters from every region of the country. A large banner reading "No North, No South, No Distinction in Politics, No Sex in Citizenship" hung over the speakers' platform, announcing the bold reconciling and liberating themes of the convention. In her autobiography Willard described the event as "the most remarkable in the history of the Temperance Reform." The rising power of the Prohibition Party's new political ideals, especially its inclusion of women in leadership positions, she believed, marked it as a "moral watershed."[1]

Party chair Samuel Dickie[2] asked Willard to deliver the Decoration Day Address, the centerpiece of the convention, before an audience that included five hundred members of "The Army of the Blue and the Gray," a group of Civil War veterans from both North and South who supported the Prohibition Party. The massive crowd of some five thousand people in Tomlinson Hall was among the most enthusiastic Willard faced outside the WCTU. According to the *Indianapolis Journal,* when introduced, she touched off a standing ovation that lasted "more than a minute," and her speech itself was "interrupted continually by applause."[3] Willard built on the patriotic fervor of the crowd and tailored her speech to the veterans in her audience, emphasizing the theme of reconciliation between former enemies. Employing poems, songs, and narratives of Civil War heroes and recalling the deep sentiments and passions the war had generated on both sides, she begged them to move on from their grief and unite in the common causes of temperance and women's suffrage. She called on both women and men from South and North to enlist in a war different from the destructive one the nation had lived through only two decades earlier, one in which their guns would be ballots and their bullets, ideas.

Neither the Republican nor the Democratic Party, Willard insisted, could put the war behind them and move on to confront the looming threat of the liquor power or to embrace the opportunity of working toward women's suffrage. Only the Prohibition Party—"The Greatest Party"—placed those two aims at the very forefront of their agenda, along with a concern for the rights of wage workers. As she had done in many previous speeches to her own organization, she invoked the powerful symbol of home and rallied the temperance forces in its defense.

Willard ended her speech with a reminder of the party's commitment to women's equality. She took those sentiments and her sense of their enthusiastic reception into the evening meeting of the party's Committee on Resolutions where she and others argued to include a women's suffrage plank in the party platform. A compromise measure was reached that endorsed women's suffrage limited by an educational requirement. On the convention floor the following day, debate over women's suffrage was heated. Several male delegates spoke against including the plank, convinced that it was politically unwise to link the controversial issue with prohibition and that women's suffrage must wait until prohibition was won. Willard, however, closed the debate with a brief defense of women's suffrage as a right, a claim she had not made during the early 1880s, preferring to focus on the women's vote as a weapon of protection for the home. She dismissed the notion that the push for women's suffrage would follow the victory for prohibition, naming instances at the state level where this had not happened. Instead, she called for the simultaneous support of both issues, a strategy the convention adopted. Although omission of the suffrage plank had been advocated by only a small minority of delegates, the *Chicago Tribune* credited Willard's speech with winning the day for women's suffrage.[4]

The text of "The Greatest Party" is from *Our Day* 1 (June 1888), 505–10. It can also be found in Willard, *Glimpses,* 447–52.

* * *

Here side by side sit the Blue and the Gray. No other than the Prohibition Party ever dared to be so great as to ordain a scene like this. I speak the words of truth—and soberness.

What a circle we have here! Sweep the compasses of thought through its circumference. Prohibition, first of all, the fixed point whence we calculate all others. The Blue and the Gray, the workingmen, the women. Enclosed and shielded by this circle is the home—that goes without saying; and beyond its shining curve is the saloon, out-matched, out-witted, and out-voted, which, in a republic, is best of all. For the fiat of the greatest party has gone forth, and we are here simply to set our seals to it: no saloon in politics or law, no sectionalism in law or politics, no sex in citizenship, but liberty, equality, fraternity in politics and law, now and forevermore.

This is our platform in a nutshell, and it is a platform of four ideas at least.

When, in all history, were such matchless issues espoused by such magnanimous men?

There are two other parties; big but not great; multitudinous, not masterful. Their tissue is adipose, not muscular. The issues of the one are made literally out of whole cloth, of all-wool tariff, warranted to wash in yet one more campaign, and the ensanguined shirt warranted never to be washed at all. Those of the other are spoils and Bourbonism.[5] They will soon rally their respective clans to their stereotyped, old-fashioned conventions in Chicago and St. Louis, prepared to fight, bleed, and die for their country and its offices once more. Not a woman will be in their delegations. A woman might displace some man. Not a word about the home. No decisive utterance as to the greatest of our national perils.

Probably women would not attend these conventions, even were their presence sought. They certainly could not hold their own at the bar of the saloon, while in the greatest party they are only required to hold their own at the bar of public opinion.

Meanwhile, as if to set before these brethren a loftier example, the greatest party welcomes here the home folks to equal opportunities and honors, and rallies here a remnant of the noble veterans who have learned that it is good to forgive, best to forget, attesting by this splendid and fraternal object lesson, that one party spells "nation" with the tallest kind of a capital "N"—one that indeed includes "the *people* of these United States"—and that the Blue and the Gray are to us emblems of nothing less than the blue sky that bends its tender arch above us all, and the gray ocean that enfolds one country and one flag.

> Angels look downward from the skies
> Upon no holier ground,
> Than where defeated valor lies
> By generous foemen crowned.

How [Ulysses S.] Grant would have rejoiced to look upon a scene like this—he whose most memorable words were, "Let us have peace!" by whose sick bed sat General [Simon Bolivar] Buckner of the Confederate army, and to whose recent birthday celebration rallied Fitz Hugh Lee and other Southern braves!

The leaders of the party that was great when great Lincoln was its chief are pleased in these days of its fatal degeneracy to call us "the Saint Johnites." He is our patron saint—Heaven bless him!—who laid himself upon the altar of our sacred cause, and in the flame of partisan wrath that followed the defeat of 1884 proved to be a whole burnt offering, yet I present him to you here tonight, one of the most gallant Union soldiers, "without the smell of fire upon his garments."

That party dare not gather Blue and Gray at its convention, lest they should spoil its ammunition and tip one chief plank of its platform into the last ditch. What would it do if thus ruthlessly deprived of that timeworn utterance about a "free ballot and a fair count," which in its long years of supremacy it has proved itself impotent to secure, while the greatest party, by dividing the white vote into two hostile camps on the prohibition issue, is opening a straight path for the black man to the polls?

The women who uniformed their sons in Southern gray, and said, like the Spartan mother of old, "Come ye as conquerors or come ye no more," are here tonight with those other women who belted Northern swords upon their boys in blue, with words as pitiless and brave. The women who embroidered stars and stripes upon the blessed flag that symbolized their love and faith, today have only gentle words for those who decked their "bonny flag of stars and bars" with tenderness as true and faith as fervent. The greatest party seats these women side by side tonight, and we all wear our snowy badge of peace about the hearts that hate no more, while we clasp hands in a compact never to be broken, and solemnly declare, before high heaven, our equal hatred of the rum power and our equal loyalty to God and home and native land.

What hath God wrought? Surely a winsome thing is the human heart. It went against the grain for us to hate each other, did it not, dear Southern friends and allies? Never in history was there a war involving so little personal animosity. The French by nature hate the English and speak about "perfidious Albion," and we know that "lands intersected by a narrow frith [estuary] abhor each other," but our great unsevered continent was meant for an unsevered people, and "man breaks not the medal when God cuts the die." One Anglo-Saxon race, having one heritage of a queenly language and a heroic history of hardship mutually borne—it was hard for us to hate each other. The soldiers learned this first, brave and chivalric fellows, and they helped to teach us stay-at-homes the gracious lesson of fraternity. How often was the rude wreath of leaves placed on the grave of a Confederate by the Union soldier who had killed and yet had wept over him! The fury of the noncombatant was almost the only fury that survived Grant's brotherly words to Lee at Appomattox.

Devoted to the stars and stripes, the sentiment of patriotism having been, from childhood, like a fire in the bones with me, I have wept over the flag for love of which great [Thomas Jonathan] Stonewall Jackson and gallant Albert Sydney Johnston died. Nor do I envy the Northern patriot who can read without a tugging of the heart that wondrous poem by Father [Abram Joseph] Ryan the Southern Catholic priest, about "The Sword of Lee," and I can hardly trust myself to repeat his requiem of the Southern flag.

Fold that banner, for 'tis weary;
Round its staff 'tis floating dreary,
Furl it, fold it; it is best;
For there's not a man to wave it,
And there's not a sword to save it,
And there's not one left to lave it
In the blood that heroes gave it,
And its foes now scorn and brave it;
Furl it, hide it, let it rest.

Furl that banner, furl it sadly;
Once ten thousands hailed it gladly,
And ten thousands wildly, madly
Swore it should forever wave.
Swore that foeman's sword should never,
Hearts like their entwined dissever,
Till that flag should float forever
O'er their freedom or their grave.

Furl that banner, softly, slowly;
Treat it gently, it is holy,
For it droops above the dead.
Touch it not, unfold it never,
Let it drop there furled forever,
For its people's hopes are dead.

Not that I loved that flag. No, indeed. I loved the slave too well not to desire its downfall; but then, so many brave hearts bled for it, so many gentle women wept, that I could be sincerely sorry for their grief, and yet be loyal to an emancipated race and my own glorious North. When the troops were mustered out in 1865, we little dreamed that less than ten years later the home guards of the land would be mustered into the war of the crusade. God bless the Crusade state [Ohio], the veteran of our army!

As the sequel of that mighty movement, God's Pentecost of power upon the nations, behold the women who, only a year ago, went to the polls to persuade men to cast their ballot for prohibition in Oregon and Texas, in Michigan and Tennessee. If the voters of the greatest party are true to us as we have been and will be true to them, ten years hence we will help those who were beaten in four states that stood for constitutional prohibition in 1885, with our guns that are ballots, as we are now helping with our bullets that are ideas.

I never expected to speak with pride about the solid South as such, but surely I may do this now that it is becoming solid for the "dry ticket," and you who dwell there may be glad that the Northern heart is fired once more, this time with the same war cry as that which fires the Southern, and it is "protection for our homes." That is the spell to conjure by. That is the rallying call of North and

South, Protestant and Catholic, of white and black, of men and women equally. Bourbon Democrat and Radical Republican will seek in vain to stifle this swift-swelling chorus, that "Chorus of the Union," for which great Lincoln vainly prayed in his first inaugural. Do you not recall his marvelous concluding sentence (I quote from memory): "The mystic chords of memory, stretching from many a sacred hearth and patriot's grave all over this broad land, shall once more swell the chorus of the Union when again touched, as surely they will be, by the better angel of our nature." That angel is the temperance reform, and the fulfillment of that prophecy we have lived to see.

The greatest party stands for nationalism as against sectionalism; it stands for the noblest aims and aspirations of the wageworker as against monopolies that dare to profane that holy word, "trust"; it stands for the future in politics as against the past, the home vote with an educational test as against the saloon vote with a beer-breath as its credentials; and best of all, it stands for the everlasting and ab-solute prohibition of sin as against any alliance between sin and the government. For while the greatest party will never hesitate to be the champion of these causes good and great, so closely linked with its own central purposes, neither must it fail to put prohibition by law and prohibition by politics so far in the lead that no can-did man can for a moment question the august supremacy of these overmastering issues. We are firmly persuaded that the separation of the people into two distinct armies, one voting for men who will outlaw the poison curse, and the other for men who will legalize it, must come, and that such separation cannot come too soon. We are not here to speak harsh words of armies rallied under other ensigns, but simply to declare that in this great emergency we cannot depend on them. Party machinery and the ambition of party leaders today stand between the people and their opportunity. We would clear the track for prohibition. We are bound to do it. For that were we born and for that came we into this world.

When I think of Lexington and Paul Revere; when I think of Bunker Hill and the dark redoubt where General [Joseph] Warren died; when I think of [George] Washington, that greatest of Southerners, upon his knees in prayer at Valley Forge; when I think of Stonewall Jackson praying before he fought; of Robert E. Lee and Sidney Johnston's stainless shields; when I remember [Philip] Sheridan's ride (alas! That the hero of Winchester hears the stealthy steps of the Pale Horse whose unrelenting Rider comes to bear him away from a grateful and admir-ing people into the Silent Land), and [William T.] Sherman's march to the sea with the boys in blue behind him, and Grant fighting the battle out and on to the glorious triumph of our Northern arms, then my heart prophesies with all a patriot's gratitude, America will win as against the awful tyranny of King Alcohol and King Gambrinus, and proud am I to have a part in it, for thank God I—I, too, am an American.

Bound together by one mutual faith in Mary T. Lathrap of Michigan and Sallie F. Chapin of South Carolina; cemented by the martyr blood of Iowa's George

B. Haddock and Mississippi's Roderick Dhu Gambrell; made one by the pride we feel for these grand old pioneers, John Russell, the father of our party; James Black, its earliest presidential candidate; Gideon Stewart and H. A. Thompson; St. John and Daniel, the heroes of a latter day and a more dreadful crisis; Green Clay Smith and Samuel Dickie, Hopkins and Brooks, Clinton B. Fisk and George W. Bain, and glorious old Neal Dow, the father of prohibition for the world,[6] surely temperance people of the North and South may well say each to the other, "Where thou goest I will go; where thou lodgest I will lodge; thy people shall be my people, and thy God my God. The Lord do so to me and more, also, if aught but death part thee and me" [Ruth 1:16–17].

Here upon Indiana's genial soil, midway between the sections that shall ere long be sections no more, but part of the greatest party's family circle, gracious and great, let us unitedly say to the fire-eaters of the South on the one side and the chasm-diggers of the North on the other:

> Oh, meaner folks of narrower souls,
> Heirs of ignoble thought,
> Stirs not the campfire's blackened coals,
> Blood-drenched by those who fought,
> Lest out of heaven a fire shall yet
> Bear God's own vengeance forth
> On those who once again would set
> Discord 'twixt South and North.

In the spring of 1863 two great armies were encamped on either side of the Rappahannock River, one dressed in blue and one in gray. As twilight fell, the bands of music on the Union side began to play the martial strains, "The Star Spangled Banner" and "Rally 'Round the Flag," and that musical challenge was taken up by those on the other side, who responded with the "Bonnie Blue Flag" and "Away Down South in Dixie." After a while it was borne in upon the soul of a single soldier in one of those bands of music to begin a sweeter and more tender air, and slowly as he played it they joined with all the instruments on the Union side until finally a great an mighty chorus swelled up and down our army, "Home Sweet Home." When they had finished there was no challenge over yonder, and every confederate band had taken up that lovely air, so attuned to all that is holiest and dearest, and one great chorus of two great hosts went up to God; and when they had finished came from the boys in gray a challenge, "Three cheers for home," and as these cheers went resounding through the skies from both sides of the river, "Something upon the soldier's cheek washed off the stain of powder."

Fellow soldiers in the fight for a clear brain, I am proud to belong to an army which makes kindred of those who once stood in arms against each other. Let us cherish North Carolina's motto from Isaiah's words: "Fear not, I am with thee; I will bring thy seed from the east and gather them from the west; I will say to the north *give up,* and to the south *keep not back,* bring my sons from afar, and my daughters from the ends of the earth" [Isaiah 43:5–6]. I am glad of these good times, and I think we women are in them, equal members of the greatest party, as we have been since the day of its birth.

> It shall shine more and more
> Till its glory like noontide shall be.
> It shall shine more and more
> Till the home from the dramshop is free.
> It shall shine more and more
> Till the nation Christ's glory shall see.

Notes

1. Willard, *Glimpses,* 437.

2. Canadian born Samuel Dickie (1851–1925) was the Prohibition National Committee chair from 1887–1900. Though active politically—he was the Prohibition candidate for governor of Michigan in 1886—he was ineligible to be the party's presidential candidate because of his foreign birth. From 1901–21 he was president of Albion College in Michigan.

3. *Indianapolis Journal,* May 31, 1888, in scrapbook 32, Frances E. Willard Memorial Library.

4. *Chicago Tribune,* June 1, 1888. The *Indianapolis Sentinel,* June 1, 1888, carried a partial transcript of Willard's extemporaneous comments that closed the debate.

5. *Bourbonism* was a term used after the Civil War to describe the conservative southern Democratic Party that supported segregationist politics and was allied with the liquor interests.

6. Here Willard intoned the names of prominent northern and southern women and men, all active in the temperance cause and the Prohibition Party. Mary Torrance Lathrap (1853–95) was the Michigan WCTU president and a powerful temperance and women's suffrage orator. Sallie Chapin was noted earlier. George Haddock (1832–86) of Iowa and Roderick Dhu Gambrell (1865–87) of Mississippi were both antisaloon activists murdered for their reform efforts in the late 1880s. Most of the other men that Willard names were national Prohibition Party candidates for president and vice president: James Black (1823–93) of Pennsylvania and John Russell (1822–1912) of Michigan in 1872; Green Clay Smith (1832–95) of Kentucky and Gideon Stewart (1824–1909) of Ohio in 1876; Neal Dow of Maine and Henry Adams Thompson of Ohio in 1880; John P. St. John of Kansas and William Daniel (1826–97) of Maryland in 1884; and Clinton B. Fisk (1828–90) of New Jersey and John Anderson Brooks (1836–97) of Missouri in 1888. Dickie was noted earlier. Alphonso Alva Hopkins (1843–1918) was editor of the *Voice,* the major temperance newspaper from 1884–1912. Hopkins, as well as George W. Bain (1840–97), was also a popular and effective temperance lecturer.

FOURTEEN

"The Dawn of Woman's Day," October 4, 1888

In the fall of 1888 Willard delivered her inaugural address, "The Dawn of Woman's Day," as president of the newly founded Chicago Women's League. This local umbrella organization, formed through alliances with fifty-seven existing women's groups in the Chicago area, was the outgrowth of a similar movement to coordinate the efforts of women's organizations at the national and international levels. According to *The History of Woman Suffrage,* Elizabeth Cady Stanton initiated the founding of an International Council of Women among women leaders meeting in Liverpool, England, in 1883. In 1888 at the International Council of Women meeting in Washington, D.C., a National Council of Women for the United States was formed. Frances Willard was elected president of this National Council, a position which placed her at the head of virtually all of America's organized women.

Energized by their vision of organized women's possibilities, Willard, and other founders of the National Council of Women,[1] set to work building a network of state and local women's councils or leagues that could unite the leaders of the various women's organizations working at each of these levels. Willard hoped to re-create, on a much broader scale, the structure of the WCTU where the local unions provided the grassroots strength, yet the combined power of these unions at the state and national level gave legitimacy as a national voice for temperance and other reforms. These efforts bore immediate fruit in Chicago, where there was a strong tradition of women's activism. During the summer of 1888, press coverage of the abysmal working conditions of women and children in that city had encouraged women's labor organizations to look for ways to extend the influence of their unions. The leaders of these organizations combined with those of other reform efforts in the city to form the Chicago Woman's League.

On October 4, 1888, when the league held its inaugural meeting, numerous reports were given on topics ranging from the working conditions of women in Chicago's factories and shops to the development of kindergartens within the city. According to the *Inter-Ocean,* however, "The principle feature of the meeting was the reading of the inaugural address by the President, Miss Frances E. Willard."[2]

The address announced the broadening of Willard's reform vision; guided by the "star that is JUSTICE," she called women to act "wherever there is a sister more downtrodden than any other." The speech articulated the means, goals, and effects of harnessing and organizing the philanthropic impulse of women—what she called the "mother-love" of the nation. Introducing her listeners to the charge of the National Council of Women—to band together with other women workers to transform society, Willard went on to explain the wisdom of extending its principles to the state and local levels. She hoped that organizations such as the National Council would be the last step in women's "training for our true position as the equal partners of men in the great world and its work."

The address explored the many benefits of women's new levels of organization. In addition to strengthening the power of their appeals to governmental bodies to enact reforms, such united efforts would also lift women out of the parochial world views that often resulted from a single-minded focus on one particular issue or reform. The Chicago Woman's League would also have practical benefits for the everyday lives of women since bringing women together for work outside the home would necessitate various changes to deal with the work women had traditionally done within the home. More than any other in her corpus, this speech illustrated Willard's optimism that modern inventions would revolutionize the ways people cared for their homes and families. Public laundries, a catering system, and paid teams of housekeepers would increase the health, happiness, and beauty of Chicago's homes.

Willard's call for women's united action to improve the conditions of the workplace and home as well as to broaden the perspective of reform-minded women reached beyond Chicago to a national audience with its publication in the WCTU's *Union Signal* and the reform journal *Our Day.* Through her message she intended to inspire "each village, town, and city" to establish its own council of women. The speech evidenced, in its incipient form, a Christian Socialist perspective as she advised using pooled resources to correct the nation's injustices. Willard would continue to develop this perspective throughout the next decade.

Excerpts from "The Dawn of Woman's Day" are from *Our Day,* 2 (November 1888), 345–60.

* * *

There is a prayer, uttered or unexpressed, that brings us face to face, and it is this: "Help me to heal the heart-break of humanity." The measureless injustice that surrounds us like an atmosphere and the fathomless misery that broods over us like a malaria make many a murmuring heart cry out:

> Had I God's power or He my love,
> We'd have a different world from this we see.

But the philosophic mind perceives that everywhere God works by means, and that evermore the Christ-spirit must be incarnate or it cannot carry out its miracles of healing. In the order of evolution it is first of all embodied in the individual, then in the home, then in society, then in the State, and some day shall be in that Universal Republic of which the Laureate [Alfred Lord Tennyson] sings, when

> The flags shall all be furled
> In the Parliament of Man, the Federation of the World.

Our meeting here hastens that coming consummation. Mother-love works magic for humanity, but organized mother-love works miracles. Mother-hearted women are called to be the saviors of the race. I speak it reverently, as a loyal worshiper of Him who said, "Mother, behold thy Son" [John 19:26].

New Organizations of Women

We all know that organization is the one great thought of nature. It is the difference between chaos and order; it is the incessant occupation of God. But, next to God, the greatest organizer on this earth is the mother. She who sends forth from the sanctuary of her own being a little child has organized a great spiritual world, and set it moving in the orbit of unchanging law. Hence woman, by her organism, is the greatest organizer ever organized by our beneficent Creator.

But in the nature of the case, the mother, patiently preoccupied in deeds of love for those about her, has been slowest of all to reflect on her own innate powers, and has not until recently so much as dreamed of the resistless force of the world's aggregated motherhood. When I was graduated from college in 1859 there was not on the face of the earth, I venture to say—certainly there was not in my native land, the most progressive land of all—a national society of women. We worked on in weakness and seclusion, in loneliness and isolation. But we learned at last the gracious secret that has transformed the world for men and made them masters. We learned the mighty difference between the wide, open hand with individual fingers impotent because separate, and the condensed, constructive, organized power of those fingers when combined. We learned that floating timbers on the sea are not more futile as compared with the same timbers when organized into a ship than are solitary human beings as compared with the same persons when organized and instructed, unified and equipped in societies and guilds. The mighty work done to mitigate the horrors of our Civil War first revealed to us and to our brothers the latent power of the nation's womanhood; next came the holy zeal of the Women's Foreign Missionary Societies; then the heavenly enthusiasm of the Woman's Temperance Crusade, with its marvelous sequel, the Woman's Christian Temperance Unions; then the beautiful younger sister, the Woman's Home Missionary Society, while the Women's Christian Association and Congress, the women's clubs, industrial and educational unions, relief corps, protective agencies, the mighty labor movement, and the countless societies for local help to the sick, the friendless, and the poor abundantly testify to that *esprit de corps* which we women have at last acquired and are now so sure to utilize for purposes of blessing vastly wider, more pervasive, and more varied than we could at first have dared to undertake or dreamed of compassing.

Mother-Hearts as Leaders of Reform

From this time on the world will have in it no active, organic force so strong for its uplifting as its organized mother-hearts. You will notice the breadth of my generalization. I do not say "all mothers," because all women who are technically mothers are not "mother-hearted," while many a woman is so, from whom the crisscross currents of the world have withheld her holiest crown. . . .

It has required more than a generation of training within the sheltering circle of the church, where most of us have had our schooling in organized endeavor, to prepare us for so large a thought as was launched at Washington, D. C., last spring in the International Council. We knew that by the law of fittest survival, each group of women working together according to a plan develops its own leadership. But there and then began the widest evolution possible to us as women and the last in our slow process of training for our true position as the equal partners of men in the great world and its work. . . .

Platform of Woman's World's Council

It is the unanimous voice of this council that all institutions of learning, and of professional instruction, including schools of theology, law, and medicine, should, in the interest of humanity, be as freely opened to women as to men; that opportunities for industrial training should be as generally and liberally provided for one sex as for the other. The representatives of organized womanhood in this council will steadily demand that in all avocations in which both men and women engage equal wages shall be paid for equal work; and, finally, that an enlightened society should adopt, as the only adequate expression of the high civilization which it is its office to establish and maintain, an identical standard of personal purity and morality for men and women.

The general declaration of the National Council of the United States as well as of the World's Council was as follows:

> We women, sincerely believing that the best good of our homes and nation will be advanced by our own greater unity of thought, sympathy, and purpose, and that an organized movement of women will best conserve the highest good of the family and the state, do hereby band ourselves together in a confederation

of workers committed to the overthrow of all forms of ignorance and injustice and to the application of the Golden Rule to society, custom, and law. This council is organized in the interest of no one propaganda, and has no power over its auxiliaries beyond that of suggestion and sympathy; therefore no society voting to become auxiliary to this council shall thereby render itself liable to be interfered with in respect to its complete organic unity, independence, and methods of work, or be committed to any principle or method of any other society, or to any utterance or act of the council itself, beyond compliance with the terms of this constitution.

How Women Are Organizing

No sooner was this new thought launched on the seething waves of journalism than good women everywhere began to say to one another: "If unification is strength in the national movements of women, why not in the States, and why not in each city, town, and village? If, as the Council Women said in their preamble, such an organization 'will incalculably increase the world's sum total of womanly courage, efficiency, and *esprit de corps,* widen our horizon, correct the tendency to an exaggerated impression of the value of one's own work as compared with that of others, and put the wisdom and experience of each at the service of all,' then let us all have councils, local and state, and let us have them speedily."

Here in Chicago seventy societies have already responded to the call and fifty-seven have allied themselves with the new movement. In Kansas a state woman's council was organized, as I suppose, this week, and another will be in Ohio the 11th of this month. I have never known a movement among women so enthusiastic and spontaneous. The time for it has fully come; the clock of God has struck the hour, and the best manhood of the manliest nation reaches out a brother's hand of help to us as we move forward bearing woman's white flag of peace, inscribed, "For Home and for Humanity." This is the latest outgrowth of that gospel which raises woman up and with her lifts toward Heaven the world.

Some of the Reflex Results

Let us think for a little while about the results to be expected from this movement. Naturally they will be twofold: First, the reflex influence of such association upon the members themselves. For instance: Here is a woman devoted to self-culture. She learns, not to put aside her Plato, but to alternate its study with that of Helen Campbell's *Prisoners of Poverty* and to divide her time at the art gallery with her visits to the white slaves.[3] Here is a woman who is so devoted to the Waif's Mission that she takes no time for books. Her association with the self-culturist leads her to ask for *Emerson's Essays* at the Public Library, and perhaps to advance so far beyond her former horizon as to join a Robert Browning club.[4] Here is a home missionary woman devoted to the Bohemians, not of journalism, but of Pilsen on the *Nord Seit*.[5] She is assigned to duty with a foreign missionary woman, and from association with her discovers that electricity and steel have shrunk the world till it is hardly bigger than an orange, that the Bohemian beyond the sea needs looking after just as badly as his brother on this side, while the zenanas [harems] of India and the Congo atrocities in Africa[6] become so vivid in recital as to seem knocking for relief at her door. Meanwhile the foreign missionary woman at her side makes the useful discovery that the telescope of observation by which she was wont to bring the distant near can be adjusted as a microscope, magnifying to her perceptions the tenement-house horrors of her own city. Here is a temperance woman who solemnly believed that prohibition was the be-all of the republic's hopes and the end-all of its sorrows; but the Knight of Labor woman at her elbow convinced her that better economic conditions enter into that colossal problem and prevailed on her to read Edward Bellamy's[7] wonderful book, entitled *Looking Backward,* while the working woman graciously accepted in return a copy of the platform of the Prohibition party, which appeared to be quite edifying reading. Here again is a Republican woman placed alongside a Democratic woman, and as true yokefellows they go on a legal embassy from the Women's to the City Council, and whatever their opinion of their respective parties may be, from what they there perceive they will be pretty sure to gain from one another a more hopeful view of those two great marching armies of civilization, whose guns are ballots and whose bullets are ideas.

Here is a Protestant woman who thinks there is no good in Catholics, never was, and never will be, but she is placed on the Public Library Committee with a communicant of the Cathedral, and finds her "so much like other folks" that she would really have supposed her to be a devout Presbyterian, while the Catholic sister comes into kindly fellowship with her Baptist committeewoman, and will never again believe but that Protestants are really reputable people and quite likely to be saved.

Thus in a thousand ways the blessed education into a tolerant spirit goes swiftly on; the cobwebs of ignorance are brushed away; the rusty chains of prejudice are filed in two, and sectarianism is replaced by sisterly love; meanwhile the horizon of the heart is widened because the outlook of the brain is elevated, and into the lonesome little coves, inlets, and bays flow the strong, healthful tides of life's cosmopolitan sea.

But this is only the beginning. These women in council will not be theorists—they will be above all else practitioners in that word's widest sense. They will have no use for any philosophy of life that cannot be translated in terms of good works as well as of good will. Their deeds will all be "deeds of weekday holiness, nor will they ever chance to learn that aught is easier than to bless." In the wide realm of human misery they will have one guiding star and that is JUSTICE. Wherever there is a sister more downtrodden than any other, more helpless and forgotten, there by the law of spiritual gravitation they will delight to invest the weight of their power and the momentum of their united enthusiasm.

Effects on the Home

But while we believe the reflex influence of the Woman's League upon its members will be of incalculable value to them all, we are chiefly concerned today with its reaction upon the five great organized forces by which the council is environed—namely, the home, the school, society, the church, and government.

The united wisdom and work of Chicago's organized womanhood directed upon Chicago homes will mean a better knowledge of sanitation and hygiene as applied to home architecture, ventilation, drainage, light, heat, diet, and dress adornings. If the best and broadest-natured housekeepers, or, as I like a thousand times better to call them, the homemakers of our city, could put their heads together over this problem of the modern home, as their husbands do over the problem of rapid street-car transit and the bridge question, I believe that such an impetus would be given to invention and such encouragement to enterprise that the following improvements would be wrought out within ten years:

Hot water and steam-heated air supplied to every house as gas is now from common reservoirs; a public laundry system, so complete as to drive the wash-tub out of every kitchen, banishing forever the reign of a steamy, sudsy, indigo-blue Monday; and a caterer's system so complete as to send the cooking-stove into perpetual exile. If men had these problems on hand, complicated with the unspeakable servant-girl problem, they would have solved them by a syndicate long before this, putting no end of money in their purses and no end of misery outside of home's four walls. The servant-girl question will erelong be answered by not having servant-girls. The relations of the maid-of-all-work to the average household are abnormal, if not to a degree inhuman. They ought to be abolished, and will be in the growing unrest and uplift of the wage-worker on the one hand and the growing tendency of the employer to look upon this woman as a convenient "Celtic apparatus" on the other. Invention, enterprise, and associated effort, stimulated by the united wit and wisdom of united housekeepers, will lead us out of this wilderness.

Cooperative Housekeeping

I often think, when rejoicing in the homelike amenities of a vestibule train, with its day-coach, dining-car, and sleeper, that if George M. Pullman[8] could be induced by a council of women to give five years of his wonderful brain to this problem of household comfort off the rails, counseling with the housekeepers, as he would be wise enough to do, he might crown his splendid life by carrying into the average home the same wholesale comforts and elegances with which he now regales the traveling public. Only in that case we must petition him to spare us the diffusive atmosphere of that horrible smoker's annex. He would have his house porters who would come around regularly and set everything to rights, build fires in the open grate, just for the beauty and coziness thereof, and clear up the house generally; his pneumatic tubes through which to send the meals ordered by telephone, and waiters detailed, so many to the block, to serve and gather up the fragments of the same, at far less cost than now, taking the wholesale contract by the year, while the average excellence of viands prepared by experts would be far higher than at present, with a proportionate increase in the health and happiness of the families thus served. To preserve the individuality, the privacy, and sanctity of home while diminishing its cost and friction is the problem that women in council must set themselves to solve. Notable homemakers, ready for the next thing, and not afraid of it because it is the next and not the last, should be organized into a standing committee on this subject.

Specialists in Household Industry

What is done on a large scale places the doer on a vantage-ground financially, socially, legally, and every way. The boardinghouse, that sepulchre of domestic happiness, would disappear to the incalculable advantage of husband, mother, and child, and the notable women who have a genius for affairs and now conduct our boardinghouses would find a broader field in the supervision of apartment houses and other details of the better housekeeping arrangements herein pro-posed, while the bachelor who now leads the sorry life of "a young man about town" would find his pathway to the marriage altar far less hedged about with financial briars and brambles, a "home of his own"—that dearest wish of every true man's heart—having become possible on easy terms.

Specialists in industry everywhere command respect and have a first mortgage on success, but the infinite variety of industries that a maid-of-all-work must carry on, whose thankless task is never done and seldom well done, ought at this advanced stage of invention and enterprise to follow the otherwise almost universal law of corporate direction. Each branch of her never-ending duties is capable of being so administered as to make it a great business controlled by the best brains and handled by trained experts.

The only class that yet retains the badge of servitude in its name of servant girl deserves the utmost consideration at the hands of women well to do, for what other class has placed us upon such a vantage ground? While I believe that the tendency of the time is toward such a scientific rectification of household duties as will render the office of maid-of-all-work obsolete, I believe that for the present distress a training school for domestics would be a boon to housekeepers and a capital help for hired helpers which this league of women might well lend its great influence to establish and maintain.

It has been justly said that many now living have seen in the last eight years changes for the better that the previous eight centuries have hardly noticed. "The tendency of today is to afford to each individual in the community a service that would once have been attainable only to the man of large wealth. In all directions the tendency is toward making the advantages of the few the privilege of all, and the all can collectively afford a better service than the few." When the public learns that it can do anything better and cheaper by concerted action, it will not be slow to make new applications of that lesson, and household industries will be differentiated and specialized to a degree that will solve the servant-girl question to the advantage of all concerned and assign the well-disposed and capable among such girls to the fast multiplying trades and occupations now opening to women on every hand.

"And the earth helped the woman" [Revelation 12:16], is one of the Bible's grandest prophecies, fulfilled for us and yet to be far more perfectly fulfilled in the material inventions whereby woman shall be relieved from the drudgery of daily toil and lifted to the level of her highest and her holiest ministries.

But with these varied cares and perpetual annoyances removed, how will the homemaker of the well-to-do classes employ her time? In the care of her children, the companionship of her husband, and in works of philanthropy, by which the coming epoch shall be hastened forward when there shall be no classes that are not well-to-do.

But there remains abundant territory to be possessed in home's illimitable realm. Women in council working to improve that sanctuary of their hearts will find grievous inequalities in the laws that relate to property as between husband and wife; they will find that in most of the states a wife cannot bring a civil suit for damages against her husband; that as a rule the crime of despoiling a woman of her honor is not punished so heavily as the stealing of a cow; that in general the protection of the person ranks far behind protection of the purse; that in all the thirty-eight states but four still make the father the natural guardian of the children, and that as against all but his wife he can will away the guardianship of his child, whether born or unborn, while she cannot will away hers as against all but her husband.

To show how gladly good men help us toward better law let me recite an incident. In the winter of 1856–57 Judge Waite[9] was sitting in his law office in this city when a woman came in and said her husband was about to convey the homestead and have her put out of doors. She asked if this could legally be done. The judge told her he feared it could be, but would examine carefully. She came in the next day, and he was obliged to tell the poor woman that her husband could take away her home. But Judge Waite immediately drafted a bill to prevent such action in this or any case, sent it to a member of the State Senate, and it was passed at once, and was the first or among the first statutes of the kind in the United States. So that we must not only say that "The earth helps the woman," but that the good and true man everywhere is more than glad to help her.

The Child's Right to Be Well-Born

A great world is looming into sight, like some splendid ship long-waited for—the world of heredity, of prenatal influence, of infantile environment. The greatest right of which we can conceive, the right of the child to be well-born, is being slowly, surely recognized. Poor old humanity, so tugged by fortune and weary with disaster, turns to the cradle at last and perceives it has been the Pandora's box of every ill and the Fortunatus casket of every joy that life has known. When the mother learns the divine secrets of her power, when she selects in the partner of her life the father of her child, and for its sacred sake rejects the man of unclean lips because of the alcohol and the tobacco taint, and shuns as she would a leper the man who has been false to any other woman no matter how depraved; when he who seeks life's highest sanctities in the relationships of husband and father shuns as he would if thoughtful of his future son the woman with wasp waist that renders motherhood a torture and dwarfs the possibilities of childhood, French heels that throw the vital organs out of their normal place, and sacred charms revealed by dresses *décolleté* [with low necklines], insisting on a wife who has good health and a strong physique as the only sure foundation of his home-hopes, then shall the blessed prophecy of the world's peace come true; the conquered lion of lust shall lie down at the feet of the white lamb of purity and a little child shall lead them [Isaiah 11:6].

Woman's Part in Legislation

Society and government are two circles which interplay like rainbows round a fountain, and that fountain is the home. Women in league or council will bring their united power to bear wherever in the operation of an unjust law, whether it be of custom or of legislation, any woman is defrauded of her right. Let us picture them in action: The Municipal Council is in session; but the Board of Directors of the Women's Council is in session also; it represents not some single, isolated, and comparatively uninfluential society, but the united forces of Chicago's organized womanhood. We want an ordinance giving better protection to shop and factory girls; providing more carefully for their physical health, comfort, and convenience, guarding them so far as possible from moral disaster and disease. Through our office secretary we have sent out petitions to every woman's society in the city asking for this ordinance and pledging its enforcement by means of women inspectors from our own number who will serve without fee or reward. The petitions come back signed by tens of thousands. All reputable employers are with us in this effort, and the wage-workers of the city are well pleased to have our help, hence the voting majority that makes and unmakes city councils is on our side.

Woman's Possible Political Influence

Thus panoplied with the power of organization of numbers or a majority among the voters, and, best of all, pleading a cause that tends towards human brotherhood, the Women's Council goes before the City Council and wins the day. But without the law-enforcer back of the law, it is like a rusty sword in a still more rusty scabbard. Already the working-girls of Chicago have much more law upon their side than is utilized for their defense. But there has been no eye to pity, and no hand to save. Now you are here, the women whose opulent and forceful lives have been from a thousand springs of opportunity and blessing; you are here with the arrest of thought in your brains and the enthusiasm of humanity in your hearts; let us bring the solid weight and total momentum of Chicago's organized womanhood to bear upon the problem of a better and a happier life for working-girls. For one, I promise, overwhelmed with cares and duties as I am, to give one afternoon in the week as an inspector to see that the laws we have and mean to get for these women are carried into execution. Nor do I see anything generous about the offer. It will help me as much as it can possibly help those to whom I minister. . . . And we, going straight to those who need our help, shall learn a thousand ways of helping that we do not dream of now, while the public sentiment we can arouse and educate will wonderfully hasten the better day. We must be willing to go forward upon this untried pathway just a step at a time. The whole question of tenement-house misery will open before us, and we shall yet find remedies; the unutterable problem of Chicago's haunts of infamy will be understood and studied as it has not been before; the right of workingmen to one day in seven for rest; the people's right to outlaw the liquor saloon as well as the gambling saloon—these and cognate forms of philanthropy will claim our courage and devotion.

State Councils of Women

Think for a moment of all this upon a larger scale. When each village, town, and city of our state shall have its league or council of good women, they can do for their localities what we hope to do for ours. But we must set them the example. As President of the Women's National Council, I earnestly hope they will move at once along these lines of organization, which mean power, and when the legislature meets next winter the State Council of Illinois ought to meet also, bringing the combined influence of us all to bear in asking for such legislation as our committee on legal work agree upon, and no bill should go before the legislature that is not backed up by the State Council of Women. We should have our representatives constantly at the capital—the State Council regularly holding its sessions there, and asking unitedly for the things that have heretofore been asked for only by separate societies. A law for the better protection of women; for raising the age of consent; for the teaching of hygiene in all grades of the public schools, with especial reference to stimulants and narcotics; for compulsory education; also for appropriations in aid of the industrial school for girls and other institutions to which our philanthropic women are devoted—we must together strive for these.

Locally, a Woman's League should, in the interest of that mothering which is the central idea of our new movement, seek to secure for women admission to all school committees, library associations, and boards entrusted with the care of the defective, dependent, and delinquent classes; all professional and business associations; all colleges and professional schools that have not yet set before us an open door of ingress: and each local league should have the power to call in the united influence of its own state league or of the National Council if its own influence did not suffice.

In the development of this movement I am confident that it will impart to women such a sense of strength and courage that their corporate self-respect will so increase that such theatrical bills as we now see displayed will not be permitted for an hour without our potent protest; and the exhibition of women's forms and faces in the saloons and cigar stores, which women's self-respect will never let them enter, and the disgraceful literature now for sale on so many public newsstands, will not be tolerated by the womanhood of any town or city. . . .

Dear friends, you know the story of Androcles and the lion; how the poor animal came limping out of the forest, knowing the gentleness of Androcles and unable longer to endure the pain of the sharp thorn it carried. To me that lion is a figure of humanity in its rough strength and staggering misery as it turns toward mother-hearted women for relief. I wish that we might have as a seal and emblem of our society the picture of a woman healing a lion's hurt. You know, as the sequel of the story, that when, long afterward, Androcles was condemned to fight with a lion in the arena, it proved to be his former friend, who received him with every demonstration of tenderness and loyalty.

Let us work on with the HUMAN rather than the WOMAN question as our deepest motive, and in the individual no less than the collective struggle of our lives we shall discover friends where foes were feared.

Notes

1. In addition to Willard, the founders of the National Council of Women included Susan B. Anthony (1820–1906), Clara Barton (1821–1912), Lucy Stone Blackwell (1818–93), Julia Ward Howe (1819–1910), May Wright Sewell (1844–1920), and Elizabeth Cady Stanton (1815–1902).

2. *Chicago Inter-Ocean,* October 5, 1888.

3. Helen Stuart Campbell (1839–1918) was a journalist who reported on a number of reforms during the last quarter of the nineteenth century. *Prisoners of Poverty,* illustrated

her ability to describe urban poverty, especially that faced by women workers. *The Union Signal,* the WCTU's weekly newspaper, published many of her articles. Although the term *white slave* was more familiar in the late nineteenth century as a designation for prostitutes, reformers and labor organizers used it often in a broader sense to signify exploited wage workers.

4. Literary clubs were very popular among middle-class American women in the last third of the nineteenth century. They often named their clubs after popular literary figures, as in this example, named for beloved British poet Robert Browning (1812–89).

5. The reference here is to the Czech immigrant neighborhood on the near south side of Chicago.

6. In 1885 King Leopold II of Belgium took control of a vast area of Africa. Under his rule, forced labor and violence devastated the population. From 1888 through 1908 an estimated 20 percent of the population was killed.

7. Bellamy (1850–98) was the author of *Looking Backward* (1888), a utopian novel whose ideas quickly inspired the creation of Nationalist Clubs whose members met to discuss the novel and to promote its socialist vision. Several members of the Boston Nationalist Club, including Bellamy himself, later formed the Society of Christian Socialists (1889) and began publishing the monthly reform journal *The Dawn.* Willard became an associate editor for that journal.

8. George Pullman (1831–97), industrialist and inventor of the luxurious railroad car that bore his name, built a town for his factory workers complete with schools, shops, a library, and hotel. The Pullman name would later become infamous among labor reformers when his wage cuts prompted unionization of railworkers and eventually a general railroad strike (1894), one of the most famous labor protests of the nineteenth century.

9. Charles Burlingame Waite (1824–1909) was a Chicago judge who, along with his lawyer wife, Catharine Van Valkenburg Waite (president of the International Women's Bar Association), supported the Illinois Equal Suffrage Association and worked to reform laws pertaining to women's property and other rights.

FIFTEEN

Tenth Presidential Address, November 8, 1889

In November 1889 Willard welcomed the WCTU to Chicago, her headquarters, in her tenth annual address as president of the organization. Delivered to a large crowd in the Battery D Armory, the very length of the published address—at seventy-six pages—attested to the broadening of the WCTU's expanding "Do Everything" agenda. By the close of the first decade of her presidency, the annual message had begun to resemble the U. S. president's state of the union address, reporting on every aspect of the WCTU's work and commenting on all issues of vital importance to its reform aims. The presidential address was, most significantly, where Willard analyzed challenges she saw to national well-being and charted new directions for her organization to take to confront those challenges.

Early in the address, Willard vividly described many of the changes Americans faced in a rapidly urbanizing and industrializing society with an unprecedented influx of immigrants, many from southern and eastern European cultures very different from those of earlier northern European settlers. It was filled with shocking statistics that demonstrated the large numbers of foreign-born in major cities; alarming reports on the threatening presence of anarchists; corrupt politics at all levels of government; the rise in drinking, smoking, and crime and their cost to the public; and the high population of persons, especially young men, who were unchurched and, thus, uninfluenced by Protestant values.

Imbedded in this fearful litany, however, was a ringing indictment of Gilded Age economic practices, based on a more subtle analysis than Willard had previously been equipped to make. During the last half of the 1880s, she evidenced a growing ability to approach many issues in a more complicated and sophisticated way. She increasingly sought the knowledge and advice of those she termed "experts": political economists, labor leaders, reforming politicians, investigative journalists, staff of municipal charity boards and both religious and secular benevolence agencies, and civic betterment leaders, all of whom were examples of a new breed of activists devoted to understanding and addressing the complex, interlocking causes of urban poverty.

Willard's own study of causes opened her eyes to the great injustices within America's unrestrained capitalism. She saw the displacement of workers by machines, and the troubling accumulations of capital, as well as the collusion of big business and politics that maintained this unjust system. Among the solutions to these challenges, Willard endorsed the program of the Nationalists—the "new labor reformers," inspired by their reading of Edward Bellamy's utopian novel *Looking Backward,* published the previous year—and inserted their entire manifesto into her presidential address. During the next decade, she would make the vision of Christian Socialism her own and continue to champion its goals in spite of its unpopularity with Americans, including most members of her own organization.

Willard's growing comprehension of the terrible conditions in which wage workers labored led to a virtual sea change in her understanding of the link between intemperance and poverty. With this speech she began to reject the traditional notion that intemperance caused poverty, a position that she and many others had previously maintained. Instead, she suggested, inhumane working conditions and the resulting despair of workers were a prime cause of intemperance. Furthermore, she implied that the WCTU and other temperance organizations would do well to cooperate with labor leaders struggling to reform working conditions, thus attacking the problem of intemperance as well. By the late 1880s, Willard insisted that what she viewed as the three great reforms of the era—temperance, labor, and women's rights—were inextricably linked together. This idea became one of the central themes of her second decade as president of the WCTU. The interrelated nature of these reforms meant that her organization must work for all three in as many ways as it could devise.

Excerpts from the text of Willard's tenth presidential address are found in "President's Annual Address" in *Minutes of the N. W. C.T.U.* (Chicago: Woman's Temperance Publication Association, 1889), 94–98, 110–12, 114–18, 123–28, 131, 133–35.

* * *

The Situation

Patriotism has always been part and parcel of my religion. From the first flag I ever saw, made for me by my mother when I was a little prairie girl, out of an old pillow-case with red calico stripes sewed on, and gilt paper stars pinned in the corner, I have always looked upon America as the Majestic Mother whom her grateful daughters should gladly live to serve or die to save. This fact I mention because I know the annals of our lives, beloved comrades, would reveal the same sacred passion of the patriot. God always has one more arrow in His quiver, one more force as yet untried, and this convention of white ribbon women covering the entire continent by its representative delegations, is one of God's condensations of celestial power. Surely the time is ripe for it, and the occasion fit! You are in Chicago; the Cronin murder trial is in full blast; the National flag was hissed and the red flag of the Commune applauded not far from here but a few weeks ago.[1] For the experiment of free government in our large towns and cities is a failure loudly confessed by men themselves. Nor are the reasons for this monumental catastrophe mysterious.

America has become the dumping ground of European cities. The emigration has steadily deteriorated in proportion as its quantity has grown. This is a fact so notorious that our reputable foreign population now protests against the present wholesale exodus from European slums more bitterly than we do.

Today we have a hundred thousand anarchists among us in this country who claim to have twenty-five thousand drilled soldiers at their call, as many as the entire regular army of the United States. It has been truly said that the explosion of a little nitroglycerine under a few water mains would make our great city uninhabitable; the blowing up of a few railway bridges would bring famine; the pumping of atmospheric air into the gas mains and the application of a match would tear up every street and level every house.

The multiplication of inventions, the enormous accumulations of capital, the corporate combinations and octopus grip of the "Trusts" render our wage workers uneasy. A new machine may any day make the work of scores of men superfluous. "Bread or blood" is the inscription on many a concealed red flag and the motive of many a hidden bomb. Note the sullen look on grimy faces in mine and manufactory and on the streets;—read the labor organs of the day, and see if well-to-do Americans are not asleep on the edge of a volcano.

Over 800 papers printed in foreign languages circulate constantly throughout the nation, a majority of which contain ideas concerning home and women, temperance and the Sabbath, that are European and revolutionary, not American and Christian. At Castle Garden eighty-four large steamships land their passengers each month, thirty-two of these steamers being from Great Britain and Ireland. In the First Ward of New York, where Castle Garden stands, are five churches and chapels and four hundred liquor saloons, "and this is their welcome home." In May of last year, one hundred and forty-three thousand emigrants landed at Castle Garden. A million feet yearly sound the signal of an ominous invasion on our wharves as these strange people come. Whether this swift tattoo shall prove to be the reveille of hope or the requiem of despair for America, doth not yet appear, and depends decisively upon the amount of Christian endeavor that is put forth in the next quarter of a century. Twenty-six per cent of our entire population is either foreign born or of foreign parentage. Of one hundred persons in New York City, only twelve are born of American parentage, and in Chicago only nine out of one hundred. You see we women have entered on foreign missionary work without crossing the sea to do so.

In San Francisco, with three hundred and fifty thousand inhabitants, only forty thousand go to church. In "Pilsen," the Bohemian quarter of Chicago, the entire church facilities would accommodate, sitting and standing, about twenty-five hundred persons, but there are not less than forty thousand inhabitants. The largest missionary work done in this foreign city, that forms a section of Chicago, is by disciples of Robert Ingersoll.[2] His writing the people have in their own language. Indeed, his books have been translated into every European tongue, several languages of India, Chinese, Japanese, and others. The man in this country who relishes these books is apt to read them in saloons on Sunday with a pipe in his mouth and in his hand a mug of beer. Nearly half a million Chicagoans would be kept out of church for lack of sittings, had they no other reason for remaining absent, but even under the magic method of High License all who wish sittings in the *saloon* can be accommodated.

There are seven million young men in America today, of whom over five million never darken a church door. Seventy-five out of every one hundred of these young men do not attend church; ninety-five out of every hundred do not belong to the church and ninety-seven out of every hundred do nothing to spread Christianity. But on the other hand, sixty-seven out of every one hundred criminals are young men, and young men are the chief patrons of the saloon, the gambling house, the haunt of infamy. It was noticed recently that into a single saloon in Cincinnati and within a single hour went 252 men, 236 of whom—or all but sixteen—were young men. As a result the death rate steadily increases from 14 to 25 years of age, their evil habits reporting themselves in deteriorated bodies and distempered souls at the age when they should have attained their manly prime.

We spend fifteen hundred millions a year for liquor and tobacco—ten times as much as for education and religion. We have two hundred and fifty saloons, enough to form a line from Chicago to New York, and in making alcoholic beverages we waste enough grain annually to pave a street a thousand miles long with loaves of bread. East of the Mississippi we have one saloon for every 107 voters; west of it, in the eleven mountain states and territories, one for every forty-three. . . .

We have seventy thousand criminals, and while our population doubles every twenty-five years, the number of criminals doubles every ten. It is but just to say that this increase is almost wholly among the native-born, the proportion of foreign-born being about what it was ten years ago. We have over 492 towns and cities containing over five thousand persons each. They make up one-fourth of the population and contain a standing army of fifteen thousand policemen. These men cost us fifteen millions per year and make on an average fifty arrests each. Figure out the cost of each arrest and see if prohibition would not be a great economy.

The ratio of women prisoners to men prisoners is as one to ten, of foreign born to native born nearly double; the average age a little more than twenty-nine and one-half years. About five per cent of our entire population is placed under arrest each year, and in that period about one hundred thousand persons are put in the common jail for the first time. We have at present with us four thousand murderers, five thousand convicted of assault, nine thousand burglars, seventeen thousand common thieves—these are some of the figures of our degradation.

Light is thrown upon the temptation to crime in great cities by the fact that in Chicago we have women who make twelve shirts for 75 cents and furnish their own thread; women who "finish off" a costly cloak for 4 cents; children that work twelve hours a day for a dollar a week. "Alas that gold should be so dear and flesh and blood so cheap!". . . .

For the ills of such an emigration and the degeneracy of our people as proved by the defeat this year of prohibition in six states, there is one remedy—one only—and that is Christianity in action; not fashionable church-membership, but actual Christian living and Christ-like reaction on the world around us. But so long as religion is kept like canned fruit, bottled up at a fixed price of pew rent or other contribution, so long will the crime list continue to increase. God be thanked that the womanhood of Christendom begins to go out into the highway and hedge, shaking into the laps of the people the rich, ripe fruit of the gospel tree without money and without price!. . . .

National Prohibition

The whole practical philosophy of a National constitutional prohibitory amendment is thus stated by its great author, Senator Blair:[3] "There are good motives and impulses and sufficient means in the world for its redemption from want and suffering, and for the distribution of happiness to all, if we would only give combined and intelligent direction to the disorganized masses of mind and heart and hand and money which are now fighting, like the mobs of liberty, for the best ends, but without comprehensive and definite plans of action."

Senator Blair's Amendment to the National Constitution is as follows:

ARTICLE XVI.

Section I. The manufacture, importation, exportation, transportation and sale of all alcoholic liquors to be used as beverages shall be, and hereby is forever prohibited in the United States, and in every place subject to their jurisdiction.

Section II. Congress shall enforce this article by appropriate legislation.

This is the keystone to the arch; the goal toward which every eye is strained, as the home-protection veterans move forward. Let us all be thoroughly familiar with the argument of the far-sighted statesman who was raised up for us just after the Crusade and has stood like a rock for this amendment amid the surging tides of foes without and fears within. [Blair's] great book, *The Temperance Problem: or Man and Alcohol,* is now published by the W.T.P.A. [Woman's Temperance Publishing Association]; which with the *Guide to National Constitutional Prohibition* by our legal adviser, Mrs. Ada M. Bittenbender,[4] will make us all intelligent upon this theme, and I hope that a general rally for enrollment and petition work may be made according to the plans so carefully formulated by this wise white-ribbon lawyer and true hearted leader.

According to a recent estimate there have been nineteen prohibitory amendment struggles since 1880 in which the total vote against is less than a majority of all those qualified to vote, by about four hundred thousand. It is about two million out of a total vote on the question of four million eight hundred thousand. Of this number, total constitutional prohibition secured one million seven hundred and fifty thousand. As the word vote means a *vow*, let us be thankful that we have substantial reason to believe that this enormous number is vowed to the outlawing of the liquor traffic and from the stay-at-home voters and, better still, the on-coming voters now in our Loyal Temperance Legions, let us patiently recruit the comparatively small number yet to be convinced, before our sacred Cause shall attain the princely power of the majority, and prohibition be rooted in the Constitution of these United States. . . .

The Labor Question

The colossal Labor Question looms up more and more; its correlations with the Temperance Question are being candidly considered, and as the two armies approach nearer to each other, they discover that uniform and weapons are curiously alike. No voice has rung out clearer for the prohibition of the Sunday saloon than that of Terence V. Powderly, the leader of the wage workers,[5] whose fame is burnished by every blow that falls on him from foes within and foes without the labor camp. It is being proved that intemperance is most prevalent where the hours of toil are long, because overwork drives men to drinking; hence the eight hour law finds steadily more favor with our temperance people. The fate of the factory girls is being thought about, and "the slavish overwork that drives them into the saloons at night," when "they come out so tired, thirsty and exhausted from working steadily so long and breathing the noxious effluvia from the grease and other ingredients used in the mills." This is especially true of eastern factories, and temperance people might wisely clasp hands with the labor reformers who in Chicago and elsewhere are securing the appointment of women inspectors, whose field should extend to all places where women are employed.

Riches and rich people are naturally exclusive. Genius is hospitable in mind as well as heart; it is universal in its sympathies, a type and a forerunner of what average humanity shall yet become. Delivered from the everlasting struggle for life's three necessities, food, clothes and shelter (for it is a magnificent fact that the fourth necessity, something to drink, has full and free natural supply!), human beings will enjoy their first opportunity for individual development; for the culture of their best and highest gifts. Nobody has the smallest conception of what mankind shall grow to be when the first question is never "How shall I live?" but always "How can I best develop my highest possibilities?" This will come only when all avenues of training are freely open to us all, and every opportunity of growth is at the beck of each.

That the aims of the new labor reformers called "Nationalists" may be more clearly seen, I publish them in their own language:

> Society is awakening to new light upon Social Problems. We do not see all light. We know no sudden panacea that will cure all social ills; we do not believe that it is yet day; but do believe that it is Dawn, that we may see at least in what direction the day will break. Thither we point, gladly communicating to others what light we have, more gladly welcoming all further light from any who may see more. The following are the positions in which we see the light.
>
> First. *The basing* of all social, political, and industrial relations on the Fatherhood of God and the Brotherhood of Man, in the spirit and according to the teachings of Jesus Christ.
>
> Second. *Beginning with the inner and working toward the outer.* We see small hope in simple system. The spirit giveth life. Systems are important aid, but only aids. National life must be educated, character must be developed, before any system can bear good fruit. We would remember this; we would begin with the inner life. We would not seek to systematize humanity unto perfection, but to Christianize society into Brotherhood.
>
> Third. *Molding the Social Order.* Christianity does not concern the individual alone. Christ preached a social gospel. There is a Social Law of God. Men today forget this. As individuals they strive to apply their Christianity in business, and largely fail. Business itself today is wrong. It rests upon a negation of the social law. Each man is for himself, each company for itself. It is based on competitive strife for profits. This is the exact opposite of Christianity. Christianity says: "Let no man seek his own, but each his neighbor's good." To attempt therefore, to apply Christianity to modern business is to attempt to be Christian in an unChristian way: it is to build obedience to Christ on the sands of disobedience. *It cannot be done.* We must change the system. We must found business upon Social Law. Combination must take the place of competition; we must have a system in which business shall be carried on, not for private profits, but for the public good. We must apply our Christianity to the Social Order.
>
> Fourth. We view the *lack of social order as the main cause of present social ills.* We find here the main cause of the evils that today threaten society and the Church: plutocracy, mammon worship, pauperism, poverty, unbelief, immorality, intemperance, prostitution, crime. Reforms upon these especial lines can therefore only alleviate, not cure, the cause being left untouched.
>
> Fifth. *The development of Christian Socialism our need today.* We mean by this no fixed, cast-iron system of any nature, no magic panacea of any description, no sudden transformation of any sort, but (1) contentment to proceed one step at

a time; (2) leaving to science and experience the exact form that society should adopt, yet (3) ever gradually and thoughtfully proceeding toward the general goal of association; an association (1) fraternal and not paternal; (2) democratic and not tyrannical; (3) developing true individuality, and not ignoring it; (4) land and all resources of the earth to be held under some system as the gift of God equally to all His children; (5) capital and all means of industry to be held and controlled in some way by the community as a whole, and operated for the benefit of the community equitably in all its parts; thus realizing at last the ideal of Christian Socialism, the Fatherhood of God, the Brotherhood of Man, the spirit of Jesus Christ. . . .

Invention doubles the manufacturing power of the civilized world every seven years. For example, a type-setting machine has just been invented which will reduce the demand for compositors fifty per cent. Anarchists say they will destroy machinery, but that would be idiotic, not to say fiendish. Instead of that, we must reduce the hours of labor, and as monopolies multiply, humanity will in some future age be very likely to declare just one huge monopoly, and that will be Humanity itself. We shall then have simply swung around to the New Testament basis, and reached the day when all men's weal is made to be each man's care, *by the very construction of society and constitution of government.*

"The community of the early Christians, as described in the book of Acts [4:32–37], was, I suppose," said James Freeman Clarke,[6] that great student of religions, "the best society the world has ever seen, the highest social condition yet attained by human beings. That was the divine compensation which they had for their poverty, persecution, and danger." All this will come, not in our day, but slowly and surely as Christianity leavens the lump of poor old human nature, and the wish I have for you as for myself, is that we may put a shoulder to the heavy and unwilling wheel.

The wage workers have this year given a fresh demonstration of what total abstinence can do to tone down the terrors of the greatest strike yet known—that of the London dock men. There was no violence worth mentioning, and yet the strikers were in want of bread. But their great leader John Burns[7] is, like Mr. Powderly, totally free from the drink habit, and he urged the men to keep clear of the gin shops. They even secured 1,200 signatures to the pledge, while the strike was going on and pleaded with the men to be considerate toward their wives and children, and to lead pure lives. I sometimes think it looks as if modern chivalry were threatening to make its home with the leaders of the modern labor movement.

The most significant word that we, as temperance experts, can send to our future allies of the labor camp is this: You say that you must combine to control legislation in your interest; but meantime you support the saloon, and that controls legislation in its own interest, which is opposed to yours. Come with us and let us put down the saloon as the initial step in the mighty labor movement. . . .

Physical Culture

.... Women's everlastingly befrilled, bedizened and bedraggled style of dress is today doing more harm to children unborn, born and dying, than all other causes that compel public attention. With ligatured lungs and liver as our past inheritance and present slavery, the wonder is that such small heads can carry all we know! Catch [Thomas Alva] Edison and constrict him inside a wasp-waistcoat, and be assured you'll get no more inventions; bind a bustle upon [Otto von] Bismarck, and farewell to German unity; coerce Robert Browning into corsets, and you'll have no more epics; put [Charles Stewart] Parnell in petticoats, and Home Rule [for Ireland] is a lost cause; treat Powderly in the same fashion, and the powder mine of failure will blow up the Labor Movement. Niggardly waists and niggardly brains go together. The emancipation of one will always keep pace with the other; a ligature around the vital organs at the smallest diameter of the womanly figure means an impoverished blood supply in the brain, and may explain why women scream when they see a mouse, and why they are so terribly afraid of a term which should be their glory, as it is that of their brothers—viz., *strong-minded.*

Our degradation in the line of bandaging the waist has reached such a point, that Helen Campbell says it is a requisite in fashionable London stores to have the women clerks not larger around than twenty inches, "and eighteen-inch waists are preferred." Look at the monstrous deformity produced by constrictive surgery as applied to the average fashion-plate; and think what belittlement of power and happiness it means to the poor creatures who will wear these waists, and to their children! We shall see, I hope, something less humiliating in *Harper's Bazar* than its immemorial abominations of "fashionable style," now that so true a Christian woman as Margaret Sangster[8] edits that otherwise excellent paper. ...

Bonneted women are not in normal conditions for thought; high-heeled women are not in normal conditions for motherhood. Each of the constrictions and contortions involved by these crimes in dress is a distinct violation of loving laws given by our Heavenly Father for our highest happiness and growth. I wonder that men, in their broader outlook, and magisterial power, do not forbid this thing by statute, in the interest of their sons that are to be.

But ethics and aesthetics must go side by side in the blessed work of dress reform, for that is Nature's way. The pioneers did not see this, and their "bloomers" speedily dropped into innocuous desuetude. But the moderns—led by Mrs. Annie Jenness Miller ... ,[9]—have sat at Nature's feet, and on my recent eastern trips I learned what I know to be true in progressive Chicago—that the best are also coming to be the bravest women, that among them there is an absolute craze for getting rid of corsets, and that the divided skirt is worn by tens of thousands whom you might not suspect of so much good sense and courage.

Much as I am devoted to the ballot for woman, I would today rather head a crusade against bandaged waists, street-sweeping skirts, and camel's-hump bustles than—do I live to say it?—yea, verily, *than to vote* at Chicago's next election for a Sunday-closing mayor!

Notes

1. Willard referred to the May 1889 murder of Dr. Patrick Henry Cronin, the Chicago leader of one of the factions of the United Brotherhood, an Irish-American secret society. The trial of Cronin's alleged murderer was occurring during the WCTU convention. The red flag of the Commune, a symbol of those who supported the violent overthrow of capitalism, was carried by many socialist and anarchist groups that attended the numerous labor demonstrations occurring in Chicago from the 1870s on. Both incidents are examples of the kind of ethnic and labor unrest that worried middle-class Americans in Chicago and other large cities during the last quarter of the nineteenth century.

2. Robert Ingersoll (1833–99), a popular orator during the last quarter of the nineteenth century, toured the country speaking against Christianity and championing agnosticism. As Willard indicated, his speeches and writings influenced many to question their faith.

3. Henry William Blair (1834–1920), senator from New Hampshire, was a great supporter of temperance measures throughout his political career.

4. Bittenbender (1848–1925) was superintendent of legislation and petitions for the National WCTU. She lobbied on behalf of the National Prohibition amendment and the bill revising statutory rape laws by raising the age of consent to sixteen years in Washington, D.C. This latter reform was a catalyst for new age of consent legislation in many states across the nation.

5. Terence Vincent Powderly (1849–1924) was the General Master Workman of the Knights of Labor, the most powerful labor union during the mid-1880s. His espousal of temperance for himself and his organization and his support of women's suffrage persuaded Willard to align the WCTU with Powderly and the Knights.

6. James Freeman Clarke (1810–88), Unitarian minister and Transcendentalist scholar, was the author of *Ten Great Religions,* an early comparative study.

7. John Elliot Burns (1858–1943) was a British labor leader. He was a major figure in the London Dock Worker's Strike of 1889, which was a turning point in the history of British labor, bringing skilled and unskilled workers together within the union movement.

8. Margaret Munson Sangster (1838–1912) was the editor of *Harper's Bazar* from 1889 to 1899.

9. Annie Jenness Miller (1859–?) was one of the most prominent dress reformers of the era and a popular lecturer on sensible dress and women's health issues. She was co-owner of a women's magazine that featured many articles on these reforms.

SIXTEEN

"Women and Organization," February 23, 1891

When the National Council of Women held its first triennial meeting in Albaugh's Opera House in Washington, D.C., in late February, 1891, Willard addressed delegates from forty national women's organizations representing seven hundred thousand American women. During her preceding three-year term as president of the council, she had worked to develop a network of local, state, and national women's organizations that could address, with a united voice, issues of common concern to the nation's women. Her presidential address rearticulated her belief that organizing women on a broad reform platform would unleash a powerful force for positive social change. At the same time, she urged women to go beyond the simple act of meeting together solely to educate themselves, and to actually take up the hard work of accomplishing their reform goals through united effort. The address also celebrated the growing sense of sisterhood and tolerance of difference emerging from work with the National Council. For example, Willard pointed to the fact that, though they disagreed about theology, she worked side by side with Elizabeth Cady Stanton, president of the newly reunified National American Woman Suffrage Association.

This National Council of Women was different from previous gatherings of women because it aimed to create a representative government for women parallel to the existing national legislature peopled solely by men. The council, she argued, would "*legislate* for Womanhood, for Childhood, and the Home." Economic reform would be foremost among their legislative changes. Her call for better protection of women's property rights and for monetary recognition of women's labor in the home was coupled with her call for broad labor reforms. Once again, Willard's emerging vision of Christian Socialism was at the core of the economic arguments. Only when the necessities for survival were given to all people as an investment in their future contributions to society would all people be able to develop and share their gifts.

It was a radical vision and, according to Willard, women were crucial to its realization. She believed that women, certainly through nurture and perhaps by birth, were synthesizers and unifiers with an "instinct of otherhood," rather than analytic and committed to individualism and selfhood—as she believed most men had been trained to be. As a result, women's presence and perspective was essential to fueling such broad social transformation. Full participation of women in the political and legislative leadership of the nation was therefore necessary.

The address closed with a section titled "Women in Religion" in which Willard exhibited her ecumenical spirit and aimed to transcend the theological differences that could be divisive among women working for reform and to encourage work toward common goals. Asserting a theory of learning promoted by physiologist William B. Carpenter, she acknowledged that new ideas were often hard for human minds to accept. Rather than getting caught up in the kinds of theoretical conflicts that had led men to divide into at least 140 separate religious groups and to substitute a corrupted political system for what could have been true government, she insisted, women and enlightened men should instead focus on "religious living." Willard commended the reform work of individuals ranging from Catholic Cardinal John Henry Newman to labor reformer Terence Powderly, to women's rights leader Susan B. Anthony, as illustrating the new age of united work for reform which aimed to "bring in the brotherhood and sisterhood of humanity."

Willard's work with the National Council of Women was part of this broad reform agenda. Commending her efforts as the presiding officer at the council, the *Boston Traveller* commented that she had a special talent for bringing women together. "Grand and noble woman that she is," they wrote, Willard "never truly showed how broad and liberal she really is until this week. There is a place in her heart for every woman who works for any cause, if she is in earnest. Miss Willard is the apostle of love between women of conflicting interests."[1]

The following excerpts are from the pamphlet "Address of Frances E. Willard, President of the Woman's National Council of the United States, at its First Triennial Meeting, Albaugh's Opera House, Washington, D.C., February 22–25, 1891," 1–3, 5–10, 15, 16, 17, 18, 19, 31, 32–35.

* * *

Beloved Friends and Comrades in a Sacred Cause:

A difference of opinion on one question must not prevent us from working unitedly in those on which we can agree.

These words from the opening address before the International Council[2] convened in this auditorium three years ago were the keynote of a most tuneful chorus. The name of her who uttered words so harmonious is Elizabeth Cady Stanton, and it shall live forever in the annals of woman's heroic struggle up from sexhood into humanhood.

Our friends have said that, as President of the National American Woman

Suffrage Association [NAWSA], Mrs. Stanton leads the largest army of women outside, and I the largest one inside, the realm of a conservative theology. However this may be, I rejoice to see the day when, with distinctly avowed loyalty to my Methodist faith, and as distinctly avowed respect for the sincerity with which she holds to views quite different, I can clasp hands in loyal comradeship with one whose dauntless voice rang out over the Nation for "woman's rights" when I was but a romping girl upon a prairie farm.

It has taken women of brains and purpose over forty years to find out that they could be true to the faith born with them (nourished at the bosom where their infant heads were pillowed, and taught them at their mother's knee, until its fibers are part and parcel of their own), and yet in the thickening battle for "the liberty wherewith Christ maketh free," [Galatians 5:1] could keep step with any soldier and heed the voice of any captain who was fighting

> "For the cause that lacks assistance
> 'Gainst the wrong that needs resistance,
> For the future in the distance
> And a woman's right to do."

"Would that Blucher or night were come," said Wellington at Waterloo, and surely night without a morning would have come ere this in the great final battle for the overthrow of that proud usurping Napoleon, better known as Brute Force, had not the two divisions of the conquering army of womanhood [National American Woman Suffrage Association and the National WCTU] effected a junction in the last decades of this last Old World century.[3]

In saying this let me distinctly disavow any banding together of women as malcontents or hostiles toward the correlated other half of the human race. Brute force, to my mind, means custom as opposed to reason, prejudice as the antagonist of fair play, and precedent as the foe of common sense. This classification blots out the sex line altogether; for, alas, what a horde of well-meaning women it arrays against the ideas for which this Council stands and huzza for the army of great hearts it sets in array among men, as our valiant allies in the thick of the fight!

It was a beautiful saying of the earlier Methodists, when they avowed a holy life: "I feel nothing contrary to love." But the widening march of Christianity has given a wonderfully practical sense to such words, and we actually mean here today that whatever in custom or law is contrary to that love of one's neighbor which would give to him or her all the rights and privileges that one's self enjoys, is but a relic of brute force, and is to be cast out as evil.

And because woman in some of our American Commonwealths is still so related to the law that the father can will away an unborn child, and that a girl of seven or ten years old is held to be the equal partner in a crime where another and a stronger is the principal; because she is in so many ways hampered and harmed by laws and customs pertaining to the past, we reach out hands of help especially to her that she may overtake the swift-marching procession of progress, for its sake that it may not slacken its speed on her account as much as for hers that she be not left behind. We thus represent the human rather than the woman question, and our voices unite to do that which the president of our New York Sorosis so beautifully said in a late letter to the Sorosis of Bombay:

"Tell them the world was made for woman, too!"[4]

Every atom says to every other one, "Combine," and, doing so, they change chaos into order. When every woman shall say to every other, and every workman shall say to every other, "Combine," the war dragon shall be slain, the poverty viper shall be exterminated, the gold-bug transfixed by a silver pin, the saloon drowned out, and the last white slave liberated from the woods of Wisconsin and the bagnios [brothels] of Chicago and Washington.[5] For combination is "a game that two can play at"; the millionaires have taught us how, and the labor tortoise is fast overtaking the capitalistic hare.

What was it Mrs. Stanton said? "A difference of opinion on one question must not prevent us from working unitedly in those on which we can agree." Illustrations of this great principle (so long universally recognized by men, whether Jew or Gentile, orthodox or heterodox, in all their humanitarian and patriotic work) are more conspicuously manifest in the programme of this Council than ever before in the forty-year long annals of the woman movement, for here we have nearly forty different societies represented by delegates either regular or fraternal. . . .

Let me then frankly say that I believe we should organize a miniature council in every town and city, confederating these in every state, and instructing the state council to send delegates to the national council. The plan would be to let these delegates form a lower and the heads of national societies an upper house, whose concurrent vote should be essential to the enunciation of any principle, or the adoption of any plan. The president of this society should be (as has already been wisely ordained by this council) eligible for but one term, and should have power to choose her own cabinet from the seven ablest women of the country, representing the industries, education, professions, philanthropies, reforms, and the religious and political work of women. We should thus have within the national government, as carried on by men, a republic of women, duly organized and officered, not in any wise antagonistic to men, but conducted in their interest as much as in our own, and tending toward such mutual fellowship among women, such breadth of knowledge and sympathy as should establish solidarity of sentiment and purpose throughout the nation of women workers, put a premium upon organized as against isolated efforts for human betterment, minify the sense of selfhood and magnify that of otherhood, training and tutoring women for the next great step in the evolution of humanity, when men and women shall sit side by side in government and the nations shall learn war no more [Isaiah 2:4].

The Upper Council, as it might be called, would, by this plan, consist of two delegates from each society which, in its judgment, was national in scope or value, one being the president of that society, the other chosen by ballot at its last annual meeting preceding the session of the council (which I would have convened biennially). This Upper Council would answer to the Senate of the United States, and the Lower Council, made up of delegates chosen by the forty-four state councils from their auxiliaries, would be analogous to the House of Representatives. We should thus have an organization that would include all the various groups of women hitherto isolated (and as a consequence, in some degree provincial), while its basis would be so broad, its aims so far-reaching, and its plan so unique that no other society could consider its realm in any wise encroached upon.

The same democratic basis of organization should extend to the local council—*i.e.,* each should be made up of two delegates from each local society of women in the city, town or village, one being the president of said local society and the other chosen by ballot of that society. The state council should be made up of two delegates each, chosen in like manner from the local councils, these to form a lower house in the state council, and the presidents, with one other representative of each state society, to form the Upper Council in each state, the president and vice-president of the National Council to be elected biennially by a popular vote of all members of all local societies tributary to the National Council. We have wished for a method of inducing women to cast their ballots on a large scale; this would be quite sure to arouse an enthusiasm that would "call out the vote"....

"Something solid, and superior to any existing society, is what we want." This is the commentary of women with whom I have talked, and the foregoing outline is offered as a possible help toward meeting this very natural and reasonable requirement. Such a national society would, indeed, incalculably increase the world's sum total of womanly courage, efficiency, and *esprit de corps;* widening our horizon, correcting the tendency to an exaggerated impression of one's own work as compared with that of others, and putting the wisdom and expertness of each at the service of all. Nor would it require a vast amount of effort to bring such a great movement into being, for the work of organizing is already done, and the correlating of societies now formed could be divided among our leaders, each one taking a state or a number of chief towns and cities.

Being organized in the interest of no specific propaganda, this great Association would unite in cordial sympathy all existing societies of women, that with a mighty aggregate of power we might move in directions upon which we could agree.

Moreover, the tendency would be vastly to increase the interest of individual women in associated work and the desire of local societies to be federated nationally, individual women and isolated societies of women being ineligible to membership in the councils, whether local, state, or national.

But the greatest single advantage will perhaps be this, that while each society devoted to a specific end will continue to pursue these by its own methods, every organization will have the moral support of all others and will be in a position to add its influence to that of all others, for such outside movements of beneficence as it may approve. For instance, without a dissenting voice, the International Council of 1888 put itself on record to the following effect:

> It is the unanimous voice of the Council that all institutions of learning and of professional instruction, including schools of theology, law, and medicine, should, in the interests of humanity, be as freely opened to women as to men; that opportunities for industrial training should be as generally and as liberally provided for one sex as for the other, and the representatives of organized womanhood in this Council will steadily demand that in all avocations in which both men and women engage equal wages shall be paid for equal work; and, finally, that an enlightened society should demand, as the only adequate expression of the high civilization which it is its office to establish and maintain, an identical standard of personal purity and morality for men and women.

Probably there is not an intelligent woman in America who would not subscribe to this declaration. The only point of possible difference would be the opening of theological schools to women; and since Oberlin and Hartford, Boston and Evanston theological seminaries have done this and it does not necessarily involve the ordination of women, that difference would not be likely to arise.

Were there such a council of women in town and city, state and nation, we should have our representatives constantly at the state and national capitals, and should ask unitedly for advantages that have heretofore been asked for only by separate societies. Laws for the better protection of women, married and single; laws protecting the property rights of married women and giving them equal power with their husbands over their children; laws making the kindergarten a part of the public school system; requiring lessons in physical culture and gymnastics to be given in all grades of the public school with special reference to health and purity of personal habitudes; national and state appropriations for common school and industrial education, and appropriations for institutions helpful to women—surely we might together strive for all of these.

Locally a woman's council should, in the interest of that "mothering" which is the central idea of our new movement, seek to secure for women admission to all school committees, library associations, hospital and other institutional boards entrusted with the care of the defective, dependent, and delinquent classes; also to boards of trustees in school and college and all professional and business associations; also to all college and professional schools that have not yet set before us an open door; and each local council should have the power to call in the united influence of its own state council, or, in special instances, of the National Council, if its own influence did not suffice.

I am confident that the development of this movement will impart to women such a sense of strength and courage, and their corporate self-respect will so increase, that such theatrical bills as we now see displayed will not be permitted for an hour, without our potent protest; and the exhibitions of women's forms and faces in the saloons and cigar stores, which women's self-respect will never let them enter, and the disgraceful literature now for sale on so many public newsstands, will not be tolerated by the womanhood of any town or city. An "Anatomical Museum" that I often pass on a Chicago street bears the words: "Gentlemen only admitted." Why do women passively accept these flaunting assumptions that men are expected to derive pleasure from objects that they would not for a moment permit their wives to see? Some day women will not accept them passively, and then these base exhibitions will cease, for women will purify every place they enter, and they will enter every place. Catholic and Protestant women would come to a better understanding of each other through working thus for mutual interests; Jew and Gentile would rejoice in the manifold aims of a practical Christianity; women who work because they must; women, true-souled enough to work because they ought, or, best of all, great-souled enough to work because they love humanity, will all meet on one broad platform large enough and strong enough to furnish standing room for all. Later on, who knows but that by means of this same Council we women might free ourselves from that stupendous bondage which is the basis of all others—the unhealthfulness of fashionable dress! "Courage is as contagious as cowardice," and the courage of a council of women may yet lead us into the liberty of a costume tasteful as it is reasonable, and healthful as it is chaste.

Another practical outcome that might be looked for from such a confederation of women's efforts in religious and philanthropic, educational and industrial work, might be the establishment in every town and city of headquarters for women's work of every kind. There they could have a home for their enterprises, a hall for their meetings, and, by building on the plan that Mrs. Carse[6] suggests, and we are carrying out in Chicago, they could, from the rental of such a building, realize money for their work. The recent gift from the projectors of Glen Echo (the great Chautauqua adjoining Washington, D. C.) of ample grounds on which to locate a National Temple for this Council, marks another epoch in the movement to "arise and build," which is the latest material evolution of our mighty cause.

Still another great advantage would be the wide attention given to conclusions reached by such a representative body of women. The best ideas of leaders are now entombed in their annual addresses, leaflets, and books intended for a single society. But literature issued by the National Council would command the well-nigh universal attention of intelligent women, and would furnish such a fund of facts, statistics, and results of the individual and associated study of reformers now isolated in their work, as would be of incalculable value to students of the many and widely-varied enterprises to which women are devoting themselves with so much zeal. In this connection, let me say that to develop the great quality of corporate as well as individual self-respect, I believe no single study would do more than that of Frances Power Cobbe's noble book on *The Duties of Women*.[7]

It ought to be in the hands of every woman who has taken for her motto loyalty to "heart within, and God o'erhead," and surely it ought to be in the hands of every one who has not this high aim, while I am certain that every man who lives would be a nobler husband, son, and citizen of the great world if he would give this book his thoughtful study.

A little girl has defined a secret as "something which somebody says in a whisper to everybody," and my secret thought concerning organization among women has been here uttered in what I hope may prove to be what Fanny Fern designated as the whispered voice—namely, "one loud enough to be heard in South America."[8] I wish that at least this council would ask its officers to consider and report upon this plan some time within the present year, giving them power to act.

A pan of milk sours in a thunderstorm, and must stand still ere cream will come. So is it with our minds. Their sober second thought is best attained in solitude. We have long met to read essays, make speeches and prepare petitions; let us hereafter meet, in this great Council, to *legislate* for Womanhood, for Childhood and the Home. Men have told us solemnly, have told us often and in good faith, no doubt, that "they would grant whatever the women of the Nation asked." Our time to ask *unitedly* has waited long, but it is here at last. [Johann Wolfgang von] Goethe has said, "Talent is nurtured best in solitude, but character on life's tempestuous sea," and to make the world wider for women and happier for humanity the wonder-working powers of organization are essential, the chaos of individuality giving place to the cosmos of aggregated influence and power.

He who climbs, sees. Poets tell us of

> The one far off, divine event,
> Toward which the whole creation moves,

and in this mighty movement toward the power that organization only can bestow, what end have we in view? Is it fame, fortune, leadership? Not as I read women's hearts, who have known them long and well. It is for love's sake—for the bringing in of peace on earth, goodwill to men [Luke 2:14]. The two supreme attractions in nature are those of gravitation and cohesion. That of cohesion attracts atom to atom, that of gravitation attracts all atoms to a common center. We find in this the most conclusive figure of the supremacy of love to God over any human love, the true relation of human to the love divine, and the conclusive proof that in organizing for the greatest number's greatest good, we do but "think God's thoughts after Him."

Women Plus Time

... [L]et us ... see what forty years have wrought along the picket line of our advance—actual participation in the government. Nineteen thousand women voted in Boston alone on a decisive school question in 1888, and in a driving snowstorm. Women have the ballot now on school questions in twenty-two states, have municipal and school suffrage in Kansas and Oklahoma; while by constitutional enactment, ratified by a vote of eight to one among the people, they are fully disenthralled in the free mountain state of Wyoming. . . .

The first ballots ever cast by women for the election of a national ruler will be those of Wyoming women in 1892. A happy man indeed ought that next President to be should the candidate for which a majority of enfranchised women vote come to the throne of power, and from his administration women would have much to hope—at least in post-office promotions! Our expectation of justice is not in the lily-handed men of college, court, and cloister, but in the farmers whose "higher education" has been the Grange, and in the mechanics trained by trades unions and the Knights of Labor. These are the men who have been known to go on strike because sewing women toiled at starving rates; who stand stoutly by their motto, "Equal pay for equal work"; who declare in their platforms that we shall have the ballot, and who are the force that shall yet bring about an evenness between the eight-hour day of the husband and the sixteen-hour day of the wife! . . .

Cooperative Happiness

In the epoch on which we have entered labor will doubtless come to be the only potentate, and, "for value received," will have the skilled toil of the human species as its sole basis of any "specie payment"; "a note of hand" having no offset save the human hand at work. For man added to nature, is all the capital there is on earth; and "the best that any mortal hath is that which every mortal shares." But nature belongs equally to all men; hence the only genuine capital and changeless medium of exchange, always up to par value is labor itself, and there will eventually be no more antagonism between capital and labor than between the right hand and the left. Labor is the intelligent and beneficent reaction of man upon nature. This reaction sets force enough in motion to float him in all waters and carry him across all continents. His daily labor, then, is the natural equivalent he furnishes for food and clothing, fuel and shelter, and it is the supreme interest of the state to prepare the individual in head, hand, and heart to put forth his highest power. Carried to its legitimate conclusion, this is the socialism of Christ; the Golden Rule in action; the basis of that golden age which shall succeed this age of gold. . . .

Women are beginning to study the labor question, that whale to which politicians are now throwing tubs, and which spouts so foamily in the deep sea of living issues. Women, as a class, have been the world's chief toilers; it is a world-old proverb that "their work is never done." But the value put upon that work is pointedly illustrated in the reply recently given by an ancient Seminole to one of our white ribboners who visited the reservation of that tribe in Florida, where she saw oxen grazing and a horse roaming the pasture, while two women were grinding at the mill, pushing its wheels laboriously by hand. Turning to the old Indian chief who sat by, the temperance woman said, with pent-up indignation: "Why don't you yoke the oxen or harness the horses and let them turn the mill?" The "calm view" set forth in his answer contains a whole body of evidence touching the woman question. Hear him:

Horse cost money; ox cost money; *squaw cost nothing.*

After all, there were tons of philosophy in the phrase; for, by the laws of mind, each person in a community is estimated according to his relation to the chief popular standard of value. Today, in this commercial civilization of ours, money is that standard. Hence the emancipation of women must come, first of all, along industrial lines. She must, in her skilled head and hands, represent financial values. Today the standard is gold; tomorrow it will be gifts; the next day character. But, in the slow, systematic process of evolution it is only through financial freedom, that she will rise to that truer freedom which is the measure of all her faculties in trained, harmonious, and helpful exercise. . . .

Women in Religion

. . . Some people take their religion on the square, and others on the bias. It is largely a question of nature and environment. For those who do not like the square, the bias is perhaps good. Doubtless both have the root of the matter in them if both go at it with a true purpose towards God and man, but the seamless robe is the only true ideal. Folks with a new notion in their heads remind me of a bird flying about with a straw in its bill. One would think that but one swallow made a summer, and one straw would build a nest. But the truth is, the nest of the human soul has not only many a straw in it, but twigs, bits of leaves, scarlet threads and downy shreds of wool, and much besides. It has taken all the ages of light, of evolution, of nature, and of the great human heart itself to build the nest called Christianity, in which so many souls have found a home. And is it finished? Not by any means. There shall come other builders, and in other swift-revolving ages man shall still be the student of God and of humanity. Yea, and in other worlds, up toward which we gaze as they gleam in the great sky the building will go on. But we are all like children. When we find anything new, some pretty leaf, some bright scrap of a thread, we are delighted with it, and want everyone to see it; we think this the latest, the last, the best. The white sunlight of God's truth falls through the stained glass window of the human brain and takes the color of our individuality.

"The logic of new theories," says the physiologist [William B.] Carpenter,[9] "is very differently estimated by different individuals, all equally desirous of arriving at the truth, according to their conformity or disaccordance with that *aggregate of preformed opinion* which has grown up in the mind of each. For just as we try whether a new piece of furniture which is offered us does or does not fit into a certain recess in our apartment, and accept or decline it accordingly, so we try a new proposition which is offered to our mental acceptance. If it at once fits into some recess in our fabric of thought, we give our assent to it by admitting it to its appropriate place. Otherwise, the mind automatically rejects it."

If only we could remember this and so cherish that charity, one toward another, which can alone warm and embellish human life, that would be a long stride forward in all that relates to everyday Christianity. For myself, I am a firm believer that the Way, the Truth, and the Life [John 14:6] are shown to us in Christianity, and that God was manifest in the flesh [1 Timothy 3:16]. But the differences come in when we would apply this transcendent declaration, not to the facts of everyday life, but to the theories that men call creeds.

One of the crucial tests of our Christianity is this: What does the "hired girl" think about our kind of religion? Never was nobler tribute paid to character than when the body servant of Alexander H. Stevens[10] said of him, as he wept beside the statesman's bier, "Mas'r Alick was kinder to dogs than most folks is to men." Dress parade is one thing, everyday doing quite another, and the verdict of the most dependent in our circle is the final verdict as to whether we are magnificent or mean.

Silence concerning injuries and contradictions is the most smothering blanket that ever was woven or spun. Ill will and the manifestation thereof never yet caused anybody to do the thing we wished to have him do. But goodwill can conquer anything. No man will double up his fists to fight the atmosphere. The sweet south wind of Love is the only strategist that never lost a battle. "Love is the Holy Ghost within, and hate the unpardonable sin." George Eliot said that sometime it would be as natural to show goodwill to others, and as instinctive, as it is to put out one's hand for help when one is falling.

Some one has recently said, "After all, religion is the only interesting thing." How interesting, let the late census reveal. We are there informed that the people of these United States disagree so widely in their concepts of God and immortality, duty and destiny, reward and punishment that they are separated by their creeds into one hundred and forty distinct groups. Now add to this the various creeds into which nonchurch members are separated, from the Positivists of London, whose "Temple" was once wittily described as including "three persons and no God," to the Spiritualists, whose name is legion. Then enumerate the orthodox, the heterodox, and the "New Departure men" in each group of scientists, and, returning to the church groups, take account of the fact that almost every one of the one hundred and forty has as many well-defined shades of opinion as the fearful and wonderful "Establishment" of England classed as "High," "Broad," and "Low" church (or "Attitudinarians, Latitudinarians, and Platitudinarians"), and what a fearful totality of beliefs and unbeliefs is this into which the destructive criticism of the incomplete masculine mind has brought us! Surely the wizard's broth is as bad as the witch's ever can be, in politics as a substitute for government and ecclesiasticism as a substitute for religion.

I rejoice that women reformers do not claim the ability to renovate the existing condition of things in church and state, but their contention is that if the analytic method of man's thought and the synthetic method of woman's were combined, humanity would then have brought all of its tithes into the storehouse [Malachi 3:10] of the common good, and God would pour us out the blessing that has always been potential but could only become actual when the conditions were supplied that lie in the changeless nature of things. For:

> The sweet persuasion of His voice
> Respects our sanctity of will;
> He giveth day—we have our choice
> To walk in darkness still.

In all this discord about religious theory there has been very little controversy about religious living. Cardinal Newman and General Booth, Terence V. Powderly, the master workman, and William Morris, the poet; Frances Power Cobbe and Margaret Bottome, Lady Henry Somerset and Susan B. Anthony are all bent upon one beautiful result—they would bring in the brotherhood and sisterhood of humanity; they would hasten the coming upon earth of the kingdom of heaven.[11]

Notes

1. *Boston Traveller,* March 2, 1891, in WCTU series, reel 37, frame 119.

2. In the spring of 1888 the International Council of Women met in Washington, D.C., with Elizabeth Cady Stanton (1815–1902) presiding. Stanton's and Willard's addresses at that first council can be found in the *Report of the International Council of Women* (Washington, D.C: R.H. Darby, 1888).

3. Willard referred here to the famous Battle of Waterloo (1815) that led to Napoleon Bonaparte's downfall.

4. Sorosis, first organized by journalist Jane Cunningham Croly (1829–1901) in New York in 1868, as a club for professional women, soon spread nationally and internationally among middle-class women as an organization aimed both at self-improvement (including, in some cases, career development) and volunteerism.

5. Here Willard referred to two major reform concerns of the era, noting her support for the free silver economic reform that argued against the U.S. treasury's gold standard, and her concern over recent exposés of enforced prostitution, especially in lumber camps.

6. Matilda B. Carse (1835–1917) was the longtime president of the Chicago Central WCTU, founder of the Woman's Temperance Publishing Association, and the major mover behind the WCTU's Women's Temple building project.

7. Cobbe (1822–1904) was a British author and reformer. Her book *The Duties of Women* (1881) was widely read among WCTU members.

8. Fanny Fern was a pseudonym for popular author Sara Willis Parton (1811–72).

9. William Benjamin Carpenter (1813–85), British physiologist and naturalist, was a

leading figure in the emerging science of brain function. His promotion of the Gilchrist lectures brought science to the working class.

10. Alexander H. Stevens (1812–83), member of the U. S. Congress, vice-president of the Confederacy and, later, governor of Georgia.

11. Each of these figures was admired by Willard for what they had written or spoken about living a useful life. Catholic Cardinal John Henry Newman (1801–90) of Great Britain wrote eloquently of the conscience as the internal proof of God and good works as an external sign of the workings of the conscience. Labor leader Powderly was noted earlier. William Morris (1834–96) was a British poet and craftsman who became an advocate for socialism. British author, Cobbe, was noted earlier. New York native Margaret McDonald Bottome (1827–1906) was president of the King's Daughters and Sons, an organization committed to self-improvement and Christian service. Philanthropist Isabels Lady Henry Somerset (1851–1921) was president of the British Women's Temperance Association and became an ally, patron, and close friend to Willard from late 1891 until Willard's death in 1898. In 1891 Susan B. Anthony, noted earlier, was serving as vice-president of the National American Woman Suffrage Association.

SEVENTEEN

"The Coming Brotherhood," August 1892

By the time Willard's article "The Coming Brotherhood" appeared in *The Arena,* a widely read reform journal, her support of labor and commitment to Christian socialism were firm. From 1886 when she first suggested that WCTU members consider ways in which the organization could help "ameliorate the deepening battle between capital and labor,"[1] she had continued to denounce the nation's unjust economic situation. In the face of middle- and upper-class opposition to labor, Willard urged her organization to study present economic conditions, espouse most of labor's aims, and join with workers and reformers to bring about a more equitable economic future. That same year, Willard publicly endorsed the Knights of Labor, then the largest union in the country. Like the WCTU, the Knights pursued a broad reform agenda with three linked components: temperance, the woman question, and the goals of the labor movement.

Echoing the muckrakers such as Helen Campbell, whose exposés of the terrible working conditions faced by wage laborers began to appear frequently in newspapers and magazines by the mid-1880s, Willard offered graphic descriptions of labor's exploitation to inspire action on the part of her constituency. For nearly two decades, she had been rallying women against the liquor industry and the male-dominated political system. Now she focused her critique on the strong laissez-faire economic policy elaborated by influential economists and vociferously championed by business and government, who were opposed to most forms of what they viewed as paternalism. Taking a stand against this dominant view, Willard announced that she and the WCTU "believe[d] in a paternal and a maternal government," one that would put in place local, state, and national regulatory systems designed to protect workers, especially women workers, and prevent the deplorable working conditions she described.

Writing as the past president of the National Council of Women, Willard called on organized women—especially middle- and upper-class women—to join with their sisters in labor unions in opposing the exploitation of workers. For Willard, the united action of reformers and workers of both sexes occurring in Chicago and elsewhere was a clear sign of the "coming brotherhood" that would inaugurate a new age based on the principles of justice and equality. The advent of a new economic order in America was one of the most persistent and inspiring themes of the second half of her WCTU presidency. Influenced by Edward Bellamy and his utopian socialistic novel *Looking Backward,* as well as her study of the work of political and economic theorists, Willard called for the institution of a radical alternative to what she and other reformers during the social gospel era saw as a cutthroat capitalism. She envisioned this new order as a form of Christian socialism in which all of the country's natural resources, industry, transportation, and utilities would be jointly owned and administered by the people—"We, Us, & Co."—through a representative government free from the manipulations of big business and corrupt politicians.

This new economic/political/social system would be inspired by the ethical teachings of Jesus, particularly the Golden Rule. Willard had noted in 1887 that, with the encouragement of the Knights of Labor, workers were reading the Bible as a "marvelous textbook of political economy," rather than ignoring biblical teachings except to ridicule them.[2] "God grant that the doctrine of Christ, which is 'fair dealing to others as you would yourself be done by,' may soon be put in practice toward every working woman and man in America," she exclaimed at the close of her article. She and other reformers of the era prophesied the creation of "a Heaven out of this world." Although such an ambitious vision must have seemed like an unattainable goal to many—perhaps most—of her readers, Willard believed that it could indeed become a reality, if only right-thinking men and women would band together to bring it about. In this article and in many speeches Willard delivered during the 1890s, she sounded a powerful rallying cry to her followers, enlisting them in the struggle to make this ideal world a reality.

The text of "The Coming Brotherhood" appeared in *The Arena* VI (August 1892), 317–24. The article was also published as a pamphlet and in a slightly different version by the Woman's Temperance Publishing Association (n.d., but probably 1892).

* * *

The synonym for knight is "chevalier"—that comes from the French "cheval," a horse, because the chevalier was a soldier and rode on horseback. Those who tilled the ground were called villains; they went afoot, and were also termed "clodhoppers." The knights thought themselves of great account, because they could gallop off to the wars on horseback; for war was the aristocratic profession, and labor was something very low down. But the good Book predicts the time when men shall "beat their swords into ploughshares, and their spears into pruning hooks" [Isaiah 2:4]. In these latter days, the word "knight" has been joined with "labor," and thus has been formed the right relationship. The true knight, the true chevalier, the true gentleman is the one who works, and not the one who goes off fighting and killing people, and devastating the world. We once required war, but in the process of evolution have come to a better civilization, and something of worth has been done for the country in giving it the idea of the "knight" as part and parcel of "labor," bringing those two words which have been opposites, into one thought, and proving that the laboring man can be a true gentleman, in all that goes to make up the beautiful significance of that word.

Many and urgent are the questions that the working men and women of today must help to decide. But whatever may be said of methods in general, and of special methods, as "strikes," in particular, as a temperance woman, I am confident that the best strike is to strike against the saloon, and then to strike against all politicians and parties that do wrong to the workingmen. Those are the two strikes that will pay.

There are enough saloons in America, if they were set in a row, to keep one company without a break, along a street reaching from Chicago to New York. In the eleven mountain states of the Union, in the West, there is a saloon for every forty-three voters. The boycott of the saloon is the greatest thing and the most helpful thing that has ever come to the Knights of Labor, or any similar organization. In one of the towns of Illinois, a banker put his private mark on the money he paid out on Saturday night to the wage-workers of the town who patronized his bank; and on Monday nights, of the seven hundred dollars paid out and marked privately, over three hundred dollars had come back to him from the saloons of that town! There is nothing that cramps, belittles, and dwarfs the possibilities of the labor movement in America like the saloons; and some guilds of workingmen show that they know this, by boycotting the saloons and all liquor dealers, not allowing them to be counted with reputable men, whose work brings back a good return.

Legitimate traffic is like the oak tree; in its branches the birds gather and make their pleasant music; under its shade the weary herds and flocks find rest and shelter. There is scarcely anything living that cannot get good out of an oak tree. It is like legitimate industry; every other industry is helped and benefited by it. But the liquor traffic is like the upas tree, forsaken by every living thing, because it is the deadly foe of every living thing, and drips not dew, but poison. The labor question is a mighty issue, but wage-workers would do well to study with it the temperance question; they would remember that nine hundred millions a year are expended by our people in America across the counters of saloons and in the liquor traffic,—nine hundred million dollars, to say nothing of the money that is lost by those who would be at work except for the temptation of the saloon.

If the women of the nation had the ballot, they and the good men of the nation would hold the balance of power. As white-ribboners, we believe that these great reforms must come in through the ballot box. We believe that because they are physically weaker, women, by the very instinct of self-protection, are the enemy of the liquor shops, because the manly arm that was meant to be their protection, when uncontrolled by the guiding brain and frenzied by alcohol, becomes their dread. We believe it makes no difference whether a woman is Protestant or Catholic, whether she is black or white, cultured or ignorant, native or foreign-born; but that, as a rule, women for the sake of protection for themselves, their children, and their homes, stand solidly against the dram shop. We believe that prohibition will come whenever woman has the ballot. In Washington [state] they gave women the ballot, and it was such a terror to the saloon men that they worked away with the Supreme Court, and finally succeeded in making out that they had left some punctuation mark, or else some little word, in the name of the bill, and so the Supreme Court said that the bill was not legal. What happened? There were bonfires and rejoicings in all the cities and towns and villages of Washington. There were bells ringing, not the bells in the steeples, but the ding-donging of all the old cow-bells and sheep-bells they could get. There was beer to be had on tap, furnished free by the saloon keepers, and a great jubilee from one end of the state to the other. Who got it up? The saloons. Why did they get it up? It was their celebration of the deplorable loss by women of the ballot. Tell us what the liquor men are afraid of, and the temperance people want it, and it is sure to be a safeguard of the home.

The workingmen are going to give us prohibition by their votes—but after they have driven the nail, they will need the hammer of woman's ballot to rap it into place, so that it will hold strong, steady, and sure.

Another vital issue in the labor question is the wages of women.

> "Alas! That gold should be so dear,
> And flesh and blood so cheap!"

We read about women who make twelve shirts for seventy-five cents, and furnish their own thread, in Chicago; about women that finish off an elegant cloak for four cents; about children that work twelve hours a day for a dollar a week; about some women who are glad to get the chance that offers six cents for four hours' work. Things like that our papers are full of, and other things too bad to describe. It is pitiful to read words like these: "We have six children at home; I give all my money to mother. Father is a builder, and is laid off for the best part of the year, and I don't have a cent for myself; I give it for meat and groceries. My sister is younger than I. She works on neckties. Fun? You ask me if I have fun? I've no time for it. I'd a great deal rather be a boy. They have a better time. They keep their money. Girls have to give up all they make to the home folks."

Now, many people say they do not believe in a paternal government. But we believe in a paternal and a maternal government, and that if a few more women had something to do with affairs, there would not be so many white slaves in Chicago, New York, and all along shore.

The women's clubs can do something in this line. If they would hold a convention on the subject of white slaves, if they would work up a petition to the city councils, something would come of it. Let the petition ask that there shall be women appointed as inspectors; that there shall be a municipal ordinance, providing that in a given city there shall be women to serve without salary—well-to-do women, who would much better invest their time in this manner than to swing in hammocks and read story books—to be appointed to visit these places where women work, and make official reports to the majority in every city, demand that there shall be a fire escape to every building where there are wage-workers, instead of having them piled in and killed and burned as thoughtlessly as if they were so many sardines in a box. Then let it be put down, as another section of the law, that there shall be just so many in a room of a certain size, and no more. Why, in some places, the girls are told they must take short threads; for if they don't, their needles will go into the eyes of those who sit in front! Then the law should provide that they shall have their lunchroom, and not be obliged to stand up, huddled together like so many sheep, to nibble away at their lunch; also that they shall have an hour, and not a half-hour, at noon, and that there shall be the best sanitary conditions and conveniences.

But the law is nothing unless you have an enforcer. Let the women enforce the laws; and let the men and women sitting in their clubs and saying what a wonderful country this is, that a woman can dress so cheaply, that the sewing machine has made such a difference that you hardly have anything to pay for your clothes, and have so much more time and money to improve your mind—let those women know how it is they get their collars and cuffs so cheap; let them look into the wan faces of the women who make these garments and receive these prices for their work. Women are too good hearted to tolerate all this, if they once know the cause. Bring them face to face with the situation, and they will soon work up such a public opinion that the rates and hours of wages will be changed for the better.

Already much has been done in the way of having a police matron at every police station. Before this, women were arrested by whom? By men. Tried by whom? By men. Sentenced by whom? By juries of men. And taken to the Bridewell [prison] by whom? By men. They never saw anybody but men. It came into the hearts of women who had never thought of it before, "Now why don't we have some woman at the police station, to be kind and friendly to these women?" The point gained in Chicago, the agitation spread to other cities, and success was ours in almost every large city of the nation. If temperance women could inaugurate all that, what could all the women's societies, united, do for the white slaves of Chicago and other cities?

In order to get your minds stirred up, by way of remembrance, read *The Prisoners of Poverty*, by Helen Campbell. When I was in Boston, in the winter of 1888, I read in the papers that some of the professors of Harvard University had been having a great deal of talk with a socialist. His name was Laurence Gronlund.[3] He was a Dane, and those men said he was the most sensible socialist they ever saw.

Many think every socialist an anarchist, but here was one who was reputable! I had the pleasure of an interview with him, and I was wonderfully interested in his ideas. He said to me, "People generally will not read my book, because it is dry; but there's a wonderfully gifted man who has put my book into a story, and the name is *Looking Backward*." So I read that; and Edward Bellamy, its author says that from the year 2000 he looked backward to the year 1887, and he saw, from that blessed and wonderful time, the terrible condition we are in now; he tells what might be done, as if it had really happened. Of course there are characters in the story, and there's a spice of romance, and all that; but it is to me a wonderful book. I do not see why what is in it should not some day come to pass. If men would say, "Let us have no enmity let us have no outrage, let us have mutualism, let us have collectivism, let us have arbitration, let us have cooperation instead of the wage system, and let it come, not by revolution, but by evolution," I think it might be slowly but steadily wrought out. The best part of this evolution will be the little white papers dropped into the ballot box. That is the way it is to be done.

Away in San Francisco some men got up a Bible class to study Christ's Sermon on the Mount. They had been conning in the Epistles that part where it said, "Servants, obey your masters" [Colossians 3:22], "Wives be in subjection to your husbands" [1 Peter 3:1], and all that went very nicely; but when they began to take up the Sermon on the Mount, the Golden Rule, "Do unto others as ye would they should do unto you" [Matthew 7:12], that was hardtack; it broke their teeth, spiritually speaking. Then came, "He that would have you go with him a mile, go with him twain" [Matthew 5:41], "To him that smites you on the right cheek, turn the left" [Matthew 5:39], "Give to him that asketh of thee, and from him that would borrow of thee, turn not thou away" [Matthew 5:42], "Give, and it shall be given to you,"[Luke 6:38], "Lend, hoping to receive nothing again"[Luke 6:35]—at this the Bible class adjourned, and they said of the Bible class teacher (who really thought this meant what it said, and took it literally), that he was a crank, and they wouldn't go any longer to such a Bible class. So they went home, justified in their own conceit, as John Habberton[4] tells us in one of his bright books.

Workingmen are reading the New Testament. They are in these days studying about that wonderful character, the Carpenter's Son. They are learning about His ideal of brotherhood, and what kind of a world we could make this, if we set out on the principles that He taught, and on the principles that He lived. I am glad that they are studying the temperance question, studying the woman question, and studying the New Testament. They are thinking whether we could not make a Heaven out of this world. There are rich men who find that it is for their interest to have a great big "trust," and a great big "monopoly." Perhaps the people will some time discover that two can play that game. The people may find that the trust, with "We, Us & Co." for its name, might make things go into a sort of brotherhood in this country, and that it would be brought through the ballot box.

Work is getting to be aristocratic; and not to work, dishonorable. It is not uncharitable to say that a person who does nothing is a drone to the hive, and does not amount to anything; it is the sweat of the brain and the sweat of the brow that make us Somebody, with a capital S, instead of Nobody, with a capital N. Then let us be glad that we are workers with God, who never ceases in His benefactions. We live in a world where every insect and bird and living creature is always doing something, because to do something is to be happy; and so, when the time comes that the true aristocrats shall make the world something like a home, and not altogether like a desert; when they come to their kingdom; when they have the opportunity for the culture of their minds, as well as the development of their hands, which they ought to have; when there are no grades in society except the grades of moral excellence, grades of industry, grades of intellectual nobility; when there is no wealth that makes aristocracy, but when what we are, what we have done, fixes our places in the world, then I believe we shall see the world that Christ came to create. We are going to see it far sooner than we think, because we are living in a time when ideas travel almost as quickly as a flash of lightning. Every throb of sympathy from the heart toward the "white slaves," every outraged sense of justice that ever stirred a human heart has helped to bring about this great time of deliverance. We have talked about charity. I am glad to live in a day when we are talking about justice! What we women want is simply justice. All that the laboring man wants is justice and fair dealing. All that these "white slaves" ask, is that they shall not be slaves; that rich merchants shall not give so much for missions, as if they were great Christian philanthropists, yet all the time put the thumbscrews of everlasting stinginess on these poor girls. That thing has got to be done away with, and that right early! People's eyes are being opened. God grant that the doctrine of Christ, which is "fair dealing to others as you would yourself be done by," may soon be put in practice toward every working man and woman in America.

And yet the nation is full of real Christian men and women, who "deal justly, love mercy, and walk humbly with God" [Micah 6:8]. They heed the voice of Christ in its tender cadences, saying, "And all ye are brethren!" [Acts 7:26]. God grant their number be multiplied! Even men of the world admit that London's four hundred city missionaries mean more for peace and quiet than four thousand police would mean. Even secularists applaud the splendid humanitarian work of the W.C.T.U. and the Salvation Army. Even infidels admit that McAll's Mission, in Paris, prevents barricades and riots, by teaching the French workman a more excellent way to the brotherhood of which he dreams.

Let me give you my "shorter catechism" of Political Economy from Ruskin: "There is no Wealth but Life. Life, including all its power of love, of joy, and admiration. That country is the richest which nourishes the greatest number of noble and happy human beings; that man is richest who, having perfected the functions of his own life to the utmost, has also the widest helpful influence both personal and, by means of his possessions, over the lives of others. A strange political economy; the only one, nevertheless, that ever was or can be; all political economy founded on self-interest being but the fulfillment of that which once brought schism into the policy of angels and ruin into the economy of Heaven."[5]

Notes

1. Willard, "President's Annual Address" in *Minutes of the National Woman's Christian Temperance Union* (Chicago: Woman's Temperance Publication Association, 1886), 85.

2. Willard, "President's [1887] Annual Address" in *Minutes of the National Woman's Christian Temperance Union* (Chicago: Woman's Temperance Publishing Association, 1888), 91.

3. Gronlund (1846–99) emigrated to the United States in 1867 and became a lawyer, reformer, and a leader in the Socialist Labor Party. His book, *The Cooperative Commonwealth* (1884), set forth German socialist economic principles.

4. John Habberton (1842–1921) was a prolific author of popular novels during the last half of the nineteenth century.

5. The final quotation in this article is from British art critic and social reformer John Ruskin's (1819–1900) essay "Ad Valorem" in *Unto This Last*. See Ruskin, *Sesame and Lilies, Unto This Last, and the Political Economy* (London: Cassell, 1910), 90.

EIGHTEEN

Address at Exeter Hall, January 9, 1893

Frances Willard's public reception and speech in London's Exeter Hall at the beginning of 1893 underscored her status as one of only a handful of internationally recognized reform leaders. As president of both the American WCTU and the World's WCTU, Willard held international credentials, and from 1892 to the end of her life, she was increasingly concerned with reform issues at a global level, spending nearly as much time abroad as she did in the United States. In fact, Willard biographer Ruth Bordin maintains that from 1892 until late in 1896, Willard's "real home" was England rather than Evanston, Illinois.[1] Her residencies at Eastnor Castle and Reigate Priory came through the invitation of their owner Lady Henry Somerset, president of the British Women's Temperance Association (BWTA).[2] Willard had first met Isabel Somerset in the fall of 1891 during preparations for the first World's WCTU convention in Boston. Somerset made the trip to the United States expressly to meet Willard and to study the organizational methods and work of the National WCTU. Willard and Somerset quickly became colleagues and friends, and their relationship had a significant influence on both the WCTU and the British women's temperance movement.

Throughout the 1890s, on the national and international stage, Willard vigorously maintained her belief in a broad reform agenda. During 1891–92 she had worked closely with other U.S. political and reform leaders, including representatives from the Populist movement, the Prohibition Party, labor organizations, Nationalist clubs, the WCTU, and others, to create a coalition of reform groups to mount a strong third-party challenge in the 1892 presidential election. Though this effort failed, Willard managed to carry her message of coalition building and broad-based reform to Great Britain. Throughout her tours of England she argued for her "Do Everything" policy and aimed to form alliances with others who agreed that the three most pressing reforms of the era, temperance, the woman question, and the aims of organized labor, were inextricably intertwined. Willard encouraged Somerset and her organization to look beyond the use of simple moral appeals for temperance and instead to consider a broad range of targeted activities, including suffrage and political work to further the cause of temperance as well as other reforms. Conservatives within the BWTA objected to Willard's influence and methods, but eventually the organization took on a range of reforms mirroring many of the efforts of the WCTU in America.

On the evening of Willard's first public welcome to England, Exeter Hall was packed to overflowing, with four thousand people crowded into the main room and fifteen hundred more in the lower hall.[3] Canon Samuel Wilberforce, the Bishop of Oxford, presided over the meeting, which consisted of several addresses of welcome, the presentation of various testimonials, and the address by Willard. Somerset later described the participants: "On the platform sat members of Parliament, dignitaries of our own church [Church of England], and temperance leaders from the Catholic Church, leaders of the Labor movement and of the Salvation Army, and delegations from the Methodist, Baptist and Congregational Churches and the Society of Friends. The chief Jewish rabbi sent a congratulatory letter and signed the address of welcome, which was also signed by hundreds of local branches of the British Women's Temperance Association."[4] The *Daily News* praised Willard's "unadorned" eloquence, noting that "her quaint Americanisms, homely practicability and quiet earnestness ha[d] a wonderful effect upon the audience." "From first to last," the paper declared, the Exeter Hall meeting "was a magnificent success."[5]

Indeed, Willard's Exeter Hall address was so successful that she soon received numerous invitations for speaking engagements and interviews. During the next few months Willard would share a similar message in places such as Liverpool, Manchester, Glasgow, Lutton, Southhampton, Portsmouth, and Cambridge.[6] The warmth of her reception was repeated in city after city and her appeal for broad-based reform helped re-energize women's reform efforts throughout Great Britain.

Excerpts of the Exeter Hall address appeared in both of Gordon's biographies of Willard,[7] but the following version from the WCTU series, reel 40, frame 56, is the most complete.

* * *

Most of us have in the course of our life looked with wondering and delighted gaze upon the "Happy Family" of Barnum.[8] If we are not a happy family here tonight and nothing to pay in order to see it, then I should like to know where you would go to find one? Can you show me an audience, that among forty-six different philanthropic guilds represented upon its platform, has the Vegetarians on one side balanced by the Butchers' Total Abstinence Society on the other? (Loud cheers.)

As you have been talking to me, my generous brothers and sisters, I have said to myself "For the first time in my life I am glad that I did not vote in America within the last two years, for I might have been led to vote in favour of the McKinley Tariff,[9] and how sheepish I should feel now." (Cheers.) As I looked round I felt the sense of a great home circle in your good hearts and kindly hand-clasps. It reminded me of the principle that Benjamin Franklin enunciated on a certain important occasion when he observed: "I tell you, my friends, we have got to all hang together or we shall all hang separately"[10]—(cheers)—and you will bear me witness that we do hang together and you are proud of us because we do. I do not know that I was ever more pleased than I am tonight that I can trace my undiluted ancestry back nine generations to an honest yeoman of Kent.

"Brave hearts from Severn and from Clyde and from the banks of Shannon," I come to you from the Mississippi valley, and in that "whispering corn" of which my beloved friend and our great leader has spoken, I used to sit on my little four-legged wooden cricket [stool] hidden away that nobody should know, reading out of poets and philosophers things that caused me to believe more than I knew, and I do it yet. I do not know, Brother Raper,[11] that Prohibition will capture old England, and salt it down with the "inviolate sea" as a boundary—but I believe it will; I do not know that the strong hand of labour will ever grasp the helm of state—but I believe it will; I do not know that the double standard in the habitudes of life for men and women will be exchanged for a white life for two[12] on the part of the Anglo-Saxon race—but I believe it will; I do not know that women will bless and brighten every place they enter, and they will enter every place—but I believe they will. (Cheers.) The welcome of their presence and their power is to be the touchstone.

When I come back here seventeen years hence, I shall be hale and hearty and seventy-two years of age, please notice—I have long had a notion in my head that I would speak right out and tell my age every time I had the chance, because I thought there was a sort of superstition that women did not like to tell their ages and we want to shine away all the superstitions that we can. (Hear, hear.) It is said that gratitude is a lively expectation of favours to come, but I have had so many favours tonight that I can never again be grateful under that definition. Some philosopher has said that the Gods approve the depth and not the tumult of the soul, and so amid all your generous tokens and expressions of kindness and goodwill, I have tried to hold myself as steady as I could, but it has not been a very easy task.

I have pictured in my mind three children—the three that I knew best—standing in an old weather-beaten barn away by the Rock River of a Sunday when the circuit rider did not come around—(brother Mark Guy Pearse[13] understands that). It was a misty, moisty morning and cloudy was the weather—(a little like London on occasions!)—and in this lonesome barn door stood three children—I was in the middle, my brother Oliver on one side, and my younger sister Mary on the other, and I remember saying in a sort of peevish voice (for I was the feeble one and the slight one that they thought would never live to grow up):

"Do you think that we shall ever go anywhere or see anybody, or be anything?" and my generous hearted brother Oliver, who has made me always a friend of men, because he was my ideal man,—(cheers)—said "Don't you mind, Frank, you just behave yourself the best you can, and I should not wonder if you came to something yet." He was always patting me on the shoulder, always helping me along. We read the same books: we shared the same sports, and all of a sudden all unnoticed he seemed to cross a sort of invisible line—I do not yet know where it was, but the almanac said that according to the reckoning he was twenty-one. The day after came that great assize in my country when they were to vote for or against John C. Fremont,[14] the "pathfinder" through the woods, who was, we hoped, to lead us in the anti-slavery victory, and my brother Oliver put on his best Sunday-go-to-meeting clothes, and went in the old farm wagon with father, who was in favour of free speech, free soil, free labour and free men—(cheers)—and the two of them jogged off to the polls.

Standing by the window, a simple country lassie, not a bit strong minded, and altogether ignorant of the world, I felt something hurt me in my throat, and then I turned to my little sister Mary who stood beside me, and said "Don't you think we ought to go with them? Don't you think it would be better for the country?" (Laughter and cheers.) I thought that women ought to have the ballot when I used to pay the hard-earned taxes on my mother's cottage home, but I never said it to anybody in public, I had not courage, but when it came to this great thought that women might help the temperance cause by combining their ballots with those of good men—(cheers)—then I could hesitate no longer. For the sake of the mothers who in the cradle's shadow kneel tonight beside their infant sons, I have the courage to speak out, and I know that whenever these words have been spoken by the lips of men and women in dead earnest, that the great heart of humanity has been comforted and tens of thousands have said "That is the larger hope." (Cheers.)

I am sorry Father Nugent is not here, but I was glad the Canon thundered. Why the name of Wilberforce has been shut up in my heart since ever I had a heart. For in my dear old home we were anti-slavery people from the beginning. All my kinsfolk, Brother Horton—(cheers)—were educated in that tremendously radical institution Oberlin College, founded by Congregationalists thirty years before any other discovered that for educational purposes it made no difference whether a person had a dark or a light complexion, whether a person were boy or girl, youth or maiden. These snug round boxes on the top of everybody's head were all Finney and Mahan took account of at Oberlin.[15]

We must clasp hands with Catholics if we would win this temperance battle. We had no end of Catholics on our old farm; perhaps that is where I learnt not to be afraid of them. I presume we had a hundred different ones during the time we were living in the country, and I want to tell you a story of one of them named Mike [Tullay]. I taught him to read and write; he was a good-hearted young fellow, who came over at twenty-three years of age, very lonesome and very eager to learn. After many years of absence, when I had gone into the temperance work and had a few silver threads on my forehead, I got a letter from Mike, not with much care taken as to punctuation, and there were some slips in the grammar and I being a school ma'am could have touched up the spelling a little. But I will tell you what was in this epistle. He wrote after well-nigh thirty years: "I have got a good wife and a big farm of my own, my boys are going to school, I shall send them to college and the girl too. I went to the polls this last autumn because I was a-thinking that you had not a vote to bless yourself with. I left the Democratic Party and voted the Prohibition ticket in your name, and I thought I'd write and tell you." So you will imagine that I thought pretty well of that Catholic to say the least. Last year I attended the Catholic Total Abstinence Society, and was received just as warmly and kindly as I have been here tonight. About the creed I did not think as they did, nor did they on all subjects agree with me, but we thought just alike concerning total abstinence and prohibition. And the beauty of this gathering tonight where so many are represented, is that we have had the wit to shut off certain parts of our brain just as a photographer puts his screens here and there and shuts off the light from the plate.

On a green hill far away was the great scene of history where, on a wide-armed cross, was lifted up that Figure whose radiant love shining out through all the generations since, has brought me and you together; given us our blessed temperance reform; is lifting Labour to its throne of power; has made men so mild that they are willing to let women share the world along with them.

And that reminds me that I wanted to speak a word about the *gentle* Czar. Have you heard of him?—the *gentle* Czar? This one of whom I speak had at one time absolute power. He dwelt in his own world, woman was his vassal altogether; she could not help herself, and had not wit enough perhaps to want to do so. But behold the Czar said, "Since woman has a brain, it is God's token that she should sit down with her brother at the banquet of Minerva." So you invited us to school and then we came tripping along like singing birds after a thunder storm. No vote except that of this hydra-headed Czar ever opened a school for women to get their brains nurtured and cultured. I read that in Edinburgh (which classic city I hope to visit in a week or two,) the trustees had by order of this Czar, invited women to join the College of Arts, and instead of the young men being crusty about it they were received with loud huzzas. In my own country, in some of the states and towns, the women have the municipal ballot; they have it under restriction in England. Who gave it to them? The gentle Czar. The Barons at Runnymede had to force their charter [Magna Carta] from King John, but the baronesses of this age have but to say: "Would not you like us to come and help?" and the gentle Czar extends his scepter, when lo, the doors are opened wide.

So I have no quarrel with men, and I have two reasons for thinking that they have been full of wisdom in letting us into the kingdom—for we want a fair division of the world into two equal parts. Please take notice, an undivided half is what the women want; they do not want to go off and set up for themselves and take their half, but to let it remain for evermore an undivided half. I believe men have let us into the kingdom because they have had six thousand years of experience, and consider themselves tolerably capable of taking care of number one. (Cheers.) In the second place I think that they are well assured in their own spirits that nobody living is quite so much interested to do them justice, and to look after them in a very motherly way as these very women folk!

There is between us but one great river of blood, one great battery of brain—our interests are for ever indivisible, for every woman that I ever knew was some man's daughter and every man I ever saw was some woman's son, and most of the men that I have been associated with in Christian work were "mother's boys." That is the best kind of boy, whether he belongs to the children of a larger growth or whether he is still in the bewildered period of the first and second decades. I believe that the bogies and the scare-crows that some folks have set up saying these ogres would make war between men and women are fast being consigned to the very last ditch of conservatism. We are not a bit frightened here tonight, are we? All of you that are not frightened, you my brothers with a basso-profundo voice, or a tenor it may be, who are not frightened because women are coming into the kingdom, just sing out "no." (Loud cheers and a chorus of "no.") I do not dare to take the voice of the women yet because they have not been sufficiently tested, but if I had them in a Temperance Convention by themselves you may be sure I would.

It is the thought and hope of the temperance reformer that by means of organisation those who are down will get up. We call it in America the "combine." Do you have that expression, the "combine," in England? We do not mean anything good by it in my country. The "combine" of "coal barons" as we call them that will not allow any more coal to be mined than is sufficient to keep the price up whether our noses are blue and the tips of our fingers are cold or not. The "combine" means a great monopoly, but we have found out at last that it is a game that two can play at and we believe that combination is the watchword of the hour for the labour movement, the temperance movement and the women's movement, the three parts of a tremendous whole. We believe that there is just one company that will never go into bankruptcy; would not you be glad to know what it is? We believe there is just one firm that will never make an assignment, one firm that will never go out of business, and it is the firm of "W. U. and C." [We, Us & Company] I pin my faith to that firm's sleeve and to no other.

Under the forms of organisation women are beginning to find out their power. The hand with its open fingers is rather an imbecile object, but if you bring it to a focus it is the emblem of man's greatest personal power. And it is because of discovering this that we are forming these kindly groups of white ribboners the world around—because "it is easier taking hold of hands." And we believe in the "do everything" policy. Some people have said that it is a "scatteration" policy, but

I am willing to sink or swim, live or die, survive or perish under the working of the "do everything" policy. By this we mean what they did at the Battle of Boyne [1690]: "Whenever you see a head hit it." Wherever the liquor traffic is entrenched there put in an appearance and send out the ammunition of your Gatling gun rattling its fires along the entire field. That has been our method from the beginning.

The liquor traffic is intrenched in the customs of society—go out after it then with the pledge of total abstinence for others' sake. The liquor traffic is protected by the people's ignorance—go after it into the Sunday schools and public schools with a "Thus saith Nature, thus saith Reason, thus saith the Lord." The liquor traffic is safeguarded by the law; go after it into legislature and parliament, and give them no rest for the sole of their feet till they give you a better law than you have yet achieved. But laws are made by men, not by abstractions, and men are elected by parties. Then do not be the least afraid, but go out among the parties and see which of them will take up your cause and then stick to that one. Parties are built up from units of humanity, and they need a stronger contingent of moral power. Let us then bring that contingent to the front; bring up the home guards and add them to the army.

There are two serpents, intemperance and impurity, that have enclosed and are struggling with the infant Hercules of Christian civilization. Let us strike at both, for purity and total abstinence must go together; the two must rise or fall together, and when we find that the Siamese twins of civilization are purity and abstinence, when we find that we must foster both, or each will die, then we shall have widened our course as God wants to see it widened.

As my friend W[illiam] T. Stead stood here just now it reminded me of the time when he came out of jail and they presented to him in Exeter Hall a Bible from the Y.M.C.A. I have ever since that time honoured the Hall more than I did before, though I confess to you that I should have thought it the acme of my hopes even to be inside it, let alone being greeted as I have been tonight.

In this work of the "do everything" policy we do not employ committees. No committee was deputed to build the ark, for if one had been the ark would have been on the stocks till now. Mrs. Hannah Whitall-Smith,[16] who sits on the platform beside me, said in her Quaker fashion something wonderfully true, in one of our conventions. I was appointing her on a committee when she rose, and with a sublime disregard of Parliamentary usage said, "If thee wants me to accomplish anything put me on a committee with two others, one of them a permanent invalid, and the other always out of town." From that day on we have had a single woman responsible for a single work, and we have fifty distinct departments of work, in which our great-hearted women are engaged. This plan has been admirably carried out in the United States, in Australia and Canada, and I believe that it will be in England, as the British Women's Temperance Association voted this classified method at its Council last spring.

I wish to thank you for the courtesy, kindness, and goodwill that you have shown to me and the cause I represent in England, and to say that after all you have done and said, I do not think even you, ingenious friends, could have thought out more to say and do in anybody's honour than we Yankees showed to Lady Henry Somerset. (Cheers.) She was welcomed in my land in a style that you here would call "royal." We are a little afraid over there, you know, of the people that have titles to which they are born, and I being a daughter of the Puritans, was especially afraid, but I make a great exception in her case. I think she will do to "belong," and she has concluded that I will do to "belong," so with my dear friend and trusty helper, Anna Gordon, we go happily about our work singing the white ribbon song to any who will hear, "Let us all belong," because that is the key note to the "combine" that is going to be the power in this great world of the firm of "W. U. and C."

And now may I conclude with the words of Tiny Tim, "God bless us every one!" May we have power to feel that there are but two words in the language of all the earth, and they are, *God and Humanity.* The old catechism said, "What is the chief end of man? To glorify God and enjoy Him for ever." The blessed Christianity in action of our own day says, and I reverently repeat the words: "What is the chief end of God?" "To glorify man and enjoy him for ever." And it is the clear brains of man into which that light of God can shine of which my gifted brother Woolley[17] spoke, that sacred "white light of truth." Alcoholized brains are like coloured glass. We cannot transmit the light of the truth unless we are under the power of that holy habit—sobriety.

May every home that you love be the home of peace; may every life that you cherish escape the curse of drink; may every child that you left tonight when you came out to this great meeting grow up sweet, and pure, and true. May every man that has lent to us his attention at this hour belong to the great army of the gentle Czar who is willing to welcome women even to the throne room of government.

> "Strike, till the last armed foe expires,
> Strike for your altars and your fires!
> Strike for the green graves of your sires!
> God and your native land!" (Loud cheers.)

Notes

1. Bordin, *Frances Willard,* 190.

2. During Willard's visits in England in the 1890s, she stayed mostly at the Reigate Priory, Isabel Somerset's primary residence, located in Surrey, a suburb south of London. She also spent time at Eastnor Castle, Somerset's hereditary home in Herefordshire, northwest of London.

3. Quoted in the introduction to Gordon, *Beautiful Life,* 15.

4. *The Friend,* January 20, 1893, in WCTU series, reel 40, frame 51; Anna Gordon, *The Life of Frances Willard* (Evanston, Illinois: National WCTU, 1912), 197.

5. Quoted in the introduction to Gordon, *Beautiful Life,* 227.

6. Gordon, *Beautiful Life,* 227. See clippings from Willard's scrapbooks in WCTU series, reel 40, frames 56–312, for coverage of her activities in England up to April 1893.

7. See Gordon, *Beautiful Life,* 223–26; Gordon, *Life of Willard,* 197–201.

8. One of the traveling exhibits of P. T. Barnum (1810–91), showman and occasional temperance lecturer, included a menagerie of caged animals he called the "Happy Family."

9. The McKinley Tariff of 1890 raised tariffs on goods imported to the United States, including goods from Great Britain, by as much as fifty percent. Viewed by many as a mistake, the tariff helped provoke the U.S. economic panic of 1893.

10. Franklin (1706–90) is said to have made this remark at the signing of America's Declaration of Independence.

11. James Hayes Raper (1820–97) was a leader of the United Kingdom Alliance, a British Temperance organization, and a prominent lecturer.

12. Willard used the expression "white life" to refer to a pure life, a life of sexual fidelity in marriage and free from the taint of alcohol, tobacco, pornography, or narcotics. For a version of Willard's popular lecture titled, "A White Life for Two," see Karlyn Kohrs Campbell, ed. *Man Cannot Speak for Her, II: Key Texts of the Early Feminist Movement* (New York: Praeger, 1989), 317–38.

13. Pearse (1842–1930) was a popular Wesleyan preacher and writer as well as a temperance lecturer with the Blue Ribbon Movement.

14. Fremont (1813–90) was the antislavery candidate for president in 1856.

15. Monsignor James Nugent (1822–1905) was a leading British Catholic reformer based in Liverpool, England. Brother Horton is likely a reference to British Congregationalist theologian Robert F. Horton (1855–1934), who was active in ministry to the working poor. William Wilberforce (1759–1833) was a member of the British Parliament whose record as a leader in the British antislavery movement was highly regarded within the U.S. abolitionist movement. He was grandfather to Albert Basil Orme Wilberforce (1841–1916), the Canon and later Archdeacon of Westminster, who was an active temperance leader and often chaired temperance meetings at which Willard spoke during her time in England. Scholar and antislavery and coeducation advocate Asa Mahan (1799–1889) was the first President of Oberlin College (1835–50), who was succeeded (1851–66) by famous preacher, Charles Finney (1792–1875).

16. An American, Smith (1832–1911) was raised Quaker but became famous in the 1870s as a holiness preacher at evangelical revivals. Active in the National WCTU as the head of the Evangelism Department, she moved to England in 1886 and began work with the BWTA.

17. John Granville Woolley (1830–1922) was an American preacher and temperance lecturer. At the invitation of Lady Henry Somerset, he was in England during 1892–93 on a speaking tour.

NINETEEN

Fourteenth Presidential Address, October 16, 1893

Frances Willard's 1893 annual presidential address for the combined meeting of the National WCTU and the World's WCTU was delivered at the World's Columbian Exposition as that six-month-long World's Fair drew to a close. Though written at a time when Willard was physically ill and still grieving the loss of her mother, the address is notable for its optimistic view of the past, present, and future of the WCTU and the goals of her "Do Everything" reform agenda. The annual message was deeply influenced by Willard's immersion in British thought and culture during the months she had been in England living with Lady Henry Somerset. Among the great British thinkers she had met was philosopher and sociologist Herbert Spencer. Always a believer in evolutionary progress, Willard was attracted to Spencer's theories of individual and social development. This address was infused with his ideas and also reveals her support for the earlier progressive evolutionary perspective of Jean Baptiste Lamarck.

Despite being composed while in Great Britain, Willard's annual address was in keeping with the atmosphere of celebration surrounding the World's Columbian Exposition. That commemoration of human advancement during the four hundred years since Columbus' landing in the New World had captivated the attention of the world and reinvigorated attention to women's accomplishments as women's organizations combined to design and build the Woman's Building as the nexus for their activities throughout the fair. As one of the most prominent women in America and a Chicago luminary, Willard had served on the Fair's Board of Lady Managers and helped plan events. Though her travels and ill health rendered her a minor figure in its final development, her annual message bears the marks of the reflective stance inspired by the exposition.

Opening with a commemoration of the nearing twentieth anniversary of the birth of the Woman's Temperance Crusade, the address celebrated the unfolding of the temperance movement from the streets to scientific circles, to legislative assemblies and on into political parties. Despite its history of continuous expansion, Willard warned that some critics wished to stem the tide of movement by restricting it to outdated notions of temperance. Accusing those critics of tunnel vision and self-righteousness, she asserted the interconnectedness of the temperance, women's rights, and labor reforms. She insisted that the women of the WCTU unite to "leave the world materially, mentally, sympathetically, conscientiously, [and] spiritually," better. This goal required action on a larger front than women had previously attempted.

In the section of the annual message titled "Gospel Socialism" Willard built her case for widespread economic revolution grounded in biblical principles. Her discussion was influenced by the thinking and reading she had done on the issue while trying to convert Somerset to the principles of Christian social-ism. Eventually, both women formally joined the Fabian Society, a British-based organization convinced that capitalism was unjust and committed to the peace-ful establishment of a socialist state. Although the discussion of socialism in this address echoes her earlier sentiments concerning the complex relationship between poverty and alcohol and gives praise for working men, it also paints a harsher view of the evils of money and the deepening gulf between the rich and the poor.

Though too ill to travel back to the United States to deliver the address, Wil-lard's leadership of the National WCTU was reaffirmed by her re-election by a huge majority. Nevertheless, the ten dissenting votes signaled that her broadened view of the goals of the WCTU was not universally accepted. In fact, a review of the speech in the *Chicago Journal* voiced the fears that Willard tended "to dissipate her forces over too wide a field." Claiming that the "curse of colossal ambition" had infected the movement, the *Journal's* reporter declared that the WCTU ought to rename itself, the "Woman's Universal Reform Society."[1] The irony here, of course, is that rather than seeing this as a critique, Willard would likely have embraced just such an organization.

The following excerpts are from "The Do Everything Policy," in *Address before the Second Biennial Convention of the World's WCTU, and the Twentieth Annual Convention of the National WCTU* (Chicago: Woman's Temperance Publishing Association, 1893), 1–2, 3–4, 5, 6–7, 12, 24, 34–35, 52, 53, 54–55, 57–58, 59–60.

* * *

Beloved Comrades of the White Ribbon Army:

When we began the delicate, difficult, and dangerous operation of dissecting out the alcohol nerve from the body politic, we did not realize the intricacy of the undertaking nor the distances that must be traversed by the scalpel of investiga-tion and research. In about seventy days from now, twenty years will have elapsed since the call of battle sounded its bugle note among the homes and hearts of Hillsboro', Ohio. We have all been refreshing our knowledge of those days by reading the "Crusade Sketches" of its heroic leader, Mrs. Eliza J. Thompson,[2] "the mother of us all," and we know that but one thought, sentiment and purpose animated those saintly "Praying Bands" whose name will never die out from human history. "Brothers, we beg you not to drink and not to sell!" This was the one wailing note of these moral Paganinis, playing on one string. It caught the universal ear and set the key of that mighty orchestra, organized with so much toil and hardship, in which the tender and exalted strain of the Crusade violin still soars aloft, but upborne now by the clanging cornets of science, the deep trombones of legislation, and the thunderous drums of politics and parties. The "Do Everything Policy" was not of our choosing, but is an evolution as inevitable as any traced by the naturalist or described by the historian. Woman's genius for details, and her patient steadfastness in following the enemies of those she loves "through every lane of life," have led her to antagonize the alcohol habit and the liquor traffic *just where they are,* wherever that may be. If she does this, since they are *everywhere,* her policy will be "Do Everything."

A one-sided movement makes one-sided advocates. Virtues, like hounds, hunt in packs. Total abstinence is not the crucial virtue in life that excuses financial crookedness, defamation of character, or habits of impurity. The fact that one's father was, and one's self is, a bright and shining light in the total abstinence galaxy does not give one a vantage ground for high-handed behavior toward those who have not been trained to the special virtue that forms the central idea of the Temperance Movement. We have known persons who, because they had "never touched a drop of liquor," set themselves up as if they belonged to a royal line, but whose tongues were as biting as alcohol itself, and whose narrowness had no competitor save a straight line. An all-around movement can only be carried forward by all-around advocates; a scientific age requires the study of every subject in its correlations. It was once supposed that light, heat, and electricity were wholly separate entities; it is now believed and practically proved that they are but different modes of motion. Standing in the valley we look up and think we see an isolated mountain; climbing to its top we see that it is but one member of a range of mountains many of them of well-nigh equal altitude.

Some bright women who have opposed the "Do Everything Policy" used as their favorite illustration a flowing river, and expatiated on the ruin that would follow if that river (which represents their do-one-thing policy) were diverted into many channels, but it should be remembered that the most useful of all rivers is the Nile, and that the agricultural economy of Egypt consists in the effort to spread its waters upon as many fields as possible. It is not for the river's sake that it flows through the country but for the sake of the fertility it can bring upon adjoining fields, and this is pre-eminently true of the Temperance Reform. . . .

Let us not be disconcerted, but stand bravely by that blessed trinity of movements, Prohibition, Woman's Liberation and Labor's uplift.

Everything is not in the Temperance Reform, but the Temperance Reform should be in everything.

There is no better motto for the "Do Everything Policy," than this which we are saying by our deed: "Make a chain, for the land is full of bloody crimes and the city of violence" [Ezekiel 7:23].

If we can remember this simple rule, it will do much to unravel the mystery of the much controverted, "Do Everything Policy," viz.: *that every question of practical philanthropy or reform has its temperance aspect, and with that we are to deal.* . . .

We are too apt to think that what makes for us makes for the truth and what makes for the truth must be true. Such a circle of reasoning leaves us, so far as logic goes, in the attitude said to have been assumed by the coffin of Mohammed—suspended between earth and heaven. A reformer is very apt to fall into this line of argumentation, a tendency which is perhaps most likely to be corrected by studying the correlated movements of other groups of men and women equally excellent, and by allying to the reform of which he is an advocate as many others germane to it as may be practicable, always asking this question as the touchstone of the "natural selection" he would make: "What is the Temperance aspect of this cognate reform and what [is] its aspect toward the liquor traffic?"

The Temperance cause started out well nigh alone, but mighty forces have joined us in the long march. We are now in the midst of the Waterloo battle, and in the providence of God the Temperance army will not have to fight that out all by itself. For science has come up with its glittering contingent, political economy deploys its legions, the woman question brings an Amazonian army upon the field, and the stout ranks of labor stretch away far as the eye can reach. As in the old Waterloo against Napoleon, so now against the Napoleon of the liquor traffic, no force is adequate except the "*allied* forces."

A General Survey

There are two changeless sources of solid happiness; first, the belief in God, and second, the habit of hard work toward useful ends. The first affords a sunshiny mental atmosphere, the second keeps that ever-active engine, the brain, from working on itself. For it cannot be idle, and if its energies are not directed toward objective occupation, it will find employment in such dissection of its own powers as will weaken them, and tend toward morbid views and general bewilderment. The recoil of an engine upon itself, when that engine is the brain, means, in the last analysis, insanity. Looking out upon the world we perceive that it is continually improving as to the comforts of life, the tools of mind and hand, the inventions that help on the annihilation of time and space, and the incentives to noble character. We know that this great improvement has not *happened* but *has been caused to come to pass;* and we know that human beings are the necromancers who have wrought these wonders. If we are not wandering savages, it is because of some systematic power put forth to produce that totality of improvement which we call civilization. This was done man by man, woman by woman, step by step,

thought by thought, hand by hand. Into the vast and fruitful harvest of their sowing who have passed across the stage and out of sight, we have been welcomed
for a while, and the least that we can do is to add our increment of power to the
totality of achievement—to leave the world materially, mentally, sympathetically,
conscientiously, spiritually, as much better than we found it, as the addition of
our personality and rational effort during the years allotted to us, can cause it to
become. This is a very practical view of life, I am aware; but it is one that commends
itself to this practical age, and as I understand it, the women of the White Ribbon,
banded together in the name of "God and Home and Every Land," propose to
do just what I have described in a systematized and consecutive fashion, so long
as life and health remain to them. In view of such a purpose, our Association can
but command the respect and goodwill of all rational minds, and we do not care
what the irrational may say, because their blame is praise. . . .

The history of the reformer, whether man or woman, on any line of action is
but this; when he sees it all alone he is a fanatic; when a good many see it with
him they are enthusiasts; when all see it he is a hero. The gradations are as clearly
marked by which he ascends from zero to hero, as the lines of latitude from the
North Pole to the Equator. . . .

So far as the White Ribbon movement is concerned, this has been its best and
brightest year from the outlook of the World's W.C.T.U., and that is the only point
of view that is adequate. How little did they dream, those devoted women of the
praying bands, who with their patient footsteps bridged the distance between home
and saloon, and in their little despised groups poured out their souls to God, and
their pitiful plea to the ears of men, that the "Movement" would be systematized
twenty years later into an organization known and loved by the best men and
women in every civilized nation on the earth; and that its heroic missionaries
would be obliged to circumnavigate the globe in order to visit the outposts of
the Society. How little did they dream that in the year of the World's Columbian
Exposition well nigh half a million of children would send their autographs on
the triple pledge cards of our Loyal Temperance Legions, and Sunday School Department; that we should have a publishing house, owned and conducted by the
society itself, from which more than a hundred million pages of the literature of
light and leading should go forth this year; how little could they have conceived
of the significance that is wrapt up in the lengthening folds of the Polyglot Petition,[3] signed and circulated in fifty languages, and containing the signatures and
attestations of between three and four million of the best people that live, praying
for the abolition of the alcohol traffic, the opium traffic, and the licensed traffic in
degraded women. How little they dreamed of that great movement by which the
study of physiology and hygiene were to bring the arrest of thought to millions
of young minds concerning the true inwardness of all narcotic poisons in their
effects on the body and the brain. How "far beyond their thought" the enfranchisement of women in New Zealand and Wyoming, Kansas and "Michigan, my

Michigan!" How inconceivable to them the vision of our House Beautiful[4] reared in the heart of the world's most electric city, and sending forth its influence to the furthest corner of the globe. How little did they dream that the echo of their hymns should yet be heard and heeded by a woman whose lineage, and the prowess of whose historic name may be traced through centuries, and that not alone from the cottage and the homestead, but from the emblazoned walls of splendid castles, should be driven the cup that seems to cheer, but at the last inebriates.

But we must remember that after all, these are but the days of small beginnings compared with what twenty more years shall show. Doubtless if we could see the power to which this movement of women's hearts for the protection their hearthstones shall attain in the next generation, the inspiration of that knowledge would exhilarate us beyond that which is good for such steady patient workers as we have been, are, and wish to be; but I dare prophesy that twenty years from now woman will be fully panoplied in the politics and government of all English-speaking nations; she will find her glad footsteps impeded by no artificial barriers, but whatever she can do well she will be free to do in the enlightened age of worship, helpfulness and brotherhood, toward which we move with steps accelerated far beyond our ken. The momentum of centuries is in the widening, deepening current of the nineteenth century reform; the twentieth century's dawn shall witness our compensations and reprisals, and as these increase humanity shall pay back into the mother-heart of woman its unmeasured penitence and unfathomed regret for all that she has missed (and through her, every son and daughter that she has brought into the world), by reason of the awful mistake by which, in the age of force, man substituted *his* "thus far and no farther," in place of the "thus far and no farther" of God; one founded in a selfish and ignorant view of woman's powers, the other giving her what every sentient being ought to have—a fair field and a free course to run and be glorified. . . .

The World's W.C.T.U.

The World's W.C.T.U. is but an outline map as yet. The shading is to come; the tones are to be wrought into its texture with the perspective that shall make a picture glorious and complete. How soon this vision shall begin to dawn on human eyes depends upon each one of us—in the last analysis perhaps as much on one as on another.

Dr. Kate Bushnell[5] has justly said that as it was only by confounding the languages of the earth that man was prevented from building a tower to heaven, so the isolation of women from each other has delayed the progress of Humanity. But women are now saying "we never understood each other so well as we do in these days." There is a heart-language that they are learning in every nation, and nothing can stand before the sisterhood of woman that is now growing up around the world.

No testimony is more uniform or more cheering than that which comes from our round-the-world missionaries, showing the solidarity of sentiment among women everywhere, no matter what their complexion, language, or condition of servitude; they all believe in the White Ribbon Movement when it is explained to them, and none more heartily than the dusky-faced women of Africa, to whom our ambassadors spoke through interpreters, and who listened so long and with such acute interest that the pale-faced women from the West could not find it in their hearts to break up the meeting until an unusually late hour. The universal kindness and goodwill manifested toward our representatives, brings to our minds with pathetic significance, those sacred words, "He fashioned their hearts alike" [Psalm 33:15]. . . .

Let me mention once more that the intention of the great Polyglot petition seems to have been generally misunderstood. It is not supposed that it will produce any strong impression upon any Government or ruler, although of course even this is possible. Neither is it proposed to leave the petition in the hands of any Government to be referred in the usual parliamentary way to a committee, and there remain entombed. The object is rather, *to focus public sentiment,* and we all know that whatever does that is invaluable, and speeds the Temperance cause. People are taught by great public object lessons as well as by the slow and quiet process of home training; popular opinion is exceedingly sensitive to the impress of a demonstration, and the spectacle of a commission of honorable and distinguished Christian women, who have given their lives to the cause of Temperance and Social Purity, carrying a petition with millions of names gathered up from all corners of the globe, both Christian and Pagan, and presenting that petition in the largest public hall of a great capital will be reported by the press of a whole nation, and will set a myriad of brains at work to solve the problem, "Why did these women do this thing? What does it mean? How much in earnest they must be! What infinite pains they have bestowed, what hardships they have encountered, what public opinion they have braved! Ought not we men, who have so much more power, to take up a question like that? Is it not unmanly to leave this great reform to women?" What we want is an arrest of thought in the manly brain: and such an embassy and such a petition will greatly help to bring about the consummation.

The amount of printer's ink that will be set in motion is in itself beyond computation in value for our cause. Our policy is "The do everything policy, and do it all the time." The Petition is but one method, but it is a good one, we believe, and altogether "practical." . . .

The Quenchless Woman Question

Perhaps the novel is the barometer of women's rise. Professor Swing,[6] in his famous lecture on the novel, set forth his favorite theory that it is the apotheosis of woman, a creature far too bright and good to be cribbed, cabined and confined within the conventional limits of the sphere that man's selfishness had circumscribed for her, and hence she expanded into the wider circle of the novel, where she played the public part denied her in real life; for she was made and meant to be a thing of beauty and a joy for ever; not to her home alone, but to the great world; and this is so true that in the less-developed ages, when man's self-restraint did not permit her to be a figure on the stage, young men and beautiful were attired in women's garb to act her part. When she became the central figure of the novel, it grew to be the most fascinating of all books, hence the most widely-read, in all the wilderness of literature. But this was only a figure of things to come, and predicted her admission to all the world contains. It was a sort of dress rehearsal for her part on the stage of life, wide as the planet and high as human need and sympathy. It is to be regretted that the woman, who in these regnant days of scientific Christianity and Christian science is not only "the coming woman," but has already come, should be a character so individual that the old-line novelist cannot adapt their concept or their style to her bright, new lineaments; but we, as women, should be devoutly thankful that the novelist of the future has some forerunners, in our own country, Mrs. Elizabeth Stuart Phelps Ward,[7] and in England, George Meredith,[8] who, as one of our ablest woman journalists has said, "Shows that it is possible for women to despise inconstancy and weakness, and not to cling to unworthiness in men with that blind doting love ascribed to them; that the rigid demand of a higher moral standard for women than for men frequently has its origin in the desire of brute force for absolute possession; that the faults and the virtues of women are the faults and virtues of the race; that woman in her best estate is not an angel, nor in her worst 'worse than a bad man.'"

I wish we did not so much use the expression "emancipated woman." Its associations and history are not to our advantage. It would be far better to combine our efforts to make the term "awakened woman" current coin in the world's great exchange of speech.

Of all the fallacies ever concocted, none is more idiotic than the one indicated in the saying, "A woman's strength consists in her weakness." One might as well say that a man's purity consisted in his vileness, or that his sobriety consisted in his drunkenness! When was ever strength discounted, except by those who would have women kept in a condition of perpetual tutelage, or ignorance glorified except by those who desire her as a parasite? Nothing proves more conclusively the wretched nonsense of the conservative position on the "Woman Question" than that so noble an expression as "strong minded" should have become a synonym of reproach. It is the off-set of "weak minded," and to be weak minded is the greatest calamity that can fall upon a human being. Let us have done with this nomenclature, and the shallow wit that gives it currency, and let us insist first, last, and always that gentleness is never so attractive as when joined with strength, purity never so invincible as when leagued with intelligence, beauty never so charming as when it is seen to be the embellishment of reason and the concomitant of character. What we need to sound in the ears of girlhood is *to be brave,* and in the ears of boyhood *to be gentle.* There are not two sets of virtues; and there is but one greatness of character; it is that of him (or her) who combines the noblest traits of man and woman in nature, words, and deeds. . . .

Gospel Socialism

In every Christian there exists a socialist; and in every socialist a Christian, for, as someone has wisely said, you cannot organize a brotherhood without brothers, and it is only too apparent that there are two kinds of socialism; one gives and the other takes; one says "all thine is mine"; the other says all "mine is thine"; one says "I," the other "we"; one says "my," the other "our"; one says "down with all that's up," the other "up with all that's down." It will take several generations to change the set of brain and trend of thought, so that in place of an individual we shall have a corporate conscience; but the outcome of the Gospel and the golden rule will at last make it intuitive with us to say "*our* duty" rather than always "*my* duty," that is, we shall conceive of society as a unit which has such relations to every fraction thereof, that there could be no rest while any lacked food, clothing or shelter, or while any were so shackled by the grim circumstances of life that they were unable to develop the best that was in them both in body and mind. . . .

The statement seems almost incredible that one in five of London citizens dies in the workhouse or the insane asylum, but this is vouched for by labor leaders there, as is another fact hardly less deplorable and closely connected with the first, namely, that there are 250,000 women in London whose daily wages do not exceed fifteen pence. But we have men who can pay $5,000 to decorate a house boat for their mistresses, or can give $1,200 for a pianoforte recital by Paderewski,[9] or $1,000 for flowers to decorate a table at a banquet. These things ought to be known, and the best of it is labor leaders are determined that they shall be known. If one could do nothing more than stand at the street corners ringing a bell and dinning them into the ears of the passers by, he would be organizing a revolution—peaceful, let us hope—out of which the people would emerge into a scene as different as that when one quits the sulphurous fumes of the railway tunnel for the sweet air of the fields in the spring.

"Poverty causes intemperance and intemperance causes poverty and that is the whole of it." So said a working woman cutting the Gordian knot of this difficult question, in a single sentence by the short road of her own experience and observation. . . .

Perhaps the best definition of Socialism is that endorsed by the Trades Union Congress at its recent meeting in Belfast by a majority of 137 to 97 against. They pledged themselves "to support the principle of collective ownership and control of all the means of production and distribution." As the word Socialism is greatly misunderstood, it may be well for us to carry in our minds this definition given by experts. Lasalle, the great socialistic reformer, declared that the ethical basis of the teachings of Hegel is "devotion to universality."[10] However this may be, the sense of universality is growing in the human race and is the inspiring force of what we call "the modern spirit."

The inherent antagonism between labor and liquor was illustrated last year by the refusal of the International Labor Convention held in Glasgow to admit a delegation from the brewers, and its hearty welcome given the following day to a temperance delegation.

I charge upon the drink traffic that it keeps the people down, and capitalists and politicians know it. Nothing else could hold wage-workers where they are today except the blight that strong drink puts on all their faculties and powers. There are leaders here who could testify that capitalists have said to them, little dreaming how the utterance would in future years recoil upon their class and re-echo to the world's end, "We would rather give our men drink tickets for dangerous time (in the mines) and over-time than to give them money; we could not handle such masses of men and keep them willing to undertake such odious work, and keep them down as we are able to do now except for drink." There are those who could testify that having later on written to the owners of those mines, who lived at a distance, about the way in which the overseers were handling the men through drink, they at once withdrew their support of a mission that had been established for the miners.

But for drink the slums would rise to the level of organization in Trades Unions, and through political machinery would dethrone those who reap the fruits but have not sown the seeds of industry. But for drink the standing armies of sodden soldiery would fraternize with the people out of whose loins they sprung, whose interests are their own and whose peaceful triumph alone can save their blood from watering the furrows of continental Europe. But for drink the aristocracy, rising from its bewildered dream of self-indulgence, would note as it does not now the tottering of thrones and dynasties, and would perceive that its only salvation, not for title and fortune which *must* pass away, but for life itself, lies in making common cause with King Demos [the people], the only ruler who once set on the throne shall never abdicate. The upper classes can better abstain than the overworked and often ill-fed lower.

Who can call work for shop-girls irrelevant to the temperance movement? What is it that leads them to drink? It is wretched fare, miserable quarters at home, insufficient food, and wearying hours of ill-requited toil. If we have any justice it behooves us to look into this *cause*, and not deal for ever and a day with the *effects* of the liquor traffic, and with these alone.

We should not have the women of our nation flocking to the public-house if the women of culture and fortune would but put the wine outside their doors. We ask more of working women, ill-housed, ill-fed, ill-clad, when we take the pledge to them, than we do to the daughters of wealth who lack for nothing, and to whom intoxicants are but a pleasant stimulant, whereas the working woman often thinks at least that she finds in her bottle of beer something like food and recuperative power.

Among the poor in London there is a sort of freemasonry of which the clinking of glasses is the sign. A poor woman who cannot pay her rent often goes to the public house, tells her distress, and after they have treated her and themselves all round, her neighbors will, at the rate of a few pence each, make up the amount. If she had been a teetotaler they would have said that she was a stingy Puritan, and would have left her to herself. This terrible perversion of the social instinct of mutual help practically condemns the people in the slums to make the public house the center of their good times which they do by "starting in" for a jovial hour by taking what they deem to be a jovial glass. Teetotalers are at a discount in the slums. The people say, "we must drink to forget," and quote the Bible—"Let him drink and forget his poverty and remember his misery no more" [Proverbs 31:7]. So we cannot forget the Labor Question in the Temperance Question, and unless we show the people our interest to help ameliorate and improve their condition financially, and to raise them to a better level, they will not thank us for preaching either Christianity or teetotalism, but they will look at us as hypocrites, and perhaps not inadvisably. . . .

The dignity of labor has never been so strongly insisted upon as by speakers and writers in the last year. "Blessed be drudgery" has come to be an every day beatitude in the labor propaganda. It is openly declared that we must rehabilitate work; that it is a law of life and happiness, that if a man will not work neither shall he eat; and on the other hand if a man will work he shall eat; and in Switzerland a petition has been circulated that has attained so large a number of names that under the law of initiative and referendum a plebiscite [direct popular vote] is to be taken on the question: Shall it not be obligatory on the Government to furnish work to every citizen who is willing to do it? Under the rule of labor and solidarity it is rapidly coming to pass that there is no place for the idler on this planet, he is as bad as a thief, and as disgraceful as a beggar. The one only aristocracy is soon to be the aristocracy of honest toil; but, be it well certified, that toil shall not exceed eight hours per day.

Stanley's[11] description of the forests of Africa may well be likened to the present condition of things in the forest of humanity. A few immense over-reaching and over-mastering trees so monopolize the space that the small ones have no hope or opportunity. The growth is too thick, the shadow too great, the soil not rich enough, under the system of competition. In the forests of South Africa daylight must be let in upon the gloomy undergrowth. There must be space and freedom, we shall then have more trees and better ones, an improved climate and a habitable country.

The same laws apply to the human jungles and forests of great cities—there must be a thinning out. The wholesome influence of nature, sunbeam and sky, air, earth and water must be more intelligently and equally provided for each and all, then will come the tall, well-developed and harmonious growths, and not till then; but this means that sort of socialism which is best defined as "Christianity applied."

"The love of money is the root of all evil" [1 Timothy 6:10], and the small meannesses bred by the law of competition corrode men's characters as rust spoils steel. You can enter no hotel without perceiving that the attendants look at you with a keen, commercial eye, and determine how much attention they shall pay, or rather, expect to be paid for. They have even got the matter down to so fine a point that in Switzerland, I learn, they make special marks on the baggage of travelers which mean, in the jargon of their class, "This one gives small fees: neglect him accordingly." From the boot-black to the throne, money values are the final test of every human being's status in the world in these days; and, whether we know it or not, we are all ranged in lines in the great amphitheater of life, plebeians and patricians, not by pedigree, talent, or achievement, but by the weight of the money in our pockets, and our balance at the bank. The triumph of the Labor movement will change all that; the unit of value will be a day's work with brain or hand, honestly done and fairly measured. As an offset to that day, the one who lived it shall have shelter, food, clothing, what we call, in a word, "the comforts of life." In the effort to change from the present method, which has doubtless been necessary up to date, but which is now out-worn, the whole world is writhing like a snake that would cast its skin. Its contortions take away our security and peace, and there will be no more rest until it is torn and clothed anew.

"*Ours,* not *mine* shall be the watchword of the future."

The world is waking up to the idea that because things have been so is no sufficient reason why they always shall be. Because on state occasions there are two million dollars worth of plate on Queen Victoria's table, and a chandelier above it containing a thousand ounces of solid gold, is no reason why this should be so in the better days that we believe are at the door. Because there is at Windsor Castle fifteen million dollars worth of plate, is no reason why there will be always. Because the United States contains today over four thousand millionaires, is no reason why there should be so many of these monstrosities tomorrow. . . .

Sitting in the directors' meeting of *The Union Signal* one day, I looked from the window and saw, down the next corner, the Woman's Temple going up, already having attained its thirteenth story. A hod-carrier[12] was walking slowly along its outer wall with his heavy burden, and perhaps no object on the street was less remarked or of less interest to the passers-by, but I could not help thinking, as he plodded on, that is the way with character; we built it in littles, and without observation. It is just the steady going forward doing the duty of the minute or the hour, putting in the time and effort just when and where they are needed, and doing this right on; that is all there is of character building, or temple build-ing, or probably of planet building or of universe building, just to keep right on putting in our time and effort to the best advantage practicable at the moment. It was very encouraging to me to see him go, poor fellow, and to think that there was a certain holiness about him, because all honest work is holy. The reaction of our powers on our environment for good and helpful purposes is holiness. It is fulfilling the law of our being. It is doing what God does. Sometimes one thinks when he goes along the street and sees the grimy face of some man with a pickaxe in the ditch, who can do nothing except invest his muscular force to remove certain clods or pieces of stone out of their places, "It is a pity he has learned nothing better to do than that." But after all it was thus that every city was builded, every railroad carried to completion, and I have learned to look with a certain reverence at these men who are literally doing what Emerson spoke of in his famous words, "building better than they know," better for humanity; better, let us hope, for themselves.

Notes

1. *Chicago Journal,* October 19, 1893, in WCTU series, reel 41, frame 199.

2. Eliza Jane Trimble Thompson (1816–1905) was one of the major leaders of the Wom-an's Crusade in South Eastern Ohio in the winter of 1873–74. Her book *Hillsboro Crusade Sketches and Family Records* was formally published in 1906.

3. The Polyglot Petition was the most ambitious petitioning campaign of the National WCTU and World's WCTU. Composed by Willard in 1884 and calling for the government of every nation to prohibit trade in alcohol and opium, the petition was first presented at the International Temperance Congress in Antwerp, Belgium, in 1885. By the mid-1890s the petition, over a mile long, boasted signatures from over forty nations and claimed the endorsement of seven million people.

4. The "House Beautiful" was the WCTU's Woman's Temple, an office building in downtown Chicago. Built as space for national offices and as a source of income from rentals, this symbol of women's increasing financial power was, by 1893, seriously threat-ened due to a national economic downturn.

5. In 1891 physician Katherine Bushnell (1856–1946), active in the WCTU's Social Purity department, began to travel around the globe as an organizer for the World's WCTU. She presented the Polyglot Petition to numerous foreign governments.

6. David Swing (1830–94), a Presbyterian minister in the Chicago area, resigned from the presbytery in the mid-1870s after being charged with heresy for preaching a message of works over faith and for tolerating a Unitarian rather than Trinitarian theology. Swing established a flourishing independent ministry in Chicago, founded a kindergarten and industrial school, and supported many charities.

7. Elizabeth Stuart Phelps Ward (1844–1911), best known for her novel *The Gates Ajar,* was an American author whose fictional heroines exhibited great strength and indepen-dence.

8. George Meredith (1828–1909), British poet and author, wrote works reflecting his optimistic view of the continuous evolution of life.

9. Ignacy Jan Paderewski (1860–1941) was a prominent Polish composer and pianist.

10. Ferdinand Lasalle (1825–64), French socialist and author of *Science and the Working Man,* saw the rise of the proletariat as an advance for civilization both morally and culturally. Lasalle agreed with German philosophical idealist Georg Wilhelm Friedrich Hegel (1770–1831) that the state could be a source of right and justice.

11. Henry Morton Stanley (1841–1904), journalist with the *New York Herald,* made several expeditions to Africa.

12. A hod is a trough supported on a pole and is used to carry bricks and mortar.

TWENTY

Fifteenth Presidential Address, November 16, 1894

Frances Willard's presidential address was a central feature of the 1894 convention of the National WCTU. The meeting marked the twentieth anniversary of the organization's founding in Cleveland, and media coverage was extensive. Historian Ruth Bordin likened it to the kind of attention received by political conventions "including personal sketches of prominent delegates, press interviews with Willard and other national officers, and discussion of the Union's stand on national issues."[1] The organization certainly retained its status as the largest and most influential women's organization in the nation, and Willard was celebrated as their leader.

At over one hundred published pages in length, her annual address took up issues from total abstinence and prohibition legislation around the globe, to exploring the machinations of political parties and calling on the WCTU to establish a Department of Politics and foment a grassroots movement that would bring forth a new reform political party. But the heart of the speech coalesced around Willard's central themes of the 1890s: economic reform and women's rights. In addition to exploring these issues, the excerpts below also include Willard's defense of herself and the WCTU in the wake of Ida B. Wells's charge that the organization and Willard herself had failed to show moral courage and leadership concerning the issue of lynching in the southern states.

Although the central themes of the address were familiar to Willard's audience by the mid-1890s, their treatment here was more urgent than in earlier renditions. Highly critical of capitalists who advocated a "survival of the fittest" approach to human social and economic systems and viewed working men as a "menace," she recognized the serious challenges facing the nation. With characteristic optimism, however, she articulated many reasons for hope: she had faith that the crisis would prompt the public to take control of central national industries, such as transportation and newspapers; she believed that the nation could reinvent the economic system to produce outcomes that rewarded all workers; and she hoped that all people would soon recognize the need for the new perspectives women had to offer and would call for their active participation in the battle.

In this address we find the clearest statement of Willard's view that socialization and biology combine to create differences in the ways men and women view the world. Such differences, she was quick to add, should not lead to different treatment. "The whole question is one of equal chances, not of equal powers," she announced, thus sounding the call for equal opportunity. Not until society had provided an equally free and fertile environment for men and women could we really know anything about "their comparative ability." Expanding opportunities for women in the workplace and the broader engagement of the "average woman" in the affairs of the world, she predicted, would further prepare women to take their rightful place in government.

Unfortunately, the insight Willard possessed concerning lack of equality for women was not so evident in her discussion of racial issues, as this presidential address reveals. African American activist Ida B. Wells brought this failing to light during the mid-1890s. During her 1893 speaking tour in England, Wells had publicly accused Willard and other white reformers of being indifferent to the plight of African Americans. In particular, she cited their failure to take a vigorous stand against lynching and pointed to their perpetuation of negative stereotypes of African American men. Given the seriousness of the charge and Willard's stature as a major reform figure, Wells's accusations provoked a flurry of public discussion.[2]

Willard and the WCTU did not ignore the controversy. Wells actually attended the 1894 WCTU convention and was invited to address the group as a fraternal delegate from the African Methodist Episcopal Mite Society. However, the excerpts from the presidential address below, especially the section titled "The Colored People" give an indication of the way Willard equivocated on this issue. Willard defended the National WCTU's record of including black women on equal footing as members and leaders in the organization, articulated her support for an educational test for the ballot (rather than a restriction resting on sex, race, or property), and denounced lynching as an evil and called for the WCTU to pass a resolution declaring their stand against it. But Willard failed to recognize or call for a remedy to the inevitable disenfranchisement of blacks that would result from an educational test for voting rights. Furthermore, she persisted in her belief that "the nameless outrages perpetrated upon white women and little girls," while no justification for the lawlessness and brutality of lynching, and no excuse for white male violence against black women, nevertheless, remained a legitimate concern in the southern states. In other words Willard had missed the point of Wells's argument that lynching as a practice was not about rape, actual or alleged, but about power and terror.

These failures make clear that Willard was unable to overcome the prejudices formed during her southern tours when she was hosted by upper middle-class white women. Nevertheless Willard enjoyed the support of many African American women within the WCTU who continued to use connections with the organization to work toward their own goals.[3] The WCTU was one of only a handful of integrated women's organizations and one of only a few national organizations to regularly pass resolutions against lynching during the 1890s, yet Willard's discourse reveals that she was unable to respond to the racial issues at the core of this controversy.

The excerpts are from "President's Address," in *Minutes of the National Woman's Christian Temperance Union at the Twenty-First Annual Meeting* (Chicago: Woman's Temperance Publishing Association, 1894), 87–88, 112–19, 120–22, 123–26, 129–31.

* * *

The New Age

Returning after an absence of two years (with the exception of six weeks at the time of the Denver Convention in 1892) the outlook appears to me to have changed more than in all my life before; not even during the crisis of the Civil War did the foundations seem to be so deeply shaken. Intelligence, invention, and immigration are the three points of a triangle that encloses the ploughshare that is cutting a straight furrow through the field of our former ideals, inspirations, and intentions as a people. The end is not yet, but the beginning is surely here. One sentence from Professor Huxley's[4] great lecture at Oxford, to which I listened a year ago, is the key to the conclusions of the past: "Self-assertion is the essence of the cosmic process." To survive—to survive with ever-increasing powers—to survive no matter who or what goes under—this is the law by which evolution explains the process according to which the world has reached its present culmination of material power. Applied to social conditions this assertive effort to survive has made competition sharper than any two-edged sword, has made political economists believe the law of supply and demand to be as unchangeable as the law of gravitation or the attraction of cohesion. Under it the big fish of finance have fed upon the little ones, until a tank of whales on exhibition at summer resorts and yachting contests have become the most prominent spectacles of the world's greatest republic. Invention, unavailable until patented, and preserved from ministering to the greatest number's greatest good, has been the weapon with which the majority are beaten down and the minority hold sway. Immigration has introduced a babel of tongues and bibulosity of appetite, involving confusion worse confounded in municipal politics and social customs; while materialism, applying itself to science, has ruled out the supernatural, applying itself to government, has determined upon itself as more fitted to survive than any other, and applying itself to social conditions, has determined that if it cannot level up it will surely level down. Meanwhile, the almighty dollar has acquired a momentum and brilliancy that have lifted it to the place of the sun in the heavens, where its dazzling rays have so bewildered the beholder that he looks at nothing else, but stretches forth his hand in the determination that if he cannot have that he will have nothing.

Meantime the women of the nation, with clarified intellect and growing social amenity, are held aloof from helping to work out the intricate problems of the hour, while from the vortex of a citizenship that has proved itself impotent, many and conflicting voices call, among which the sturdy tones of the honest working man and the enlightened Christian unite in the Macedonian cry to the mothers and daughters of the land, "Come over and help us [Acts 16:9]; it is not good for man to be alone [Genesis 2:18]—we have heard it always, we know it now." There is to be a readjustment of forces in this country as surely as there is a Jehovah who said, "I will overturn and overturn" [Ezekiel 21:27]. The majority, patient and hard-working, begins to stir its stalwart form, to stretch out its strong hand, and to cry in its stentorian tones, "We want the earth, and we will have it; peaceably if we can, forcibly if we must;" and when the majority makes its decision and systematically organizes to work out its purposes into deeds, it can no more be resisted than the revolution of the earth or the tides of the sea. There is more thought to the square inch in humble homes today than in the homes of haughtiness and power.

Henry George and the "single tax;" Sidney Webb and the Fabian platform; Samuel Gompers and the Universal Federation; Powderly and Sovereign and the Knights of Labor; John Burns and the parliamentary programme; Senator Kyle and the national Labor Day; Ben Tillett and the Christian propaganda; Carroll D. Wright with his facts and figures; Tom Mann and Keir Hardie with their new party of the people; William T. Stead with his dissection of the most characteristic city of the century; Archbishop Ireland and Lady Henry Somerset with their propaganda of temperance and purity—these are the persons and these are the themes that hold the thought of the masses of the Anglo-Saxon race today.[5] The beliefs of these great leaders are the sun-crowned peaks that have first received the light which steadily and soon will illuminate the valleys of human toil and tribulation. Whatever is not true concerning the onward march of which England and America are the outposts on this globe today, one thing is sure; its soldiers sing no more the song of "The Girl I left Behind Me," for the daughters of the regiment march side by side with the regiment itself. All these apostles of the new light and the larger hope are saying to womanhood that which Ruth said to Naomi, "Where thou goest I will go, thy people shall be my people, and thy God my God" [Ruth 1:16], and they are declaring also in this great battle that the brain of the "Happy Warrior" must be kept clear. The new Hercules is an athlete who knows that a level head and the white life will alone speed him to the goal and crown him with the laurel leaf. This year the working people of the nation—its only valid and lasting aristocracy—have for the first time by the nation's decree celebrated their civic feast, marched in procession on their national Labor Day, and the declarations of their leaders and the swift witness of the press demonstrate that the rank and file were sober, thoughtful, and reasonable, throughout all its sacred hours.

The Wage-Workers' War

. . . . The true statesman is like a wise physician, and his patient is the body politic. Its symptoms will not change because he pronounces an anathema. It is rather his vocation to ascertain what caused the symptom, and to apply organic treatment to the disease of which it is the most apparent, but doubtless not the most dangerous indication. The multiplication of inventions has so changed the proportion of work to the workers who seek it, that there is not enough to go around. This is not the fault of any individual or any class, but it would seem to be an ingenious way out of the difficulty, if we could devise *more work;* and when one is newly arrived from a country in which every field is like a lawn and every roadside like a garden, where there are no wooden wharfs nor sidewalks, no forests of telegraph poles, nor stretches of hobble-de-hoy roads nor corduroy streets, it can but occur to him that if all our unemployed were engaged in amending the general appearance of things in this particular, and many others, work might be found for all, to the incalculable advantage of themselves and the country upon which they thus reacted with vigorous brawn.

But at this point comes up the whole question of finance, and a non-expert can only propound the twofold conundrum, Why do one-eighth of the people of the United States own seven-eighths of the property? Why have we tons of precious metal in our treasury vaults and hundreds of thousands of idle hands in our cities, while we lack the ingenuity to bring the two together? Men have failed to furnish an answer which helps the people in the present emergency. Possibly some woman financier will be raised up who could lead us out of this dilemma.

Everybody knows that strikes are the token of a widespread discontent among those who face the specter of hunger and homelessness, when they dare to try conclusions with the capitalists, with whose reserve power they can by no means compete. We can but feel that it is a great mistake to regard the wage-earning class as a menace to the country, when in fact they are themselves the country, nor do we believe that as a class they have been guilty of endangering or destroying life and property. Their great movement entrains, by the very velocity with which it goes forward, a "following" that does not represent its spirit or intention, for the dregs of society are in its wake.

Thus the anarchist with his fusee [flare], the incendiary with his torch, and assassin with his dagger, are hideous figures that stride along beside the solid battalions of the honest working people, many of whom look with frightened glance on the confused and hurried figures of the few, while the sturdy procession of the many, who are as true patriots, as loyal to what is good as any that make up our multitudinous republic, marches onward to a better future for mankind. We must not forget that every army has its camp followers, every party its treacherous and hair-brained leaders, and the larger the army, the more powerful the party, the greater will be the number to attach themselves to it for ignoble reasons. It is also true that as the moth to the candle, so the weak-brained are irresistibly borne onward toward the bright shining of a great new possibility that gleams in the forehead of the future. On the other hand, we must remember that it is government itself which has created and fostered trusts and corporations, and that the millionaire is the necessary apex of the pyramid that we ourselves have builded. If a man is a millionaire—and there are four thousand of them in the republic—in these days it is rather his misfortune than his fault; and that it is a misfortune, rich men are realizing painfully each day. We see the beginning of this wonderful uprising against the power of the dollar, and the next generation will see the end, as we believe; for the evil will have become so great that people will annihilate the trusts and blast the corporations, taking into their own hands these weapons too great to be wielded by any individual or corporation, and becoming themselves the only trusted, as we believe they are the only trusty, "Trust"....

For the first time there has been established in industrial history the principle of the minimum wage; namely, that the selling price of anything must be regulated on the basis of a living wage being paid to those who produce the thing, just as the selling-price of anything would necessarily be regulated by the cost of any other ingredient in its production. A living wage, of course, will differ with the different conditions of living, and with the nature of the work—a miner, because of the higher rents, dearer food, and more dangerous work, requiring a much higher living wage than an agricultural laborer. But once the principle is established that the laborer has a right to a living wage, it will be comparatively easy to decide what this shall be in any given case.

Labor has no capital except itself; hence in common honesty this labor should be regarded as a fixed factor in the cost of a product, and that should be taken into account in determining the exchange value of that product. It is but recently that any system stood condemned which by means of economic law consigned a large section of the population to existence under conditions in which they could not live as good men should....

It is not sympathy the workman needs; it is business sense and justice. Boards of conciliation and arbitration between employer and employed are what will supply the missing link for which we have been looking so long and earnestly. Wherever it has been tried, the success of this method has commended it to both the contending parties. Mr. Mundella,[6] ex-President of the British Board of Trade, is entitled to the credit of introducing the conciliation idea in England. He began life as a poor boy, working in the hosiery trade, which had for hundreds of years been hindered by horrible fights between the employers and the employed. In 1869 the manufacturers proposed to lock out their men, but Mr. Mundella said, "Let's get the leaders of the union together and talk it over." The result was the formation of a conciliation board, and the dissensions in the hosiery trade came to end, as a matter of course.

When they meet for purposes of conciliation employer and employed must be on an equal footing, must be represented in equal numbers, and the same weight must attach to the opinions of both. I do not think that these boards of conciliation will ever reach their utmost usefulness until women as well as men are elected to membership. It has long been my belief that the finest qualities of diplomacy are lodged in the brain and heart of the sex which for unnumbered centuries has been the chief member of a perpetual board of conciliation in the home, hearing complaints, adjusting differences, forming treaties of peace, administering justice, and oiling the machinery with patience and goodwill. I hope this Convention will pass a resolution urging the national as well as state and local governments to place women on their boards of conciliation. It will be a long step away from anarchy and towards "peace with honor."

The Industrial Life of Woman

Among the good and great men who are with us, heart and soul, is Honorable Carroll D. Wright, chief of the National Bureau of Statistics, and if the standard of character and purpose in every officer appointed by the United States Government were up to the level that his have illustrated, we should be in sight of the millennium. He thinks that this is the core of the whole woman question, and that while the training of her hand has, in the nature of the case, led on to her mental development and discipline, and involves as its largest outcome her complete participation in the government, the chief and most vital change that can come to woman's lot is involved in the independent possession of sovereignty over her own person, and that nothing will so surely effect this as the power of wife and mother to procure bread and raiment for herself and for her children. No writer has more pointedly anathematized the social system by which, instead of bestowing the possession of herself for a brief period upon him who will in exchange give her the money to supply immediate wants, woman in a conventional and loveless marriage makes this exchange, not for an hour, but for a lifetime. I am glad that a man so honored has said these things for us and keeps them before the public by voice and pen. He truly declares that it is the unchanging law of industry, that in its march it takes no account of the positions it overturns nor of the destinies it modifies. This public officer, unlike so many others, has proved himself a gallant "Knight of the New Chivalry."

He affirms that those who take the view that the morals of wage-earning women are not up to the standard of women under the domestic system, have put forth a statement that is absolutely false; and he insists that the exact opposite is true—that there is no higher plane of purity among any class of women in the nation than among those who have the self-respect to maintain their independence by earning their bread, and no man between the two oceans is a better informed expert; he adds that which is the most important statement, that the co-occupation of men and women has the same result upon character as coeducation; namely, it is carried on with great advantage and without any of the evil consequences which its enemies predicted. He affirms that the mingling of the sexes, either in industry or education, does not work harm to society, but on the contrary brings great good and secures that mutual respect which is essential to honorable social and family life.

When Harriet Martineau[7] visited America, in 1840, she put it upon record that she found but seven employments open to women; namely, teaching, needlework, keeping boarders, washing for the operatives in cotton mills, type-setting, work in book binderies, and household service. Today it is impossible to enumerate the variety of employments that are freely open to her, and it is safe to say there are not seven remaining from which she is debarred. While as yet she does not receive adequate pay, the reasons that lead to this inequality are transient, and with the development of skill, prestige, and political independence she will enter fully upon her heritage, as an equal independent citizen of the world, a daughter, first of God, then of humanity.

The People Must Own the Newspapers

Much as we desire the ownership by the people of the great plants now in the hands of individual or associated capitalists, there is, to my mind, no one thing that would so serve the liberties and rights of the people as that they should own the newspapers.

That the people should themselves be the proprietors of the means of locomotion and communication is by no means so important as that they should be the purveyors of their own ideas instead of taking them at second-hand.

At present the situation reminds one of the method devised at the stockyards in Chicago, by which the unsuspecting cattle from the prairies are decoyed, by a serene-eyed ox rightly named "Judas," into the yards that adjoin the shambles [slaughterhouse], whence there is no return. With branching horns and stately tread he leads them in, then turns about and betakes himself to his first position that he may decoy others of his kind into the terrible fate which he himself escapes. This is precisely what the party organs of the United States are doing. They are in a large degree subsidized by great corporations or by that greatest of corporations, a political party. They make their money and their fame that way, and the unthinking masses follow on where they lead as if hypnotized, dazed, or distempered. Their influence is the most gigantic fraud to which current affairs bear witness. If the people owned the newspapers instead of being owned by them, every penny-a-liner would have to sign his name to what he wrote instead of banking upon the editorial "we" or the misleading alias. He would then stand forth in all his native littleness, and his opinion would be taken for what it was worth. The time is as certain to come when the people will *own the newspapers* as the world is certain to advance out of a sheep-like docility to a dignified individuality, and it is a part of the mission of the W.C.T.U. to stir up a question like this, to put it before the people, and keep it there by speech and pen.

"The Ever-Feminine Draweth On". . . .

I wish that instead of using the term "Woman's Rights Woman," which is drastic and aggressive, we might employ the more descriptive and teaching phrase, "The Awakened Woman." She is today the leader of her sex, because she has answered to the call that said, "Arise, wake out of sleep, hear my voice, ye careless daughters!" [Isaiah 32:9]. A leading thinker with whom I was conversing on this subject recently—a man of strong character and wide observation—said to me: "Whatever you . . . attempt, try to get women to think—get them to be less frivolous, less occupied with trivial subjects, more earnest, larger minded, more devoted to general rather than specific ideas." And I thought: What weariness of life to such a man if, on returning to his home, he found that the rim of a teacup or the circumference of a thimble were the emblems of the circuit of talk to which he had to listen! We women have not thought enough about the dwarfing of mind and character that has come to men throughout the ages from the pitiably narrow converse of the fireside.

Going my way in life alone, so far as the natural companionship to which we are all born is concerned, the concept of the human question comes to me perhaps most naturally under the thought of a true comradeship in which reciprocity of thought, affection, and purpose should be combined into that triple cord that holds two human beings more strongly than bands of steel or sanctities of church or state. But the awakened woman who begins to see that the whole realm of thought is her heritage, and the entire world of power her kingdom as much as it is that of any other human being, and as much as her capacities render it possible to be, can only hope to see her ideals realized through the enlistment of the Average Woman. She is the key to the position. For the abstract principle of justice on which the Woman Question is really based, the Average Woman does not care a farthing; while, for the sake of justice in the concrete, she often plays the part of heroine. If she thought she ought to want the ballot, she would seek it with persevering zeal; but she honestly believes that it is more womanly to cry out against than for it.

She has been told this from press and pulpit since her earliest recollection, and she has learned the same doctrine from "her husband at home." The Average

Woman is oftentimes a member of the church, and like the rest of us falls into the error of confounding the husks of Christ's gospel embodied in theology with its kernel embodied in the Golden Rule; she is devoted and good and conventional; she usually has a home of her own, and her favorite end of all controversy is, "I have all the rights I want." She is (like some others) disgusted with the "woman-novel," and not too well pleased with platform women—at least, not until she has had the happiness of hearing them; after that, she has not infrequently been known to say, "With all thy faults I love thee still." She is attractive, kindly, and well-meaning, but dreads "The speech of people" even more than she does all the speechifying of the speaking sisterhood, even though their tireless tintin-nabulations should tinkle on until the crack of doom. She is not clear concerning the relations of cause and effect in politics and law, but she must be if women are to win the ballot. She has not studied Frances Power Cobbe on the "Duties [of Women]," nor John Stuart Mill[8] on the "Subjection of Women;" she could not for the life of her state the theory of evolution, or Henry George's heavenly vision of the Single Tax; but this same Average Woman has a lot of hard sense in the snug round box on the top of her head, and whoever counts her out, let not the progressive women do so if they expect to win. She is not imaginative, and if she believes in politics at all, it will be decidedly "practical politics," and she must be shown that as it is impossible for man to "represent" woman when the tax-gatherer comes round, when the policeman escorts her to jail, or the hangman to the gallows, so he cannot "represent" her in the drawing up of laws through whose outworking these penalties fall to her lot.

In America, Australia, and New Zealand the Average Woman has rallied to the polls to vote against the saloon, against the gambling house and den of vice. In the nature of the case she can be counted on to stand with practical solidarity against this trinity of evils that forms the fortress of temptation to her children. She is perfectly "clear in her mind" that no one has a right to set these institutions along the streets in neighborly nearness to her home, and if the power is given her she will remorselessly drive them off the pathways frequented by herself and little ones. There is no lever so long by which to lift the Average Woman above her prejudices as that of the reforms that tend to safeguard those to whom she has given birth and being. Here we have solid testimony to stand upon. An ounce of fact is worth a ton of theory, and the testimony of Sir John Hall, ex-Premier of New Zealand, and of Mrs. [Kate Malcolm Wilson] Sheppard, Superintendent of the Franchise Department in the Woman's Christian Temperance Union of that colony, abundantly proves that with the slogan, "Down with the Dramshop," we can win the adhesion to the woman's vote of the Average Woman, and that means the Average Man in whose ballot lies the promise and potency of all things governmental that we seek.

. . . . The whole question is one of equal chances, not of equal powers. We do not say the rose and violet are equal; but we give God's sunshine, showers, and shelter to them both in equal measure. The outcome of our kind care is their development, and the process is that each one will absorb what it most needs. It is our part only to furnish the material and to clear away the weeds, the briers, and stones that would impede their growth. What we insist on is that not until the environment of man and woman has been for centuries equally free and equally fertile in opportunity can any one profess to have the material for a just generalization concerning their comparative ability. Inherent nature must have fullest opportunity of self-assertion; that which is involuted must not by the smallest increment be prevented from its utmost evolution.

The question is often asked these days, What is to be the moral destiny of woman? I am not one of those who, in answering this question, would ignore the fact that the moral influence of one-half the human race, in its relation to the race as a whole, is greatly influenced by the difference of sex. None but shallow reasoners will overlook the physical basis of life, or forget the fact that though we lift our foreheads to the stars our feet are firmly planted on the earth. The holy estate of motherhood must always make the moral influence of the mother-sex a stronger conserving power than any other of which humanity is cognizant. By nature and by nurture (which as a matter of course includes inherited tendencies and the results of environment), women will, *as a class,* illustrate those virtues of gentleness, mercy, and peace upon which so largely depends their power to fulfill the functions inseparably belonging to their organization, constitution, and destiny. If this were a world of men, and of men only, the provision made for helpless infancy, with all the tender sentiments that it involves, would be unknown. The sense of other-worldliness can never be so strong among men as a class as among women, since the latter, during the most active period of their existence, walk along the edge of a plain that breaks off so suddenly for so many of them that the others must feel the more uncertain tenure of their thread of life. The breath of eternity touches the forehead of woman whenever a little child is born, and this great fact relates her differently to life, its prizes, its ambitions, its unceasing warfare; nor can women as a class fail to be mellowed in their nature by the contemplation of that mystery of dawning life with which they are more closely associated than any other thinking beings of which we know. The companionship of helpless infancy must modify the moral nature and deepen the religious hopes and aspirations of those who throughout the generations have kept watch beside the cradle. How many noble men have emphasized this truth in words like these of Dr. Holmes:[9] "From women we come at first with our pitiful infant's cry; in their arms we are cherished throughout our tenderest years; to them we return when wounded and worsted in the fierce battle; and in the ominous last hour of life our heads are pillowed on their bosoms."

Many other considerations might be adduced to show that the moral destiny of woman is always, and must be in the nature of the case, that of comforter, counselor, and conserver of the most sacred forces that center in childhood and the home. And I believe that in the larger home of Society and Government these powers will be most beneficently exercised to help bring in the reign of peace, purity and brotherhood....

The Colored People

Much misapprehension has arisen in the last year concerning the attitude of our unions toward the colored people, and an official explanation is in order.

The World's and National W.C.T.U. take no cognizance of color either in their social customs or their legislation, and have never done so. It would have been impossible for me to be interested in a movement that made any such distinction, for my ancestors on both sides were, without exception, devotedly loyal to the colored race, and my earliest recollections are of an abolition home, and an abolition college town [Oberlin, OH] of which my parents and all of my relatives who enjoyed the higher education were at one time or another either students or graduates. In the fifty states and territories that make up the National W.C.T.U. we were obliged, in order to form such a society at all, to leave the details of organization under the control of the said states and territories, and it is my understanding that in several of those at the South it was arranged by mutual and entirely amicable agreement between white and colored women that there should be two state unions whose delegates should come to the National on a plane of equality, but who should conduct their work separately within their own borders. In accepting this decision we followed the precedent we had established years before in the recognition of "state rights," and with the exception of a few extremists we have found no criticism resulting from this action, which was taken with intelligence and deliberation, and by which we are ready to stand. It is needless to say that in all the Northern and Western states colored women join the same local union as white women, and that they have always been among our national superintendents. The President of a colored state W.C.T.U. is a full voting member of our Executive Committee, just the same as the President of the white W.C.T.U. who comes from the same state; and I do not hesitate to claim that whenever a colored woman has shown zeal and intelligence she has been frankly and fully recognized in our councils. Mrs. Frances Harper[10] of Philadelphia, and Mrs. Early,[11] of Nashville, have been officers in our National W.C.T.U. In Michigan a gifted Afro-American woman is President of a district union, and her white comrades are proud of her, as are we all, and as we ought to be.[12]

And now about the lynching controversy. Some years ago on my return from the South I was interviewed by a representative of the New York *Voice*, and stated that as one result of my observations and inquiries I believed that it would be better if not only in the South but throughout the nation we had an educational rather than a color or sex limit put upon the ballot. To this opinion, without intending the slightest discrimination against any race, I still adhere. I also said that in the South the colored vote was often marshaled against the temperance people by base political leaders for their own purposes, and still hold to that statement. Furthermore, I said that the nameless outrages perpetrated upon white women and little girls were a cause of constant anxiety, and this I still believe to be true; but I wish I had said then, as I do now, that the immoralities of white men in their relations with colored women are the source of intolerable race prejudice and hatred, and that there is not a more withering curse upon the manhood of any nation than that which the eternal laws of nature visited upon those men and those homes in which the helpless bondwoman was made the victim of her master's base desire. But the bleaching of the black race which was the ever-present bar sinister of the olden time in the slaveholding states has largely ceased, and I make this statement on the testimony of well-informed Northerners who have long lived in the South, and who are, like myself, of New England ancestry and training, with all that those words imply. An average colored man when sober is loyal to the purity of white women; but when under the influence of intoxicating liquors the tendency in all men is toward a loss of self-control, and the ignorant and vicious, whether white or black, are most dangerous characters.

It is inconceivable that the W.C.T.U. will ever condone lynching, no matter what the provocation, and no matter whether its barbarous spectacle is to be seen in the North or South, in home or foreign countries. Any people that defends itself by shooting, burning, or otherwise torturing and killing any human being, for no matter what offence, works a greater retribution upon itself by the blunting of moral perception and fine feeling than can possibly work upon any poor debased wretch or monster that it thus torments into another world. Concerning the stirring up of the lynching question in Great Britain, I have thought that its reaction might have a wholesome tendency, and for this reason urge the following resolution, which was offered by Lady Henry Somerset at the last annual meeting of the British Women's Temperance Association, and unanimously adopted, and which has been adopted by many of our state unions:

> *Resolved,* That we are opposed to lynching as a method of punishment, no matter what the crime, and irrespective of the race by which the crime is committed, believing that every human being is entitled to be tried by a jury of his peers.

At the same time I strongly feel that the treatment of the Matabele and other dark-faced tribes in South Africa has been as unworthy of England as any of our dealings with the same race have ever been in the United States; and while receiving in a spirit of reciprocity the criticisms of the British press and public on the lynchings in this country, it seems to me we might as well appoint a committee on the subject of British outrages in South Africa, and present to the British minister at Washington a similar petition to that sent to Minister Bayard, London, through the influence of Miss Ida B. Wells, a bright young colored woman, whose zeal for her race has, as it seems to me, clouded her perception as to who were her friends and well-wishers in all high-minded and legitimate efforts to banish the abomination of lynching and torture from the land of the free and the home of the brave.[13] It is my firm belief that in the statements made by Miss Wells concerning white women having taken the initiative in nameless acts between the races, she has put an imputation upon half the white race in this country that is unjust, and, save in the rarest exceptional instances, wholly without foundation. This is the unanimous opinion of the most disinterested and observant leaders of opinion whom I have consulted on the subject, and I do not fear to say that the laudable efforts she is making are greatly handicapped by statements of this kind, nor to urge her as a friend and well-wisher to banish from her vocabulary all such allusions as a source of weakness to the cause she has at heart.

I hope this whole subject will be carefully considered and such action taken by this Convention as shall give no uncertain sound concerning our warm interest and fellowship with the colored people in all their aspirations toward Christian conduct, character, and education. There are 25,000 schools in the Southern states for the colored people, and at least two millions have learned to read and write. It is also estimated that real and personal property to the amount of two hundred and fifty million dollars is owned by them in the United States. I hope that strenuous efforts will be made to secure the organization of W.C.T. Unions in the colored churches. As the outcome of much thought and observation, it seems to me that we cannot as yet hope for that larger development of interest and work that results from undenominational action; we must have the pastor of each church favorable to the formation of a group of White Ribbon women; we must go to him and ask for this; we must adapt ourselves to the conditions more carefully than we have done; we must put colored women in the field, and I feel sure they will join with us heartily when they understand our purpose and intention.

Notes

1. Bordin, *Frances Willard*, 218.

2. See Carol Mattingly, *Well-Tempered Women: Nineteenth Century Temperance Rhetoric* (Carbondale: Southern Illinois University Press, 1998), chapter 4; Emilie M. Townes, *Womanist Justice, Womanist Hope* (Atlanta: Scholars Press, 1993), chapter 6; and Linda O. McMurry, *To Keep the Waters Troubled: The Life of Ida B. Wells* (New York: Oxford University Press, 1998), chapter 11.

3. For a discussion of African American women's participation in the WCTU, see Glenda Elizabeth Gilmore, *Gender and Jim Crow: Women and the Politics of White Supremacy in North Carolina, 1896–1920* (Chapel Hill: University of North Carolina, 1996), chapter 2.

4. Thomas Henry Huxley (1825–95) was a famous proponent of Darwin's evolutionary theory; Willard's reference here is probably to his 1893 essay "Evolution and Ethics."

5. Here Willard is identifying many of the major labor, socialist, and political reformers in the United States and Great Britain in the 1890s. Henry George (1839–97) published his most famous book on economics, *Progress and Poverty*, in 1879. Webb was noted earlier. Samuel

Gompers (1850–1924) was a founder and longtime president of the American Federation of Labor. In 1893, James R. Sovereign replaced Powderly (noted earlier) as the Grand Master Workman of the Knights of Labor. John Burns (1858–1943), a British Labor leader, came into prominence during the London Dock's strike of 1889 and was elected to the House of Commons in 1892. Pastor and, later, Senator James Henderson Kyle (1854–1901) was chair of the Congressional Committee on Education and Labor; in 1894 his bill to make Labor Day a national holiday was passed. Ben Tillet (1860–1943) was also a British labor leader and major figure in the London Dock's strike; he later helped found the National Transport Workers' Federation and served in the House of Commons. Carroll Davidson Wright (1840–1909) was the U.S. commissioner of labor; in this position he organized the Bureau of Labor Statistics, thus stimulating objective research on labor problems. Tom Mann (1856–1941) was a British labor organizer and orator active in the London Dock's strike and the Trade Union Congress. James Keir Hardie (1856–1915) is regarded as the first socialist member of the House of Commons; he advocated a progressive income tax, temperance, women's suffrage, and the rights of labor. Mann and Hardie were key leaders of the Independent Labour Party. Archbishop John Ireland (1838–1918) of St. Paul, Minnesota, was a total abstinence proponent and advocate of political reform. Somerset was noted earlier.

6. Anthony John Mundella (1825–97) was a manufacturer and member of the British Parliament famous for his work establishing boards of conciliation.

7. Martineau (1802–76) was a British author whose study of U.S. culture, *Society in America* (1837), and research guide, *How to Observe Morals and Manners* (1838), were foundational works in the field of empirical social science research. Her visit to the United States was actually in the mid-1830s.

8. Mill (1806–73) was a British philosopher, economist, and supporter of women's rights. His writings on women had a lasting impact on Willard's thought.

9. Oliver Wendell Holmes Sr. (1809–94) was an American physician, Harvard professor, and author of popular prose and poetry.

10. Frances E. W. Harper (1825–1911), prominent reformer, activist, and author, had been an officer of the Pennsylvania WCTU since 1875 and was National Superintendent of Work among Colored People for the National WCTU from the early 1880s.

11. Sarah J. Early (1825–1907) was National Superintendent of the Department of Colored Work for the National WCTU during the late 1880s; citing lack of support for her work, Early resigned the position in 1889.

12. This is a reference to Lucy Smith Thurman (1849–1918) who re-established the National WCTU's Department of Colored Work and became the superintendent at the 1893 convention.

13. During her speaking tour in Great Britain, African American antilynching activist Ida Bell Wells Barnett (1862–1931) had encouraged the presentation of an antilynching petition to Thomas Francis Bayard Sr. (1828–98), the U.S. Ambassador to Great Britain from 1893 to 1897. Willard, wounded by Wells's attack on her ethical stance, aimed to undermine the moral authority of such a British protest by suggesting that the United States might with equal force petition the British Ambassador to protest the British treatment of the Matabele people in southern Africa. Violence against the Matabele would climax between 1896 and 1898 with a reported nine thousand Africans killed.

TWENTY-ONE

A Wheel within a Wheel: How I Learned to Ride the Bicycle, 1895

Throughout the 1890s, Frances Willard's deteriorating health was a grave worry to her and to her organization. In an effort to build up her body's flagging energy through exercise, Willard took up bicycle riding in fall 1893 while staying with Isabel, Lady Henry Somerset in England. She used her journal to chart her progress in learning to ride, announcing on its pages: "I am bound to become mistress of that instrument."[1] Aided by friends and WCTU staff, she diligently pursued the skills she needed to become adept at bike riding. During this time, she was also busy dictating to her stenographers her reflections on the process, which were published a little more than a year later as *A Wheel within a Wheel*. This volume was a continuation of Willard's writing in the genre of women's self-improvement, similar in tone and intent to *How to Win*, although it targeted an adult readership rather than one of girls and young women.

The publication of *A Wheel within a Wheel* was part of Willard's campaign to convince women of the importance of taking responsibility for maintaining their health through exercise and attending to the needs of their bodies. Using herself as an example, she pointed out that she was only in her midfifties, and should be in far better shape than she was. "It is a pathetic reflection," she concluded, "that if one had always sedulously insisted on a certain amount of wisely adapted exercise, these symptoms [her physical slow down and mental exhaustion] might have been delayed some decades longer."[2] She found bicycle riding—along with her respite in England when she significantly curtailed her speaking and writing activities—to be an invigorating and rejuvenating experience.

Willard encouraged WCTU members to recognize how crucial it was that they establish good health habits early and maintain them into later life. "The more we can study our physical organism as a great continent with a system of springs, rivulets, and rivers of blood that must be kept in motion," she insisted in her 1894 presidential address, "the more we shall understand why exercise is to us the breath of life. Let the flow of this current be clogged, and as a penalty one's thinking is clogged, one's moral perception blurred, one's spirituality dimmed."[3]

She perceived and clearly articulated the vital interconnection between body, mind, and spirit; good physical health was the foundation on which the health of mind and spirit depended.

Willard touted bicycle riding as the perfect exercise for women. It was less expensive than other sports, such as horseback riding, and was, by the 1890s, quite socially acceptable, even fashionable, for women to pursue. Though she had received some criticism when she took up cycling, especially from family and friends who were afraid that she would injure herself and thus not be able to fulfill her responsibilities, she determined to "sound the tocsin in favor of this innocent, inspiriting, and healthful exercise so long as I have breath with which to do so."[4] Thus she added bicycling to sensible dress, other means of exercise, better food, and adequate rest as a part of her health reform agenda for women. What began for Willard as a personal quest for better health became yet another crusade for an essential component of women's well-being.

Bicycle riding had meaning for Willard beyond its significance as a facet of women's health reform, however. In the imaginative prose Willard employed in *Wheel within a Wheel,* women's success at learning to ride a bicycle became a metaphor for their larger success in life: "She who succeeds in gaining the mastery of [the bicycle] will gain the mastery of life, and by exactly the same methods and characteristics." Chief among these were daring, persistence, patience, and determination in the face of setbacks and apparent failures, and, above all, "hardihood of spirit." Such virtues were also, Willard noted, the very ones reformers must acquire to stay the course through the inevitable roadblocks they would meet on the way to achieving their reform goals. In reform work and in life as a whole, one could not go wrong by following the practical advice, which she put into the mouth of "Gladys," her bicycle: "Look up and off and on and out. . . . so shall you win, and that right speedily."

Exerpts are from Willard, *A Wheel within a Wheel: How I Learned to Ride the Bicycle* (Chicago: Woman's Temperance Publishing Association, 1895), 9–29, 72–75.

* * *

Preliminary

From my earliest recollections, and up to the ripe age of fifty-three, I had been an active and diligent worker in the world. This sounds absurd; but having almost no toys except such as I could manufacture, my first plays were but the outdoor work of active men and women on a small scale. Born with an inveterate opposition to staying in the house, I very early learned to use a carpenter's kit and a gardener's tools, and followed in my mimic way the occupations of the poulterer and the farmer, working my little field with a wooden plow of my own making, and felling saplings with an axe rigged up from the old iron of the wagon-shop.

Living in the country, far from the artificial restraints and conventions by which most girls are hedged from the activities that would develop a good physique, and endowed with the companionship of a mother who let me have my own sweet will, I "ran wild" until my sixteenth birthday, when hampering long skirts were brought, with their accompanying corset and high heels; my hair was clubbed up with pins, and I remember writing in my journal, in the first heartbreak of a young human colt taken from its pleasant pasture, "Altogether, I recognize that my occupation is gone."

From that time on I always realized and was obedient to the limitations thus imposed, though in my heart of hearts I felt their unwisdom even more than their injustice. My work then changed from my beloved and breezy outdoor world to the indoor realm of study, teaching, writing, speaking, and went on almost without a break or pain until my fifty-third year, when the loss of my mother accentuated the strain of this long period in which mental and physical life were out of balance, and I fell into a mild form of what is called nerve-wear by the patient and nervous prostration by the lookers-on. Thus ruthlessly thrown out of the usual lines of reaction with my environment, and sighing for new worlds to conquer, I determined that I would learn the bicycle.

An English naval officer had said to me, after learning it himself, "You women have no idea of the new realm of happiness which the bicycle has opened to us men." Already I knew well enough that tens of thousands who could never afford to own, feed, and stable a horse, had by this bright invention enjoyed the swiftness of motion which is perhaps the most fascinating feature of material life, the charm of a wide outlook upon the natural world, and that sense of mastery which is probably the greatest attraction in horseback-riding. But the bicycle is the steed that never tires, and is "mettlesome" in the fullest sense of the word. It is full of tricks and capers, and to hold his head steady and make him prance to suit you is no small accomplishment.

I had often mentioned in my temperance writings that the bicycle was perhaps our strongest ally in winning young men away from public-houses, because it afforded them a pleasure far more enduring, and an exhilaration as much more delightful as the natural is than the unnatural. From my observation of my own brother and hundreds of young men who have been my pupils, I have always held that a boy's heart is not set in him to do evil any more than a girl's, and that the reason our young men fall into evil ways is largely because we have not had the wit and wisdom to provide them with amusements suited to their joyous youth, by means of which they could invest their superabundant animal spirits in ways that should harm no one and help themselves to the best development and the cleanliest ways of living. So as a temperance reformer I always felt a strong attraction toward the bicycle, because it is the vehicle of so much harmless pleasure, and because the skill required in handling it obliges those who mount to keep clear heads and steady hands.

Nor could I see a reason in the world why a woman should not ride the silent steed so swift and blithesome. I knew perfectly well that, when, some ten or fifteen years ago, Miss Bertha von Hillern, a young German artist in America, took it into her head to give exhibitions of her skill in riding the bicycle, she was thought by some to be a sort of semi-monster; and liberal as our people are in their views of what women may undertake, I should have felt compromised, at that remote and benighted period, by going to see her ride, not because there was any harm in it, but solely because of what we call in homely phrase, "the speech of the people."[5] But behold! It was long ago conceded that women might ride the tricycle—indeed, one had been presented to me by my friend Colonel [Albert] Pope, of Boston, a famous manufacturer of these swift roadsters, as far back as 1886; and I had swung around the garden paths upon its saddle a few minutes every evening when work was over at my Rest Cottage home. I had even hoped to give an impetus among conservative women to this new line of physical development and outdoor happiness; but that is quite another story and will come in later. Suffice it for the present that it did me good, as it doth the upright in heart, to notice recently that the Princesses Louise and Beatrice [Queen Victoria's daughters] both ride the tricycle at Balmoral [Castle]; for I know that with the great mass of feminine humanity this precedent will have exceeding weight—and where the tricycle prophesies, the bicycle shall ere long preach the gospel of the outdoors.

For we are all unconsciously the slaves of public opinion. When the hansom carriage first came on the London streets no woman having regard to her social state and standing would have dreamed of entering one of these pavement gondolas unless accompanied by a gentleman as her escort. But in course of time a few women, of stronger individuality than the average, ventured to go unattended; later on, use wore off the glamour of the traditions which said that women must not go alone, and now none but an imbecile would hold herself to any such observance.

A trip around the world by a young woman would have been regarded a quarter of a century ago as equivalent to social outlawry; but now young women of the highest character and talent are employed by leading journals to whip around the world "on time," and one has done so in seventy-three days, another in seventy-four, while the young women recently sent out by an Edinburgh newspaper will no doubt considerably contract these figures.

As I have mentioned, Fraulein von Hillern is the first woman, so far as I know, who ever rode a bicycle, and for this she was considered to be an outcast in all classes and a traitor to the feminine guild; but now, in France, for a woman to ride a bicycle is not only "good form" but the current craze among the aristocracy. . . .

[T]here has been but little authentic talking done by four-footed animals; but that is no reason why the two-wheeled should not speak its mind, and the first utterance I have to chronicle in the softly flowing vocables of my bicycle is the following purport. I heard it as we trundled off down the Priory incline at the suburban home of Lady Henry Somerset in Reigate, England, where I was staying. It said: "Behold, I do not fail you; I am not a skittish beastie, but a sober, well-conducted roadster. I did not ask you to mount or to drive, but since you have done so you must now learn the laws of balance and exploitation. I did not invent these laws, but I have been built to conform to them, and you must suit yourself to the unchanging regulations of gravity, general and specific, as illustrated in me. Strange as the paradox may seem, you will do this best by not trying to do it at all. You must make up what you are pleased to call your mind—make it up speedily, or you will be cast in yonder mud puddle, and no blame to me and no thanks to yourself. Two things must occupy your thinking powers to the exclusion of every other thing: first, the goal; and, second, the momentum required to reach it. Do not look down like an imbecile upon the steering wheel in front of you—that would be about as wise as for a nauseated voyager to keep his optical instruments fixed upon the rolling waves. It is the curse of life that nearly everyone looks down. But the microscope will never set you free; you must glue your eyes to the telescope forever and a day. Look up and off and on and out; get forehead and foot into line, the latter acting as a rhythmic spur in the flanks of your equilibriated equine; so shall you win, and that right speedily.

It was divinely said that the kingdom of God is within you. Some make a mysticism of this declaration, but it is hard common sense; for the lesson you will learn from me is this: every kingdom over which we reign must be first formed within us on what I as a bicycle look upon as the common parade ground of individual thought."

The Process

Courtiers wittily say that horseback riding is the only thing in which a prince is apt to excel, for the reason that the horse never flatters and would as soon throw him as if he were a groom. Therefore it is only by actual mastering the art of riding that a prince can hold his place with the noblest of the four-footed animals.

Happily there is now another locomotive contrivance which is no flatterer, and which peasant and prince must master, if they do this at all, by the democratic route of honest hard work. . . . We all know the old saying, "Fire is a good servant, but a bad master." This is equally true of the bicycle: if you give it an inch—nay, a hair—it will take a yard—nay, an evolution—and you a contusion, or, like enough, a perforated kneecap.

Not a single friend encouraged me to learn the bicycle except an active-minded young schoolteacher, Miss Luther, in my hometown of Evanston [Illinois], who came several times with her wheel and gave me lessons. I also took a few lessons in a stuffy, semi-subterranean gallery in Chicago. But at fifty-three I was at more disadvantage than most people, for not only had I the impedimenta that result from the unnatural style of dress, but I also suffered from the sedentary habits of a lifetime. And then that small world (which is our real one) of those who loved me best, and who considered themselves largely responsible for my everyday methods of life, did not encourage me, but in their affectionate so-licitude—and with abundant reason—thought I should "break my bones" and "spoil my future." It must be said, however, to their everlasting praise, that they posed no objection when they saw that my will was firmly set to do this thing; on the contrary, they put me in the way of carrying out my purpose, and lent to my laborious lessons the light of their countenances reconciled. Actions speak so much louder than words that I here set before you what may be called a feminine bicycler's inauguration—at least it was mine. . . .

While staying in England, I set out to learn the safety-bicycle with its pneu-matic tires and all the rest, the gearing carefully wired in so that we shall not be entangled. "Woe is me!" was my first exclamation, naturally enough interpreted by my outriders "Whoa is me," and they "whoaed"—indeed, we did little else but "check up". . . .

The order of evolution was something like this: first, three young Englishmen, all strong-armed and accomplished bicyclers, held the machine in place while I climbed timidly into the saddle. In the second stage of my learning, two well-disposed young women put in all the power they had, until they grew red in the face, off-setting each other's pressure on the cross bar and thus maintaining the equipoise to which I was unequal. Thirdly, one walked beside me, steadying the ark as best she could by holding the center of the deadly crossbar, to let go whose handles meant chaos and collapse. Eventually I was able to hold my own if I had the moral support of my kind trainers, and it passed into a proverb among them, the short emphatic word of command I gave them at every few turns of the wheel: "Let go, but stand by." Still later everything was learned—how to sit, how to pedal, how to turn, how to dismount; but alas! how to vault into the saddle I found not; that was the coveted power that lingered long and would not yield itself.

That which caused the many failures I had in learning the bicycle had caused me failures in life; namely, a certain fearful looking for judgment; a too vivid realization of the uncertainty of everything about me; an underlying doubt—at once, however (and this is all that saved me), matched and overcome by the determination not to give in to it.

The best gains that we make come to us after an interval of rest which follows strenuous endeavor. Having, as I hoped, mastered the rudiments of bicycling, I went away to Germany and for a fortnight did not even see the winsome wheel. Returning, I had the machine brought round, and mounted with no little trepi-dation, being assisted by one of my faithful guides; but behold! I found that in advancing, turning, and descending I was much more at home than when I had last exercised that new intelligence in the muscles which had been the result of repetitions resolutely attempted and practiced long.

Another thing I found is that we carry in the mind a picture of the road; and if it is bumpy by reason of pebbles, even if we steer clear of them, we can by no means skim along as happily as when its smoothness facilitates the pleasing impression on the retina; indeed, the whole science and practice of the bicycle is "in your eye" and in your will; the rest is mere manipulation.

As I have said, in many curious particulars the bicycle is like the world. When it had thrown me painfully once (which was the extent of my downfalls during the entire process of learning, and did not prevent me from resuming my place on the back of the treacherous creature a few minutes afterward), and more especially when it threw one of my dearest friends, hurting her knee so that it was painful for a month, then for a time Gladys (the name I had given my bicycle) had gladsome ways for me no longer, but seemed the embodiment of misfortune and dread. Even so the world has often seemed in hours of darkness and despondency; its iron mechanism, its pitiless grind, its swift, silent, on-rolling gait have oppressed to pathos, if not melancholy. Fortunately, good health and plenty of oxygenated air have promptly restored the equilibrium. . . .

Gradually, item by item, I learned the location of every screw and spring, spoke and tire, and every beam and bearing that went to make up Gladys. This was not the lesson of a day, but of many days and weeks, and it had to be learned before we could get on well together. To my mind the infelicities of which we see so much in life grow out of lack of time and patience to study and adjust our natures to those of others, though we have agreed in the sight of God and man to stand by one another to the last. Many will not take the pains, they have not enough specific gravity, to balance themselves in their new environment. Indeed, I found a whole philosophy of life in the wooing and the winning of my bicycle.

Just as a strong and skillful swimmer takes the waves, so the bicycler must learn to take such waves of mental impression as the passing of a gigantic haywagon, the sudden obtrusion of black cattle with wide-branching horns, the rattling pace of high-stepping steeds, or even the swift transit of a railway train. At first she will be upset by the apparition of the smallest poodle, and not until she has attained a wide experience will she hold herself steady in the presence of a coach with four horses. But all this is a part of that equilibration of thought and action by which we conquer the universe in conquering ourselves.

I finally concluded that all failure was from a wobbling will rather than a wobbling wheel. I felt that indeed the will is the wheel of the mind—its perpetual motion having been learned when the morning stars sang together. When the wheel of the mind went well, then the rubber wheel hummed merrily; but specters of the mind there are as well as of the wheel. In the aggregate of perception there are so many ghastly and fantastical images that they must obtrude themselves at certain intervals. Probably every accident of which I had heard or read in my half-century tinged the uncertainty that I felt when we began to round the terminus bend of the broad Priory walk. And who shall say by what original energy the mind forced itself at once from the contemplation of disaster and thrust into the very moment of the foot on the pedal a concept of vigor, safety, and success? I began to feel that myself plus the bicycle equaled myself plus the world, upon whose spinning wheel we must all learn to ride, or fall into the sluiceways of oblivion and despair. That which made me succeed with the bicycle was precisely what had gained me a measure of success in life—it was the hardihood of spirit that led me to begin, the persistence of will that held me to my task, and the patience that was willing to begin again when the last stroke had failed. And so I found high moral uses in the bicycle and can commend it as a teacher without pulpit or creed. He who succeeds, or, to be more exact in handing over my experience, she who succeeds in gaining the mastery of such an animal as Gladys, will gain the mastery of life, and by exactly the same methods and characteristics.

One of the first things I learned was that unless a forward impetus were given within well-defined intervals, away we went into the gutter, rider and steed. And I said to myself: "It is the same with all reforms: sometimes they seem to lag, then they barely balance, then they begin to oscillate as if they would lose the track and tumble to one side; but all they need is a new impetus at the right moment on the right angle, and away they go again as merrily as if they had never threatened to stop at all."

On the Castle terrace[6] we went through a long, narrow curve in a turret to seek a broader esplanade. As we approached it I felt wrought up in my mind, a little uncertain in my motions; and for that reason, on a small scale, my quick imagination put before me pictures of damaging bruises against pitiless walls. But with a little unobtrusive guiding by one who knew better than I how to do it we soon came out of the dim passage on to the broad, bright terrace we sought, and in an instant my fears were as much left behind as if I had not had them. So it will be, I think, I hope—nay, I believe—when, children that we are, we tremble on the brink and fear to launch away; but we shall find that death is only a bend in the river of life that sets the current heavenward. . . .

In Conclusion

If I am asked to explain why I learned the bicycle, I should say I did it as an act of grace, if not actual religion. The cardinal doctrine laid down by my physician was, "Live out of doors and take congenial exercise;" but from the day when, at sixteen, years of age, I was enwrapped in the long skirts that impeded every footstep, I have detested walking and felt with a certain noble disdain that the conventions of life had cut me off from what in the freedom of my prairie home had been one of life's sweetest joys. Driving is not real exercise; it does not renovate the river of blood that flows so sluggishly in the veins of those who from any cause have lost the natural adjustment of brain to brawn. Horseback riding, which does promise vigorous exercise, is expensive. The bicycle, however, meets all the conditions and will ere long come within the reach of all. Therefore, in obedience to the laws of health, I learned to ride. I also wanted to help women to a wider world, for I hold that the more interests women and men can have in common, in thought, word and deed, the happier will it be for the home. Besides, there was a special value to women in the conquest of the bicycle by a woman in her fifty-third year, and one who had so many comrades in the white-ribbon army of temperance workers that her action be widely influential. Then there were three minor reasons:

I did it for pure love of adventure—a love long hampered and impeded, like a brook that runs underground, but in this enterprise bubbling up again with somewhat of its pristine freshness and taking its merry course of old.

Second, from a love of acquiring this new implement of power and literally putting it underfoot.

Last, but not least, because a good many people thought I could not do it at my age.

It is needless to say that a bicycling costume was a prerequisite. This consisted of a skirt and blouse of tweed, with belt, rolling collar, and loose cravat, the skirt three inches from the ground; a round straw hat, and walking shoes with gaiters. It was a simple, modest suit, to which no person of common sense could take exception.

As nearly as I can make out, reducing the problem to actual figures, it took me about three months, with an average of fifteen minutes practice daily, to learn, first, to pedal; second, to turn; third, to dismount; and fourth, to mount independently this most mysterious animal. January 20th [1894] will always be a red-letter bicycle day, because although I had already mounted several times with no hand on the rudder, some good friend had always stood by to lend moral support; but summoning all my force, on this day, I mounted and started off alone. . . . From that hour the spell was broken; Gladys was no more a mystery: I had learned all her kinks, had put a bridle in her teeth, and touched her smartly with the whip of victory. Consider, ye who are of a considerable chronology: in about thirteen hundred minutes, or, to put it more mildly, in twenty-two hours, or to put it most mildly of all, in less than a single day as the almanac reckons time—but practically in two days of actual practice—amid the delightful surroundings of the great outdoors, and inspired by the bird-songs, the color and fragrance of an English posy garden, in the company of devoted and pleasant comrades, I had made myself master of the most remarkable, ingenious, and inspiring motor ever yet devised upon this planet.

Moral: Go thou and do likewise!

Notes

1. Willard, Journal, October 4, 1893. Entries during October, November, and December 1893 trace Willard's progress on the bicycle.

2. Willard, 1894 Presidential Address, 160.

3. Ibid., 160–61.

4. Ibid., 161.

5. Besides giving exhibitions of bicycle riding, Bertha von Hillern (1857–?) was better known as a pedestrian who competed in women's speed-walking races. After her athletic career she took up painting in the Boston area.

6. Eastnor Castle was Isabel Somerset's hereditary home in Herefordshire, northwest of London.

TWENTY-TWO

Eighteenth Presidential Address, October 29, 1897

Frances Willard's 1897 presidential address was her last major public appearance. Just weeks after presiding over the World's WCTU convention in Toronto, Canada, she arrived in Buffalo, New York, to direct the National WCTU meetings. Although she knew that her health was failing, she could not have been fully aware that she would not live to deliver another presidential speech to her WCTU constituency. Yet this final message with its note of urgency and determination seems to have sprung from the premonition that she had very little time left. Much of the eighty-five page published text followed a familiar pattern, giving a "state of the WCTU" survey that included requests for specific actions Willard hoped her organization would implement during its next year. She wished particularly to bring to the attention of convention delegates the nation's crying need for political and municipal reform and her thoughts on how such reform could be brought about. But a different theme kept bursting into the carefully labeled sections of her text, intruding into the midst of detailed, reasoned discussions of these topics.

During the late 1880s and 1890s, Willard's Christian faith had become radicalized, as had the faith of a number of other liberal evangelical Protestants. She—and they—had embraced a social gospel, which demanded far more than the individual conversion stressed by many nineteenth-century evangelicals. Social gospelers called for a conversion of the entire social order in conformity with what she defined as "the coming of Golden Rule justice," a time in which all human beings would be brothers and sisters and the care of each would be the concern and responsibility of all. She hoped to convince listeners that this was the only course for those seeking justice and equality for all and to persuade them to join her on this long and difficult path. Many parts of the excerpts below—especially the concluding sections—resemble a sermon more than a dispassionate assessment of organizational achievements and goals for the future, as Willard struggled to enlist the support of the WCTU for her radical dream.

In the section titled "Our Patent Politics," Willard indicted America's two-party political system, laying bare the corruption, boss rule, and collusion with business that made of politics a monopoly run by the rich and powerful for their own gain. Yet Willard was not daunted because she saw the possibility of a response to this intolerable situation in the development of a "corporate conscience." Furthermore she saw signs of such a conscience emerging from concerned citizens who were coming together in a number of the nation's cities to oppose boss rule. This civic collaboration to enact good government was part of a larger municipal reform movement growing in both the United States and Europe during the last quarter of the nineteenth century, one which Willard had avidly championed for more than a decade.

In her concern for enhancing the quality of workers' lives, evidenced here in her call for the WCTU to take the lead in establishing "peoples' palaces"—urban spaces for wholesome family recreation—she was one of the early voices in a transatlantic civic reform movement that advocated such improvements as playgrounds, parks, public baths, and free libraries. Willard also joined with labor leaders and municipal reformers to advocate for the implementation of a host of other changes she saw as ameliorating the lives of workers and their families, from the eight-hour day, factory inspection, and initial forms of workmen's compensation and unemployment legislation to her demand for protection and unionization of the most vulnerable workers: domestic servants and laundry women. While many officials and conservative reformers in Europe and the United States saw municipal reform measures as moves toward creating a more ethical capitalist system that established a bulwark against a socialist takeover, Willard saw them as milestones on the peaceful progress toward the inauguration of socialism.

Speaking to an audience of women who shared her Protestant faith, Willard called on the Protestant Church to be the vanguard in the creation of a socialism founded on Christian values. It was the church's responsibility, motivated by the social teachings of Jesus, she insisted, to address the injustices of each era. Realizing that churches were often slow to take up the banner of reform, Willard exhorted the women of the WCTU to persevere in their reform efforts, no matter how difficult and dangerous it might be or how unpopular with the majority.

Just two months after delivering her presidential address, she became gravely ill, and died in mid-February 1898. Her commitment to reform would have to continue, as she imagined in the last sentence of her address, by "coming invisibly to the help of those who toil in the reforms of the future, or . . . waging battles for God upon some other star."

Excerpts are from Willard, "President's Annual Address" in *Minutes of the N.W.C.T.U.* (Chicago: Woman's Temperance Publication Association, 1897), 91–94, 102–104, 114–20, 138–39, 142–46, 148, 151–53.

* * *

Our Patent Politics

No contrast in the history of "the people's government" is more distressing than the town meeting of New England and the party caucus of the present day. In the town meeting the best men ruled; the party caucus is controlled by the worst. Each town meeting concerned itself wholly with the best interests of that town; each caucus is interlaced with every other that belongs to the same party, so that state and even national politics are represented in the smallest party gathering. This is not strange when the postmaster at every crossroads represents the national government, and gets his place through state senators or congressmen, according to the income of the post office. We are fond of saying that "the post office belongs to the people," but as at present managed it is, next to the trust, the stronghold of the party, for whether it be the silver trust, the gold trust, the Standard Oil trust, the sugar trust, the railroad trust, the telegraph trust, these groups of sharp, relentless money-makers control our political bosses in nation, state and post office politics. It pays to be "an active worker" when that "work" is the "working of the party" in the interest of the trust. The expressions (heard only in what are known as "inside financial circles") that "It cost us dear to buy up such a legislature, or to secure so and so's judicial decision," brings out the financial aspect of current politics. The entire political camp has for its object "the elimination of the individual voter by selecting for him those for whom he must vote," and the bosses select men from their own organized group. The slate of officers in each community is made out after consultation with the political expert of that community, who is in constant communication with the political bosses of that part of the state and so on to the party political bosses of the nation itself. Today the individual voter in this country is as powerless as he is in Russia; his candidate is selected, his platform written, and he goes to the polls to register the previous decision of those political manipulators who are in secret league with corporations that are perpetually seeking the job of locating water works, gas works, street cars, telephone lines, telegraph lines, and other public conveniences in every locality, and who make up so large a margin on their investments that they have money left over with which to buy up such political favors as they require. The system is a perfect as a Waltham watch; once wind it up and keep it wound, and it will turn out multi-millionaires at the top and victimized voters at the bottom, while a "republican form of government" is ground between these upper and nether millstones into dust so fine that it becomes invisible. It is high time that some excellent people got out of the book of resolutions into the book of acts. Plutarch says, "You may found cities without walls, without kings, without theaters or gymnasiums or parks, but you can never found a city without God."

It has been admirably stated that the change now coming over the study of humanity is analogous to the new departure which Galileo introduced into astronomy. Until his day the earth was thought to be the center of the solar system, but now it is known that the sun is that center, even as we are learning that the letter "I" is not the hub around which the universe revolves, but the letter "H" which stands for humanity, of which we are but fractions. Some have objected that humanity lacks a common consciousness, and therefore cannot be treated as a unit, but we are rapidly developing a corporate conscience that will be as much outraged by the violation of moral law as the heart is by the violation of the law of sympathy. . . .

The recent [1896] presidential campaign, with its Machiavellian tactics and insupportable intolerance, has had no results so valuable as that the people are awakening to feel that they do not need parties, indeed that the party is a millstone about their necks, that it is a horrible fetish, a sodden superstition. Who are the men who run these parties? They are self-constituted dictators. What does the state of New York today think of "Boss Platt,"[1] who more than any other hundred men, dominates its affairs? Surely intelligent voters do not admire him, for he is not admirable in person, intellect, heart, or conduct, but, like the master whom he serves, he is of an admirable perseverance. He set at work many years ago with the determination that he would no longer be called "Me Too Platt," and by his alliance with the liquor interests and other dangerous elements he has so changed the outlook that we now have Platt, the political Czar, and New York state is itself the great "Me Too" that goes tagging at his heels. "While the master of the house slept the enemy sowed tares" [Matthew 13:25], and the work of Platt has been to manipulate and make into a mosaic the office holders and politicians on which he virtually treads in his triumphal march to power, while the businessmen, wholly intent on laying up treasures upon earth, have let him work his will, until now all they have to do is to vote his ticket at the polls and pay in their taxes to keep his political movement well supplied with the "sinews of war." For the bosses are not in politics for fun; they, like the liquor trust, are there for the money there is in it, and so long as trust and corporations are allowed to live, and the franchise of our municipalities are given away, the people may go on voting for whom they will, but they are the puppets of the political machine, and never until they get back to the root of the matter and abolish the corporations that already prevent competition, making the people the one trusty and uncompeting trust, will our government be anything except the sham and shame that it is now. It is bad enough to exploit other people's money, but there is no depth deeper than to be an exploiter of other people's votes. But the capital of the political boss is the average voter's ballot, which he "gathers in" like a ripe pippin upon election day, and adds to that sum total which holds him in place as a dictator, and makes of our good ministers and quiet businessmen the bodyguard that runs beside his chariot.

Suppose they try to break their halter. They can do this by voting for the candidates of the opposite party, but these have been as carefully chosen by the dominating money interests that manipulate politics as were the candidates in the party from whose bondage they are trying to escape, for the trusts and corporations take care to have representatives in every party who can "look after their interests." Nothing then remains to the voter, now reduced to a position of practical imbecility, except to join with other men who have reached the point of revolution and "throw away his vote." Nay, it was the political boss who invented that phrase. The temperance woman contends that such a vote is the sacred protest and the prophetic planting of a seed that shall spring up into everlasting life.

But when a handful of protesting voters splits into two parts on questions of policy, what then? Why it has always been the work of women to reconcile contending forces, and it is conceivable that we women gathered here from every corner of the republic, and knowing the competing forces as our friends and brothers, might appoint a group of peacemakers to confer with the leaders of the Prohibition and Liberty Parties[2] in the effort to bring them together. If, however, this is impossible, our only attitude towards each must be that of sisterly goodwill and sympathy. . . .

The People's Palaces

A quickened sense of what our life is for is coming to the people; the common joy is coming to be comprehended as a part of the joy of the Lord, which is our strength [Nehemiah 8:10]; the common mind begins to see that matter and spirit are but different sides of the same shield, and is rising to the concept that between the secular and the sacred there is no line of demarcation, but that the universe is one, its forces are one, its throbbing, ever-present energy is one, and "all we are brethren." The life that now is engrosses human thought more than it has since the happy days of that Greek art which concentrates the joyous gaze of all mankind. One world at a time is insisted on, and not without reason, because if rightly used, it proves to be to human souls the gate to greater worlds beyond. There is a growing sensitiveness to the inequalities that give one man pleasure enough to spoil him and deny to another pleasure enough to save him. We are tracing that grand old word "recreation" back to its basic meaning, which is "re-creation," and that is to be made over by the new creation that comes to mind and body when we throw off the harness of our cares and for a little while live simply for the sake of living. Puritan repression and ascetic zeal have tried in vain to make the mass of mankind willing to be shut away from the charm of that great world that was given us for our home. Here again, Science comes to our aid and proves that there is no better economy than to replace the waste of brain cells, nerve and muscle tissue by an utter change of occupation. Partly, at least, from this knowledge is growing the physical culture movement, in whose benefits men and women share almost equally. To the same source may be traced the development of the Delsarte culture[3] and the deepening line of demarcation between the low and the elevating productions of the play. I did not think that with my Puritan education I should ever find myself in a theater with my heart lifted up to God in prayer; but that has happened to me several times in my period of enforced seclusion and in that city of the world [London] where doubtless the dramatic gift lends itself more than elsewhere to the development of high and tender thoughts.

Now it has long been one of the most cherished hopes of my heart that the W.C.T.U. might help to bring more of honest pleasure to the people. I believe that our women might be the hand upon the rocking-stone of many a municipality that would lead its "moneyed men" to contribute to the building of a People's Palace, which would be the natural center not for men only, but for the families of those who find that all work and no play robs life of joy. Some day it will be inexplicable to good men and women that they could make for themselves beautiful club houses, tennis and polo grounds, and never spend a penny to prepare for the poor pleasures that to them would be as great as these are to the well-to-do. For surely nothing would leave the saloon out in the cold so thoroughly as a reputable place of amusement in every town and village, and at frequent intervals in our great cities, where the people could meet for a good time with the harm taken out of it. If the building were furnished and fitted up there would be no trouble about its maintenance, for this permanent object lesson of the goodwill of their neighbors would put a premium on saving from the saloon keeper's till itself the moderate amount necessary to secure membership in the great, good natured People's Palace Company. I know such work must begin somewhere, and though we are not rich, we are trusted by our neighbors, and we can do much to set in motion benignant forces far beyond our power to handle or supply. Will not some of our local Unions in town or city make it the chief work of the coming year to get the good people who have money to found, on a small scale, a People's Palace? In London, as you all know, this was done years ago by a gifted young student of Oxford University, whose name is radiant with the gratitude of the poor, Edward Toynbee,[4] the apostle of happiness for the hopeless and the weary.

We live in an age when every human being proposes to get a good slice of the world for himself and for herself. The day of fractional living and repression is past. A truer knowledge of how the world is made, and a broader interpretation of Christianity is convincing even the most subservient that no man is better than his neighbor, except when he behaves better, and as behavior can be had by anybody that wants it, there is no reason why each should not be, in the deep sense of worth and the widest sense of worthiness, a brother to all the rest. "Fullness of life" is what we seek, as instinctively as the water of a fountain bubbles to the surface that it may be brightened and glorified by sunshine. But it is also a day in which the presence in any group of one who has the danger-habit is a serious matter. By our growing pleasure in life we purpose to banish every cause of sorrow that we can. The better sanitation of cities, whereby we are not left to the mercy of ignorance and uncleanliness, prophesies that time when it will fare ill with the man who voluntarily puts his faculties beyond his own control, making himself dizzy with distilled drinks when he ought to stand firm, or sodden with beer when he ought to be alert, or destroying himself with nicotine and blowing it into the atmosphere that more cleanly and normal people must inhale. . . .

Labor. . . .

One of the cardinal doctrines of the labor movement is the Eight Hour Law, and I greatly desire that this Convention may declare in favor of it, not only because the present hours are oppressively long, but for the reason that if eight hours were the fixed period a great many more wage workers would be employed. It is a hopeful symptom for Sabbath reform that the labor people have taken it up with so much enthusiasm; they feel that the Sabbath is their day, and that it is a species of tyranny so to arrange the business of the country that they have no period of recreation. This position is well taken, and I am glad that in the interest of human brotherhood, as well as a reverent observance of what we believe to be a divine command, the White Ribbon women can join hands with the wage workers for the protection of the pearl of days. As we have in the past heartily cooperated with all who sought this end, so let us do in the future, but we must be careful always to let it be understood that those who observe some other day than the seventh are to be respected in their belief by any law that we are working to help obtain.

The divinest right on this earth is the right of the people to take corporate care of their own affairs.

There is a commodity in the market which has the magic power of creating more than it costs to produce it. This is the labor power of the human being, of a free wage worker. He sells it for a certain amount of money, which competition reduces to the average necessities of life required to produce it; to so much food, clothing and shelter which are absolutely necessary to recuperate his lost powers on the next morning and to reproduce a new generation of wage workers after this one is gone. Almost all above this goes to the employing class, and is called "the surplus value."

The human hand will yet become the adequate emblem of the only aristocracy; it is the wizard's wand. Our great Emerson[5] said, "A little waving hand reared these huge columns," and the touch of a child's finger has set free the power that made magnificent the harbor of our great metropolis. There is no limit to the forces that man's thought will yet start into motion, so that the plains shall be diversified by hills and valleys, and the inaccessible heights lowered to the level where man may build his happy home upon them, and the poles brought within the range of pleasant weather, and the poet's famous line about "the looks that commerce with the skies," made an everyday experience, while we are signaling our sister planets, and the navigation of the air becomes as simple and home-like a thing as the swift whirl of the bicycle is now upon the street. But back of all must be that faithful little hand, directed by the "gray matter" which is the condensation of development upon this earth, and warmed at the friendly fires of a heart big with the indwelling sense of God and Brotherhood.

It looks as if electricity would bring back those better times when men did their work in their own homes, instead of flocking to the factory to make machines of themselves as they do now. In the old days one man made a whole shoe, in these he only holds the hammer that drives home a peg, or the instrument that cuts a string, and he and his occupation have become equally fractioned; but when the people can take the power that drives the wheels into their own houses, they will live a much more complete and independent life. May the day hasten when their liberty shall be given back again by the new downpour of Promethean fire.

I do not wish to know what the country does for the rich, they can take care of themselves; but what it does for the poor determines the decency, not to say the civilization of a government. How to develop the downmost man and woman— that is our problem. Nothing proves the incapacity of our rulers like the tenement house abomination. If we had statesmen this could not continue; if but one more Shaftesbury would arise in the British Parliament, or Richard H. Gilder in the New York legislature, a peaceful revolution would be set in motion.[6]

Though we have nothing to hope for as temperance people from our present government, we rejoice that they have championed, and Parliament has adopted, the bill giving universal compensation to injured wage workers, except agriculturalists. It speaks well for human nature that Lord Salisbury and Mr. Chamberlain carried the bill through, and capitalists voted for it, knowing it would cost them dear.[7]

Germany provides an insurance taken from the wages of the work-people and from their employers, whereby if ill they will have resources to fall back upon, and when old they need not go to the workhouse, but will have enough to support them in comfort.

These laws are intended "to check the socialists," and they show the good that the socialistic movement has already accomplished, and predict the infinitely greater good that is to come. The next move is likely to be the enactment of laws whereby the unemployed, who are good and respectable men and women, may have provision made for their necessities when they are out of work.

There is no class more dependent than what is called "the servant class." They with laundry women must, as a rule, rely upon the goodwill of their employers, for they have but little moral or legal protection. Oftentimes they live in rooms that have no fire, and lie down to sleep on beds that are less comfortable than those provided for their master's horses. As a rule, small provision is made for their personal cleanliness by means of baths, etc. They have no stated hours, but their work, like that of the farmer's wife, is never done. They have no understandings as to holidays, of recreation or recuperation, either during the week or during the year. In short, they are not looked after as they ought to be. We believe that the great majority who employ servants treat them with a measure of consideration and goodwill, but the fate of so many persons ought not to be dependent in anywise on the peculiarities of those who employ them. Servants should organize as other working people are organized, and there should be inspection to know whether the sanitary condition and the comfort of the rooms they inhabit is adequate to the degree of civilization we have reached.

The same should be remembered of all women who do laundry work, a most taxing and difficult employment, and one in which, so far as we can learn, they are expected to begin very early and continue until very late. There should be inspection for them as well, and we believe the time will come when there will be an eight-hour day for laundry women and servants as well as for the more independent classes of workers. Until there is a move made in this direction we are far from having reached a Christian standard in respect to the condition and lives of our fellow men and women who hold the position of servants, or, as our New England people used to say, with far more refinement, "helpers". . . .

Look about you; the products of labor are on every hand; you could not maintain for a moment a well-ordered life without them; every object in your room has on it, for discerning eyes, the mark of ingenious tools and the pressure of laborious hands. Our Mary Allen West[8] always prayed, among other things, when asked to say grace before meat, "God bless the hands that prepared this food for us." She was the only person I ever met who seemed to have given a thought to those invisible human forces on which we are dependent for our daily bread. Why is it that the men and women who made the furniture in our rooms would by no means be recognized as our equals or companions? Why is it that those who make our food are usually as much forgotten by those who eat as if they were machines like the stoves on which the food is cooked? Why is it that even the higher class of draftsmen, clerks and helpers whose toil is largely mental, have no more social recognition than if a law had barred them out? Indeed just this has happened. Is it that unyielding, unwritten law of caste which says: "Labor is under foot, money is on top; idleness is a token of refinement; pleasure is the mark of birth and breeding; whoever devotes his time to useful pursuits belongs to a tabooed class, and you cannot be in Society unless you do the things that are of no mortal use to anybody and become the sort of person whose death would be no loss to the community, but oftentimes a gain." We know that this caste law is supreme in aristocratic countries, and there must be a reason for it. That reason is not far to seek. The men and women who work for wages are generally those whose ancestors were also "working people," as we say, and for this reason they were as a rule shut out from the power to get much if any schooling, or to acquire those refinements of conduct that manifest themselves in graceful speech and attitude, attractive appearance and attire, accompanied by some knowledge of literature and art. But is it not the cruelest injustice for those whose lives are surrounded and embellished by their work to have a superabundance of the money which represents the aggregate of labor in any country, while the laborer himself is kept so steadily at work that he has no time to acquire the education and refinements of life that would make him and his family agreeable companions to the rich and cultured?

Now the reason why I am a Christian socialist comes in just here: I would take, not by force, but by the slow process of lawful acquisition through better legislation as the outcome of a wiser ballot in the hands of men and women, the entire plant that we call civilization, all that has been achieved on this continent in the four hundred years since Columbus wended his way hither, and make it the common property of all the people, requiring all to work enough with their hands to give them the finest physical development, but not to become burdensome in any case, and permitting all to share alike the advantages of education and refinement. I believe this to be perfectly practicable, indeed that any other method is simply a relic of barbarism. I believe with Frederick Maurice of England,[9] that it is infidel for anyone to say that the law of supply and demand is as changeless as the law of gravitation, which means that competition must forever prevail. I believe that competition is doomed, the trusts whose single object it is to abolish competition having proved that we are better without than with it the moment that one corporation controls the entire supply of any product; and what the socialist desires is that the corporation of humanity should control all products. Beloved comrades, this is the frictionless way, it is the higher law, it eliminates the motives for a selfish life, it enacts into our everyday living the ethics of Christ's Gospel; nothing else will do it, nothing else can bring the glad day of universal brotherhood. It will not come in our time, and those of us who believe that it will ever come shall be both cursed and laughed at; but let us work right on, investing the little increment of power that we possess to render this heavenly dream a little more likely to be realized. . . .

The Church and the Reformer

The Church conserves the fruits of victory, but has not been eager to endure reproach in the reformer's camp. An individual man or woman whose heart God has touched more deeply than the hearts of their fellows, goes forth as a pioneer, even as John Howard and Elizabeth Fry,[10] in an age when the Church was not alive to its duty toward prisoners though Christ had specifically taught it, went forth to penetrate the foulest prisons of the world. John Howard declined a dinner with the Czar of Russia that he might visit one more prison. Elizabeth Fry was told that the women of Newgate would attack her, and a cannon was loaded and ready at the gate as she entered, but she declined all protection and appeared before those miserable creatures like a vision from a fairer world. William Wilberforce[11] made himself a social outlaw because, as a Christian statesman, he sought to do away with the trade in human flesh. The Church was not ready for it, but he, a son of the Church, was ready. Josephine Butler was stoned because she spoke on the subject of personal purity long before the Church was brave enough to do a work so needed. But when the most courageous sons and daughters that the Church has nurtured at her own fireside, have gone forth, under the inspiration of the Spirit, to live up to the light that they have seen, then the Church comes along in her sweeping robes, gathers up their work and makes it part and parcel of her own organic movement. I have no quarrel with the Church; it would only disturb my spirit and do nobody any good, but this much I am free to say: Whoever does not apply Christianity to the special sins of his age, in his own person and by his own work, is, to say the least a most unscientific Christian. We apply steam, when we have manufactured it, to the specific places where it is most needed; we make it turn pistons and drive wheels. When we have caught electricity and tamed it, we will turn it on where it can do the most good—we make it light our houses, carry our messages, and carry us. When the Spirit of God has been generated in a human being, it must not be shut up in the prayer meeting or the church building, but turned on in the saloons, the gambling houses, the haunts of shame, and for this purpose the ballot is one of its most effective batteries of power. . . .

Personal Opinions. . . .

Nothing recurs to my mind with such frequency and joyous hope as this soliloquy (It was with me in the quiet woods and hills of New England; it kept time to the soft sea waves; it twinkled in my soul when I looked up into the sky's bright dome): "I wonder why we don't set at work and abolish poverty in this great generous land within the next half century. We manage our public schools and great universities as the equal property of all; we carry on our entire postal system, our water supply, our parks, streets and highways in the same manner. In some countries the railroads, telegraph and telephone lines belong to the government, and in some cities the lighting is done by the municipality. All this works well. In the most progressive cities tenement houses are built to rent to wage workers, and the old rookeries where private capital demanded the highest rents and the lowest standard of living are being torn down like the Bastille[12] of old—both being parts of the same ungodly way of dealing with that holy thing called Life. Why should we practically give away the right to build railroads and streetcar lines, to manufacture gas, erect great public buildings, and thus farm out the people's business to corporate groups of men? Why do we not make the money basis of the country, not a mound of metal, white or yellow, dug out of the ground and piled up in our treasury vaults at Washington [D.C.], but the country itself with 'I promise to pay' gleaming across its breast from Mt. Katahdin [Maine] to Mt. Shasta? [Washington]". . . .

Beloved comrades, an age is hustling to the front . . . and that is the age of the Carpenter's Son. We have worshipped Him with our words, but henceforth we must worship with deeds or be set down as infidels and hypocrites. We have murmured, "We beseech Thee to hear us, Good Lord"; hereafter it is Himself *we* have to hear saying in the same tones in which He rebuked the money-changers in the temple: "WHY CALL YE ME LORD, LORD, BUT DO NOT THE THINGS THAT I SAY?" [Luke 6:46]. We have consecrated our knees to Him when it was our hands He wanted; we have courtesied to a man-made altar when He asked our obeisance for humanity itself. Science is killing out superstition as disinfectants kill microbes; no set of men can make any other set believe that they are custodians of any charm that makes men free from sin save love to God and love to man, wrought out in the enduring form of everyday work to help others to be less miserable. A bad life is the worst of heresies. Conferences and synods, revival meetings and prayer circles will have written as their epitaph, unless they make direct, honest, hard work to help men in the daily business of life: "*Behold your house is left unto you desolate*" [Matthew 23:38]. We Christians must not sit by and let the fires of intemperance burn on; we must not permit poverty to shiver and squalor to send forth its stench and disease to fester in the heart of great populations. All this must be stopped, and we are the Christ-men and Christ-women to stop it, or else we are pitiable dreamers and deluded professors of what we don't believe. I say this as a loving and always loyal daughter of the Church, and I say it more to myself than to you, "*O that I were less at ease in Zion!* [Amos 6:1]. But by Christ's name and life I mean to be—so help me, God." . . .

We shall never climb to heaven by making it our lifelong business to save ourselves. The process is too selfish; the motto of the true Christian is coming to be, "All for each and each for all," and in the honest purpose to realize its everyday meaning we acquire "A heart at leisure from itself," *and in no other way.* . . .

Power of the Spirit

Nothing less than the uttermost devotion will ever carry the temperance reform, or any other, to its high place in the temple of victory. The way of the Cross is the only way out for any life, or for the aggregation of lives, that makes up a group of reformers. . . .

Sisters beloved, it is only when we feel ourselves at the very core and center of our consciousness, linked with the Spirit of God, that we can put life into the ingenious and varied machinery which thought, purpose and devotion have wrought out for us in the past twenty-four years. How often have we said these things to one another; how utterly do we believe them! If I did not know that they are the Bread of Life to us in all that is best of our lives and character, I should be hopeless for the holy enterprise in which we have embarked. But, by the light that never shone on sea or shore, yet transfigured the kneeling faces of those Crusade groups,

> "I have read a righteous sentence writ in blazing rows of steel,
> As ye deal with my condemners so with you my Grace shall deal;
> Let the Hero born of woman crush the serpent with His heel
>   While God is marching on."

There will be other reforms and reformers. When we are gone societies will be organized, and parties will divide on the right of men to make and carry deadly weapons, dynamite and other destructive agencies still more powerful, that human ingenuity will yet invent. They will divide on the question of shambles [slaughterhouses], and there will be an army of earnest souls socially ostracized as we are now, because they believe that the butcher should cease to kill and the sale of meat be placed under ban of law. There will be a great movement to educate the people so that they will use neither tea, coffee nor any of the numerous forms of anodynes and sedatives that are now tempting millions to deterioration and death, and which will more strongly affect the finer brain tissues of more highly developed men and women. Long after the triumph of the temperance reform has universally crystallized upon the statute books; long after the complete right of woman to herself and to the unlimited exercise of all her beneficent powers is regarded as a matter of course; long after the great trust of humanity takes to itself the earth and the fullness thereof as the equal property of all, there will remain reforms as vital as any I have mentioned, and on them the people will group themselves in separate camps even as they do today. And it is not improbable that the chief value of the little work that we have tried to do on this small planet, lies in the fact that we have been to some extent tempered by it, we have become inured to contradiction, and we may be useful either in coming invisibly to the help of those who toil in the reforms of the future, or we may be waging battles for God upon some other star.

Notes

1. Thomas Collier Platt (1833–1910) from New York was at the head of the most powerful political machine in the United States.

2. The Liberty Party here refers to what is more commonly called the Populist Party. Founded in Omaha, Nebraska, in 1892, the party of farmers and working men advocated a broad range of economic reforms.

3. The Delsartean method was developed in the midnineteenth century by French singing teacher François Delsarte (1811–71) to improve both the physical health and grace of movement of women and girls. The system became popular in the United States in the last decades of the century.

4. Willard meant Arnold Toynbee (1852–83), social reformer and economist, for whom Toynbee Hall, London's pioneering university settlement, was named.

5. Ralph Waldo Emerson (1803–82) was a famous American essayist and transcendentalist whose works were widely read and known in the nineteenth century. During her early twenties Willard was a particularly avid reader of Emerson; her speeches and writings often contain quotes and echoes from his works.

6. Willard is probably referring to Richard Watson Gilder (1844–1909) who was the editor of *Century* magazine and was also involved in many reform campaigns in New York City against Tammany Hall, the corrupt political machine that ran New York City for much of the late nineteenth century.

7. Lord Robert Salisbury (1830–1903) was England's prime minister in 1897, and Joseph Chamberlain (1836–1914) was colonial secretary.

8. Mary Allen West (1837–92) was president of the Illinois WCTU and the editor of *The Union Signal* for several years during the 1880s. At that time she and several other WCTU staff members lived in Rest Cottage, the Willard home in Evanston, Illinois, and had meals with Willard and her mother.

9. Rev. Frederick Denison Maurice (1805–72) was one of the founders of the Christian Socialist movement in England during the 1840s.

10. Both John Howard (1726–90) and Elizabeth Gurney Fry (1780–1845) were British prison reformers, Howard during the late eighteenth century and Fry in the first half of the nineteenth century.

11. William Wilberforce (1759–1833), a British antislavery reformer and member of the House of Commons, first proposed the total abolition of the slave trade.

12. The Bastille was the French prison stormed on July 14, 1789, in the protest that marked the beginning of the French Revolution.

WORKS OF FRANCES E. WILLARD

Willard was a prolific writer and speaker. This list gives her most easily available books, pamphlets, book chapters, articles, and speeches. This inventory of her speeches presents 180 of the best complete and partial texts available from nineteenth-century books, conferences, newspapers, or transcripts. Entries included in this present volume are indicated with an asterisk. The sections detailing her books, book chapters, articles, and speeches are organized in chronological order. Because of the lack of publication information available, the pamphlets are listed in alphabetical order. Willard's many articles published in the *Union Signal* are not cataloged here. Copies of the *Union Signal* and many of the resources listed here are available at the Frances Willard Memorial Library, WCTU headquarters, Evanston, Illinois (cited as WCTU headquarters) or through the Woman's Christian Temperance Union National Headquarters Historical Files (joint Ohio Historical Society and Michigan Historical Collections), *Temperance and Prohibition Papers,* microfilm edition, WCTU series (cited as WCTU series with appropriate reel and frame numbers). Based on the bibliography in Amy R. Slagell's dissertation ("A Good Woman Speaking Well: The Oratory of Frances E. Willard," unpublished dissertation, University of Wisconsin, 1992), this list will guide readers to additional primary documents that demonstrate the breadth of topics, venues, and audiences addressed during Willard's career.

Books

Nineteen Beautiful Years. New York: Harper, 1864.

**Woman and Temperance.* Hartford, Connecticut: Park, 1883.

**How to Win.* New York: Funk and Wagnalls, 1886.

Woman in the Pulpit. Chicago: Woman's Christian Temperance Publishing Association, 1888.

Glimpses of Fifty Years: The Autobiography of an American Woman. Chicago: Woman's Christian Temperance Publishing Association, 1889.

Evanston: A Classic Town: The Story of Evanston by an Old Timer. Chicago: Woman's Christian Temperance Publishing Association, 1891.

A Great Mother. Chicago: Woman's Christian Temperance Association, 1894.

Do Everything: A Handbook for the World's White Ribboners. Chicago: Woman's Temperance Publishing Association, 1895.

**A Wheel within a Wheel: How I Learned to Ride the Bicycle.* New York: F.H. Berell Co., and London: Hutchinson and Co., 1895.

Willard, Frances E., and Mary A. Livermore, eds. *A Woman of the Century: Fourteen Hundred-Seventy Biographical Sketches, Accompanied by Portraits of Leading American Women in All Walks of Life.* Buffalo: Charles Wells Moulton, 1893.

Willard, Frances E., Winslow, Helen, and White, Sallie, eds. *Occupations for Women*. New York: Success, 1897.

Pamphlets

An Appeal to Mothers. Chicago: Ruby Gilbert, n.d.
The Ballot for the Home. Boston: American Woman Suffrage Association, 1888.
A Bible Talk: The Master Calleth for Thee. Chicago: Woman's Temperance Publishing Association, 1889.
The Crusade Psalm. Chicago: Woman's Temperance Publishing Association, n.d.
Doctor and Druggist. Chicago: Ruby Gilbert, n.d.
*Hints and Helps in our Temperance Work. New York: National Temperance Society and Publication House, 1875.
History of the Woman's National Christian Temperance Union. New York: The National Temperance Society and Publication House, 1876.
Home Protection. Chicago: Ruby Gilbert, n.d.
Home Protection Manual. New York: Independent, 1879.
How to Conduct a Public Meeting. Chicago: Ruby Gilbert, n.d.
I Will to Will God's Will. Chicago: Ruby Gilbert, n.d.
Individuality of Conscience in the Voter. Chicago: Ruby Gilbert, n.d.
The Law of Habit. Chicago: Ruby Gilbert, n.d.
The Modern Temperance Movement. London: World's Woman's Christian Temperance Union, 1893.
The National Prohibition Party; or, St. John vs. the Demi-John. Chicago: Charles Fielden, n.d. (1884?).
A New Era in the Temperance Reform. Chicago: Woman's Temperance Publishing Association, n.d.
The Polyglot Petition. Chicago: Woman's Temperance Publishing Association, n.d. (1895?).
The Press for Christian Temperance. Chicago: Ruby Gilbert, n.d.
Relations of Dress to Vice. Chicago: National Woman's Christian Temperance Union, n.d.
Scientific Temperance Instruction in Public Schools. Chicago: Ruby Gilbert, n.d.
The Shoemaker and the Little White Shoes. Chicago: Ruby Gilbert, n.d.
Should Women Vote? Chicago: Ruby Gilbert, n.d.
Society and Society Women. Chicago: Ruby Gilbert, n.d.
The Story of the "Women's Whisky War". London: British Woman's Temperance Association, White Ribbon Publishing Co., n.d.
A Talk with an Inquirer About God's Idea of Sin and Way of Pardon. Boston: James H. Earle, 1878.
Temperance Jack. Chicago: Ruby Gilbert, n.d.
Temperance and the Labor Question. Chicago: Ruby Gilbert, n.d.
Turn on the Light. Chicago: Ruby Gilbert, n.d.
White Cross Manual. Chicago: Woman's Temperance Publishing Association, 1886.
A White Life For Two. Evanston: Woman's Christian Publishing Association, 1890.
A White Life for Two. Evanston: Woman's Christian Temperance Union, n.d.
A White Life for Two. Chicago: Ruby Gilbert, n.d.
Why I am a Prohibitionist. Chicago: Ruby Gilbert, n.d.

Book Chapters

"A Century's Evolution of the Temperance Reform." In *One Hundred Years of Temperance*, New York: National Temperance Society Publication House, 1886.

"Individuality in Woman." In *You and I: or Living Thoughts for Our Moral, Intellectual, and Physical Advancement, by Leading Thinkers of Today*, Detroit, Michigan: F.B. Dickerson and Co., 1887.

"Women in America." In *Story of America: Comprising the Important Events, Episodes, and Incidents Which Make Up the Record of Four Hundred Years from 1492–1892*, eds. Hamilton W. Mabie and Marshal H. Bright. Philadelphia: John C. Winston and Co., 1892.

"Work." In *Mothers and Daughters*, 2 vols., ed. G. S. Reany. London: A. W. Hall, 1893.

Articles

"Embellishment of a Country Home." In *Transactions of the Illinois State Agricultural Society*, ed. S. Francis. Springfield: Illinois: Baihache and Baker, 1859.

"I and My Mother: or a Group of Asteroids." *The Ladies Repository* 23 (March 1863), 154–58.

"Faith Victorious." Parts 1–3. *The Guide to Holiness* 53–54 (June, July, August, 1868). New York: Walter C. Palmer, 1868.

"Daniel Parish Kidder D.D." *Ladies Repository* 31 (October 1871), 297–301.

"Egypt from a Yankee Schoolmarm's Point of View." Parts 1–3. *The Woman's Magazine* 8 (February, March, April, 1885).

"Latest Evolutions of the Temperance Reform." *Demorest's Monthly Magazine* 22 (March 1886): 360–62.

"Power of Organization as Shown in the Work of the Woman's Christian Temperance Union." *Lend a Hand* 1 (March 1886): 168–72.

"Women in Journalism." *Chautauquan* 6 (July 1886): 576–79.

"The World Moves on and With it Woman." *The Woman's Magazine* 10 (January 1887): 137–40.

"Man in the Home." *Chautauquan* 7 (February 1887): 279–81.

"Philanthropists." *Chautauquan* 7 (March 1887): 348.

"Frances Power Cobbe." *Chautauquan* 7 (July 1887): 597–99.

"The Progress of Prohibition." *Our Day* 1 (January 1888): 76–79.

"The Prospective Platform of the Prohibition Party." *Our Day* 1 (March 1888): 177–83.

"National Prohibition Convention." *Our Day* 1 (June 1888): 500–4.

"Woman's Temperance Work; Its Origin and Evolution." *Literature: A Weekly Magazine* 1 (September, 1888).

"Harriet Beech Stowe at Home." *Chautauquan* 8 (February 1888): 287.

"Neal Dow at Home." *Chautauquan* 8 (May 1888): 488.

"Clubs for Ladies and Gentlemen." *Our Day* 3 (January 1889): 89–91.

"The Political Future of Prohibition." *Our Day* 3 (April 1889): 315–20.

"Some Favorite Authors." *The Woman's Magazine* 12 (April 1889): 227.

"Interview With Edward Bellamy." *Our Day* 4 (December 1889): 539–42.

"Symposium on Religious Readings." *Our Day* 4 (December 1889): 514.

"The Prospects of the Prohibition Party." *Our Day* 5 (February 1890): 185–94.

"Who Knows." *Arena* 2: (July 1890): 252.

"Indian School." *Chautauquan* 9 (February 1889): 289.

"How to Bring up a Boy." *The Ladies Home Journal* (November 1891), 8.

"The Woman's Cause is Man's." *Arena* 5 (1892): 717–24

*"The Coming Brotherhood." *Arena* 6 (1892): 317–24.

"The Young Woman in Society." *The Young Woman: A Monthly Journal and Review* 1 (February 1893): 147–49.

"Pupil and Pedagogue." *Review of Reviews* 9 (January 1894): 96.

"God and Nature." *The True Thinker: An Occasional Pamphlet Devoted to the Study of Mental, Moral, and Social Philosophy* 4 (February 1894): 114–16.

"Lady Henry Somerset at Home in London." *Outlook* 49 (April 1894): 667–68.

"The Handicap of England." *American Federationist* 1 (May 1894): 44–45.

"Suffrage for Women." *Chautauquan* 13 (January 1893): 72.

"Arousing the Public Conscience; the Age of Consent." *Arena* 11 (January 1895): 198–202.

"Temperance in England." *Outlook* 52 (July 1895): 28.

"A White Life for Two." *The Lexington Church Record* 1 (December 1895).

"The Origin of the World's WCTU." *The American Monthly Illustrated Review of Reviews* 16 (October 1897): 430–36.

Speeches

1. "Woman's Lesser Duties," April 24, 1863, Pittsburgh, Pennsylvania. Pamphlet. Pittsburgh, Pa.: W.S. Haven, 1863.

2. Address for the Evanston Temperance Alliance, March 1865. In Frances E. Willard, Journal 22, WCTU headquarters.

3. Address of the American Methodist Ladies Centenary Association, Evanston, Illinois, July 12, 1866. In the *Chicago Tribune*, July 13, 1866.

4. "The New Chivalry," March 21, 1871, Chicago, Illinois. In Frances E. Willard. *Glimpses of Fifty Years: The Autobiography of an American Woman*. Chicago: Woman's Christian Temperance Publishing Association, 1889, 576–89.

5. "Who Wins," June 14, 1873, Madison, Wisconsin. In the *Wisconsin State Journal*, June 14, 1873.

6. "A New Departure in Normal Higher Education," October 15, 1873, New York. In *Papers and Letters Presented at the First Woman's Congress of the Association for the Advancement of Women*. New York: Mrs. Wm. Ballard, 1874, 94–99.

*7. "Everybody's War," Chicago, Illinois, fall 1874. Transcript, WCTU headquarters.

8. Address at the Second Women's Congress of the Association for the Advancement of Women, October 17, 1874, Chicago, Illinois. *Chicago Tribune*, October 18, 1874.

9. "The Relation of the Teacher to the Reforms of the Day," August 5, 1875. In *Addresses and Journal of Proceedings of the National Education Association*. Salem, Ohio: Allen K. Tatem, 1875, 181–87.

10. Address Before the Woman's Temperance Convention, September 9, 1875. In WCTU series, reel 30, frame 194.

11. Speech at the Chautauqua Temperance Convention, Summer 1876, New York. In WCTU series, reel 30, frame 204.

*12. "Home Protection [I]," October 5, 1876, Philadelphia, Pa. In *Association for the Advancement of Women: Papers Read at the Fourth Congress of Women in Philadelphia* (Washington, D.C.: Todd Brothers, 1877), 81–87.

13. "Address at the Centennial Temperance Congress," summer 1876, Philadelphia, Pa. In WCTU series, reel 30, frame 204.

14. "Why Should We Pray to Christ?" spring 1877, Boston, Mass. In WCTU series, reel 30, frame 346.

15. "Peace," spring 1877, Boston, Mass. In WCTU series, reel 30, frame 347.

16. "The Sermon on the Mount," spring 1877, Boston, Mass. In WCTU series, reel 30, frame 347.

17. "As It Is Written," spring 1877, Boston, Mass. In WCTU series, reel 30, frame 347.

18. "The 'I Wills' of Christ," spring 1877, Boston, Mass. In WCTU series, reel 30, frame 347.

19. "Assurance," spring 1877, Boston, Mass. In WCTU series, reel 30, frame 348.

20. "How to Study the Bible," spring 1877, Boston, Mass. In WCTU series, reel 30, frame 349.

21. "The Body Temple of God," spring 1877, Boston, Mass. In WCTU series, reel 30, frame 348–49.

22. "Obedience," spring 1877, Boston, Mass. In WCTU series, reel 30, frame 393.

23. "What think Ye of Christ?" spring 1877, Boston, Mass. In WCTU series, reel 30, frame 350.

24. Farewell Address at the close of the Moody revival, spring 1877, Boston, Mass. In WCTU series, reel 30, frame 349.

25. Temperance Address in the Tabernacle, June 1877, Boston, Mass. In WCTU series, reel 30, frame 350.

26. Scripture talk based on Luke 10:25 the Good Samaritan, [Ohio?] 1877. In WCTU series, reel 30, frame 392.

27. Address of Welcome to the National WCTU Convention, October 24, 1877, Chicago, Ill., October 24, 1877. In *Minutes of the National Woman's Christian Temperance Union 1874–1877*. Chicago: Woman's Temperance Publication Association, 1877, 136–39.

28. Address before the House Judiciary Committee, February 1, 1878, Washington, D.C. Unidentified clipping in WCTU series, reel 30, frame 406.

29. "My Story of the Pyramids," July 1, 1878, Beloit, Wis. In WCTU series, reel 31, frame 36–37.

30. Address in Hartford, Connecticut, September 29, 1878. Reported in the *Hartford Daily Times*, September, 30, 1878. In WCTU series, reel 31, frame 36–37.

31. "Presentation of the Crusade Quilt," November, 1878, Baltimore, Md. In Frances Willard, *Woman and Temperance*, 6th ed. Chicago: Woman's Temperance Publishing Association, 1897, 77–79.

32. "Temperance Lecture," December 14, 1878, Fond Du Lac, Wis. In WCTU series, reel 31, frame 44.

*33. Address before the Illinois Senate, April 10, 1879, Springfield, Ill. Reported in the *Citizen's League*, June 14, 1879. In Scrapbook 32 at WCTU headquarters.

34. "Home Protection," Springfield, Illinois, n.d. In *The Alliance*, June 14, 1879.

*35. "Home Protection [II]," July 4, 1879, Woodstock, Conn. Reported in *The Independent*, July 10, 1879, 11–13.

36. President's Address before the Illinois State WCTU Convention, October 1, 1879, Decatur, Ill. In *The Sixth Annual Report of the WCTU of the State of Illinois*. Decatur, Ill.: Hamsher and Mosser, 1879, 15–20.

37. "Valedictory Thoughts," fall 1879. In Frances Willard, *Woman and Temperance*, 6th

ed. Chicago: Woman's Temperance Publishing Association, 1897, 380–84. (In *Woman and Temperance* Willard identifies the year as 1878, but it refers to her election as president of the National WCTU, which did not occur until 1879.)

38. "Goliath-Alcohol and Brave King David," n.d. [1879?]. Unidentified clipping in WCTU series, reel 30, frame 286.

39. "Temperance and Women," May 6, 1880, Lawrence, Kans. Reported in the *Daily Press* (Leavenworth, Kans.), May 10, 1880. In WCTU series, reel 32, frame 344.

*40. First Presidential Address before the National WCTU, October 27, 1880, Boston, Mass. In *Minutes of the Woman's National Christian Temperance Union.* N.Y.: The National Temperance Society and Publication House, 1880, 9–25.

41. "Our National Curse and Our National Deliverance," December 4, 1880, Chicago, Ill. Reported in the Chicago *Times,* December 6, 1880. In WCTU series, reel 32, frame 409.

42. Speech at Liberty Hall, Elmwood, Ill., n.d. In the *Elmwood Messenger,* December 24, 1880.

43. Address at the Public Presentation of the Lucy Hayes Memorial Portrait, March 7, 1881, Washington, D.C. In Frances Willard, *Woman and Temperance,* 6th ed. Chicago: Woman's Temperance Publishing Association, 1897, 263–71.

44. Address to President Garfield, March 8, 1881, Washington, D.C. In Frances Willard, *Woman and Temperance,* 6th ed. Chicago: Woman's Temperance Publishing Association, 1897, 280–81.

45. Temperance Address, Savannah, Ga., n.d. Reported in *The Morning News,* April 4, 1881. In WCTU series, reel 32, frame 436.

46. Address at the National Temperance Convention, June 21, 1881, Saratoga Springs, N.Y. In Frances Willard, *Woman and Temperance,* 6th ed. Chicago: Woman's Temperance Publishing Association, 1897, 569–74.

47. Impromptu Speech in Reply to Chaplain McCabe, August 1881, Lake Bluff, Ill. In Frances Willard, *Woman and Temperance,* 6th ed. Chicago: Woman's Temperance Publishing Association, 1897, 392–96.

48. "The Southern People," August 28, 1881, Lake Bluff, Ill. Reported in the National Liberator (n.d.). In WCTU series, reel 30, frame 302.

49. Second Presidential Address before the National WCTU, October 26, 1881. Washington, D.C. In *Minutes of the National Woman's Christian Temperance Union.* Brooklyn, N.Y.: Union Argus Steam Printing, 1881, Appendix 64–82.

50. Temperance Address in San Antonio, Tex., March 1882. In WCTU series, reel 32, frame 473.

51. Temperance Address in New Orleans, March 5, 1882. Reported in the New Orleans *Times-Democrat,* March 6, 1882. In WCTU series, reel 32, frame 473.

*52. "Personal Liberty," June 11, 1882, Des Moines, Iowa. Unidentified clipping, WCTU headquarters. (A revised version of "Personal Liberty" is also included in Willard's *Woman and Temperance,* 486–503.)

53. Third Presidential Address before the National WCTU, Louisville, Ky., October 25, 1882. In *Minutes of the W.N.C.T.U.,* Appendix, lxxi–lxxxv.

54. Public Lecture in San Jose, Calif., April 27, 1883. Reported in the *San Jose Mercury,* April 28, 1883. In WCTU series, reel 33, frame 324.

55. Address to the Women of San Jose, Calif., April 28, 1883. Reported in the San Jose *Morning Times,* April 29, 1883. In WCTU series, reel 35, frame 325.

56. "Speech given at the Seattle [Washington] Temperance Convention" June 26–28, 1883. In *Minutes of the Temperance Convention.* Olympia: C.B. Bagely Book and Job Printer, 1883, in WCTU series, reel 33, frame 367.

57. Address before the Colorado State WCTU Convention, August 10, 1883, Denver, Colo. Reported in the Denver *Daily News,* August 11, 1883. In WCTU series, reel 33, frame 147.

58. Speech in Dayton, Ohio, September 1883. Reported in the *Daily Democrat* September 18, 1883. In WCTU series, reel 3, frame 166.

59. Temperance Speech in Atcheson, Kansas, November 1883. Reported in *The Daily Champion,* November 13, 1883. In WCTU series, reel 3, frame 378.

60. Fourth Presidential Address before the National WCTU, Detroit October 31–November 3, 1883. In *Minutes of the N.W.C.T.U,* 45–67.

*61. Address before the Committee on Resolutions of the National Republican Convention" June, 1884. *Glimpses of Fifty Years: The Autobiography of an American Woman.* Chicago: Woman's Christian Temperance Publishing Association, 1889, 392–94.

62. "Speech Seconding the Nomination of Governor St. John for the Presidency before the Prohibition Party National Convention," July 23, 1884, Pittsburgh, Pa. In Frances E. Willard. *Glimpses of Fifty Years: The Autobiography of an American Woman.* Chicago: Woman's Christian Temperance Publishing Association, 1889, 397–400.

63. "What will you do with Jesus that is called Christ?" (October 1884?). Reported in the *St. Louis Globe Democrat* n.d. In WCTU series, reel 34, frame 328.

64. Fifth Presidential Address before the National WCTU, St. Louis, Mo., October 22–25, 1884. In *Minutes of the National Woman's Christian Temperance Union.* Chicago: Woman's Temperance Publication Association, 1884, 50–74.

65. Speech in New York City, late April, 1885. Reported in *The Voice* April 30, 1885. In WCTU series, reel 34, frame 50.

66. Sixth Presidential Address before the National WCTU, Philadelphia, Pa., October 30–November 3, 1885. In *Minutes of the National Woman's Christian Temperance Union.* Brooklyn, NY: Martin and Niper, 1885, 62–93.

67. "Temperance Address to Medical Students." Reported in the Chicago *Inter-Ocean* Dec. 26, 1885. In WCTU series, reel 36, frame 197.

*68. "Social Purity: The Latest and Greatest Crusade," April 22, 1886, Chicago, Ill. Reported in *Voice Extra,* June 1886. In WCTU series, reel 35, frames 161–66.

69. "Address at the Opening of the National Temperance Hospital," May 4, 1886, Chicago, Ill. Reported in *National Temperance Hospital Quarterly,* n.d. In scrapbook #34 at WCTU headquarters.

70. "Address at the Michigan State WCTU convention at Manistee" July, 1886. Reported in *The Center,* July 8, 1886. In WCTU series, reel 36, frame 207.

71. "The White Cross Movement" August 1, 1886. In WCTU series, reel 31, frame 450–52.

72. "The White Cross and Social Purity" August 1886. Reported in the *Chautauqua Assembly Herald,* August 4, 1886. In WCTU series, reel 36, frame 210.

73. Address to the Rock River Methodist Episcopal Conference, October 6, 1886, Evanston, Ill. Reported in the Chicago *Inter-Ocean,* October 7, 1886.

74. "Social Purity," October 1886. Reported in the St. Paul, Minn., *Daily Globe,* October 18, 1886. In WCTU series, reel 35, frame 233–34.

75. Seventh Presidential Address before the WCTU, October 22–27, 1886, Minneapolis, Minn. In *Minutes of the National Woman's Christian Temperance Union.* Chicago: Woman's Temperance Publishing Association, 1886, 70–90.

76. Address at Westminster Church, October 24, 1886. Reported in the Minneapolis *Tribune,* October 25, 1886. In WCTU series, reel 35, frame 245–246.

77. "Social Purity," January 1887. Reported in the Chicago *Inter-Ocean,* January 3, 1887. In WCTU series, reel 35, frame 203.

78. "Social Purity," January 30, 1887, Washington, D.C. Manuscript in Willard's papers at WCTU headquarters.

79. Speech in Freehold, New Jersey, February, 1887. Reported in the *Monmouth Democrat,* February 10, 1887. In WCTU series, reel 36, frame 120.

80. "Woman and Philanthropy," May 9, 1887, Chicago, Ill. Reported in the *Christian Union,* volume 35, number 25. In scrapbook #34 at WCTU headquarters.

81. "Modern Temperance Reform," unidentified clipping, 1887? In Scrapbook #34 at WCTU headquarters.

82. "Woman and the Temperance Question," September 9, 1887. In the *Journal of Social Science* 23, 76–85.

83. Speech at the New York State WCTU Convention. Reported in the *Daily Republican* October 5, 1887.

84. Speech at the Prohibition Party Convention. Reported in the *Evening Transcript* October 18, 1887. In scrapbook #34 at WCTU headquarters.

85. Speech at the Opera House, November 3, 1887, Columbia, S.C. Reported in *The Columbia Register* November 4, 1887. In scrapbook #34 at WCTU Headquarters.

86. Eighth Presidential Address before the WCTU, November 11–16, 1887, Nashville, Tenn. In *Minutes of the National Woman's Christian Temperance Union 14th Annual Meeting.* Chicago: Woman's Temperance Publishing Association, 1888, 71–95.

87. Speech at McKendree Church, November, 1887. Unidentified clipping in WCTU series, reel 35, frame 381.

88. Eulogy to John B. Finch, November 30, 1887. Unidentified clipping in scrapbook #32, WCTU headquarters.

89. "Growth of Woman's Political Influence in the Temperance Reform," March 12, 1888, Boston, Mass. In *Our Day 2,* 1888.

90. "Woman in Temperance" March 27, 1888, Washington, D.C. In *Report of the International Council of Women Assembled by the National Woman Suffrage Association.* Washington, D.C.: Rufus H. Darby, 1888, 110–14.

91. "Social Purity," March 30, 1888, Washington, D.C. In *Report of the International Council of Women Assembled by the National Woman Suffrage Association.* Washington, D.C.: Rufus H. Darby, 1888, 286–89.

92. "Women in Religion," March 31, 1888, Washington, D.C. In *Report of the International Council of Women Assembled by the National Woman Suffrage Association,* Washington, D.C.: Rufus H. Darby, 1888, 422–24.

93. "Address to the Senate Committee on Woman's Suffrage" April 2, 1888, Washington, D.C. In *Miscellaneous Documents of the Senate of the United States,* 1st session, 50th Congress II, document #114. Washington, D.C.: Government Printing Office, 1888), 19–21.

94. Speech in Chambersburg, Pa. Reported in *Franklin Repository,* April 4, 1888. In scrapbook #34 at WCTU headquarters.

*95. "The Greatest Party," May 30, 1888, Indianapolis, Ind. In *Our Day*, 1, June 1888, 505–10.

96. Address on Suffrage at the Prohibition Party Convention, May 31, 1888, Indianapolis, Ind. Reported in the *Indianapolis Sentinel*, June 1, 1888.

97. Speech before the Christian Endeavor Society in Chicago, July 7, 1888. In the Chicago *Inter-Ocean* July 8, 1888.

98. Address in Maine. Reported in the Portland *Eastern Argus*, September 5, 1888. Vol. 58 no. 207. Found in Scrapbook #34 at WCTU headquarters.

*99. "The Dawn of Woman's Day" October 4, 1888, Chicago, Ill. In *Our Day*, 2, November 1888, 345–60.

100. Ninth Presidential Address before the WCTU, October 19, 1888, New York City. In *Minutes of the National Woman's Christian Temperance Union.* Chicago: Woman's Temperance Publishing Association, 1888, 1–64.

101. "Social Purity," November 1888. In *Papers Read Before the Association for the Advancement of Women.* Fall River, Mass.:J. H. Franklin & Co., 1889, 31–44.

102. Speech in Atlanta, April 7, 1889. Reported in the Atlanta *Constitution* April 8, 1889. In scrapbook #34 at WCTU headquarters.

103. "War on Liquor," April 1889. Reported in the Mississippi *Meridian News* April 17, 1889. In scrapbook #34 at WCTU headquarters.

104. Address at the Industrial Institute and College, April 15, 1889 at Columbus, Mississippi. Reported in *The College Echo* no. 3, May 1889. In scrapbook #44 at WCTU headquarters.

105. "Principle Before Politics" Oct. 7, 1889, Springfield, Mass. Reported in *Our Message* n.d. In scrapbook #44 at WCTU headquarters.

*106. Tenth Presidential Address before the WCTU, November 8, 1889, Chicago, Ill. In *Minutes of the National Woman's Christian Temperance Union.* Chicago: Woman's Temperance Publishing Association, 1889, 92–163.

107. Speech in New Jersey, February 18, 1890. Unidentified clipping in scrapbook #44 at WCTU headquarters.

108. Speech in Washington, Pa. Reported in an unidentified newspaper dated March 3, 1890. In Scrapbook #44 at WCTU headquarters.

109. "Social Purity." Reported in the Cleveland *Leader*, April 21, 1890.

110. Speech in Burlington, Iowa, April 29, 1890. Reported in *The Hawk-Eye*, April 30, 1890. In Scrapbook #44 at WCTU headquarters.

111. "Social Purity," May 1, 1890. Reported in the Muscatine *Daily Journal*, May 2, 1890. In Scrapbook #44 at WCTU headquarters.

112. "Temperance Sunday School Lessons." Reported in *The Pittsburgh Dispatch*, June 28, 1890. In Willard's papers at WCTU headquarters.

113. "The White-Cross Movement in Education" July 9, 1890. Reported in the *National Education Association Journal of Proceedings and Addresses*, Topeka, Kans.: Clifford Baker, Kansas Publishing House, 1890. pp. 159–78.

114. Speech in Terre Haute, Indiana. Reported in *Terre Haute Gazette*, October 13, 1890. In scrapbook #38 at WCTU headquarters.

115. Speech in Chillicothe, Ohio. Reported in the Chillicothe *Daily News*, October 24, 1890. In scrapbook #38 at WCTU headquarters.

116. "Laying of the Cornerstone of the Woman's Temple," November 1, 1890. Reported in the *Union Signal*, November 6, 1890.

117. Speech in Rockford Ill. October 9, 1890. Reported in *The Republican* Oct. 10, 1890. In scrapbook #38 at WCTU headquarters.

118. Eleventh Presidential Address before the National WCTU, November 14, 1890, Atlanta, Georgia. Pamphlet. Chicago: Woman's Temperance Publishing Association, 1890.

*119. "Women and Organization," February 23, 1891, Washington, D.C. Pamphlet. "Address of Frances E. Willard, President of the Woman's National Council of the United States, at Its First Triennial Meeting, Albaugh's Opera House, Washington, D.C., February 22–25, 1891."

120. "Speech to Children's Temperance Band," February, 1891. In WCTU series, reel 39, frame 390.

121. "In Honor of H.H.C. Miller." Reported in the *Evanston Index* May 9, 1891. In WCTU series, reel 38, frame 31.

122. Address at the First Methodist Church in St. Thomas, Ontario. Reported in *The Journal*, June 12, 1891. In WCTU series reel 38, frame 42.

123. "A White Life for Two." Reported in the *Chautauqua Assembly Herald*, August 3, 1891. In WCTU series, reel 31, frame 533.

124. "Address Before the Catholic Total Abstinence Union," August 10, 1891. Reported in the *Lion's Herald* August 26, 1891. In WCTU series, reel 38, frame 325.

125. Twelfth Presidential Address before the National WCTU and First World's WCTU, November 13, 1891, Boston, Mass. In *Minutes of the National Woman's Christian Temperance Union.* Chicago: Woman's Temperance Publishing Association, 1891, 84–226.

126. "Address at Exposition Music Hall in St. Louis." Reported in *St. Louis Globe Democrat,* February 22, 1892. In WCTU series, reel 37, frame 577.

127. Address of Greeting at the Industrial Conference, February 23, 1892, St. Louis, Mo. Reported in the *St. Louis Post-Dispatch,* February 23, 1892.

128. Address on the Minority Report at the Industrial Conference, February 24, 1892, St. Louis, Mo. Reported in the *Kansas City Star,* February 24, 1892 and in unidentified clipping, WCTU series, reel 37, frame 594.

129. Speech at the Michigan State WCTU Convention. Reported in the *Detroit Free Press* May 26, 1892. In WCTU series, reel 39, frame 391.

130. Speech at the Wooley Reception. Reported in the *Rest Island and Lake City Souvenir,* July 1892. In WCTU series, reel 39, frame 323.

131. Speech in Honor of Anna Gordon," July 21, 1892. Unidentified clipping, WCTU series, reel 39, frame 248.

132. Thirteenth Presidential Address before the National WCTU, October 28, 1892, Denver, Co.

133. Speech of Commemoration and Farewell. Reported in the *Chicago Inter-Ocean* Nov. 15, 1892. In WCTU series, reel 39, frame 270.

134. Excerpt from Speech in Sunderland, England. Reported in the *Sunderland Daily Echo,* November 30, 1892. In WCTU series, reel 39, frame 279.

135. Speech in Stockton, England. Reported in *The Stockton Herald,* December 3, 1892. In WCTU series, reel, 40, frame 73.

136. Speech in Doncaster, England. Reported in *The Doncaster Gazette,* December 9, 1892. In WCTU series, reel 40, frame 77–78.

137. Speech in Birmingham, England. Reported in *The Birmingham Daily Post,* December 10, 1892. In WCTU series, reel 40, frame 79.

138. Speech in Nottingham, England. Reported in the *Nottingham Daily Express,* December 15, 1892. In WCTU series, reel 40, frame 88.

*139. Address at Exeter Hall, London, England, January 9, 1893. Unidentified clipping, in WCTU series, reel 40, frame 56–57.

140. Speech at Liverpool, England. Reported in *The Liverpool Mercury,* January 21, 1893. In WCTU series, reel 40, frame 194.

141. Speech at Manchester, England, January 24, 1893. Reported in *The Alliance News* January 27, 1893. In WCTU series, reel 40, frame 208.

142. Speech at Manchester II, January 24, 1893. Reported in *The Manchester Guardian* January 23, 1893. In WCTU series, reel 40, frame 195.

143. Speech at Glasgow, January 30(?), 1893. Unidentified clipping in WCTU series, reel 40, frames 227 and 230.

144. Speech at Plait Hall, Lutton(?) England, February 10, 1893. Reported in *The Dunstable Borough Gazette,* February 15, 1893. In WCTU series reel 40, frame 249.

145. Speech at Southampton, England. Reported in *Southampton Times and Hampshire Express* Feb/March 1893. In WCTU series, reel 40, frame 310.

146. Speech at Portsmouth, England. Reported in *The Portsmouth Evening News,* March 2, 1893. In WCTU series, reel 40, frame 311.

147. Speech at Cambridge, England, March (?)1893. Unidentified clipping, WCTU series, reel 40, frame 312.

*148. Fourteenth Presidential Address before the National WCTU and the World's WCTU, October 16, 1893, Chicago, Ill. In *Address before the Second Biennial Convention of the World's WCTU, and the Twentieth Annual Convention of the National WCTU.* Chicago: Woman's Temperance Publishing Association, 1893, 1–96.

149. Farewell Address, England. Reported in *The White Ribbon Journal* [Melbourne, Australia], July 1894. In WCTU series, reel 41, frame 44.

150. Speech at the New York Reception, June 21, 1894. Reported in *The Tribune,* June 22, 1894. In WCTU series, reel 41, frame 52.

151. Speech at the Opening of the National Prohibition Convention, July 3, 1894, Montreal, Canada. Reported in the *Daily Witness,* July 3, 1894. WCTU series, reel 41, frame 89.

152. Address at the National Prohibition Convention, July 4, 1894, Montreal, Canada. In *Daily Witness,* July 4, 1894. In WCTU series, reel 42, frame 93.

153. "Woman and Temperance," July 15, 1894, Cleveland, OH. Reported in the *Cleveland Plain Dealer* July 16, 1894.

154. Speech at the Dedication of the Willard Fountain. Reported in the *Chicago Tribune* September 29, 1894. In WCTU series, reel 41, frame 158.

*155. Fifteenth Presidential Address before the National WCTU, November 16, 1894, Cleveland, Ohio. In *Minutes of the National Woman's Christian Temperance Union.* Chicago: Woman's Temperance Publishing Association, 1894, 81–183.

156. Address at a Suffrage Fair, Boston, Mass. Reported in the *Boston Record,* December 4, 1894. In WCTU series, reel 39, frame 424.

157. Speech at a Reception for John Burns. Reported in the *Boston Herald,* January 3, 1895. In WCTU series, reel 43, frame 189.

158. Address at the Boston Social Union, January 28, 1895. Reported in the *Times Herald*, February 6, 1896. In WCTU series, reel 43, frame 215–16.

159. "The Polyglot Petition" February 15, 1895. In *The Polyglot Petition*. Chicago: Woman's Temperance Publishing Association, 1895.

160. Address in Harrisburg, Pa., October 13, 1895. Reported in the *Harrisburg Evening News,* October 14, 1895.

161. Address before the World's WCTU, June 19, 1895. In *Address by Frances E. Willard, President of the World's Woman's Christian Temperance Union at its Third Biennial Convention.* London, White Ribbon Co., 1895.

162. Address at the Social Purity Congress, October 15, 1895. In Aaron M. Powell, ed., *The National Purity Congress its Papers, Addresses, Portraits.* New York: The American Purity Alliance, 1896, 124–27.

163. Sixteenth Presidential Address before the WCTU, October 18, 1895. In *Report of the National Woman's Christian Temperance Union Convention.* Chicago: Woman's Temperance Publishing Association, 1895, 77–138.

164. "A White Life For Two," December 8, 1895, Louisville, Ky. Unidentified clipping in WCTU series, reel 43, frame 67.

165. "Address at the Tabernacle," December 15, 1895, Nashville, Tenn. Reported in the *Tennessee Methodist* (n.d.) In WCTU series, reel 43, frame 69.

166. Address in Buffalo, N.Y. Reported in the *Buffalo Express,* April 2, 1896. In WCTU series, reel 43, frame 123

167. Address in Rochester, N.Y, April 3, 1896. Reported in the *Rochester Democrat Chronicle* April 4, 1896. In WCTU series, reel 43, frame 137.

168. "Farewell Speech in Washington," April 12, 1896. Reported in the *Washington Post* April 13, 1896. WCTU series, reel 43, frame 139.

169. "Farewell Address upon Leaving for England," reported in *The True Reform,* April 23, 1896. WCTU series, reel 43, frame 171.

170. Speech before the British Woman's Temperance Association, June 1, 1896. Reported in the Philadelphia, Pa. *Christian Statesman,* July 4, 1896.

171. Speech before the British Woman's Temperance Association, June 15, 1896. Reported in the Calcutta *White Ribbon* July 5, 1896. In WCTU series, reel 43, frame 342.

172. Seventeenth Presidential Address before the National WCTU Convention, November 13, 1896, St. Louis. Mo. In *Report of the National Woman's Christian Temperance Union.* Chicago: Woman's Temperance Publishing Association, 1896, 67–79.

173. Speech in Honor of the Opening of the Cordelia Greene Library. Reported in *The Castilian,* March 12, 1897. In WCTU series, reel 43, frame 429.

174. Speech on the 23rd Anniversary of the Castile Sanitarium, March (?) 1897. Unidentified clipping in WCTU series reel 43, frame 438.

175. "Address to Massey Hall Multitude." Reported in the Toronto *Mail and Empire,* October 22, 1897.

176. Fourth Presidential Address before the World's WCTU, October 23, 1897. Toronto, Canada. In *Address before the Fourth Biennial Convention of the World's Woman's Temperance Union.* Chicago: Woman's Temperance Publishing Association, 1897

*177. Eighteenth Presidential Address before the National WCTU, October 29, 1897, Buffalo, N.Y. In *Minutes of the National Woman's Christian Temperance Union.* Chicago: Woman's Temperance Publication Association, 1897, 1–85.

178. "Thanksgiving Sermon." November 22, 1897, Chicago, Ill. Reported in the *Chicago Times Herald* Nov. 23(?) 1897. In WCTU series, reel 44, frame 408.

179. "A White Life for Two," December 19, 1897, Chicago, Ill. Reported in the Chicago *Inter-Ocean,* December 20, 1897. In WCTU series, reel 44, frame 415–16.

180. Speech in Janesville, Wis., January 2, 1898. [Last reported speech before her death.] Reported in the *Janesville Gazette,* January 3, 1898. In WCTU series, reel 44, frame 416.

INDEX

brain: 41, 53, 72, 73, 88, 89, 123, 131, 167, 181, 184, 189, 195; alcohol's effect on, 5, 20, 38, 74, 164, 176, 229; application of, 16, 135, 150, 182; brain function, 159–60n9, 173; learning, 24, 36; relation to recreation, 214, 221; women's right and need to develop, 97, 103–8, 130, 146, 173–74, 186, 198
Bristow, Benjamin H., 6
British atrocities in Africa, 130, 137n6, 204
British Women's Temperance Association (BWTA), xx, xxx, 160n11, 169–70, 175, 204
Brontë, Charlotte: *Shirley*, 105, 116n2
Brooks, John Anderson, 122–23, 124n6
brotherhood, 72, 135, 161–68, 183, 186, 203, 223, 224, 226; Brotherhood of Man, 144, 145; and sisterhood, 159
Browning, Elizabeth Barrett: "The Cry of the Human," xlv n46
Browning, Robert, 129, 137n4, 146
Buck, Mrs. Norman, 64, 65–66
Buckner, Simon Bolivar, 119
Buell, Caroline Brown, 81
Bureau of Labor Statistics, 206n5
Burke, Edmund, 74, 75n3
Burns, John Elliot, 145, 147n7, 195, 206n5
Bushnell, Katherine, 183, 190n5
Butler, Josephine, xxx, 91–92, 93, 95, 99nn4–5, 227
Byzantine art, 111

Campbell, Helen Stuart, 146, 161; *The Prisoners of Poverty*, 129, 136n3, 165
Campbell, Karlin Kohrs, xlix n28, 177n12
Canada Temperance Act (Scott Act, 1878), 49–50, 57n2
Capers, Ellison, 63
capitalism: cutthroat, 162; injustice/suffering caused by, xxxvii, 138–39, 140, 161; on survival of the fittest, 192, 194–95
Carhart, Clara H. Sully, 78
Carlyle, Thomas, 106, 116n3
Carpenter, William Benjamin, 149, 157–58, 159–60n9
Carse, Matilda B., 154, 159n6
castes, 225
Castle Garden (New York City), 140
Catholic support of temperance movement, xxiv, 22, 25n8, 41, 172–73
Catholic Total Abstinence Society, 173
Chamberlain, Joseph, 224, 230n7
Chapin, Sallie Flournoy Moore, 63, 67n5, 88, 122–23, 124n6
character: 53, 56, 108, 111, 114, 115, 155, 157, 158, 189–90, 198, 199, 200, 205, 210, 228; corroded

by capitalism, 189; as master virtue, 185–86; teaching of, 72, 144
charity, xxxv–xxxvi, xxxvii
Chicago: Czech immigrants in, 129–30, 137n5; ethnic/labor unrest in, 147n1; poverty in, xxxv; prostitutes in, 98; women's activism tradition in, 125; working conditions of women/children in, 125
Chicago Inter-Ocean, 125, 136n2
Chicago Journal, 179, 190n1
Chicago Post, xvii, 100
Chicago Tribune, 124n4
Chicago Women's League: effects on the home, 131; FW's inaugural address to, 125–36; goals of, 128–29; reflex influences on women, 129–31; and State Councils of Women, 135–36; and woman's role in legislation, 134; and woman's role in politics, 135
children, 72, 134
Chimborazo, Mount (Ecuador), 18, 25n3
Chinese foot binding, 95–96
chivalry of justice, xxxi, xxxiv, xliv n31, 56
Chrietzburg, Rev., 63
Christ, teachings of, 166–67
Christian Endeavor societies, 100
Christianity: Bible study, 166; Christian service, xxxv–xxxvi; evolution of, 157–58; home, concept of, 113–14; and the Nationalists, 144–45; and reformers, 226–28; women's enslavement vs. emancipation by, xxvi. *See also* Christian socialism; Golden Rule
Christian socialism, xxxvii–xli; Christian basis of, xxxvii–xxxviii, 217–18; described, xxxvii; economic arguments based on, 148–49; and the Fabian Society, 179; founding of, 226, 230n9; and the Golden Rule, xxxvii, xxxviii, 186, 217; and inequality, 186, 189; influence of, xl; money vs. labor/exchange value, 189, 197, 226; Nationalists on, 144–45; and pooled resources, 126, 162; poverty/suffering addressed by, xxxviii, xxxix, xli, 186; Socialism defined (Gospel socialism), 186; transformation via, xxxvii–xxxviii, xli; unpopularity of, 139. *See also* Socialism, Society of Christian Socialists
Church. *See* Christianity
Church of England Temperance Society, xxx
Citizens' League (Chicago), 51
civic betterment organizations, 48–49
civic reform movement, 218
civilization, 181–82, 226
civil liberty, 72–73
Civil War, 117–21, 123–24, 127
Clark, William, 65
Clarke, James Freeman, 145, 147n6

CAROLYN DE SWARTE GIFFORD is a visiting scholar in the gender studies program at Northwestern University. She is the author of numerous articles on American women's religious experience and reform activity, and the editor of *Writing Out My Heart: Selections from the Journal of Grances E. Willard, 1855–96*. She is the co-editor, with Wendy Deichmann Edwards, of *Gender and the Social Gospel*.

AMY R. SLAGELL is an associate professor and heads the speech communication program in the Department of English at Iowa State University. She has published several articles on nineteenth-century orators and on public speaking pedagogy. Her work has appeared in journals such as *Rhetoric and Public Affairs*, *Communication Studies*, and *Communication Education*.

The University of Illinois Press
is a founding member of the
Association of American University Presses.

———————————————————————

Composed in 10.5/13 Adobe Minion
with Minion display
by Type One, LLC
for the University of Illinois Press
Designed by Paula Newcomb
Manufactured by Thomson-Shore, Inc.

University of Illinois Press
1325 South Oak Street
Champaign, IL 61820–6903
www.press.uillinois.edu